EVOLVA ARCHITECTS — CAMBERWELL HOUSE
ANDRÉS CASILLAS DE ALBA AND EVOLVA ARQUITECTOS ASOCIADOS — DOVECOTE
AZO SEQUEIRA ARQUITECTOS ASSOCIADOS
STUDIO MK27 — CASA PLANA
VALERIO OLGIATI — VILLA ALÉM
TOM KUNDIG, OLSON KUNDIG ARCHITECTS — THE PIERRE
CHROFI — A GARDEN
PETER STUTCHBURY ARCHITECTURE — SMART DESIGN STUDIO
DURBACH BLOCK JAGGERS — INVISIBLE HOUSE
THAM & VIDEGÅRD ARKITEKTER — SUMMERHOUSE
CLINTON MURRAY AND POLLY HARBISON — BALMORAL HOUSE
ARM ARCHITECTURE — TAMARAMA HOUSE
DOMENIC ALVARO ARCHITECT — ELWOOD HOUSE
NEESON MURCUTT ARCHITECTS — SMALL HOUSE
SOU FUJIMOTO — HOUSE O
CASTLECRAG HOUSE

CONCRETE HOUSES: JOE ROLLO

The poetics of form

CONCRETE HOUSES: JOE ROLLO

Thames & Hudson

THE HOUSES

014	THE POETICS OF FORM
018	CAMBERWELL HOUSE, MELBOURNE, AUSTRALIA
036	DOVECOTE, BRAGA, PORTUGAL
052	CASA PLANA, PORTO FELIZ, BRAZIL
070	VILLA ALÉM, ALENTEJO, PORTUGAL
092	IT IS A GARDEN, NAGANO, JAPAN
116	THE PIERRE, SAN JUAN ISLANDS, USA
126	LUNE DE SANG PAVILION, NORTHERN NEW SOUTH WALES, AUSTRALIA
146	INDIGO SLAM, SYDNEY, AUSTRALIA
164	INVISIBLE HOUSE, BLUE MOUNTAINS, AUSTRALIA
180	TAMARAMA HOUSE, SYDNEY, AUSTRALIA

196	BALMORAL HOUSE, SYDNEY, AUSTRALIA
210	SUMMERHOUSE, LAGNÖ, SWEDEN
224	ELWOOD HOUSE, MELBOURNE, AUSTRALIA
234	SMALL HOUSE, SYDNEY, AUSTRALIA
248	CASTLECRAG HOUSE, SYDNEY, AUSTRALIA
256	HOUSE O, TATEYAMA, JAPAN
272	VILLA WAALRE, EINDHOVEN, NETHERLANDS
288	WHALE BEACH HOUSE, SYDNEY, AUSTRALIA
298	SKYLIGHT HOUSE, SYDNEY, AUSTRALIA
311	ABOUT THE AUTHOR ACKNOWLEDGEMENTS

Ada Louise Huxtable, 'Fallingwater: A Marriage of Nature and Art', On Architecture: Collected Reflections on a Century of Change (first published by Walker Publishing Company 2008) Bloomsbury Publishing Inc, London, 2010, p. 203.

In architecture, the building's use and setting are essential components. And there is always the matter of beauty, the most elusive and subjective measure of all. Fallingwater… meets all of the criteria…it is also spectacularly and unconventionally beautiful…so magically married to its site that it is thrilling to experience, and even see. Wright's sense of the land is uncanny; he has locked building and setting together in a visual and environmental embrace. The effect is not of nature but of nature completed.
Ada Louise Huxtable

Luis Barragán, laureate acceptance speech, The Pritzker Architecture Prize, Dumbarton Oaks, Washington D.C., 1980.

The words beauty, inspiration, magic, spellbound, enchantment, as well as the concepts of serenity, silence, intimacy and amazement. All these have nestled in my soul, and though I am fully aware that I have not done them complete justice in my work they have never ceased to be my guiding lights. Luis Barragán

Eduardo Souto de Moura, laureate acceptance speech, The Pritzker Architecture Prize, Mellon Auditorium, Washington D.C., 2011.

I learned to draw in the Italian School of Porto, the place where I was born, and in high school I decided I would become an architect. It was not that I strongly felt the pull of Architecture, but during my teenage agnostic crisis I started to wonder whether or not God should really have rested on the seventh day. Giving it a second thought, He would have realized that a site like Delphi was still lacking; the Acropolis had yet to receive the Parthenon; a swamp in Illinois needed drying so that the Farnsworth House could correctly be placed there.

Eduardo Souto de Moura

Leon Battista Alberti (1404–1472), Italian humanist, architect and principal initiator of Renaissance art theory

Beauty is the adjustment of all parts proportionately so that one cannot add or subtract or change without impairing the harmony of the whole. Leon Battista Alberti

INTRODUCTION:
THE POETICS OF FORM
JOE ROLLO

The American architecture writer and critic Ada Louise Huxtable (1921–2013) could, just as easily, have been talking about concrete structures when, in a 1973 article in *The New York Times* on plans for the twin towers of the World Trade Centre, she said of tall buildings: 'The most beautiful…are not only big, they are bold; that is the essence and logic of their structural and visual reality. They are bone-beautiful, and the best wear skins that express that fact with the strength and subtlety of great art.' That just about describes perfectly most of the houses published here in *Concrete Houses*. Each has that rare quality that all good architecture exudes: grace of form. What elevates them to another level is the choice of concrete as the principal structural and architectural material.

Produced in immense quantities, concrete is the second most consumed substance on Earth, after water. Once taken for granted as the stuff of aqueducts and power plants, pavements and car parks, concrete has become the building material of choice for those architects and engineers who understand not only its versatility, strength and thermal qualities, but also its potential for shape-making, limited only by the restrictions of formwork and the imagination of its ideators. Witness the almost impossibly beautiful concrete houses and buildings of Tadao Ando. Marvel at the engineering-as-architecture of Cecil Balmond, whose outside-the-square take on the role of engineering in architecture has enabled many architects to realise seminal buildings, such as Rem Koolhaas's Bordeaux Villa – a suspended concrete box at whose heart is a platform that moves freely between its three levels to create a constantly changing architectural landscape – and Lord Norman Foster and Michel Virlogeux's Millau Viaduct in southern France – at 343 metres the tallest cable-stayed bridge in the world, supported on seven mighty concrete pillars, the tallest of which stands at almost 245 metres.

As precise and abstract a material as it is today, concrete is also ancient in its quality. The Romans discovered it by chance more than 2000 years ago, when they found that mixing volcanic ash deposits, from Pozzuoli near Naples, and limestone aggregates with water made a cementing compound – they called it *concretus* – that could be used to span vaults, stiffen walls and serve as foundations. They used it extensively, in structures such as the domed roofs of the baths at Pompei, the foundations of Rome's Colosseum and, most spectacularly, in one of the most beautiful buildings on Earth, the Pantheon, where crushed pumice was mixed with ash from Pozzuoli to lighten the massive dome that spans 43 metres, a feat unbeaten for seven centuries.

The houses in this book have been selected from *C+A* magazine, an international magazine of concrete architecture I conceived in 2004, and which I continue to edit for Cement Concrete and

Aggregates Australia, the organisation representing those industries. The magazine celebrates the use of concrete in architecture by publishing inspirational works from some of the world's best architects. The likes of Álvaro Siza, Eduardo Souto de Moura, Zaha Hadid, Fumihiko Maki, Peter Zumthor, Toyo Ito, David Chipperfield, Herzog & de Meuron, and Kazuyo Sejima and Ryue Nishizawa have all graced its pages. As for houses, they have come from the likes of Sou Fujimoto, Tom Kundig, Valerio Olgiati, Marcio Kogan, Fernando Menis, Mário Sequeira, Hiroi Ariyama and Megumi Matsubara, as well as Australians such as Peter Stutchbury, Alex Popov, Ian McDougall, Neil Durbach, Tony Chenchow, William Smart, John Choi and Clinton Murray. The premise for the magazine is straightforward: employ the highest quality photography, drawings and words (mine and those of the architects) to describe the power, grace and poetry of each featured building.

It is always the quality of the architecture, and only that, that makes the cut into the magazine. Mário Sequeira's Dovecote, in Braga, Portugal, for example (featured on the cover of this book). Here, Sequeira replaced a dilapidated bird coop with a tiny cubby house, struck entirely in concrete, seemingly floating lightly over a stone wall. Or Peter Stutchbury's Invisible House, along the brow of an escarpment at the edge of the majestic Blue Mountains, west of Sydney, with views that go on forever; the house a sheltering plane of raw concrete, on top of and under which is an arrangement of living, dining and cooking zones, bedrooms, an artist's studio and more.

Valerio Olgiati's Villa Além, situated beside a cork forest in the Alentejo region of southern Portugal, is a building – an imbalance of roofed and unroofed space – of rusticated, board-marked concrete within a walled garden, the tops of the walls peeling outwards rather 'like petals that open to the sky', according to Olgiati. Closer to home, William Smart's extravagant Indigo Slam in Chippendale, at the edge of the Sydney CBD, is an exercise in curve and counter curve, purposely designed to manipulate light and views and privacy, the concrete facade alive to the changes wrought by light, shade, sun and cloud; the interior remarkable for a spectacular hall and civic-scaled grand stair that climbs four flights to a height of 14 metres.

Impressive, too, is Elwood House, Ian McDougall's 'decorated cave-house' at Elwood in Melbourne, with its dance of almost impossibly smooth, flared concrete pillars carefully positioned to articulate and subdivide a single ground-floor plane; the columns scattered both to take structural loads and to draw the eye unimpeded toward a Moorish-inspired garden courtyard just outside its glass walls. Then there is Tom Kundig's The Pierre, a mix of rawness and refinement on Lopez Island in the San Juan Islands in the US state of Washington, that at first sight appears to have been gouged from the rock outcrop into which it is wedged. Here, looking out to the Salish Sea, is a house of concrete, glass and reclaimed timber siding, in which details large and small have been exquisitely designed and realised to make a civilised weekend shelter and protective vault for its owner's collections of art.

Concrete offers the possibility of an unlimited exploration of structure and shape. It has conviction, strength and directness, but plasticity, too, which makes the possibilities for form-making almost endless. It is hardly surprising, then, that in the hands of the talented architects described here, the incontrovertible fusion of concrete's plasticity and brute force can be turned into architecture of lyric beauty, intensity and timelessness. As much as this book is a showcase for concrete, it is also a showcase for leading-edge residential design, which is about the poetics of form in architecture.

THE HOUSES

018

Photographs: John Gollings and Jeremy Weihrauch

CAMBERWELL HOUSE

CAMBERWELL HOUSE
MELBOURNE, AUSTRALIA, 2015
ANDRÉS CASILLAS DE ALBA AND EVOLVA ARCHITECTS

There are two stories behind this house in the leafy Melbourne suburb of Camberwell. One is of its owner, a prominent plastic surgeon specialising in craniofacial conditions affecting children. He was a member of the highly specialised team of surgeons who, in 2009, separated the Bangladeshi conjoined twins Krishna and Trishna in a 27-hour operation at Melbourne's Royal Children's Hospital. The other story is of his and his wife's shared obsession with the architecture of the great Mexican architect Luis Barragán.

Their interest dates back to around 1991 when, while working and training in Mexico City, they became familiar with Barragán's own remarkable house in Tacubaya and experienced firsthand some of the houses of Andrés Casillas de Alba, who worked with Barragán from 1964 to 1968, before forging a successful career of his own. Casillas collaborated on Barragán's signature work, the Cuadra San Cristóbal house and stables (1966), at Los Clubes in the suburbs of Mexico City. Since 1994, he has overseen restoration works on the Barragán House, now listed as a UNESCO World Heritage site. Earlier in his career, Casillas attended the Ulm School of Design in Germany, a successor to the Bauhaus, and in the late 50s worked in the Milan studio of Italian architects Mangiarotti and Morassutti.

Determined to have a Barragán-inspired house in Melbourne, the couple commissioned Casillas in 2003 to design a house for them in a tree-lined street remarkable only for a streetscape of unremarkable late Edwardian houses. Originally conceived as a modernist structure in white-painted, rough-cast render, in the manner of Barragán, there soon came a shift to constructing the house from in situ reinforced concrete. This decision was influenced by the surgeon and his wife's growing interest in the concrete buildings of Tadao Ando (they had travelled to Japan to study Ando's buildings and see firsthand the quality of his concrete finishes) and the fact that one of Casillas's own later projects was realised in off-form concrete. When reminded that Barragán never worked in concrete, they answer that if Barragán were alive and still practising today 'he would almost certainly be working with concrete'.

From the street, the house reads as an uncompromising concrete box, monumental and all but impenetrable, save for a large opening – a window – to one side. The building stands at the edge of a reflecting pool, approached across a series of stepping blocks of Mexican volcanic rock from the same quarry used by Barragán. On a crisp, blue-sky day, with the house reflected in the pond, its austerity breaking the monotony of its polite surroundings, you can only wonder at what the neighbours must be thinking.

There's one small clue, a giveaway, pointing to the house being from the hand of Casillas de Alba: high on one corner at the front, perched on the top of a parapet, sits a stylised dove, a *paloma*, cast in concrete. The dove, its wings spread heavenward, has been used as a signature motif in many of Casillas's buildings. Somewhat Middle-Eastern or North African in appearance, you wonder at its origins until you learn that in 1958 Casillas spent time in Isfahan, Iran, working on urban planning projects.

The interior layout of the house follows a centuries-old Spanish quadrangular arrangement, with all private spaces (bedrooms and bathrooms) opening off a central, soaring living space. Compression and release, contraction and expansion are the main game here. Once past a large pivoted front door with a stable-door window to one side to allow light and air in as required, the house is a study in extreme minimalism. The low entrance explodes into a soaring 5-metre interior hall, rising to 9 metres at one end where a clerestory window draws northern light into the house. The box is a mix of reinforced concrete walls and white-painted plaster surfaces. The effect is one of coolness and tranquility. Bedrooms are located to one side of a lower 'street' paved in the specially quarried and cut Mexican volcanic stone, while the main living space is reached via a few steps, as if you were climbing onto a stage. A large cruciform window to the east, not unlike the great window in the Barragán House, dominates this space. In a play of light and shade, early morning sunshine casts shadows deep into the room through this window. Douglas fir wood planks, 450 millimetres wide, specially sourced and milled in Denmark, line the floor. Narrow, concealed stairs at one end of the space lead to a study, more living space and the main bedroom suite, which appears to be hung from the edge of the concrete box. Stable-door openings, one painted vivid pink, offer glimpses into and out of the house as required. Views from inside are directed out towards a simple garden and swimming pool given privacy by concrete walls. There is a small guest suite under the house, with its own sunken concrete courtyard.

The house is decorated with signature pieces of furniture designed by Barragán – commissioned from tradesmen who worked with the architect – including chairs and lamps. Desktops and library surfaces are of sabino wood, a type of water cypress native to Mexico. Artworks by artists favoured by the architect, in particular gilded canvases by Mathias Goeritz (still made by the same family of artists used by Barragán) and paintings by Chucho Reyes. Pilar Climent's art and furniture, inspired by Barragán's architecture, have been installed in the house. Dozens of tall terracotta pots, just as you would see in Barragán projects, are grouped in clumps in the garden.

Rooted in the aesthetic of Barragán's modernism and Casillas de Alba's innate understanding of the dramatic effect of light and shade in architecture, this house is suited to the Australian condition. To have inserted it in the midst of a conservative streetscape demonstrates how successfully old and new architecture can coexist.

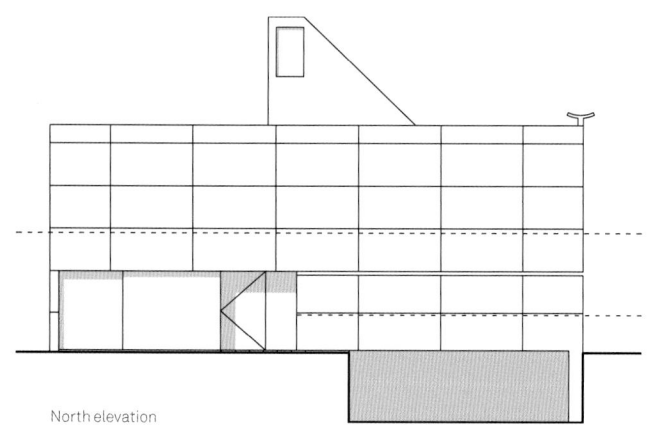

North elevation

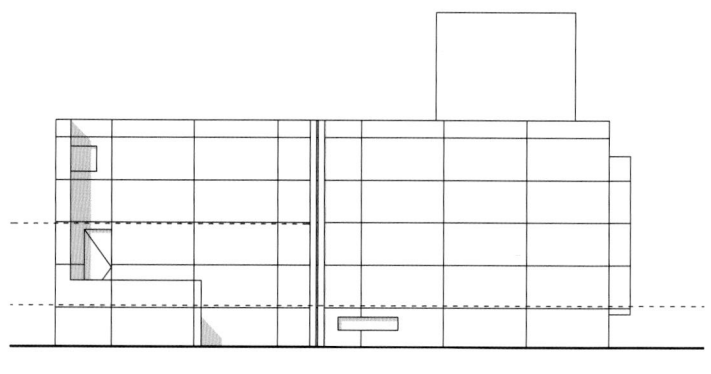

South elevation

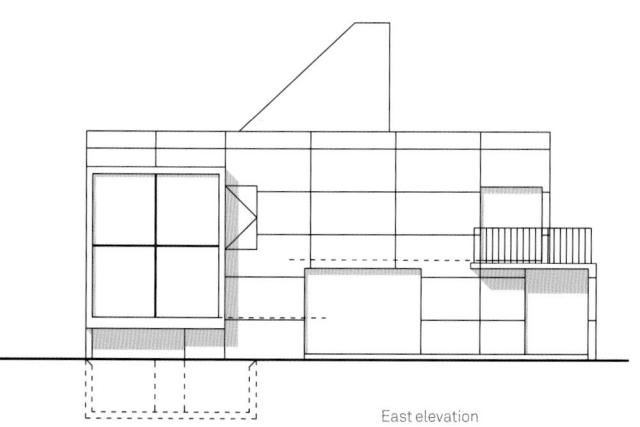

East elevation

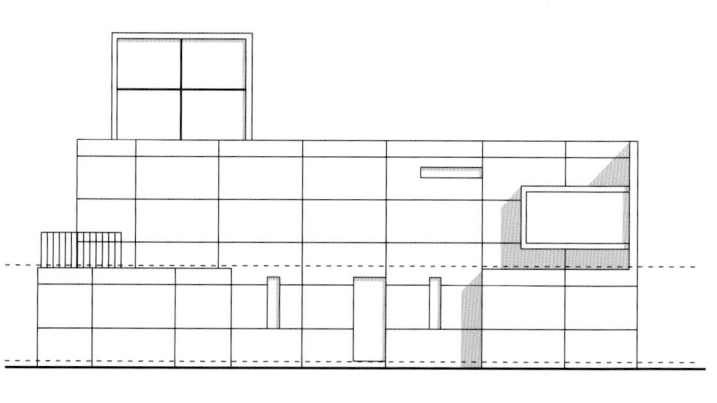

West elevation

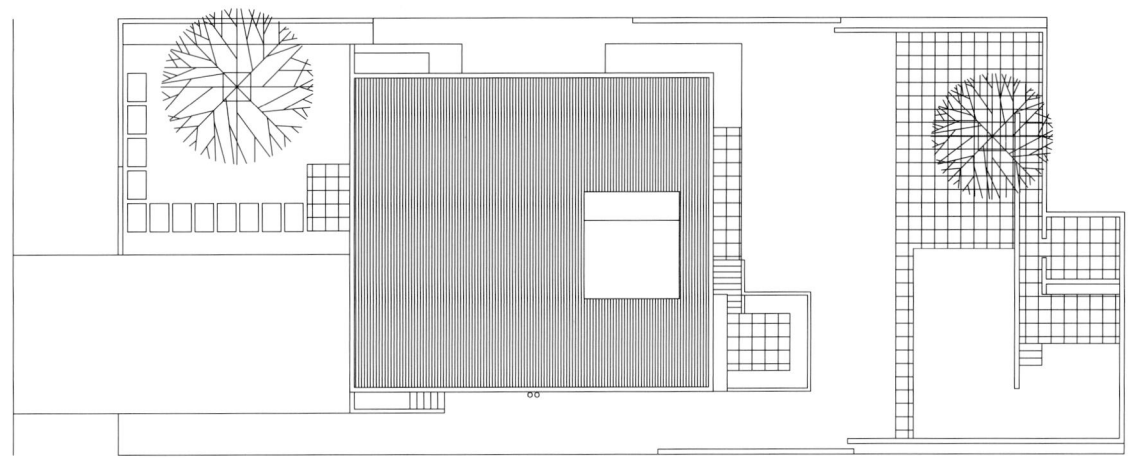

Site plan

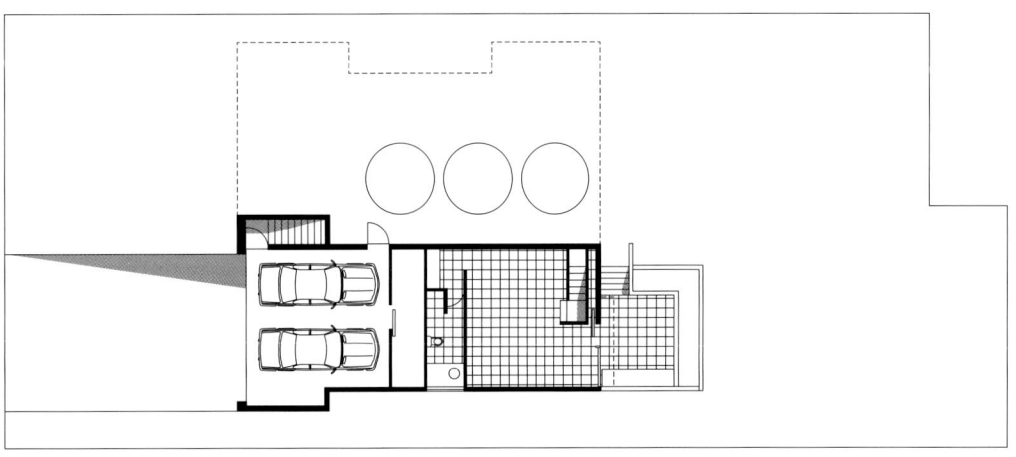

Lower ground floor plan

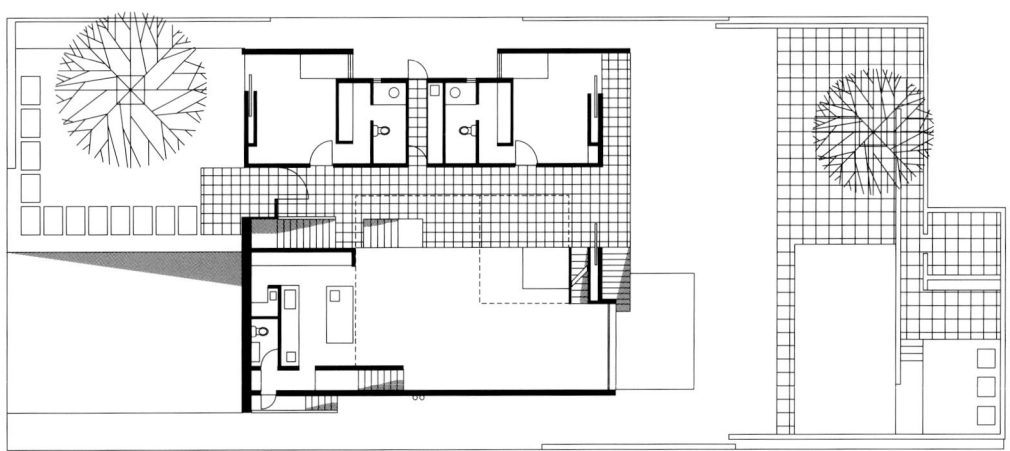

Ground floor plan

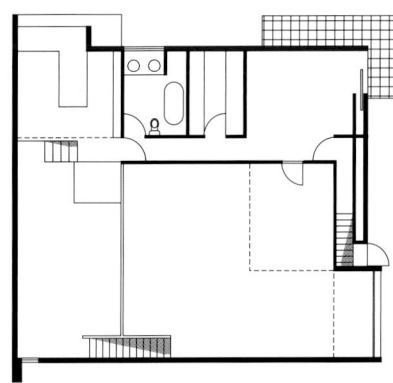

First floor plan

A house made of concrete on an ordinary lot in Melbourne, peeking out here and there, its neighbours determined by middle-class aspirations, at once eclectic and conventional. What Casillas proposes is an almost closed volume on the outside, which immediately marks its distance – as so often in the architect's work – from the surrounding context of pretentiousness and vulgarity. *Juan Palomar, architect and authority on the work of Andrés Casillas de Alba*

    A Barragán-inspired house on a tree-lined street remarkable only for a streetscape of unremarkable late Edwardian houses…an uncompromising concrete box, monumental and all but impenetrable, save for one large opening – a window – to one side…you can only wonder at what the neighbours must be thinking.

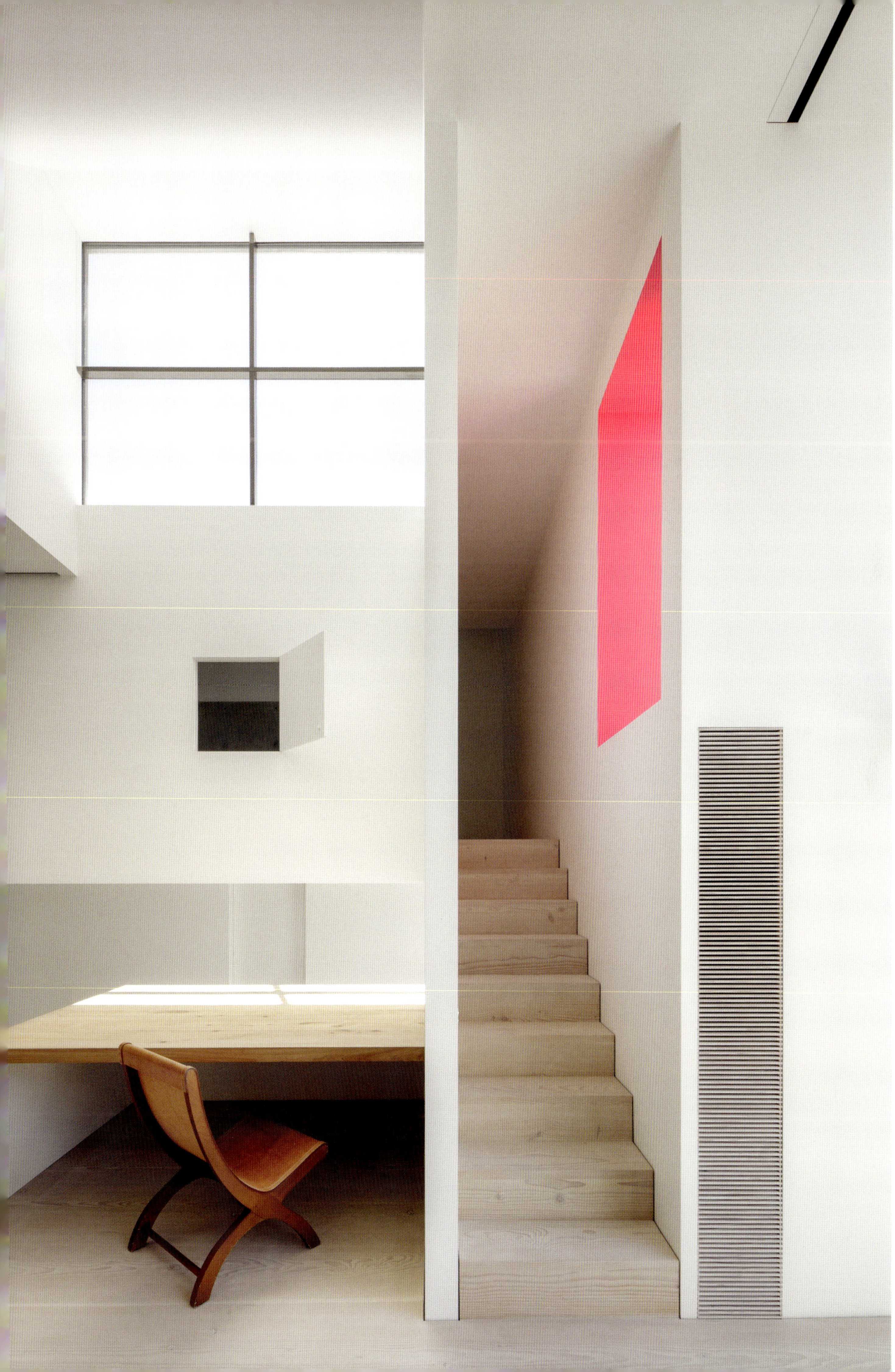

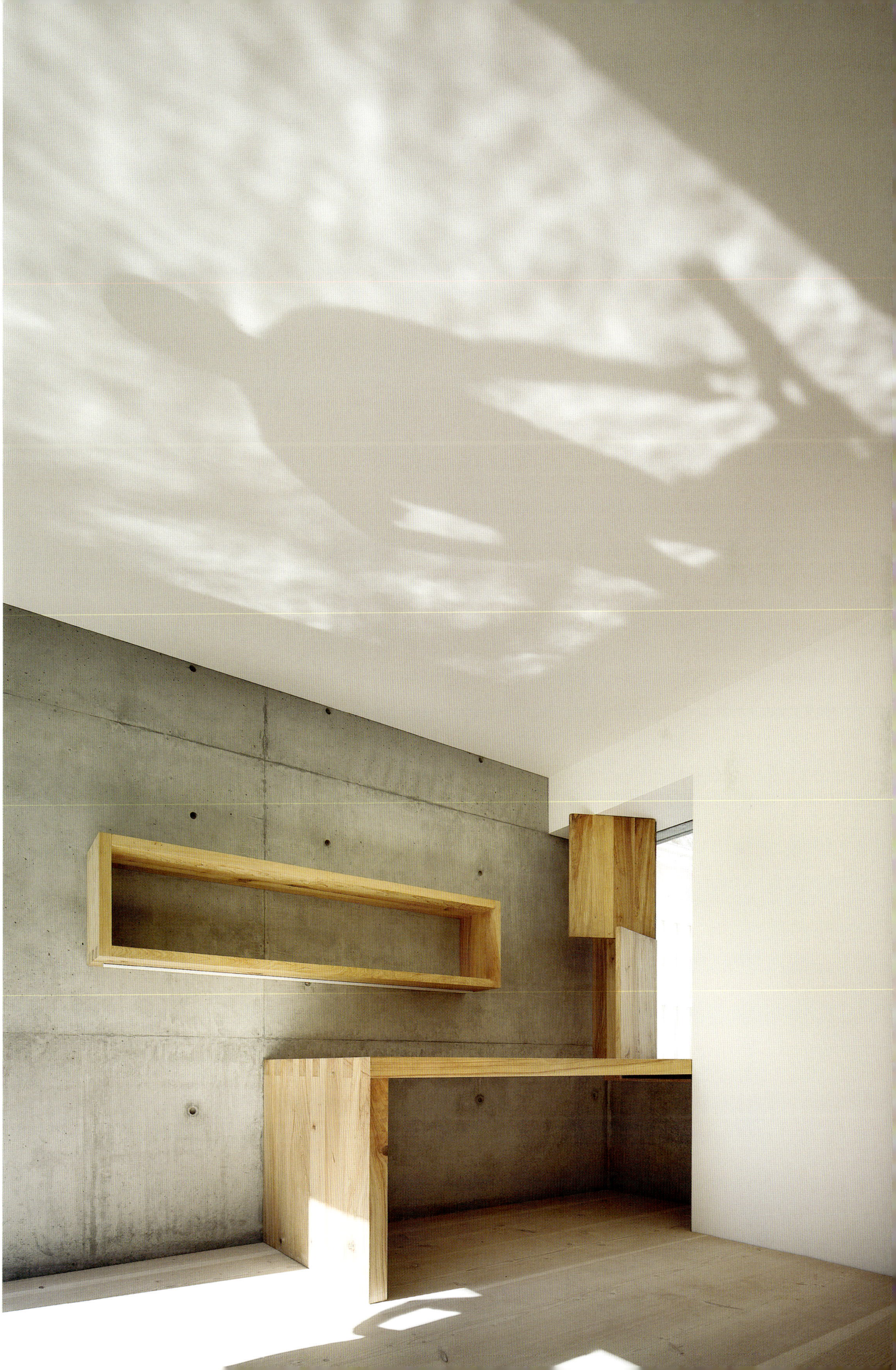

Photographs/Nelson Garrido

036

DOVECOTE

DOVECOTE
BRAGA, PORTUGAL, 2016
AZO SEQUEIRA ARQUITECTOS ASSOCIADOS

Sometimes, it is the small building that resonates most clearly. Like the bus station at Casar de Cáceres in Spain by architect Justo Garcia Rubio from 2007. Few structures demonstrate the fluidity and plasticity of concrete more than this little building in the north of the Extremadura region of western Spain. Located on a corner next to the town's municipal gardens, between a kindergarten and a school, and at the end of a path leading to the town cemetery, this sculptural beauty sweeps and swoops, folding and refolding upon itself in a seamless wave of paper-thin white concrete. Contained within its sinuous folds are the bus station's entire program: floor, walls, ceiling, roof, waiting room and drive-through shelter for buses, all struck as a ribbon of in situ concrete. Its scale is modest, matching that of its surrounding urban context, but the gesture is monumental. All pieces of a city's minutiae, those small details that help determine the feel and fabric of a place, should be as good as this.

This playroom – a tiny cubby house, really – brings to mind the Casar de Cáceres bus station and the requirements often needed for successful architecture: an architect prepared to think outside the box and a client disposed to ideas. Designed by Mário Sequeira of AZO Sequeira Arquitectos Associados, the building replaces an old dovecote that stood derelict for many years in the garden of his client's home in Soutelo on the outskirts of the city of Braga in north-west Portugal. Located close to a swimming pool, the clients wanted a space they could use for different purposes without losing the essence of the original dovecote. Sequeira proposed a new playroom with a balneary (a shower room) below as a contemporary take on the idea of a dovecote, struck entirely of in situ board-marked concrete.

Raised on a single concrete pier, the little building floats above an open shower and change room connected to the swimming pool nearby. Central to the brief was retention of some of the memories of the original dovecote. 'We wanted a playroom inspired by magic, fantasy and also by childhood dreams. We decided to transform the old dovecote into a minimal concrete tree house that represented memories and fantasies of purity of form, light and peace, and memories of the old dovecote with its triangular openings as the fly-in, fly-out points for the family's flight of doves,' Sequeira says. The result is a minimalist room with walls, floor and gabled roof of in situ concrete. A sliding door, reached via stone steps, a steel-framed window with a sliding shutter and a triangular opening at one end of the gable, as a nod to the structure's former life, make up the entire program of the new building. The shower room, with toilet and wash-basin, is partially enclosed by a section of the stone wall that once housed the lower level of the dovecote. Sitting behind a boundary wall, the balneary is all but invisible from a distance. Viewed from afar, however, the dovecote is raised sufficiently to appear as if to be levitating above the top edge of the wall. Sequeira's cubby house demonstrates that good architecture need not be big to be writ large. It shows, too, the potential for innovation and invention when you bring together the skills of an architect with the courage to fail and the support of an enlightened and equally courageous client prepared to go along for the ride.

Ground floor   First floor   0   1m

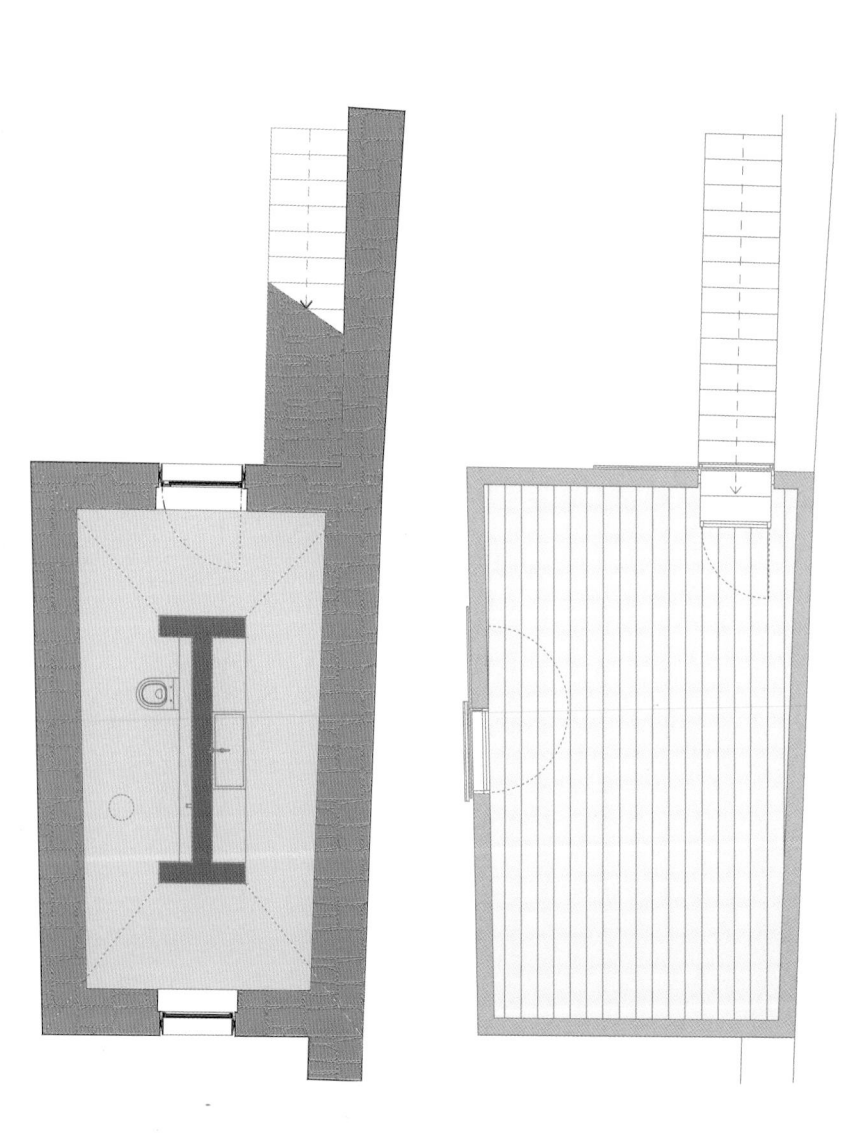

North elevation

Cross-section

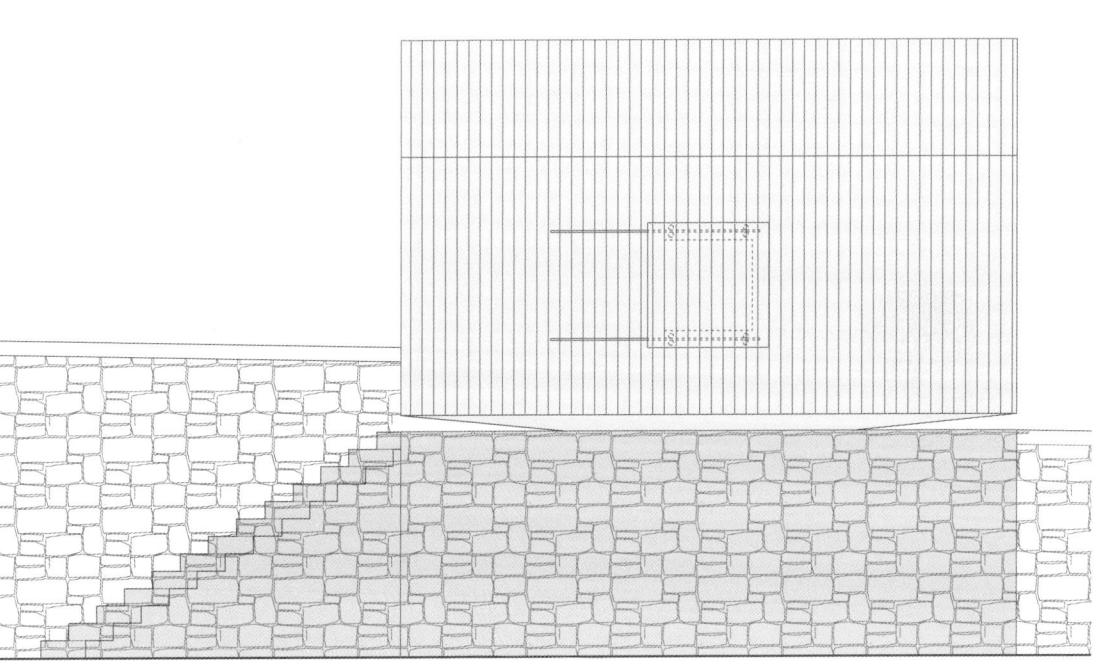

0   1m

West elevation

40 _ 41

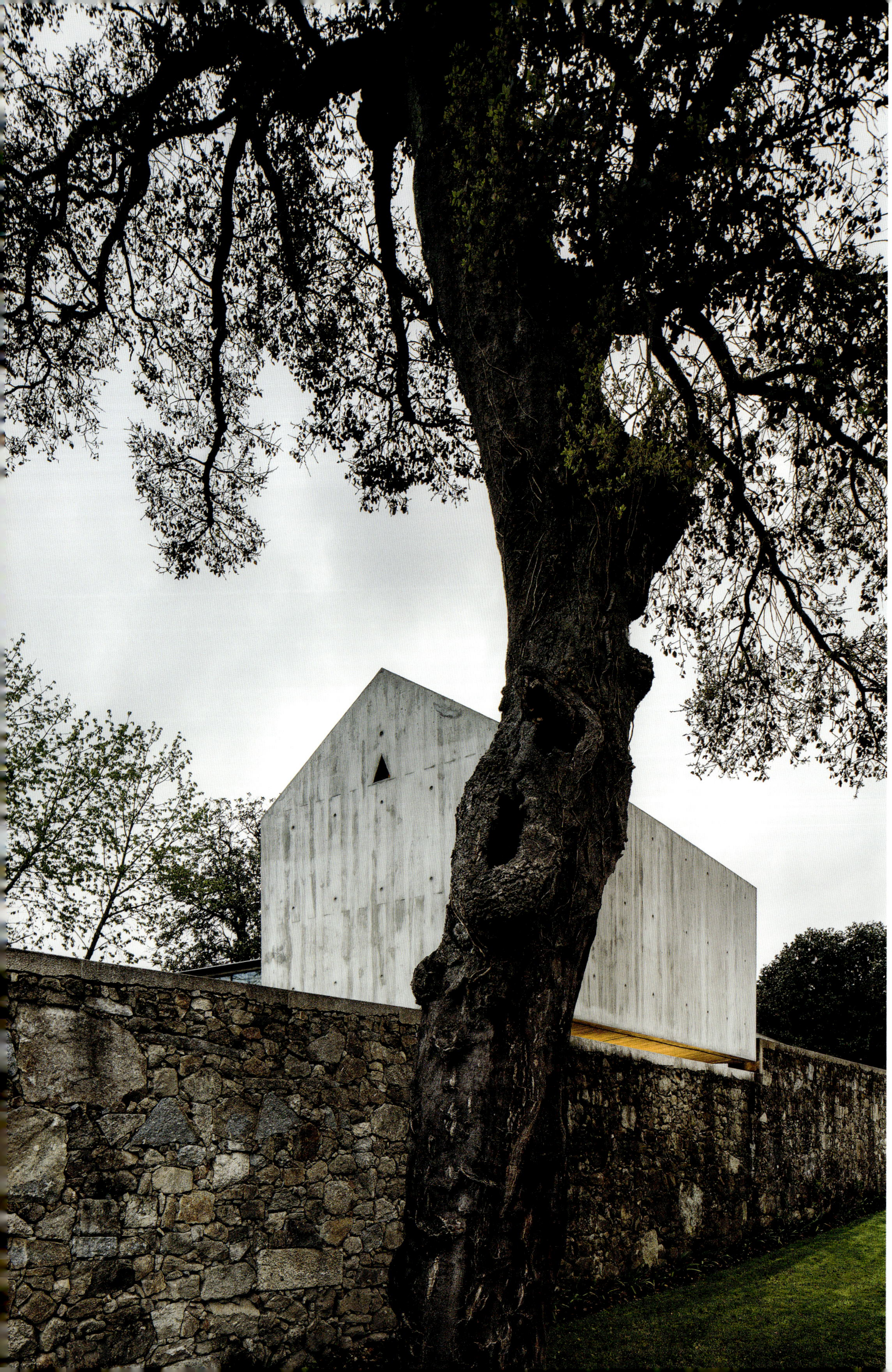

Raised on a single concrete pier, the dovecote floats over an open shower and change room connected to the swimming pool nearby. A minimalist tree house with walls, floor and gabled roof struck as one of in situ concrete…demonstrates that good architecture need not be big to be writ large.

> We wanted a play room inspired by magic, fantasy and also by childhood dreams…to transform the old dovecote into a minimal concrete tree house that represented memories and fantasies of purity of form, light and peace. *Mário Sequeira*

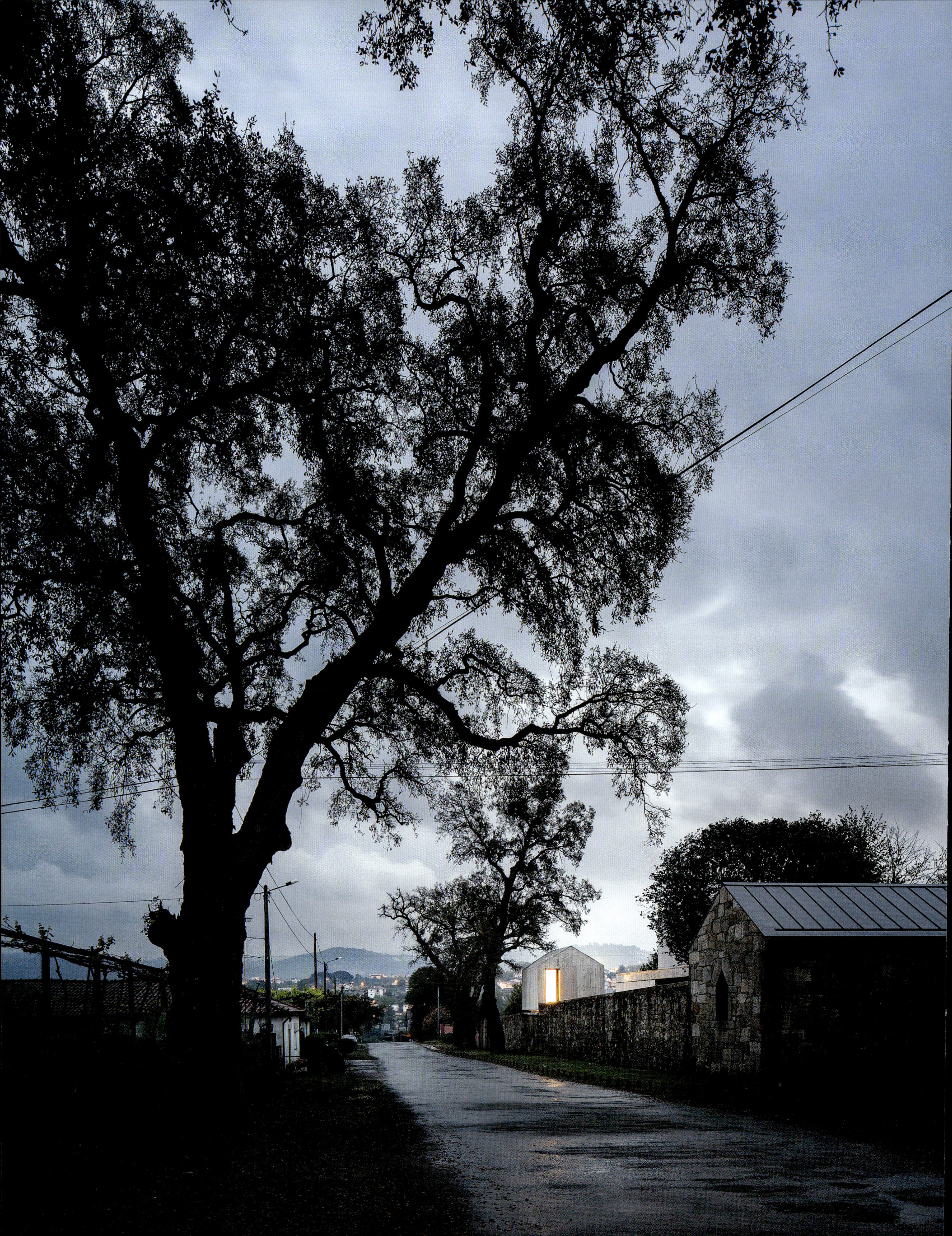

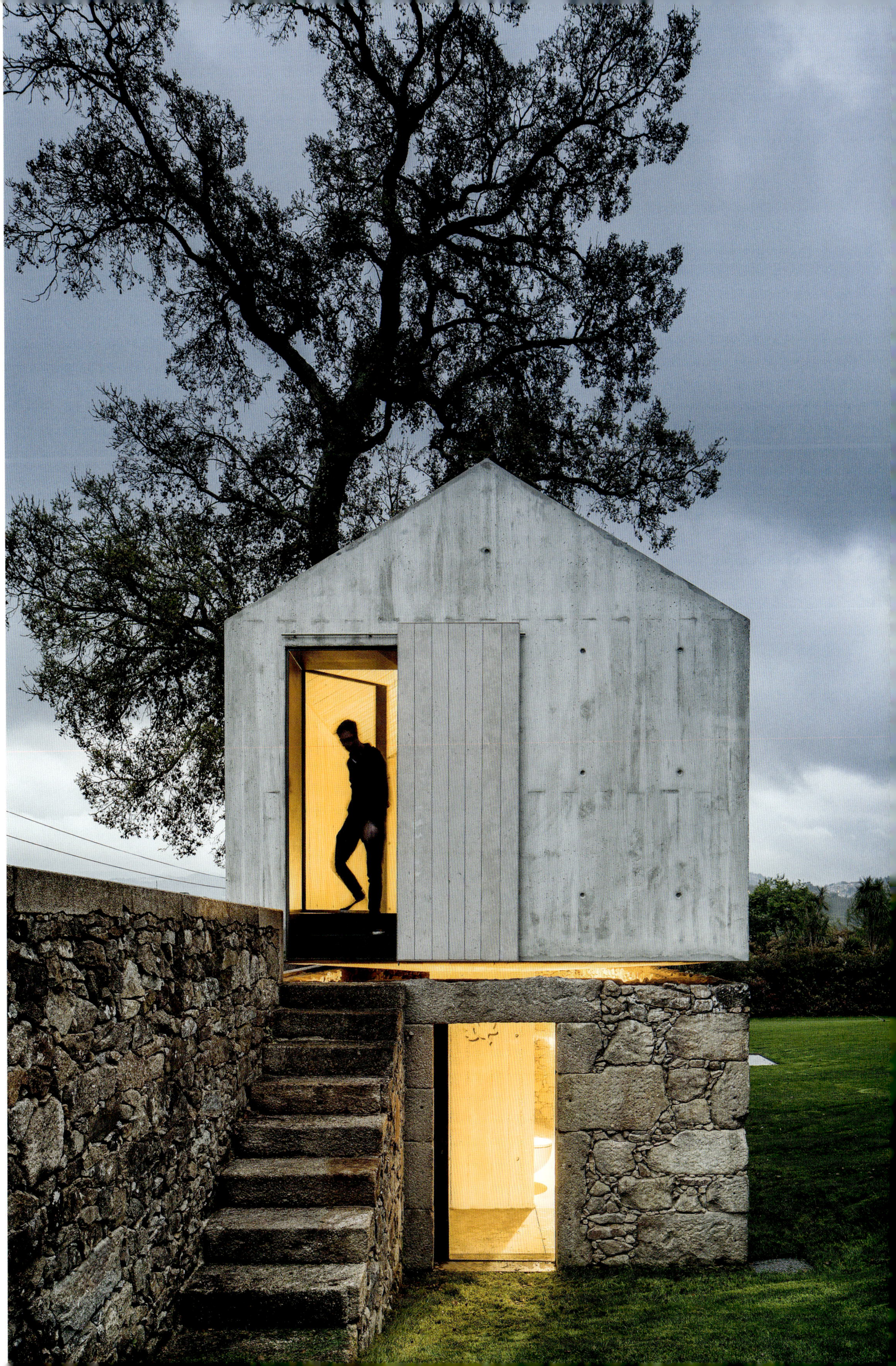

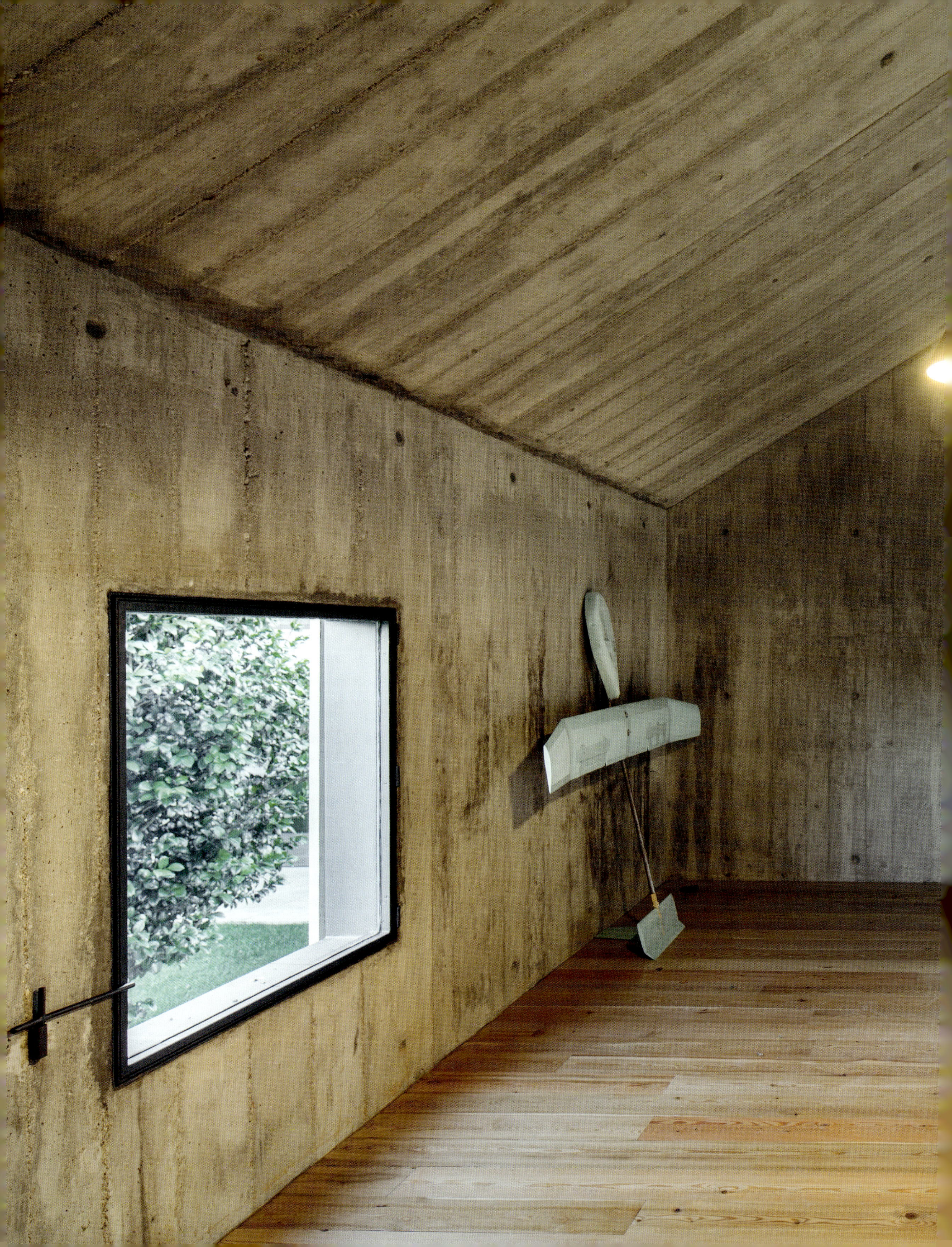

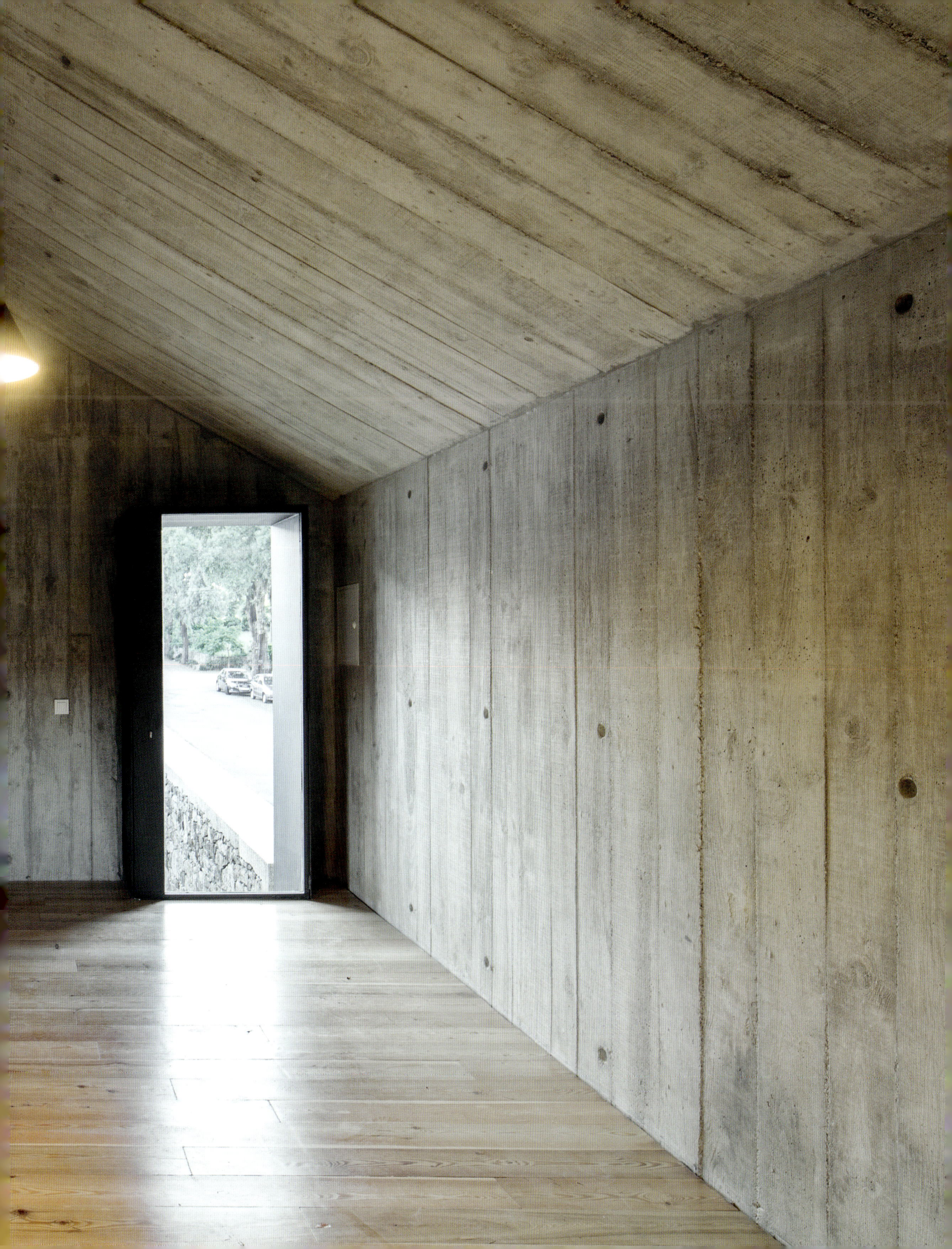

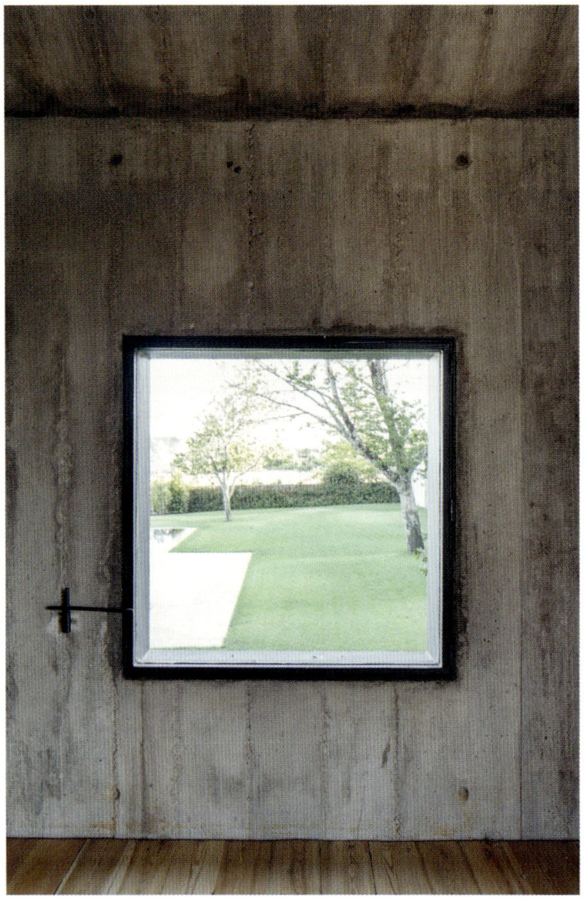
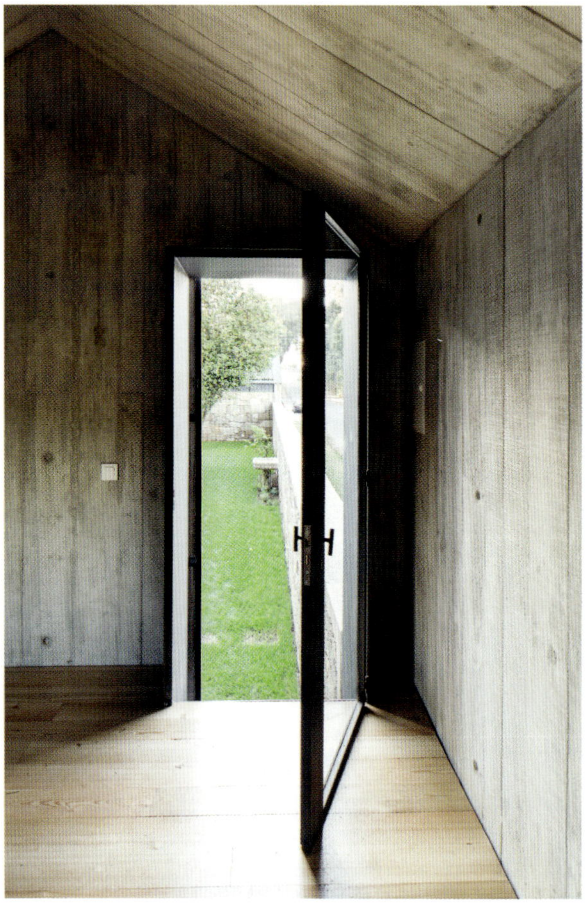

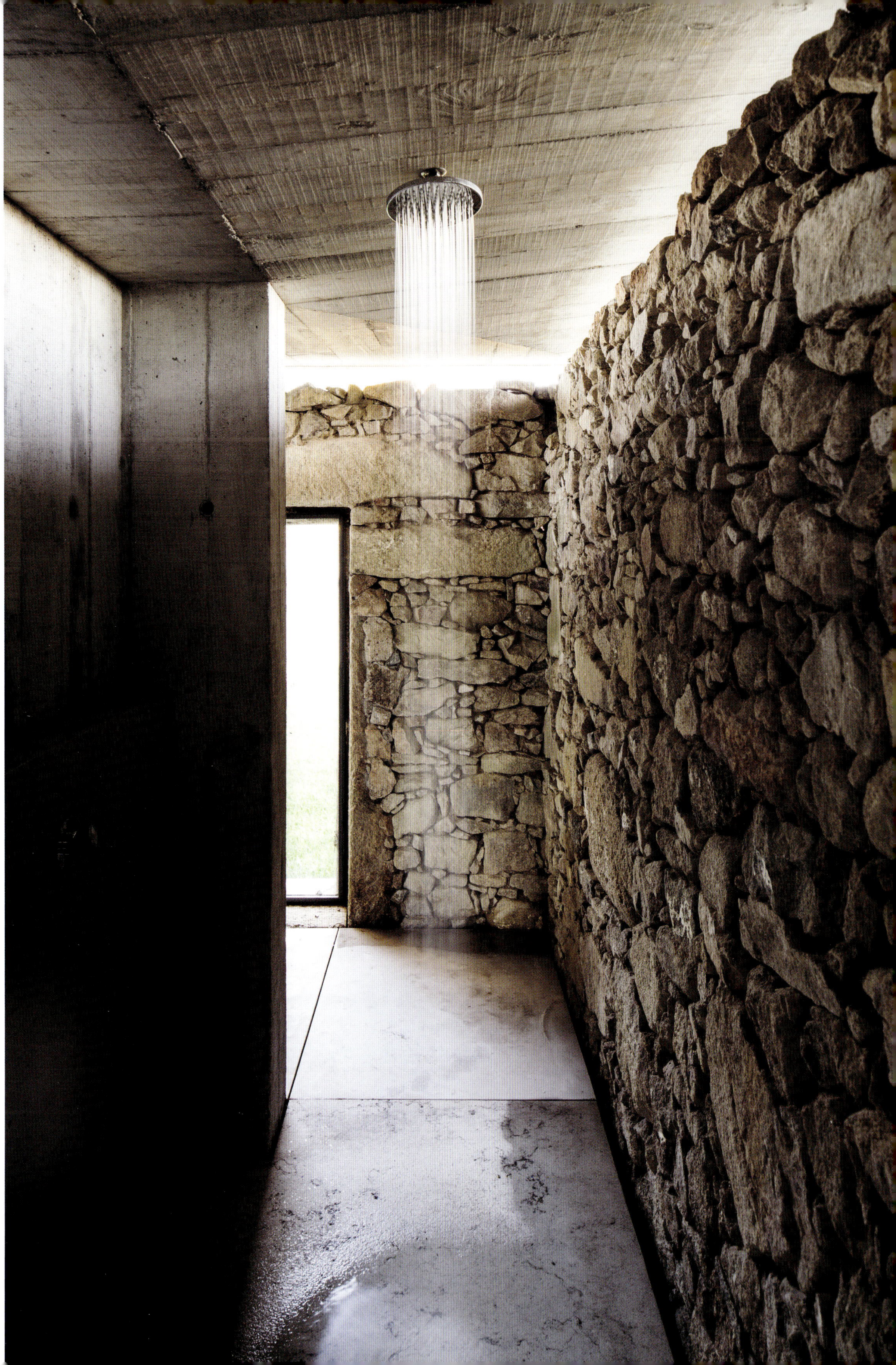

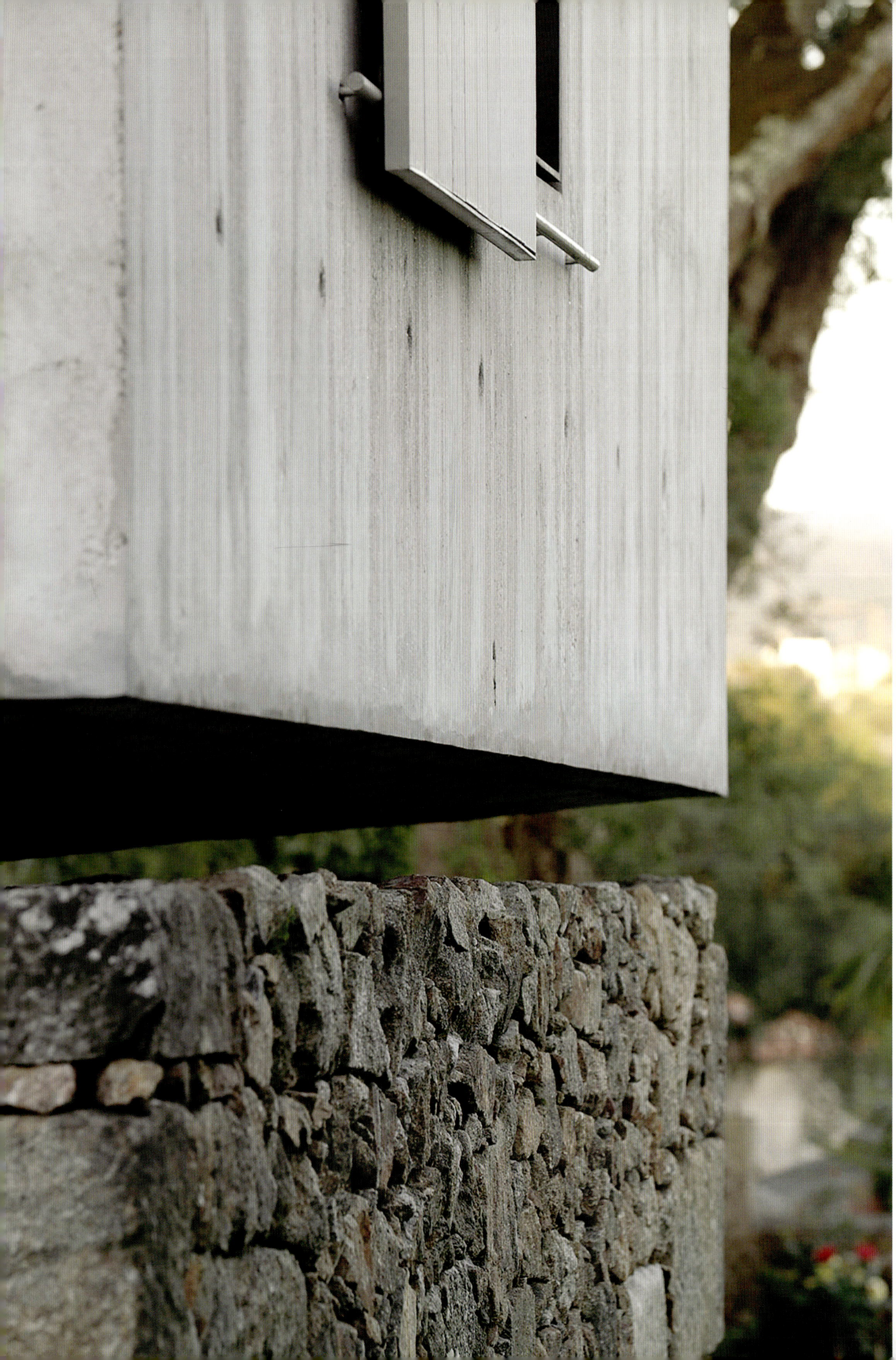

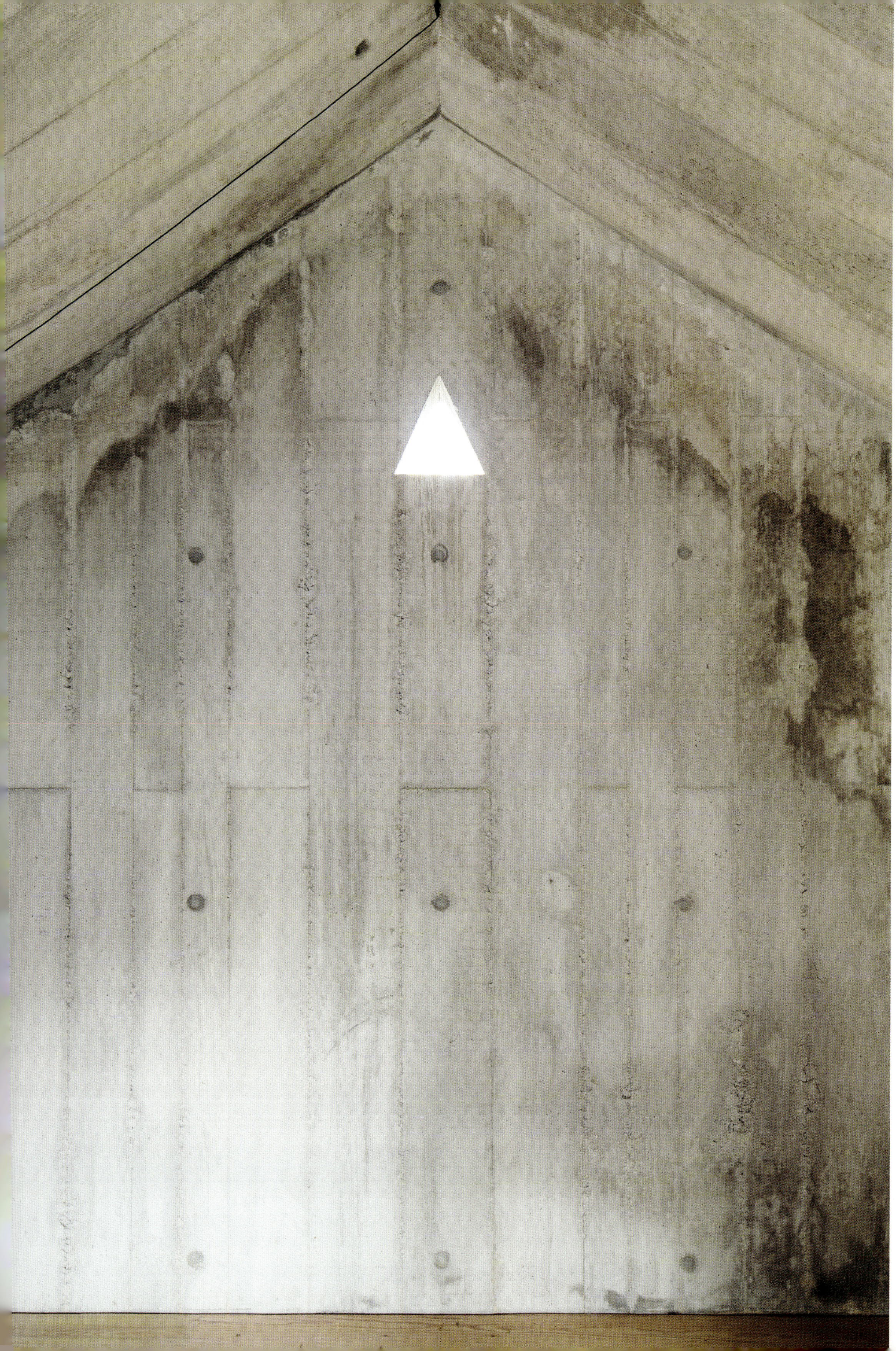

Photographs: Fernando Guerra

052

CASA PLANA

CASA PLANA
PORTO FELIZ, BRAZIL, 2018
STUDIO MK27

Fans of the work of Brazilian architect Marcio Kogan, of Studio MK27, will know his is an architecture of horizontality, of bold and refined houses of low profiles, overlapping planes of in situ concrete, uninterrupted sight lines and rich interiors fashioned from Brazilian wood. No contemporary, living architect better embodies the qualities of Brazilian modernism than Kogan, whose work ranges across architecture, exhibition design and widescreen cinematography.

Utterly at ease within their tropical surroundings, Kogan's houses combine a love of formal simplicity and rich materiality, and radiant connections between interior and exterior spaces. His buildings inhabit their sites as unobtrusively as possible, while maintaining their connection to the landscape and vegetation surrounding them. His work, too, celebrates the plasticity and expressiveness of concrete.

Long fascinated with filmmaking and widescreen cinematography, his houses are, in his own words, 'architecture in cinematic widescreen', as in this house in the countryside at Porto Feliz, two hours by car from São Paulo, Brazil, designed in collaboration with architect Lair Reis. Though large, at around 1000 square metres, the planning is simple and direct: a central hallway divides the house into two distinct volumes, both oriented north to south. On one side, facing east, are the kitchen, staff bedrooms and a gym. Family bedrooms and bathrooms are located on the other side of the corridor, with views to the west and out to a garden and lake beyond.

While this axial route functions as a warm, wood-panelled gallery for the owners' photography collection, its dark compressed space dramatises the arrival at a large, glazed pavilion-like room where family and friends can gather. Located at the southern end of the house, this space can be opened up completely with sliding glass doors, transforming it into an expansive indoor–outdoor terrace, opening onto a long rectangular swimming pool.

What is remarkable here is that the house is dominated by a spectacular roof plane of board-marked in situ concrete, measuring 67.8 metres x 17.3 metres, raised on thirteen slender cruciform steel posts and concrete pillars. The roof functions as a sheltering plane projecting past the perimeter walls of the house, extending to shelter living and dining areas to the south and car parking to the north. The concrete roof, sown with grass and accessible to gardeners only via a stepladder, serves as an efficient thermal blanket, helping keep the building cool in summer and warm in winter.

'This type of insertion on the plot demanded care and attention with the design of the rooftop, which has become the fifth facade of the building,' Kogan says. 'This was an exercise in composition and selection of the equipment to be placed there, such as solar panels and skylights. The green roof mimics the surrounding lawn as well as contributes to the thermal comfort of the house.'

In a departure from the studio's usual formality, a freestanding, perforated red-brick wall swoops around the house in serpentine curves along the east elevation as a means of shielding the house from the street without isolating it entirely. The wall, probably the first curve in the history of the studio, borders a garden. 'Paradoxically, the wall defines the different relationships between internal and external spaces...[it] is at times concave and at others convex, embracing the entrance garden and creating transparencies as well as offering protection from the street,' Kogan says. 'Its texture contributes to a cozy atmosphere and creates light filters with kinetic effects as the day passes.' A basement space, accessed only through an external bunker-like entrance, contains the plant and equipment for the pool, as well as a changing room and a non-potable water reservoir for the re-use of rainwater.

Floors are paved in Brazilian basalt, walls are sheathed in yellow Brazilian freijo wood panelling, but it is the concrete roof, floating lightly over the rectangular glass perimeter enclosure, that is the highlight of this house.

Ground floor

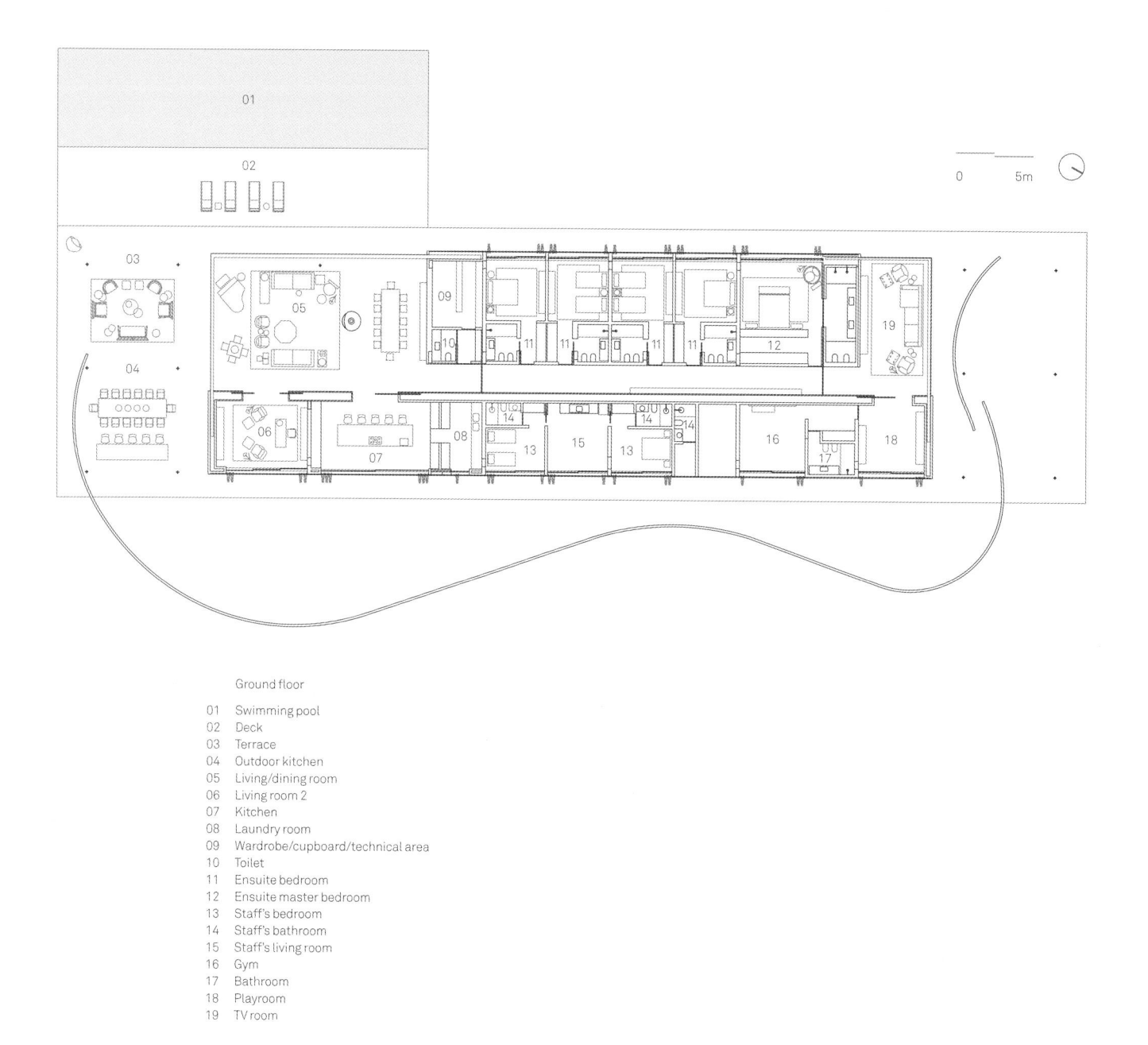

01 Swimming pool
02 Deck
03 Terrace
04 Outdoor kitchen
05 Living/dining room
06 Living room 2
07 Kitchen
08 Laundry room
09 Wardrobe/cupboard/technical area
10 Toilet
11 Ensuite bedroom
12 Ensuite master bedroom
13 Staff's bedroom
14 Staff's bathroom
15 Staff's living room
16 Gym
17 Bathroom
18 Playroom
19 TV room

0   5m

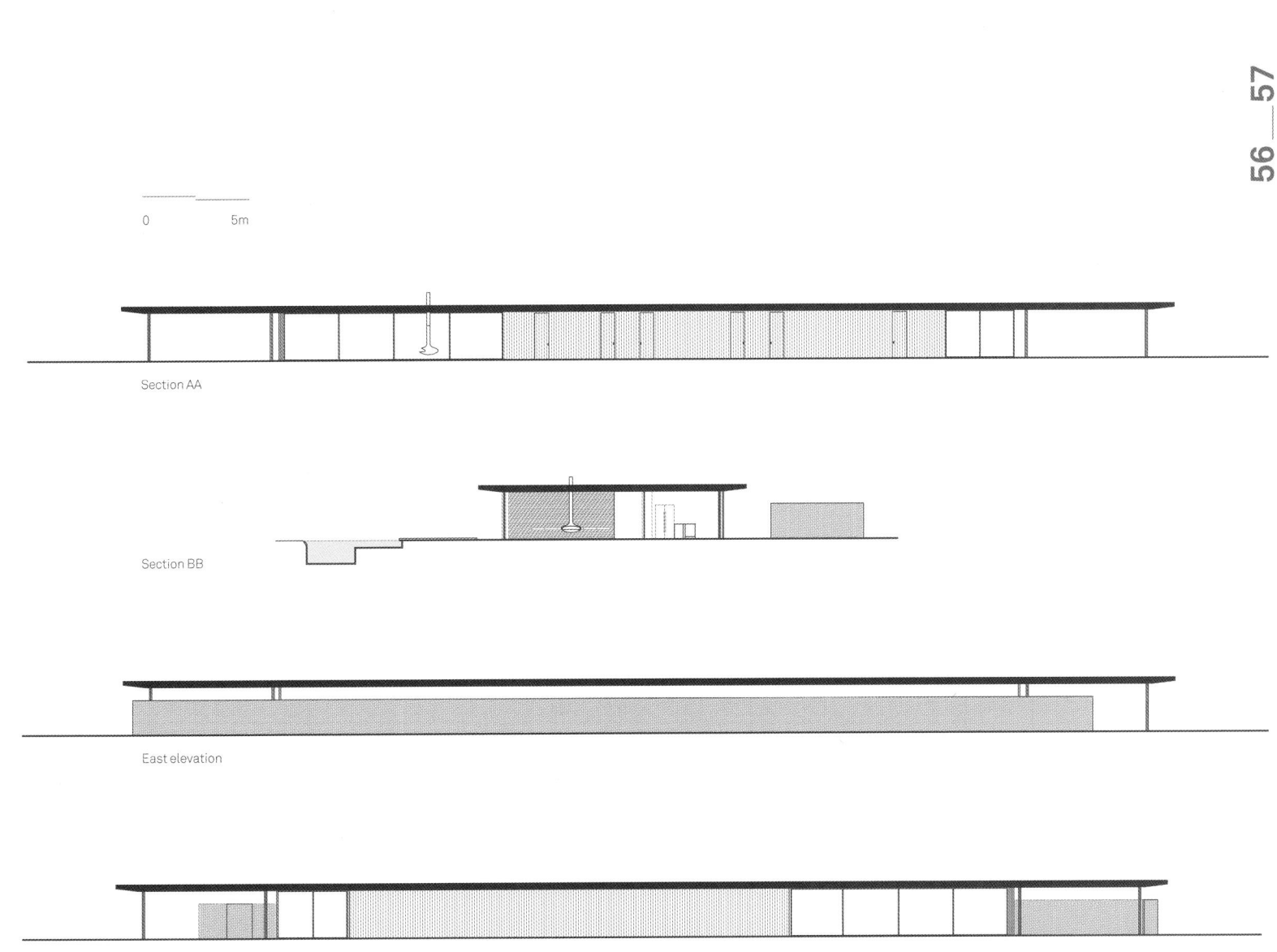

Section AA

Section BB

East elevation

West elevation

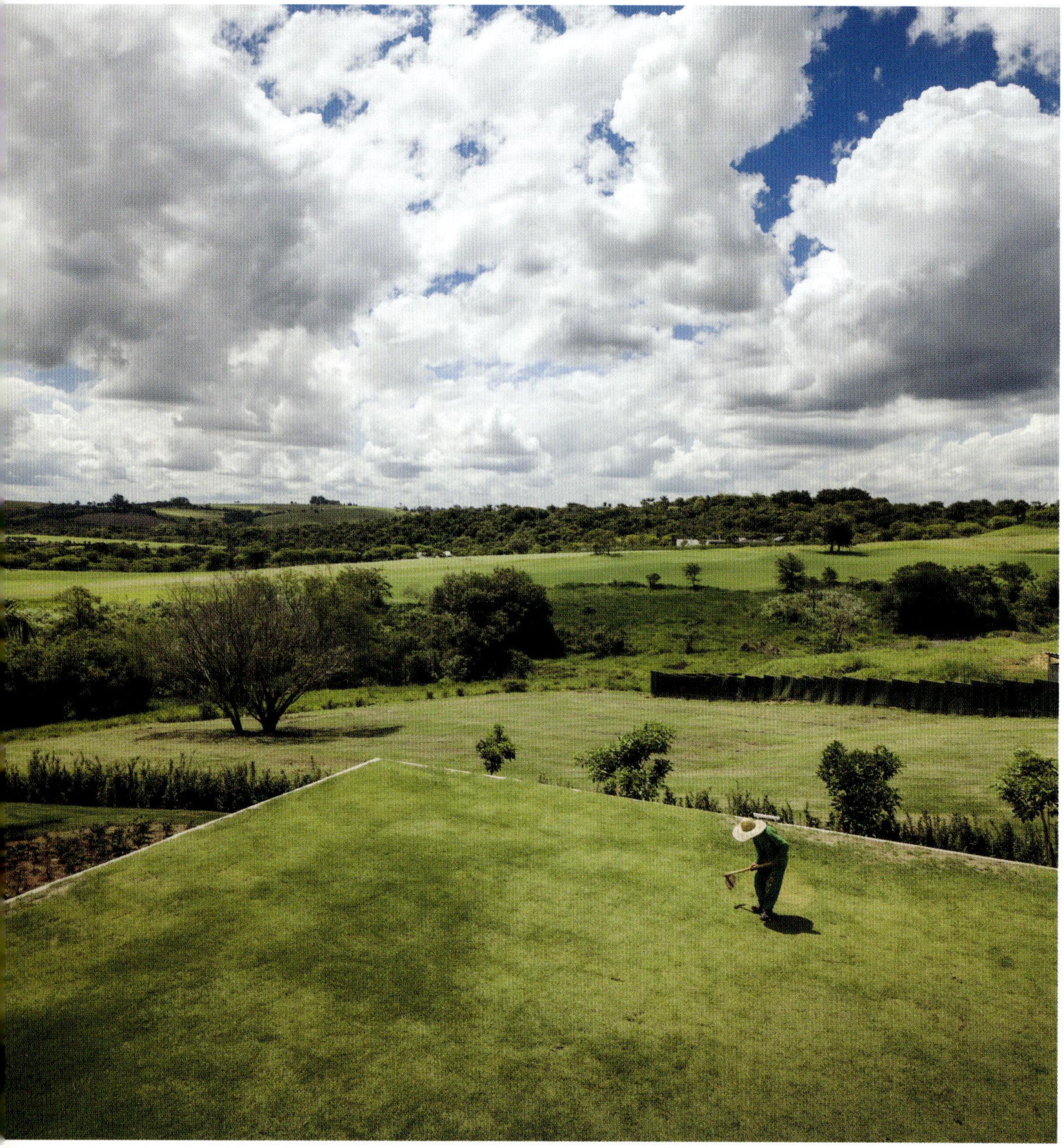

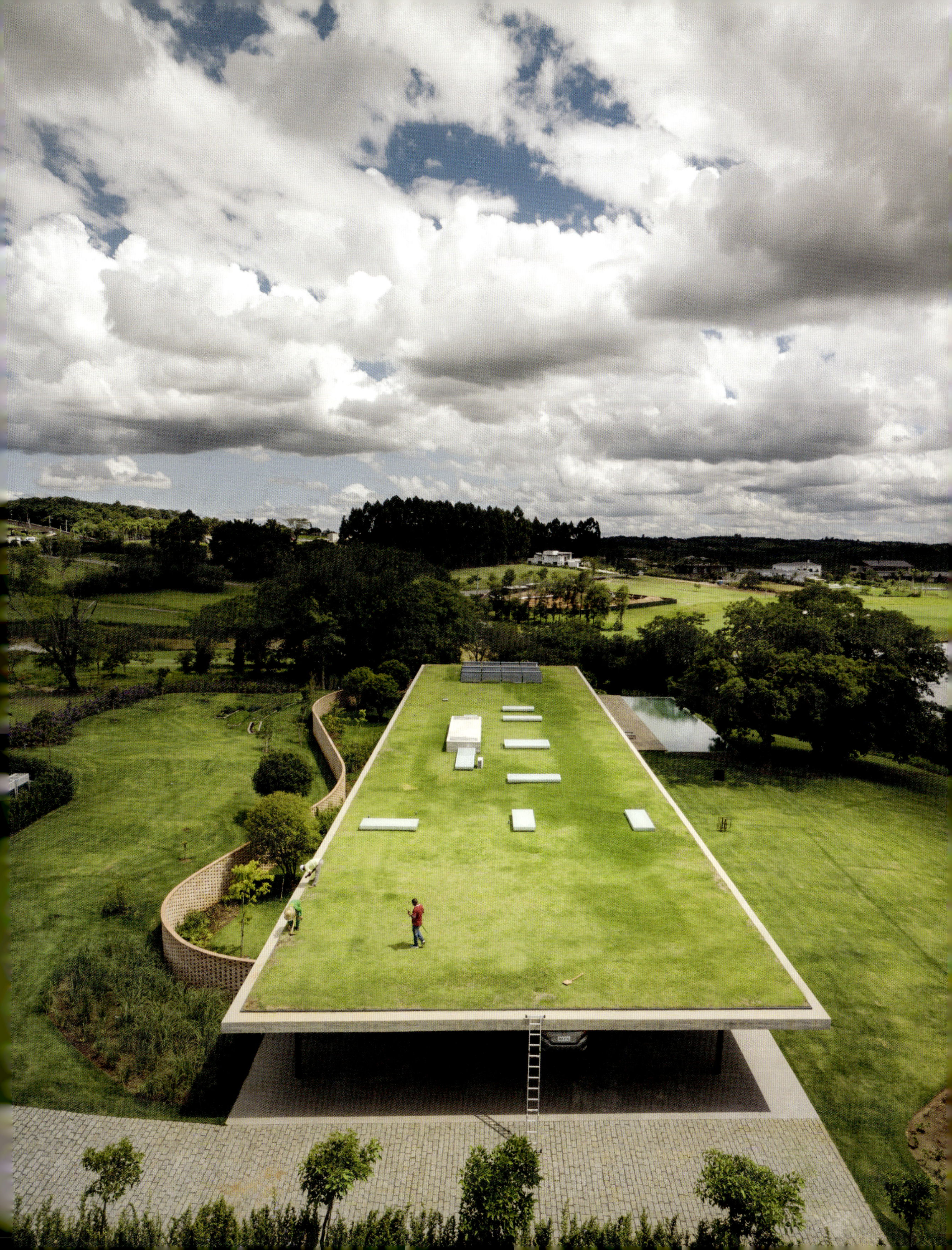

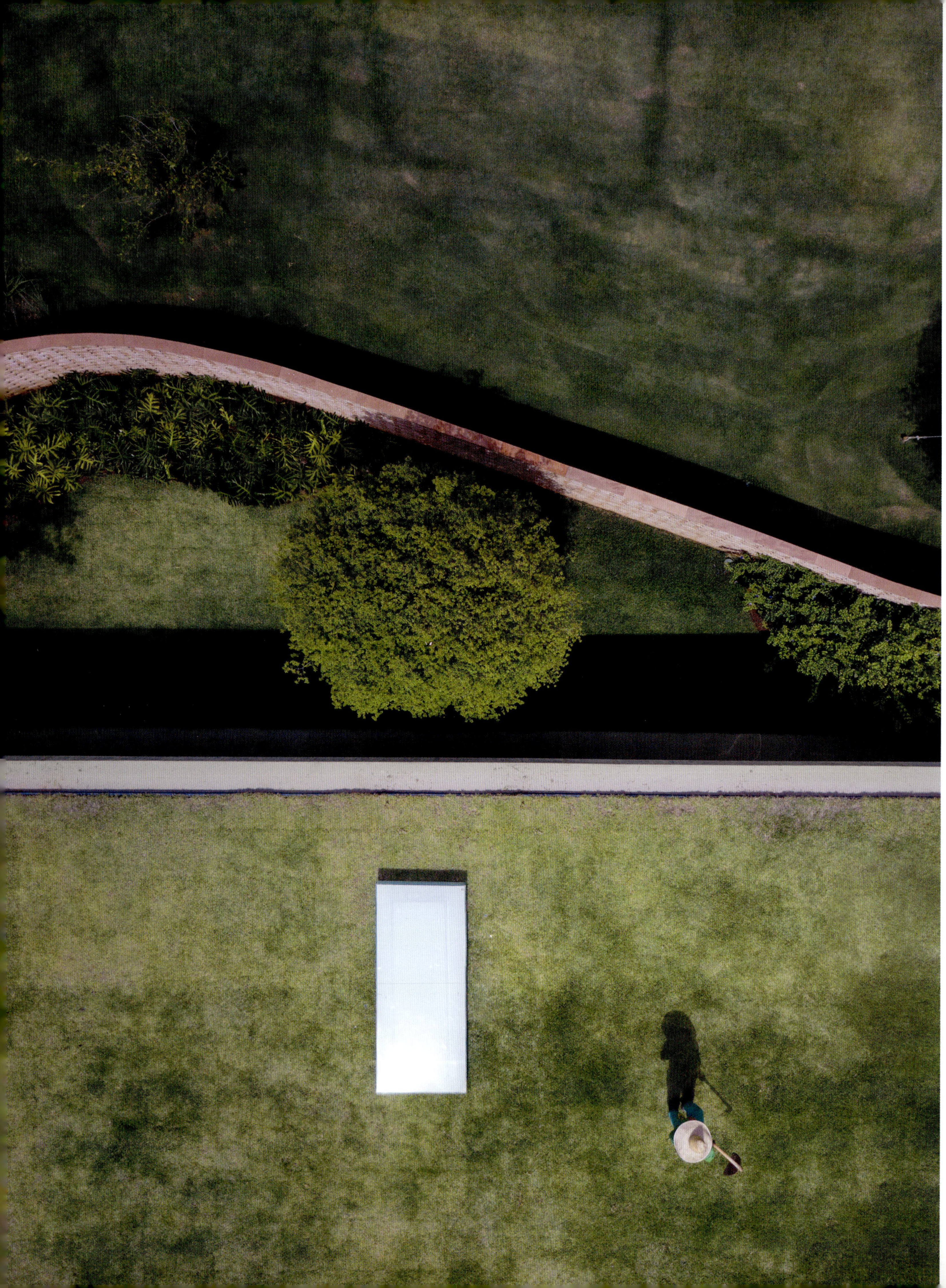

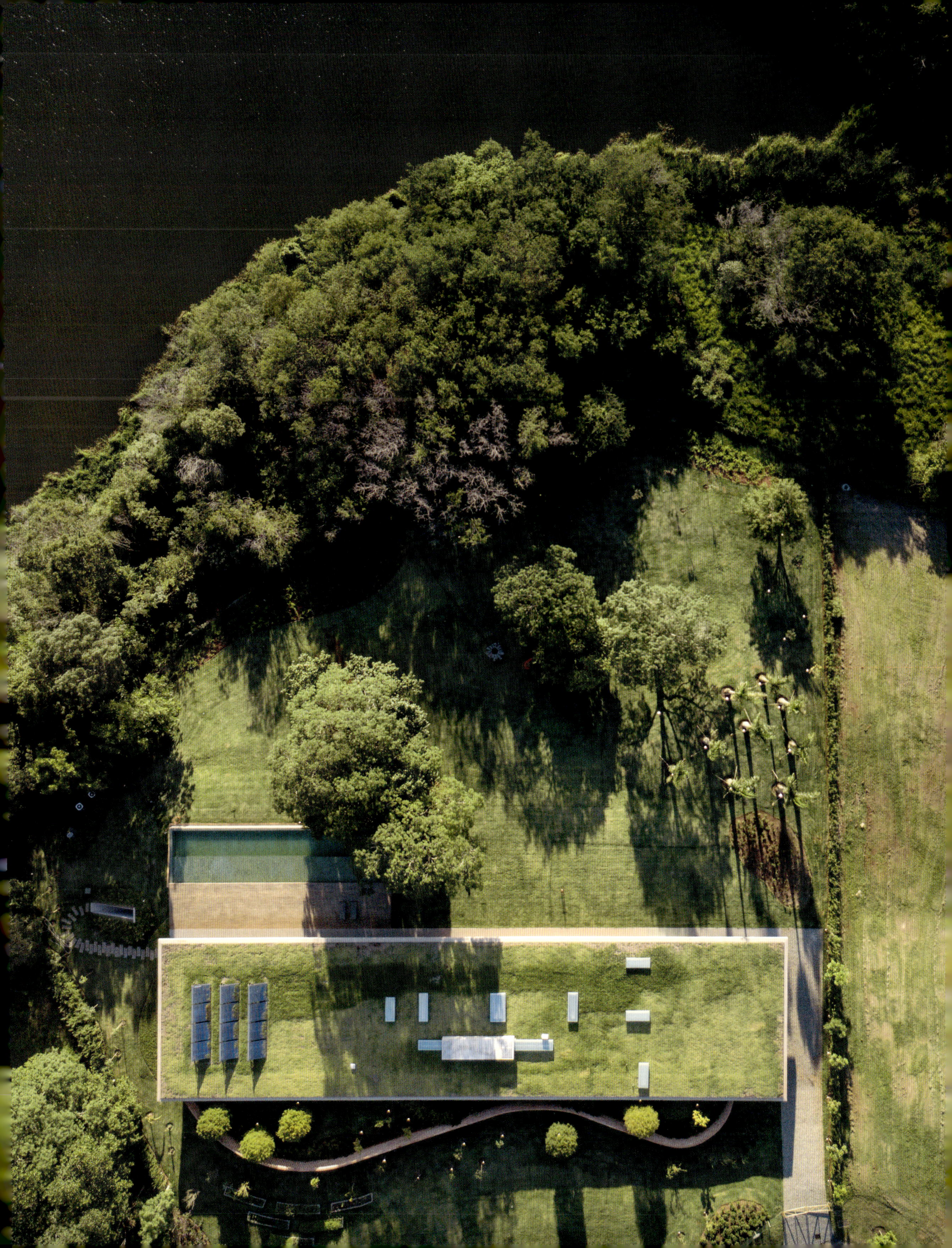

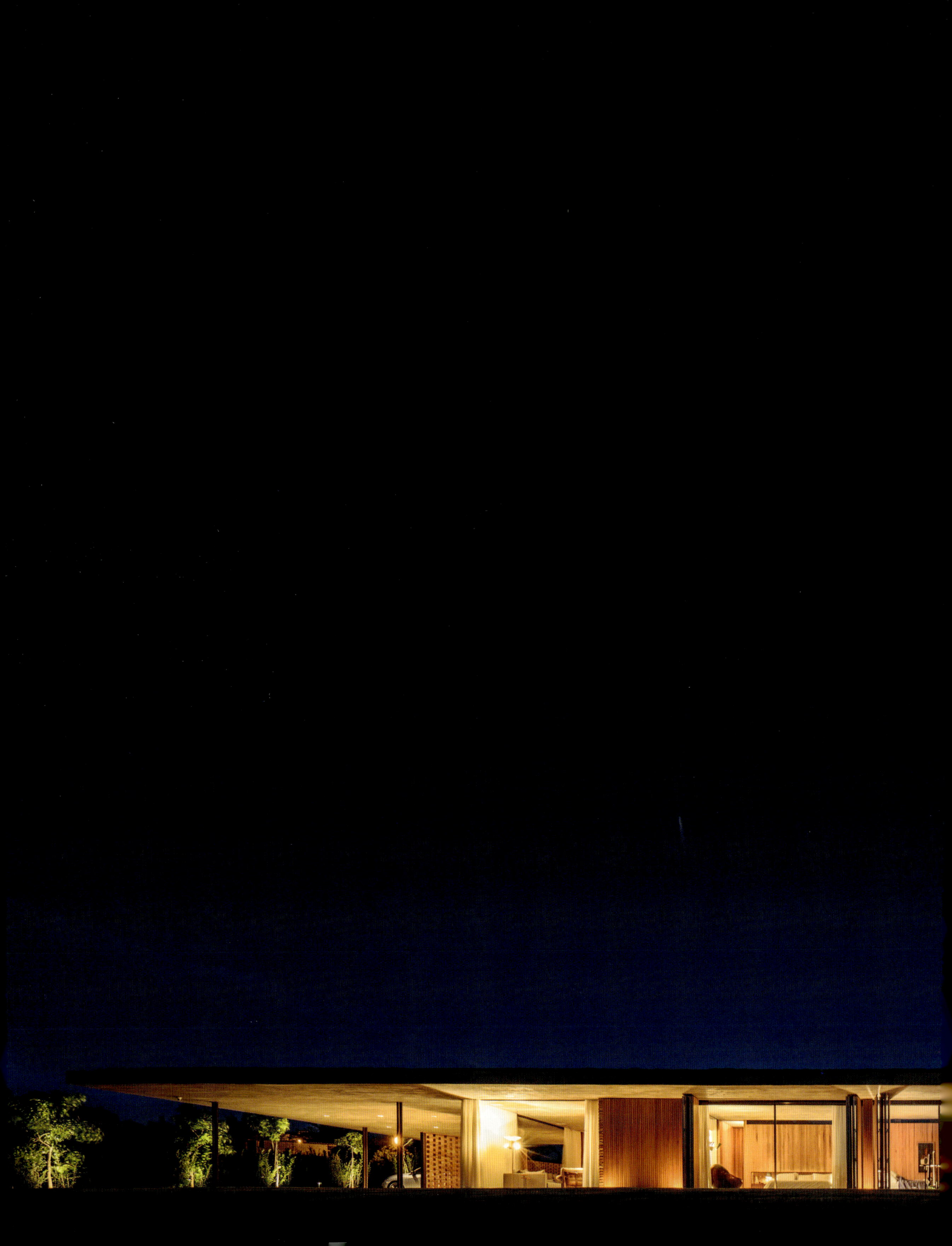

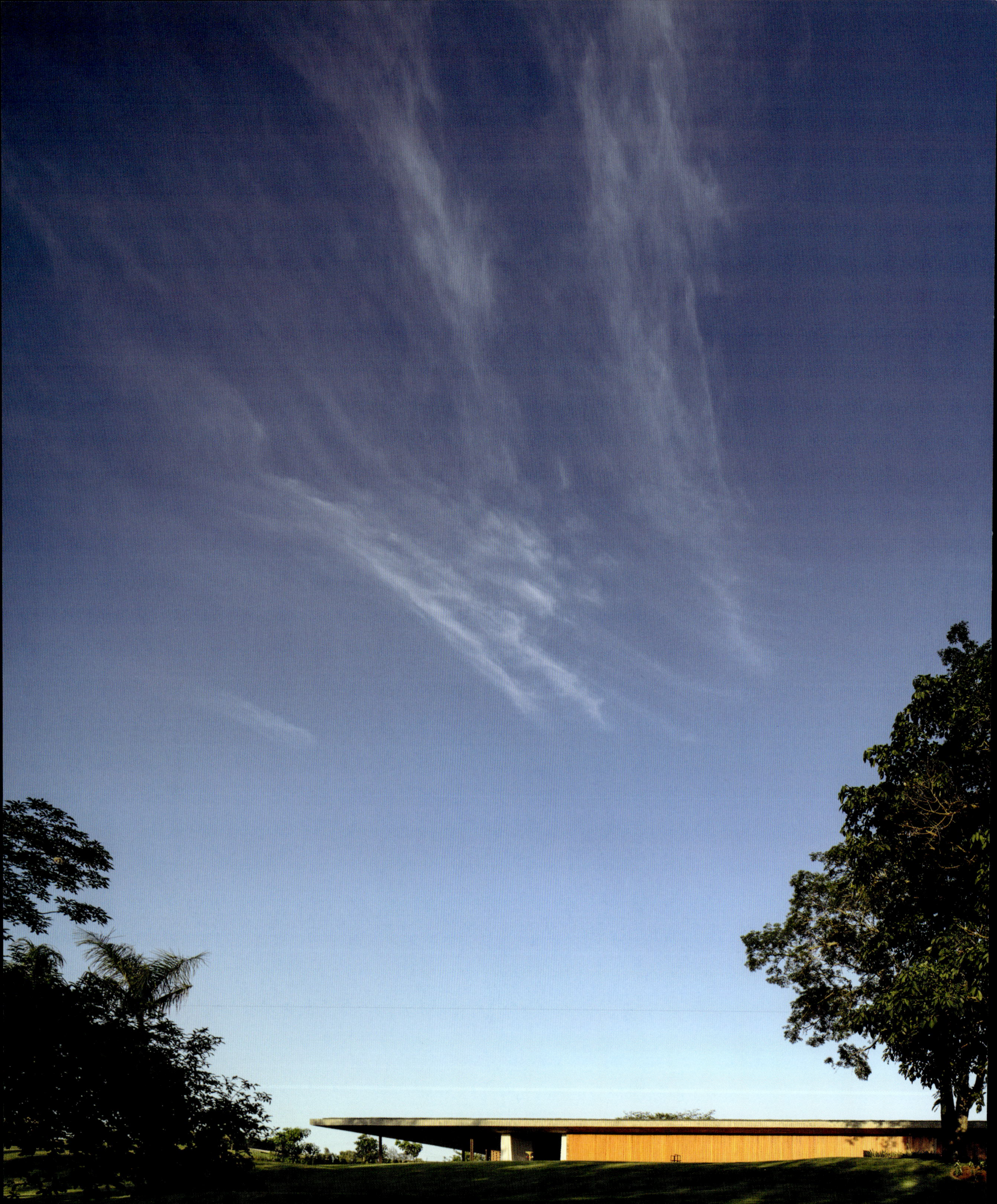

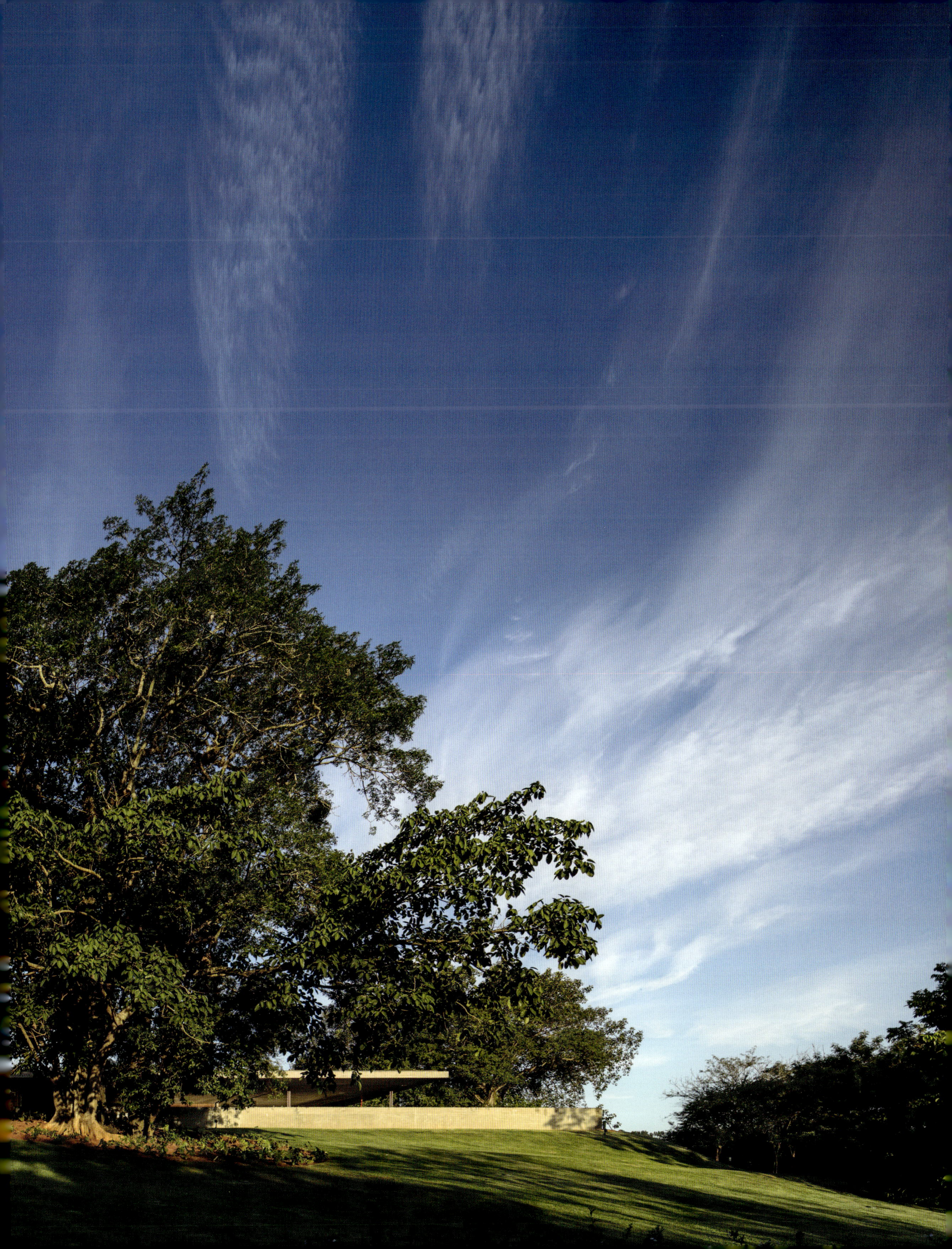

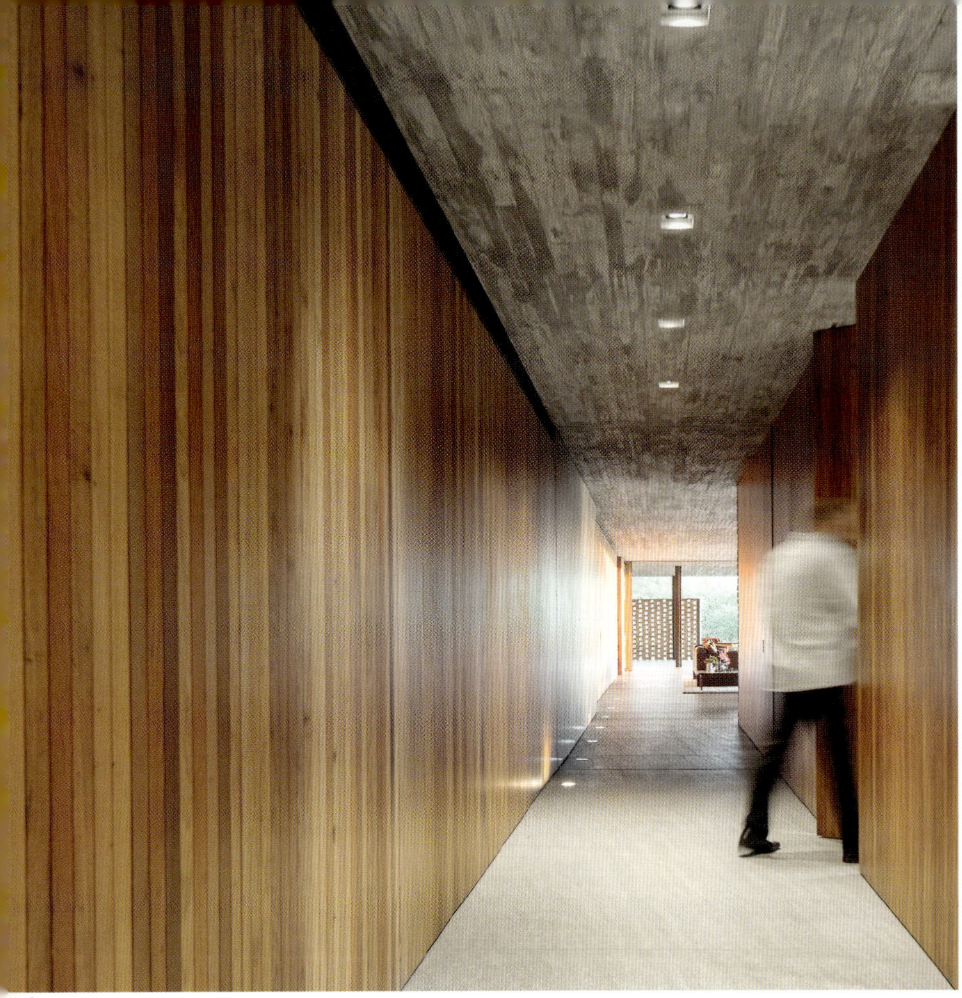

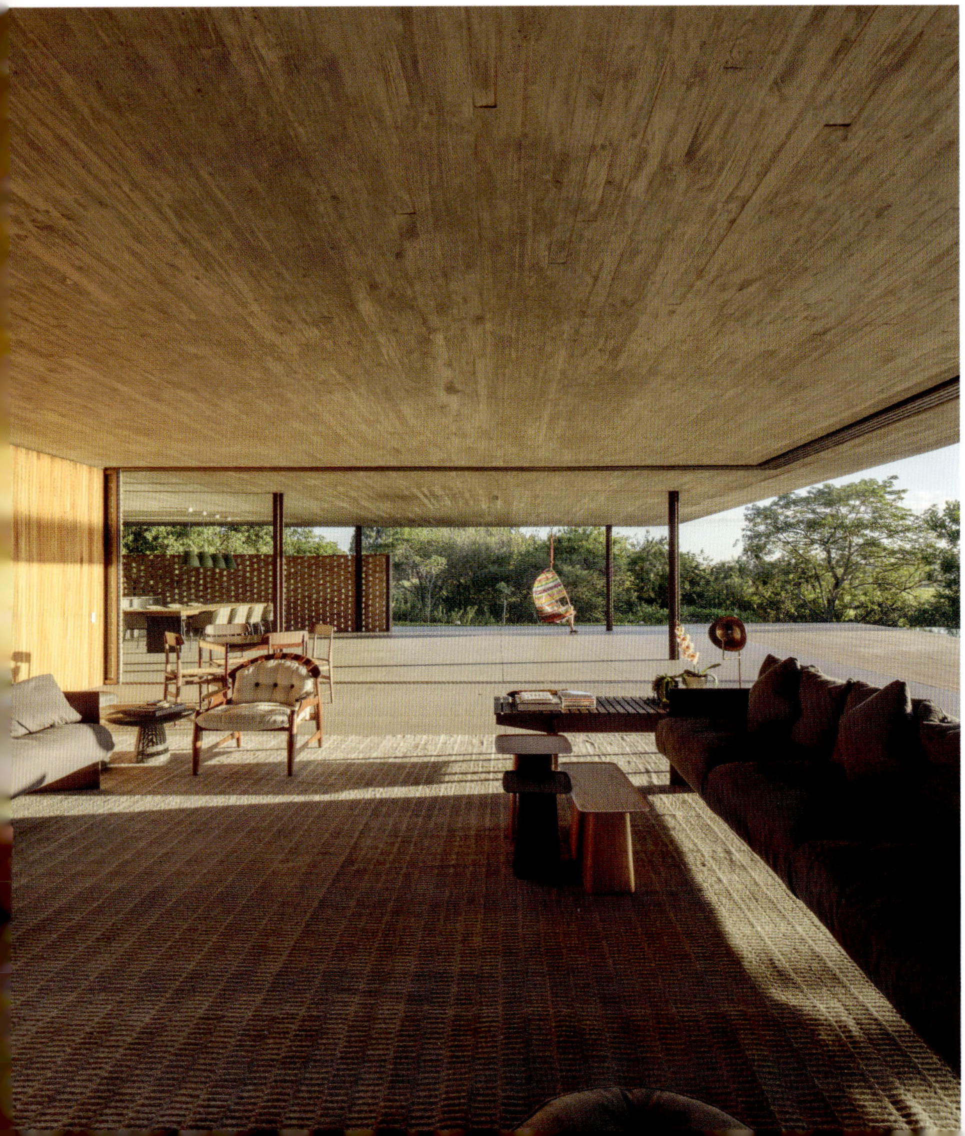

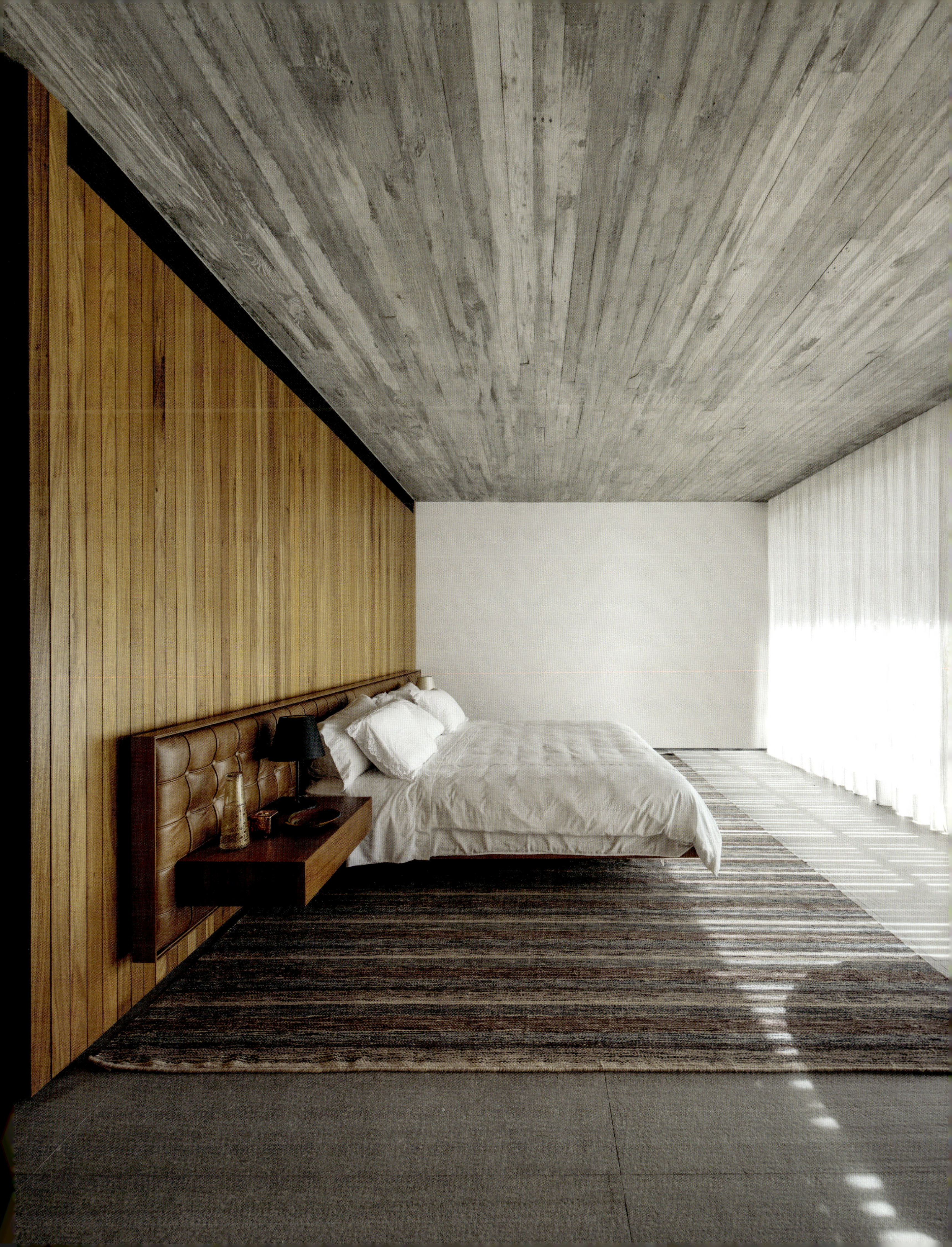

Surrounding the rigid, formal distribution of spaces, there is a brick, winding wall arranged in solids and voids. Paradoxically, the wall defines the different relationships between internal and external spaces. The wall, which is usually a symbol of division and isolation, is at times concave and at others convex, embracing the entrance garden and creating transparencies as well as offering protection from the street. Its texture contributes to a cozy atmosphere and creates light filters with kinetic effects as the day passes. *Marcio Kogan*

This type of insertion on the plot demanded care and attention with the design of the rooftop, which has become the fifth facade of the building. This was an exercise in composition and selection of equipment to be placed there, such as solar panels and skylights. The green roof mimics the surrounding lawn as well as contributes to the thermal comfort of the house. *Marcio Kogan*

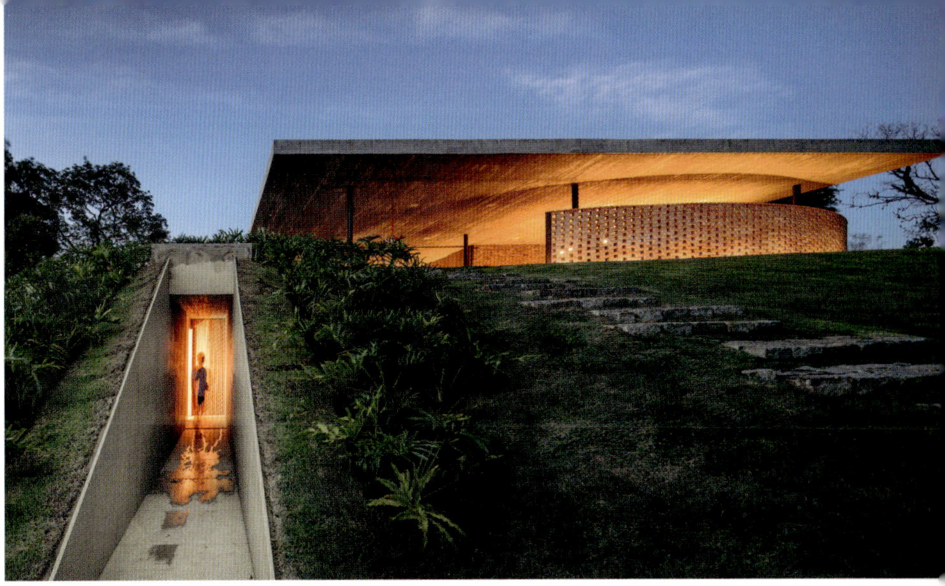

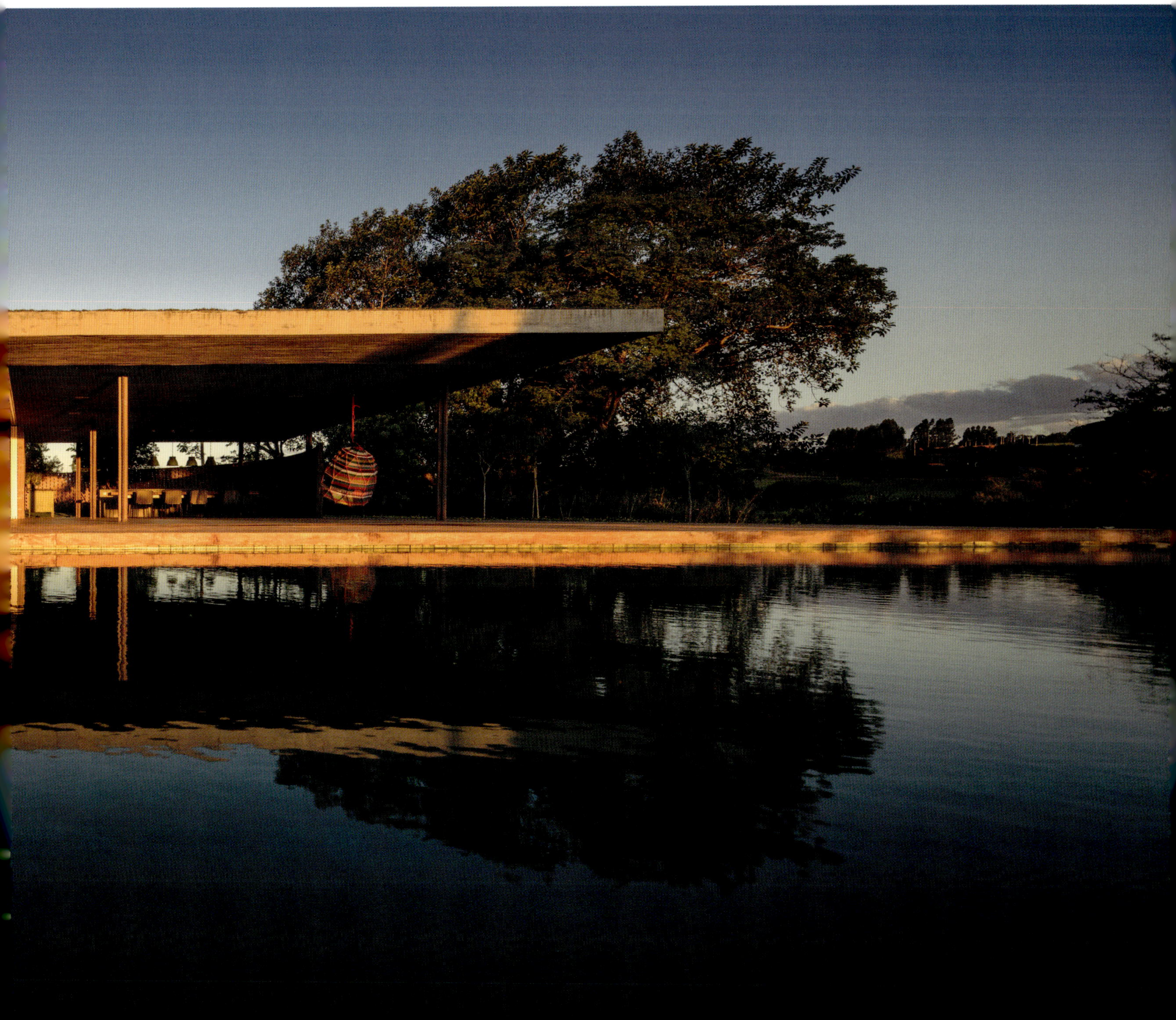

070

Photographs: Archive Olgiati

VILLA ALÉM

VILLA ALÉM
ALENTEJO, PORTUGAL, 2014
VALERIO OLGIATI

If you've had the good fortune of visiting the Court of the Myrtles, Patio de los Arrayanes, at the Alhambra in Granada, you will understand the inspiration for Swiss architect Valerio Olgiati's Villa Além in Portugal. Twice as long as it is wide, the majestic enclosed court and garden are set out in a series of parallel bands comprising a central pond framed either side by paths and plantings of myrtle bushes. The walls are sheer; the roofed colonnades at either end designed to provide the sultan and his court with places from which to survey the garden, sheltered from the searing summer heat.

Olgiati's take on this notion, in the remote and wildly beautiful Alentejo region of southern Portugal, about 10 kilometres inland from the Atlantic Ocean, retains much of the Alhambra court's essential organisation, an imbalance of roofed and unroofed space, although on a smaller scale. The house has been laid out on a north–south axis with only one roofed section at the northern end, the residential component, comprising just 20 per cent of the building's total area.

Set near the crest of a rural hill within a forest of cork trees, all distinction between the building's covered and uncovered parts is concealed from the outside world. On approach, the only reading of the house and garden is one of inscrutability. All that you can see is defined by one material: rough board-marked concrete of a ruddy colour, not unlike the colours of the earth from which it rises.

The perimeter walls rise to not much more than head height before the large flaps of concrete fold over, rather like an open cardboard box or, to use Olgiati's description, 'like petals that open and close to the sky'. The concrete flaps are there for shade but also to create tension inside the enclosure, the long axis of which is defined by a centrally located marble-lined pool designed for swimming rather than goldfish. This is flanked on either side by exotic plantings and trees which, in time, will take on a jungle-like density, framing the long view closely. The device of garden and wall lends the building a startling monumental character.

Openings in three of the perimeter walls afford views to the wider landscape beyond the enclosure. The house inhabits the northern end, across a single level. Struck entirely in board-marked in situ concrete, as of a single piece, the house comprises a living zone, with an in situ concrete sofa on which to sit and survey the framed scene outside. The effect is cinematic. Extending along the length of the pool, through the opening in the far wall and out to a range of mountains, the vista communicates a sense of your location within multiple scales of enclosure.

A kitchen also opens out onto the courtyard, while an office is networked to Olgiati's atelier in Flims, Switzerland, to enable him and his wife to work while in residence in Portugal for long periods. Here, a single opening in the concrete, on the west elevation and well out of sight of the main approach, provides a view to the wider world outside. Each of these spaces is tweaked slightly: there's a peak in the roof of the office, while the back wall of the living room cants inward slightly, mimicking the folded concrete flaps of the perimeter walls outside.

There is a distinct sense of the processional in this project, too: the long journey required to reach the building, and the use of the courtyard as a transitional space between the exterior and the house proper. It is in the elaborate labyrinthine internal planning, however, that you find this impulse most pointedly inscribed. Great lengths have been taken to extend the distance travelled from room to room. For instance, the kitchen and studio are not connected directly with the living room as you'd expect, but are linked by a brief tunnel-like passage. The northerly part of the house contains three bedrooms, and here the journey is most circuitous: each room reached along a narrow corridor, barely lit, providing a processional route around a hairpin bend, until reaching the west wall.

As in earlier projects by Olgiati — Atelier Bardill in Scharans and an apartment block in Zug, both in Switzerland — oval openings in concrete slabs over tiny internal courtyards provide the only natural light into the bedrooms. The courtyards are bare, save for discs of sunlight travelling across them through the course of the day to mesmerising effect.

Section

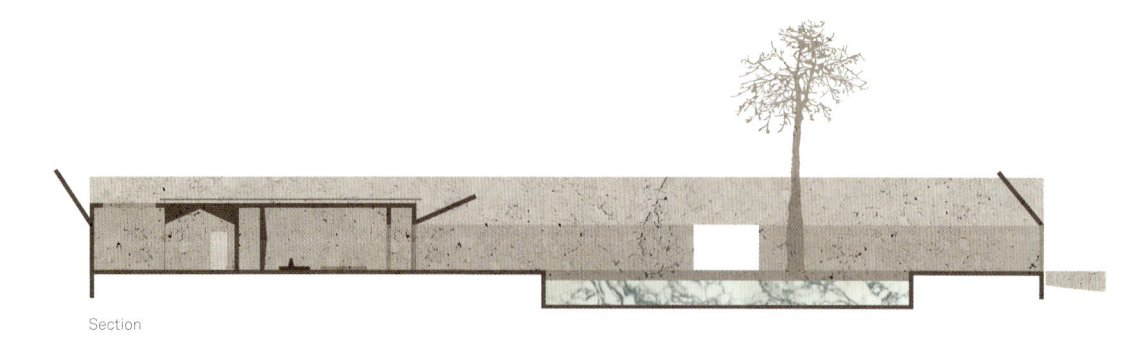

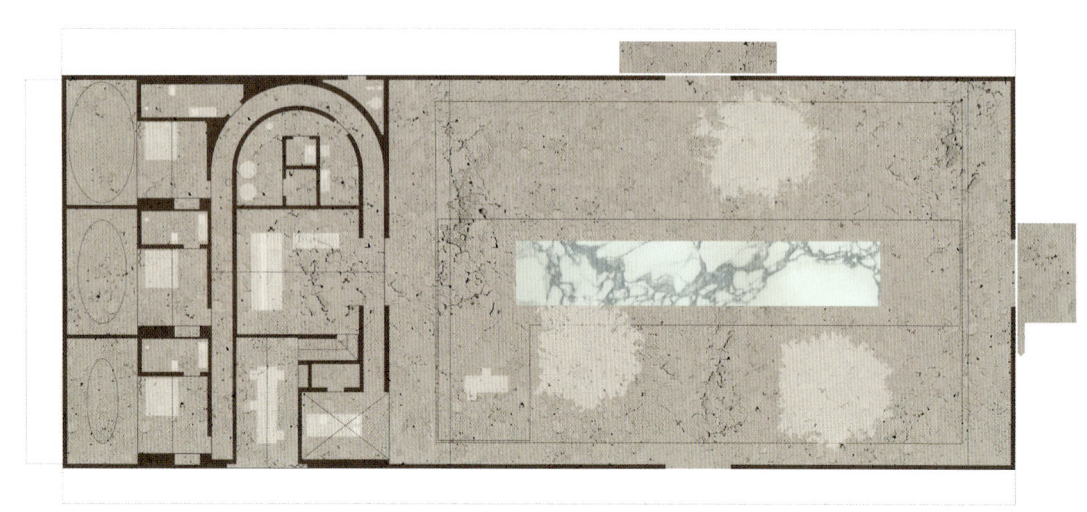

Plan

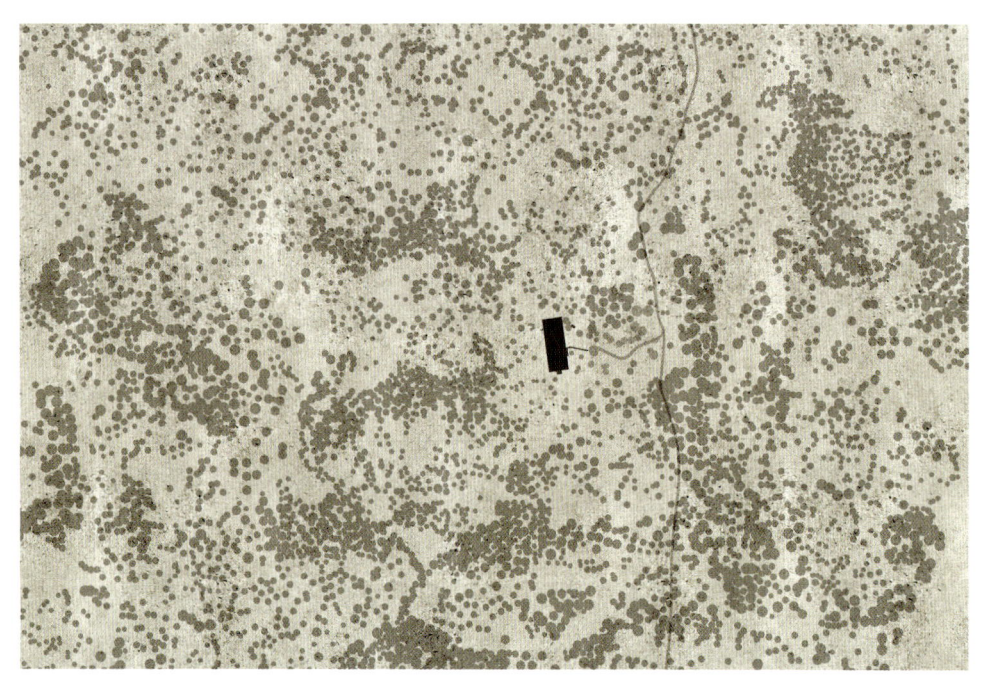

Site plan

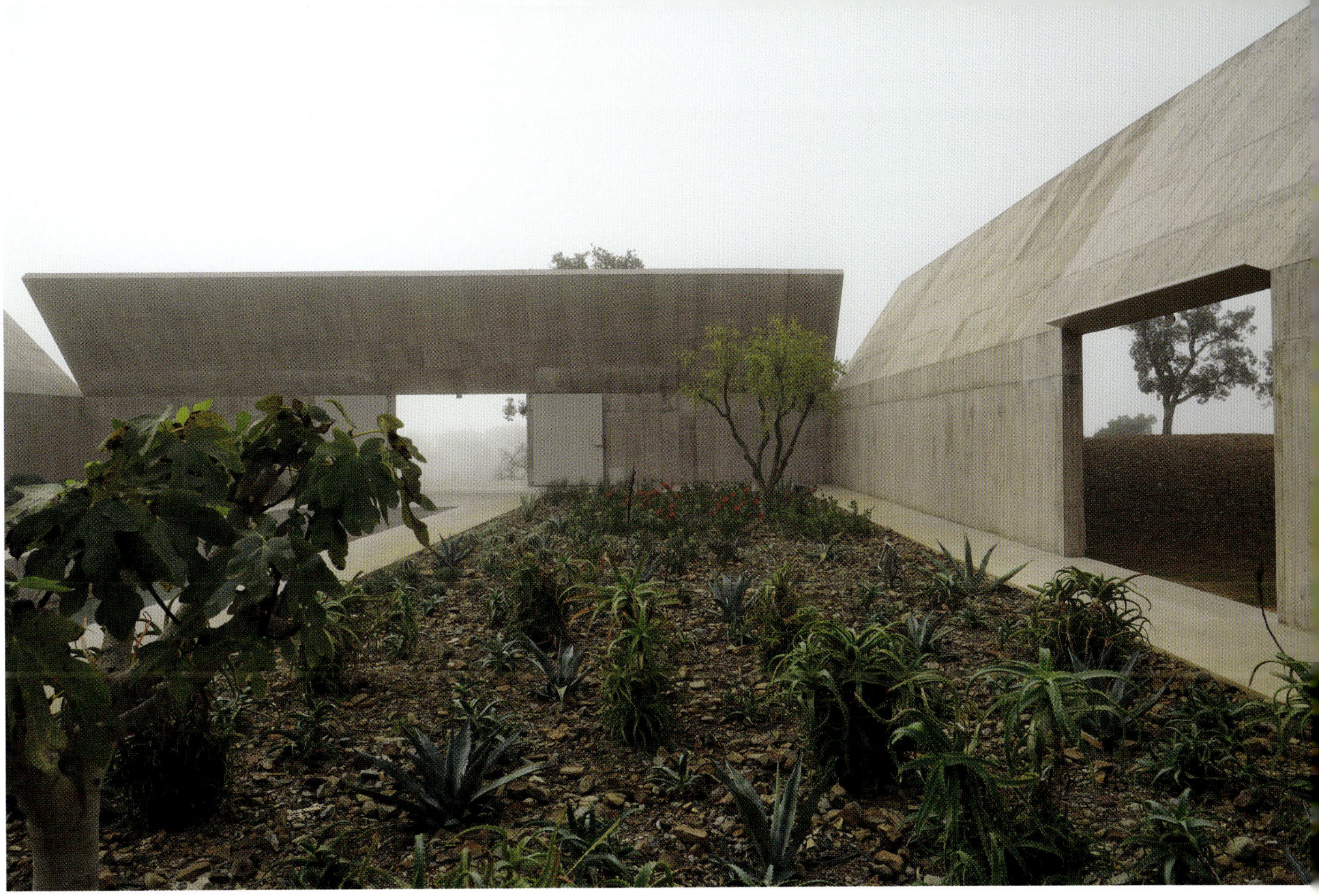

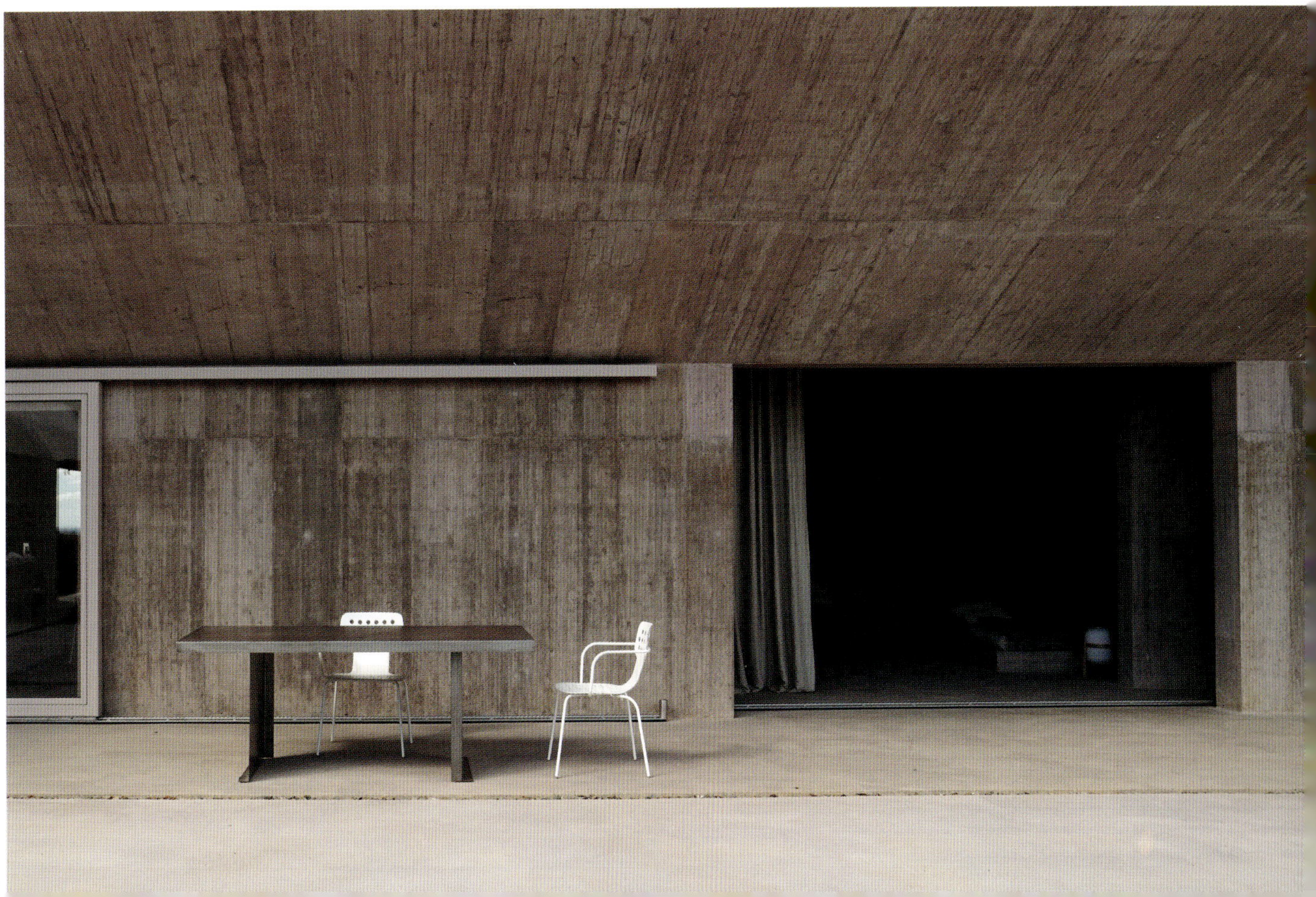

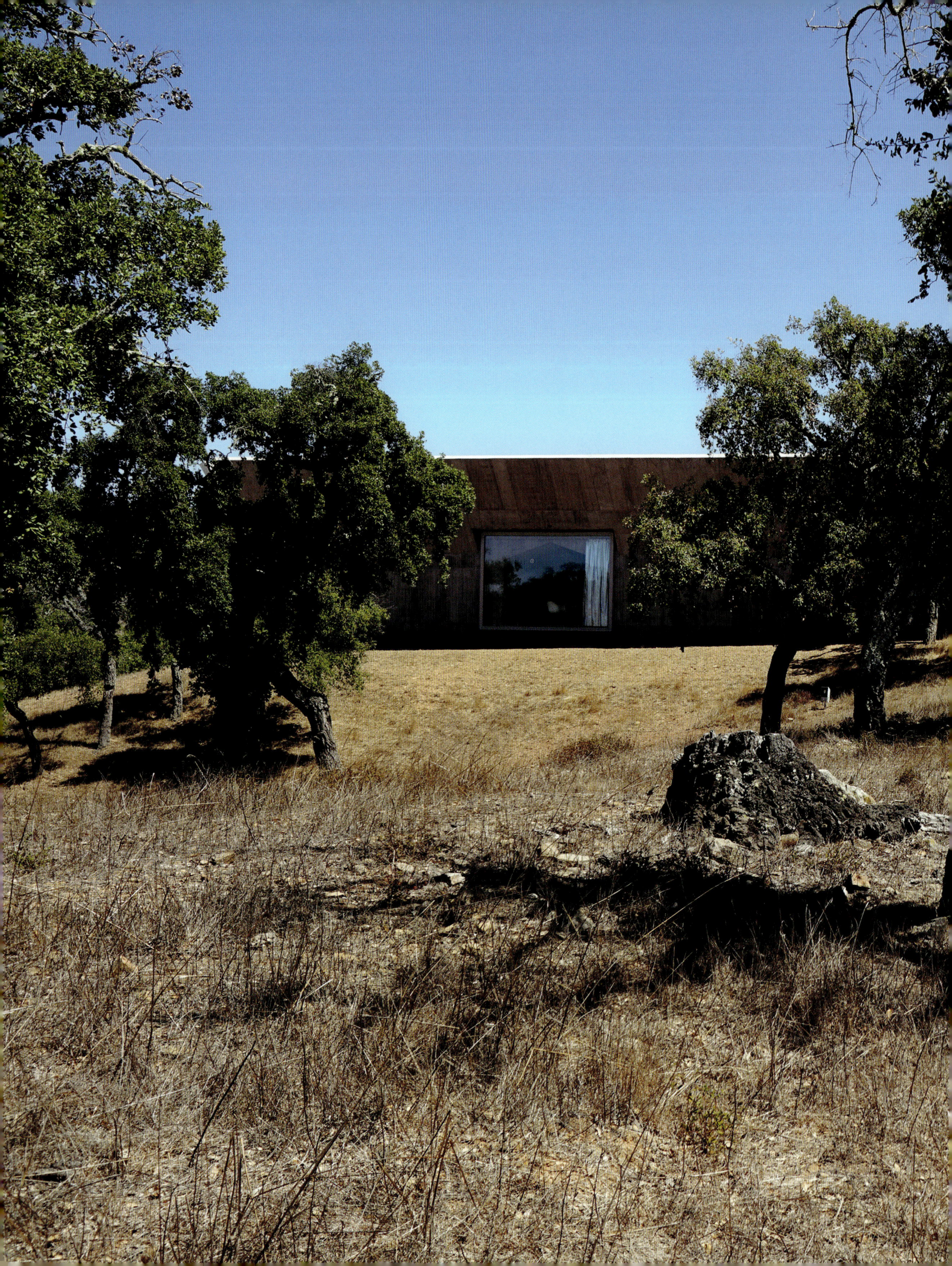

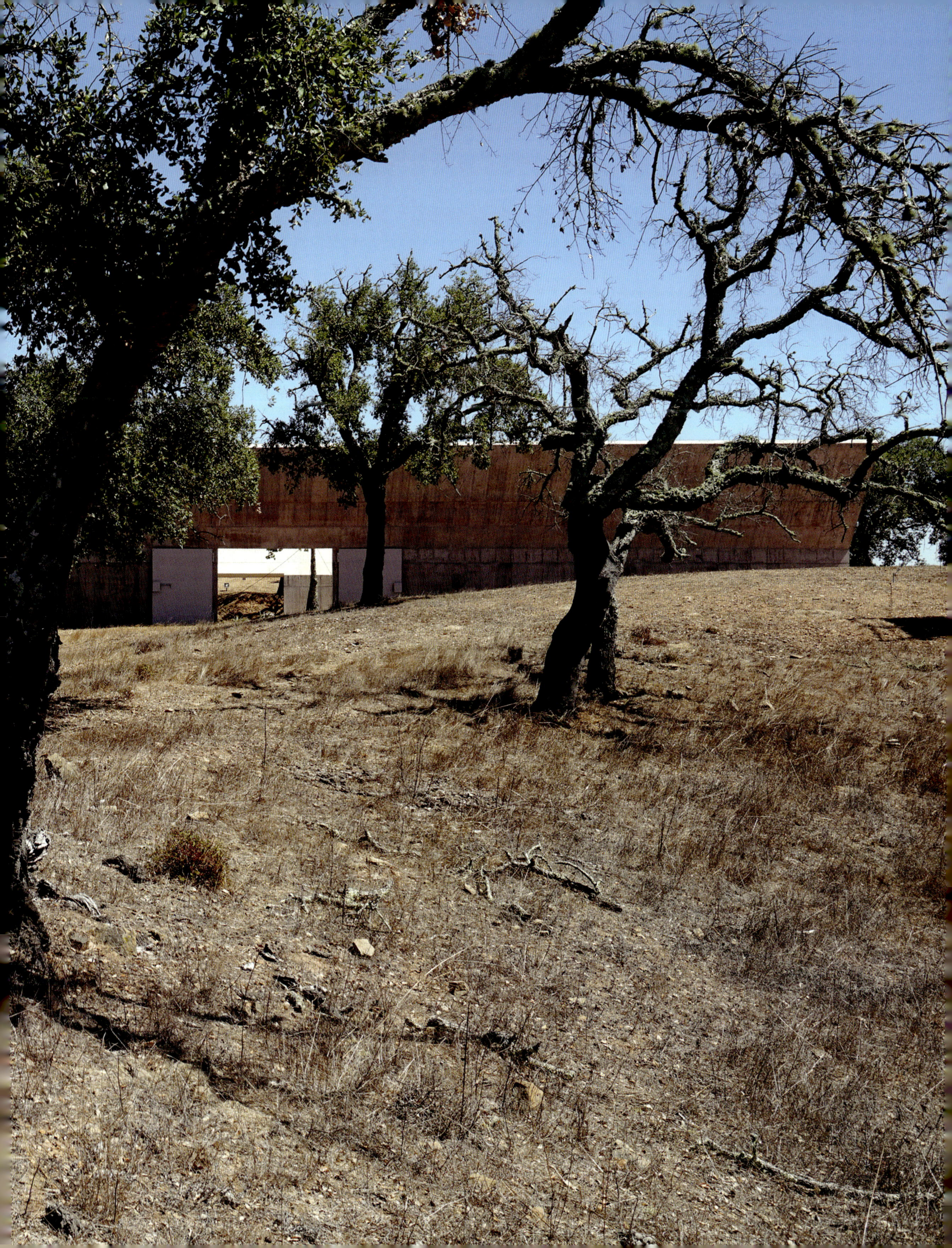

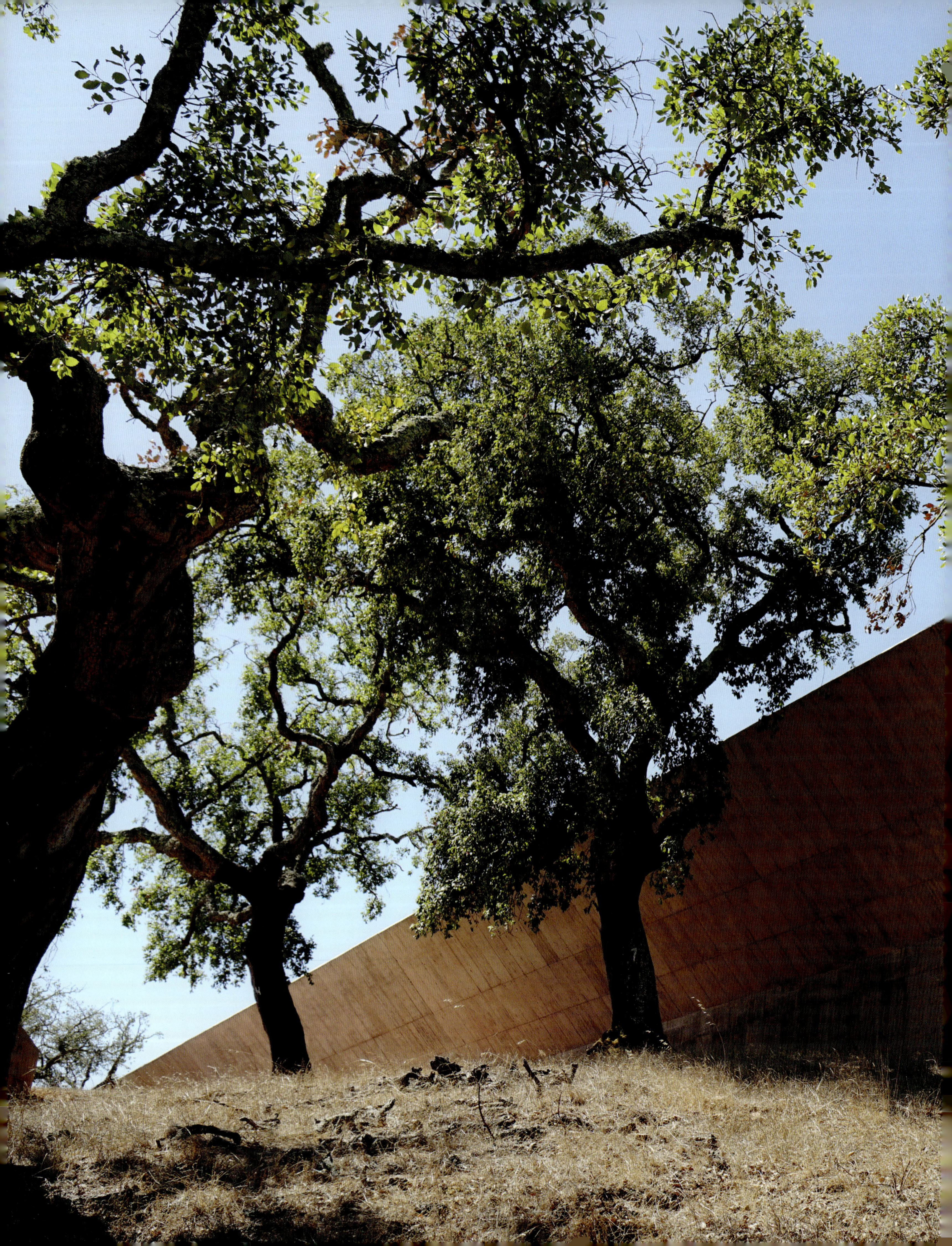

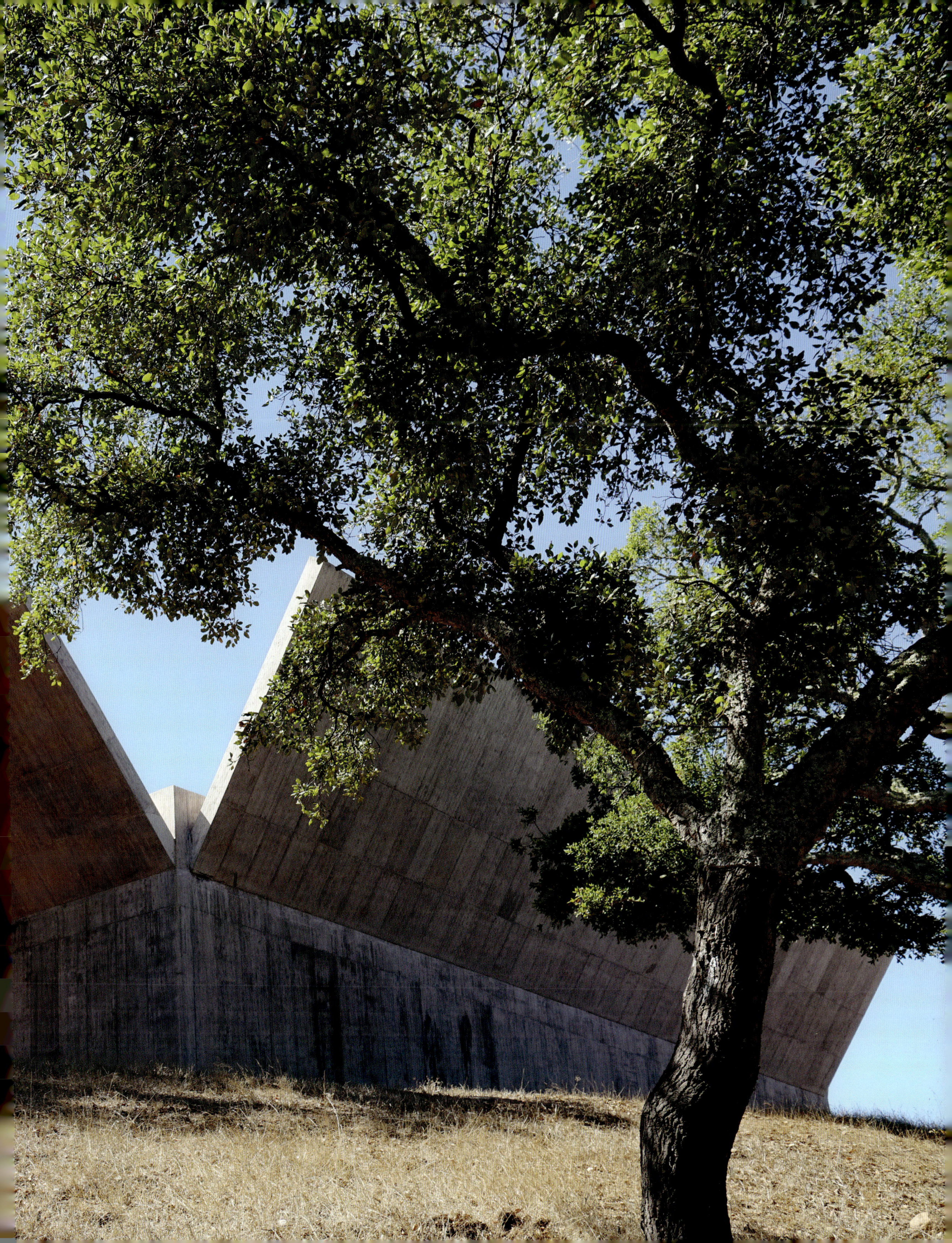

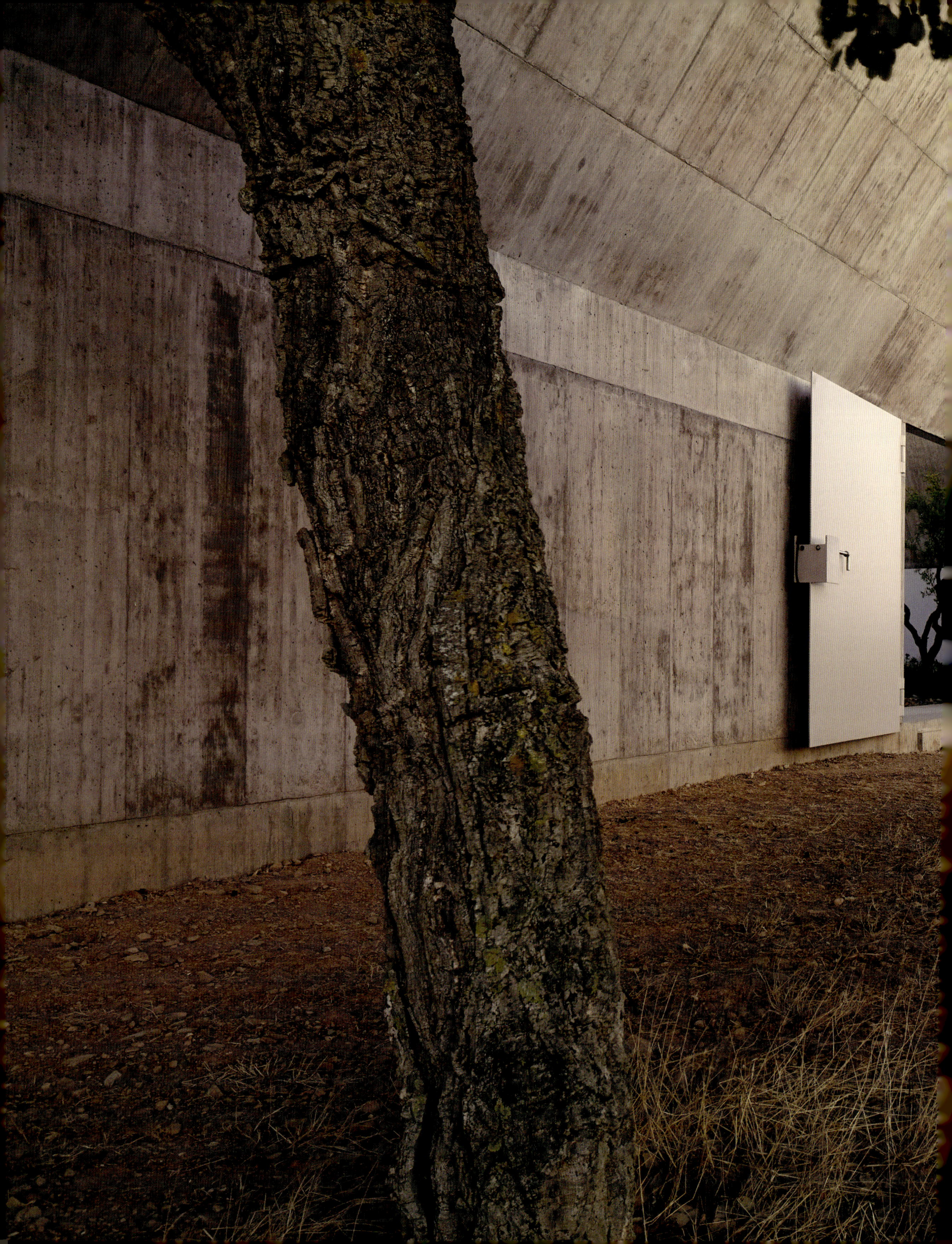

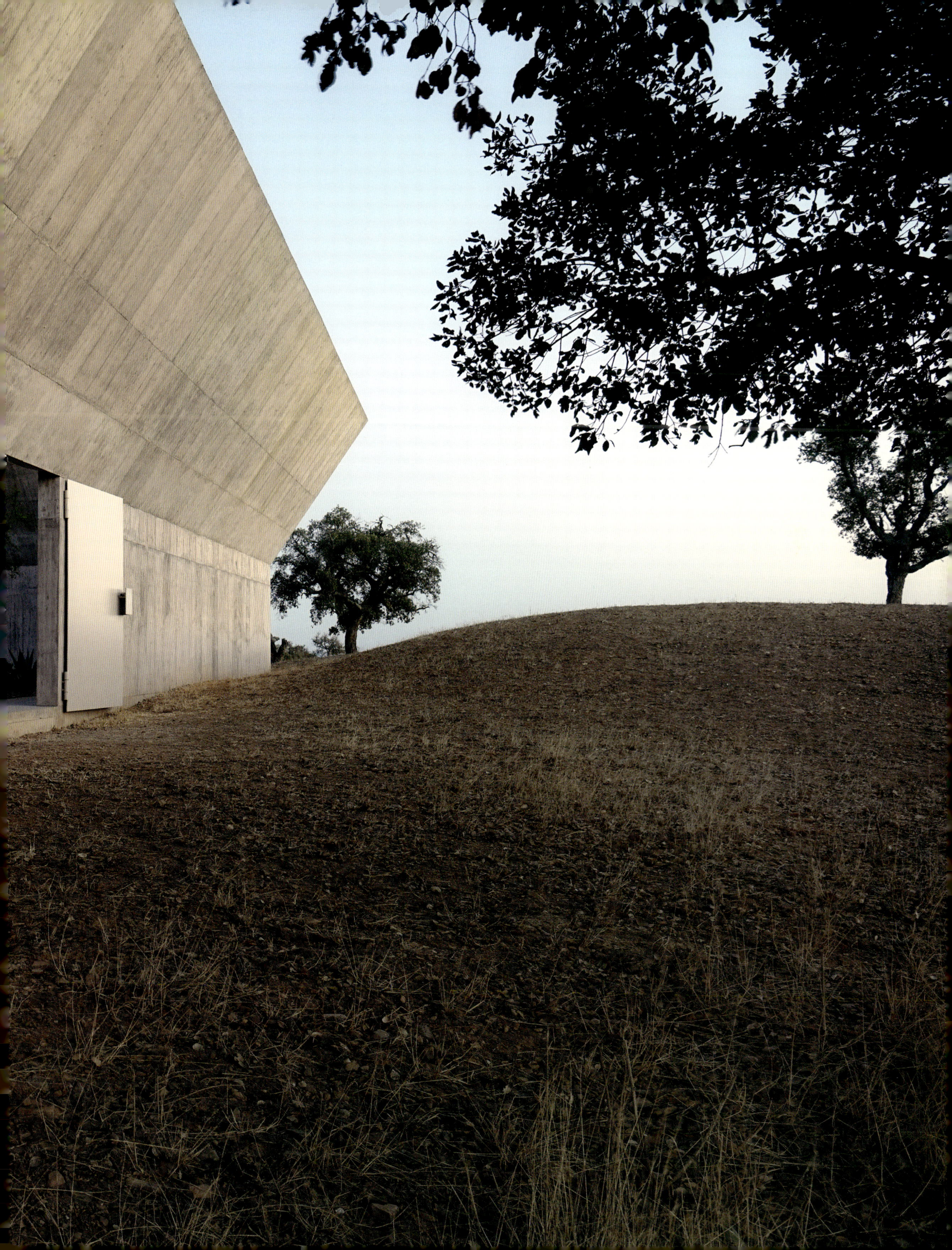

The living room is located at the end of a strict axis...it overlooks the pool
and offers a view through the southern door in the garden wall across a flat and
empty landscape. *Valerio Olgiati*

> The primary intention here is to create a secluded garden. The surrounding walls
> are up to 5.5 metres high to provide the necessary shade and the entire impression
> created is one of a desert: dry, stony and dusty. *Valerio Olgiati*

82 _ 83

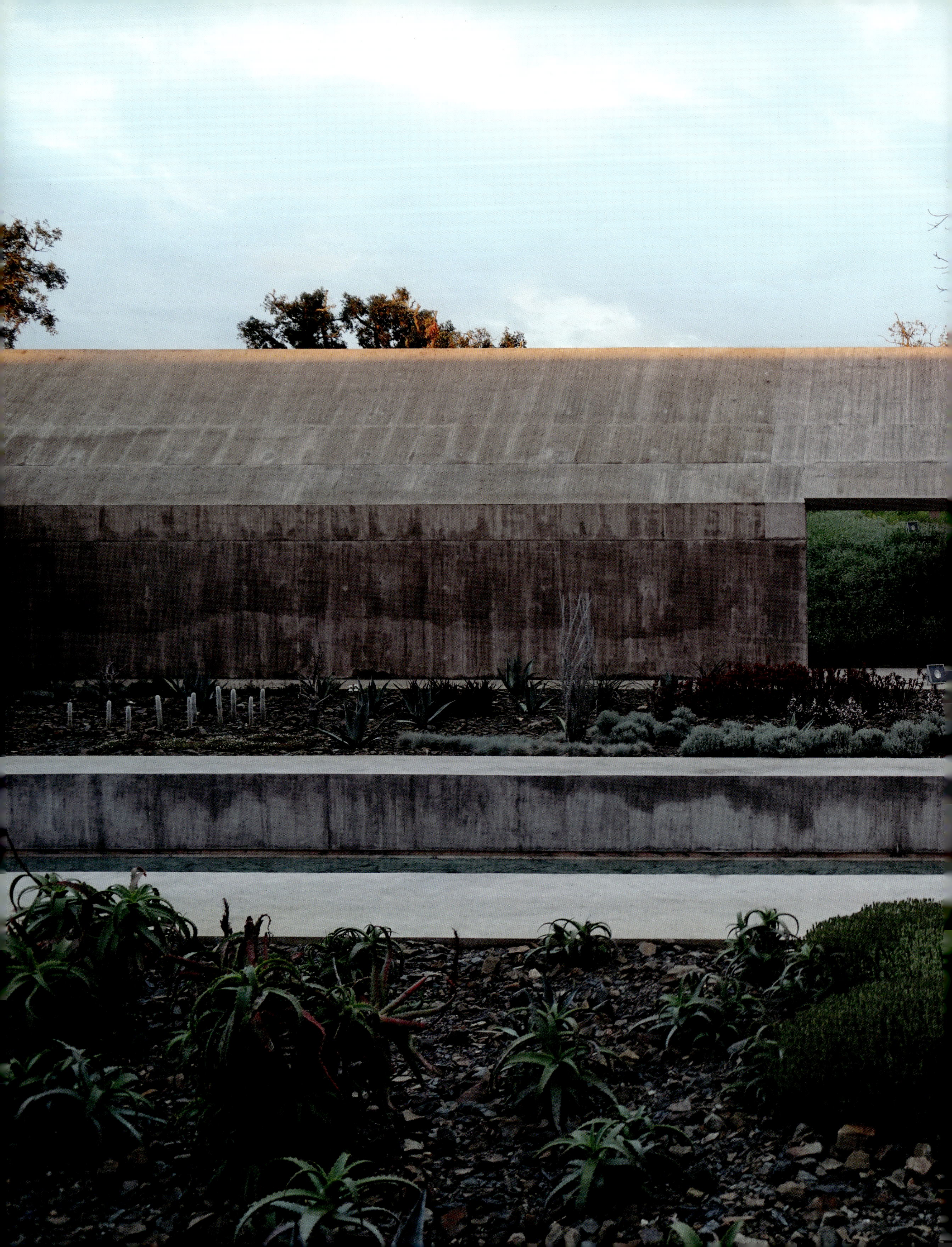

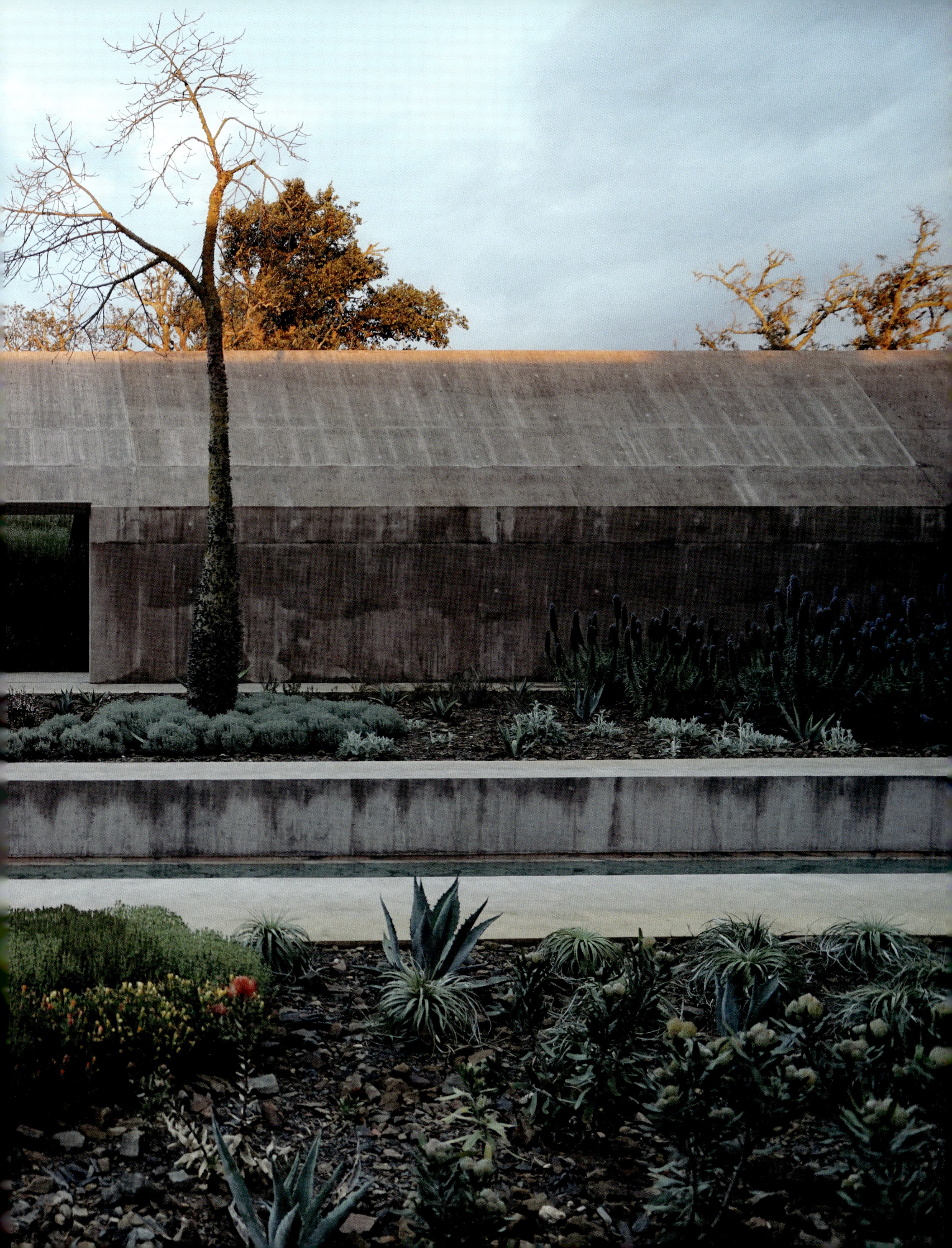

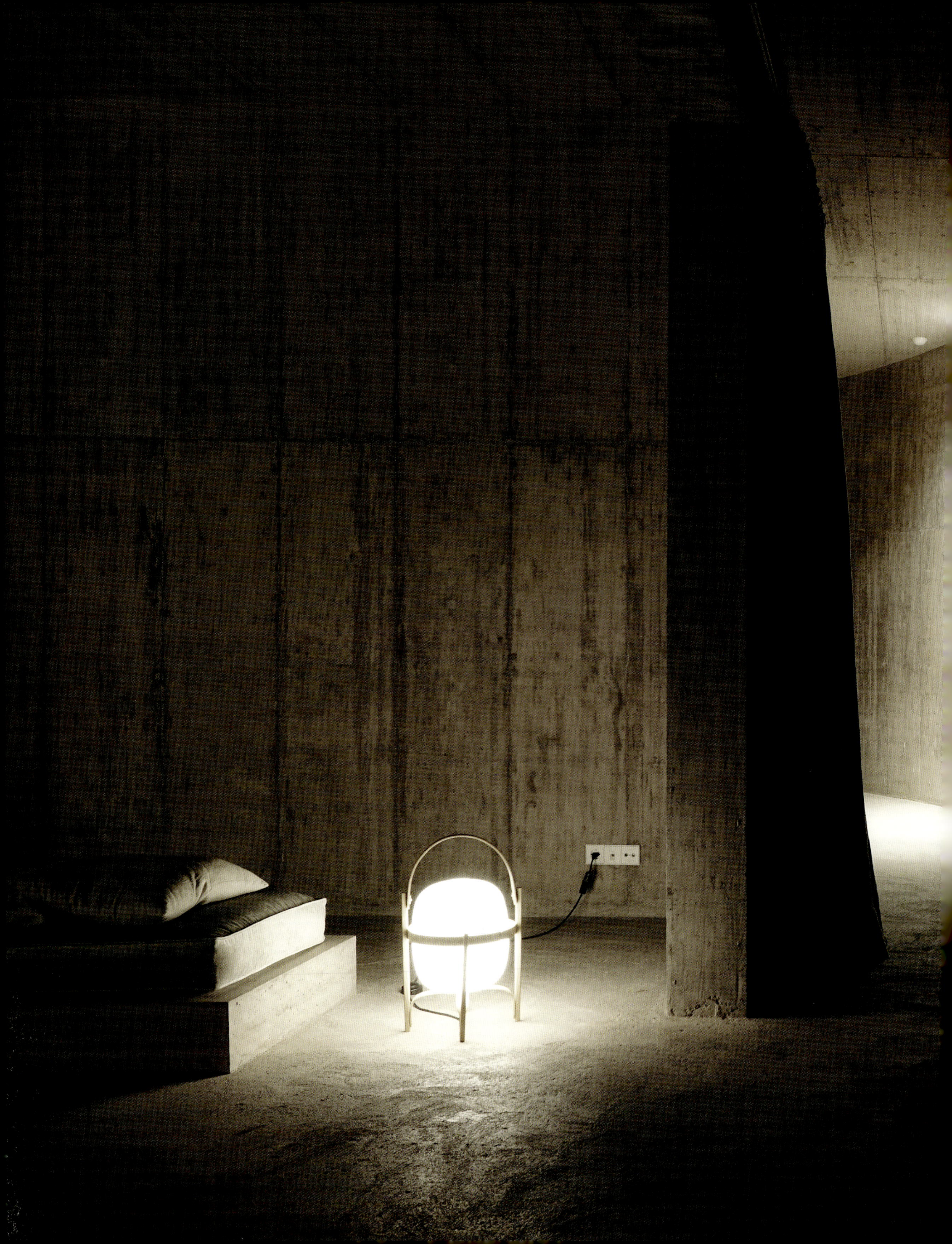

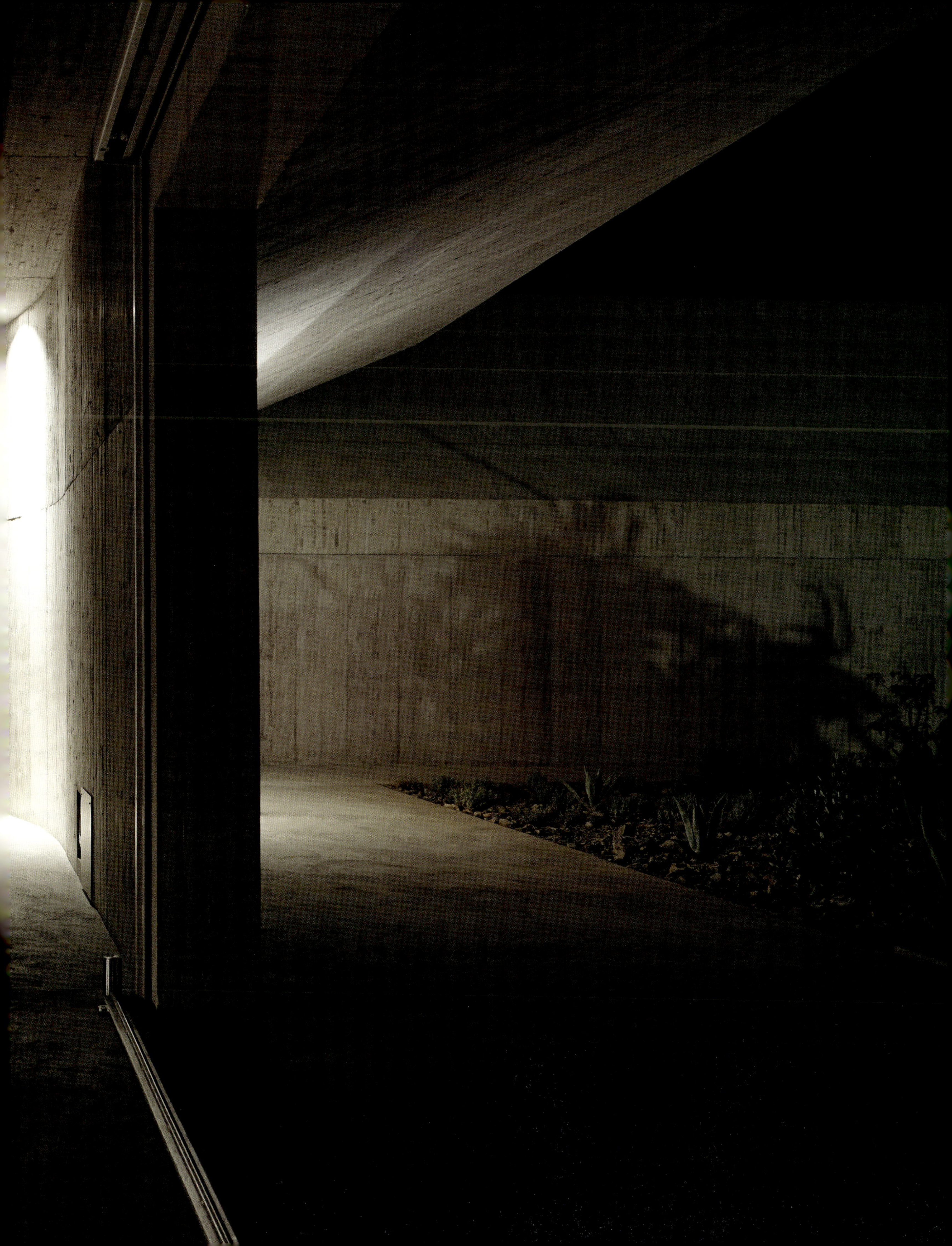

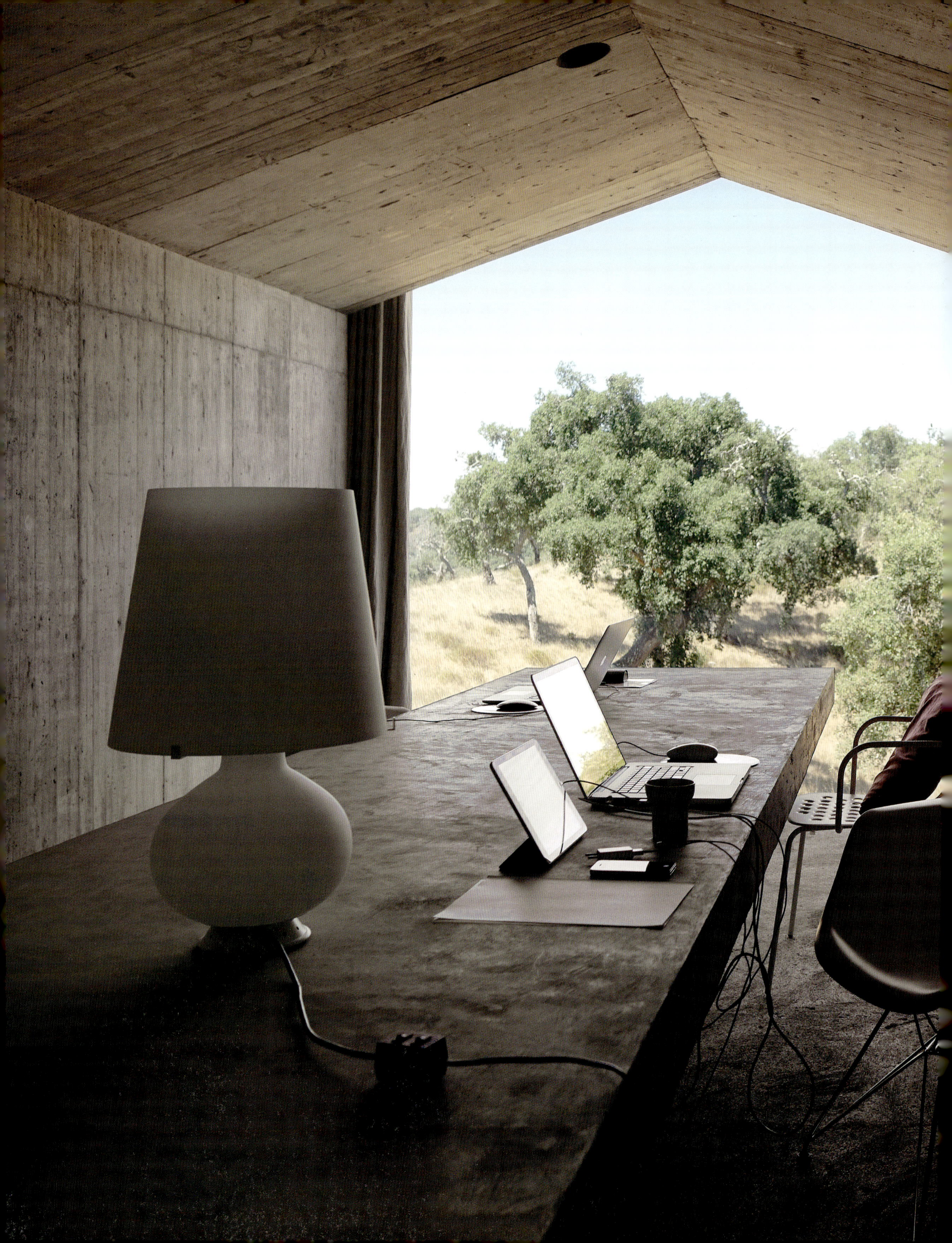

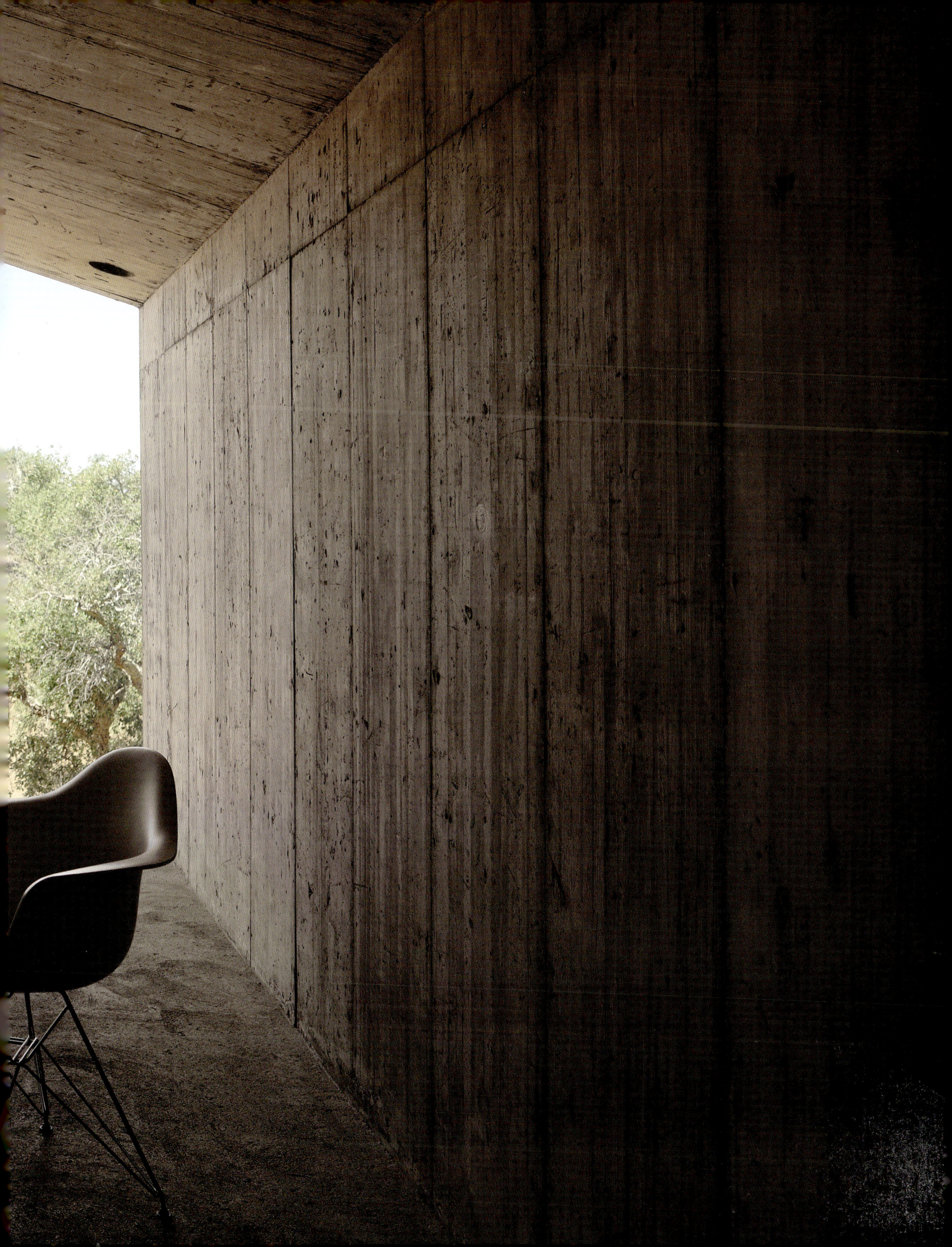

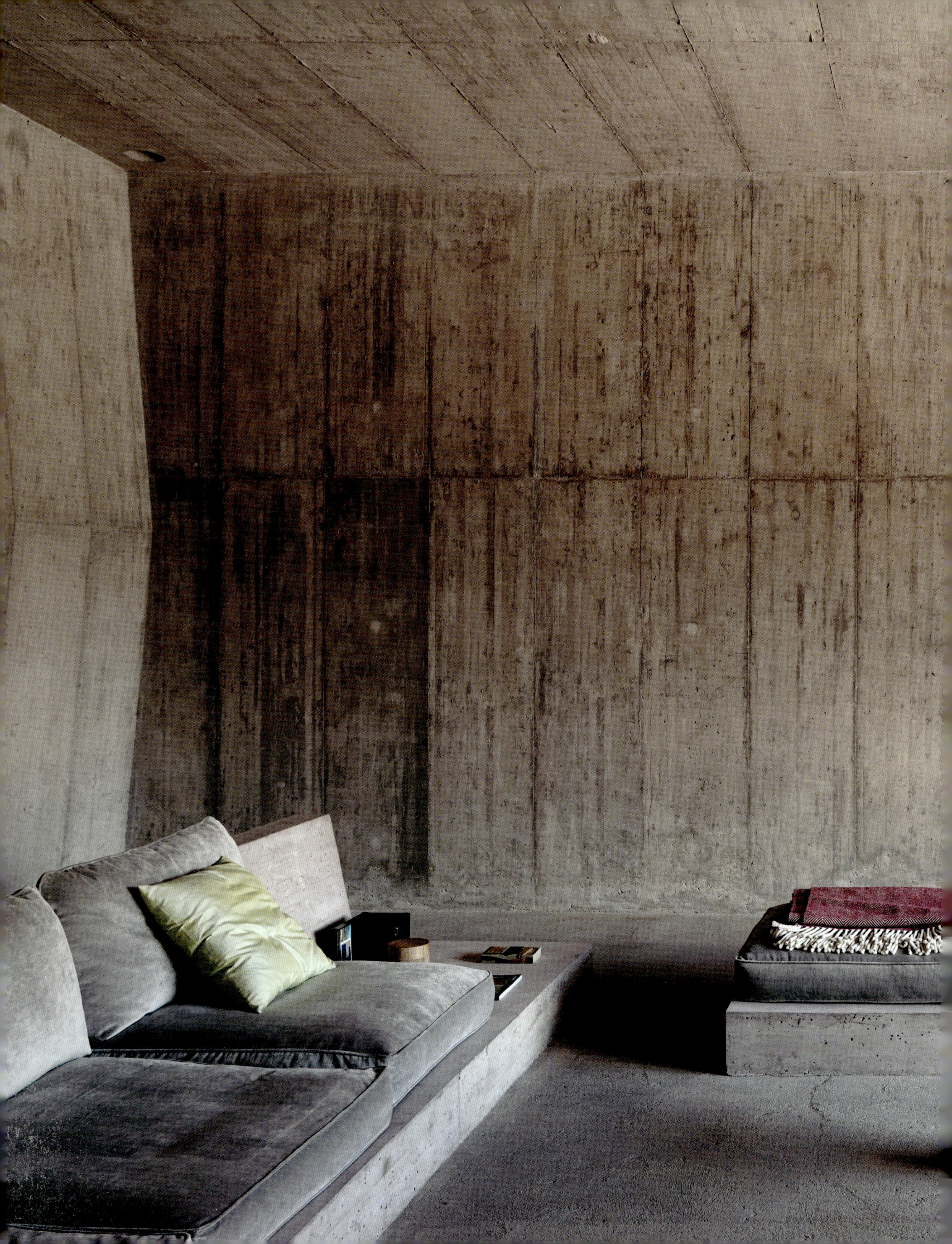

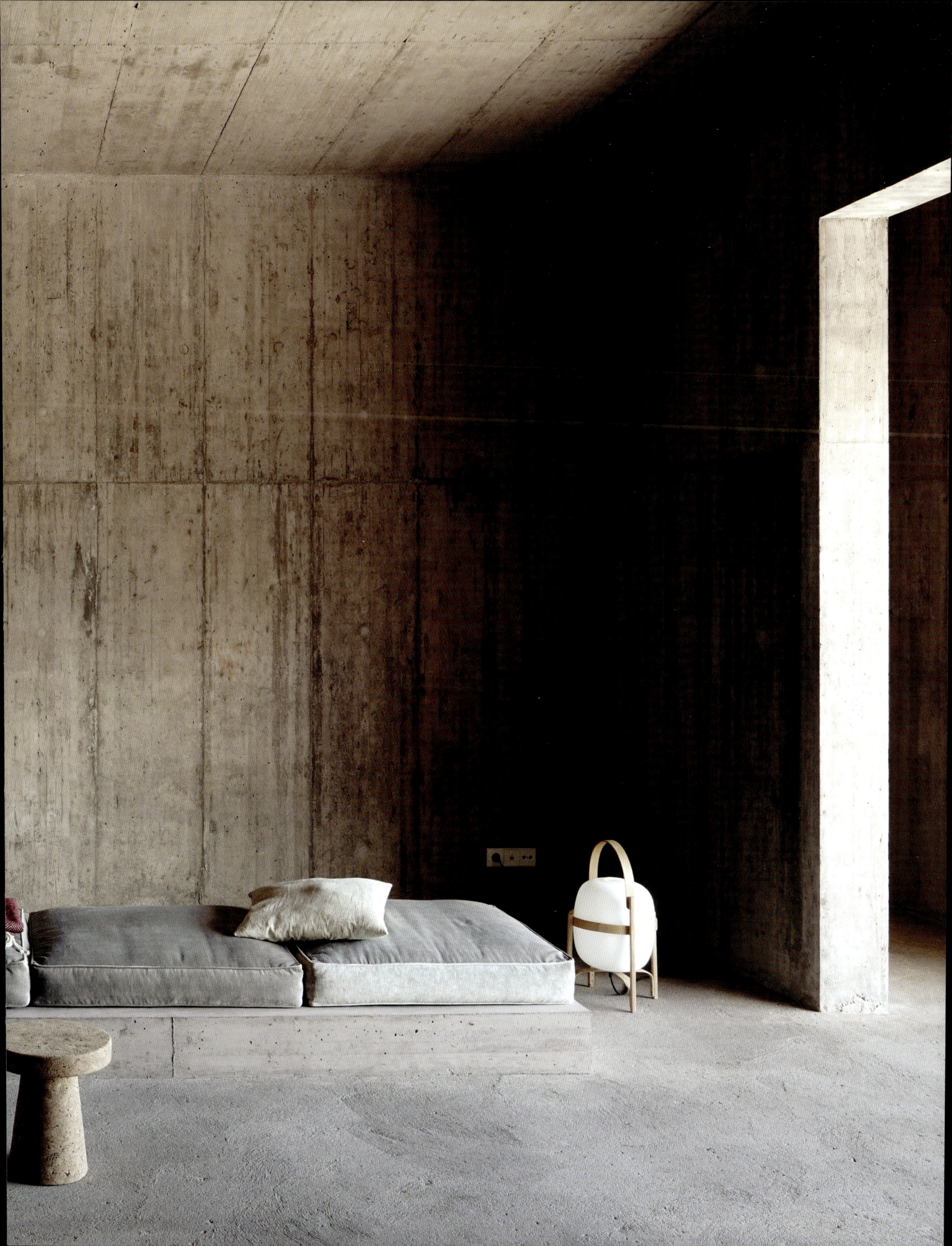

092

Photographs: Daici Ano

IT IS A GARDEN

IT IS A GARDEN
NAGANO, JAPAN, 2016
ASSISTANT

This house, by Japanese architects Hiroi Ariyama and Megumi Matsubara of ASSISTANT, a Tokyo-based practice, stands in the forest of Karuizawa, in the mountains near Nagano, Japan. Designed as a guest house, with a private art gallery for its owner's extensive collection, the single-level building, square in plan, is defined by five courtyards opened to the sky and the dense forest immediately outside its walls. It surrounds and is surrounded by the trees and plants of the forest.

Made of reinforced concrete, roof planes fold inwards to draw and bounce light, as well as the shadows of the surrounding nature, directly into the house. Ceilings of almost flawless white concrete are designed to create a rhythmic geometry to support the simplicity of the exterior. All rooms face into the courtyards, each of which is distinct in character and designed to receive light and shade at different times of the day. The concept of vertical interplay of the sun through the courtyards, juxtaposed with transversal connections to the forest outside, is critical to the design of the house, in which volumes have been made to receive those elements across all dimensions: the slant of light at ever-changing angles, the shadows cast by the forest, and *komorebi* – the effect of light filtered through foliage – make a garden of dappled shadows dancing across the floor at the pace of the moving sunlight and wind. Expansive glass walls and windows project kaleidoscopic reflections from every courtyard. The result is dynamic: a house of no walls, open to the sky and the ever-changing forest outside its 'invisible' boundaries.

Architect Megumi Matsubara has spent years working between Morocco and Japan, constantly travelling between the two countries. It is her direct experience and understanding of the two cultures, and of the relationship between light and shadow and space, that has been integrated into the primary concept for this house. It is a hybrid of the traditional Japanese relationship to nature, which is horizontal, borrowing from surrounding landscapes, and that of Islamic culture, which is vertical, inviting light in from above. Conscious use of large expanses of glass as well as strict structural integrity to draw light from above are at play here. Complex phenomena occur within the resulting interior spaces.

'In order to welcome light in, concrete and glass became the two main materials for this house,' Matsubara says. 'We simplified the materials in order to receive the complex phenomena in the architecture. Concrete receives light and shadows without blinding one's eyes. Glass reflects kaleidoscopic images, amplifying delicate phenomena designed to occur within the house. As opposed to the closed look from outside, once entering inside, the interior space is ultimately connected to the surrounding nature. The contrast makes the link to nature stronger and more intimate. Our role is to bring about this balance, so that architecture speaks of itself through the whisper of all those inhabitants. It is this quality of eventful void that we believe in, that we continue to challenge towards further awareness of space.'

Spaces around the five courtyards are designed according to the times of day and the coursing of natural light entering the house. 'For example, the gallery space is located at the corner that receives the first rays of sunshine, and the master bedroom is located just across the same courtyard from which the gallery walls receive the sunlight every morning,' Matsubara says. 'The sleeper does not see the sunrise cast on the bed but every morning, waking up, sees the gallery wall with his favourite works of art lit up by the fresh morning light. You wake up to the sunrise, see the reflections of nature and hear the singing of birds and rustle of leaves. Besides this, there are shifts of days and seasons, the changing colour of the sky. Everything is moving within and around the house in harmonious complexity. The sun creates delicate and delightful phenomena, moving freely inside the house, entertaining and embracing the visitors as a perfect host. The sun rises and sets. The moon waxes and wanes. This unbroken rhythm of light, to which we submit the entire architecture, defines this house.'

Site/roof plan

0 10m

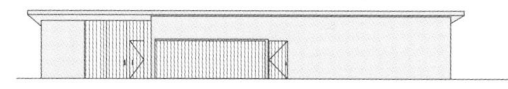

North elevation

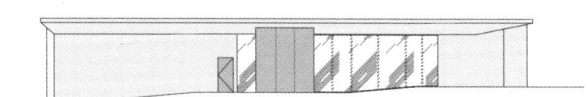

East elevation

South elevation

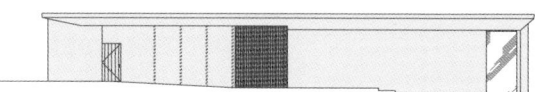

West elevation

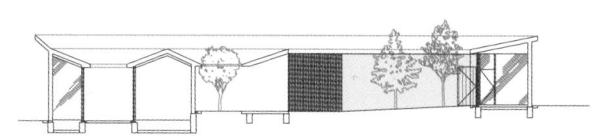

Section AA

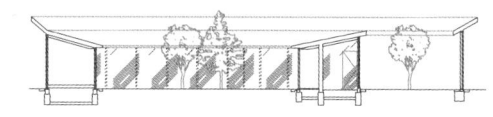

Section BB

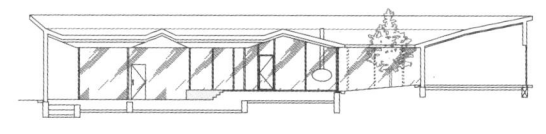

Section CC

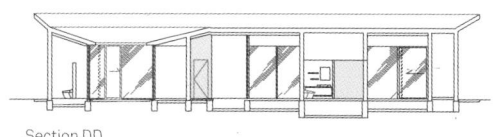

Section DD

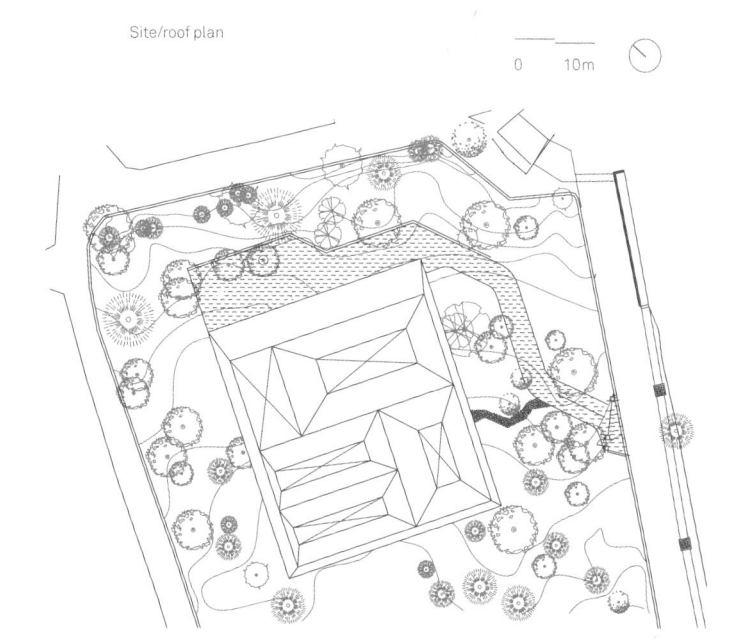

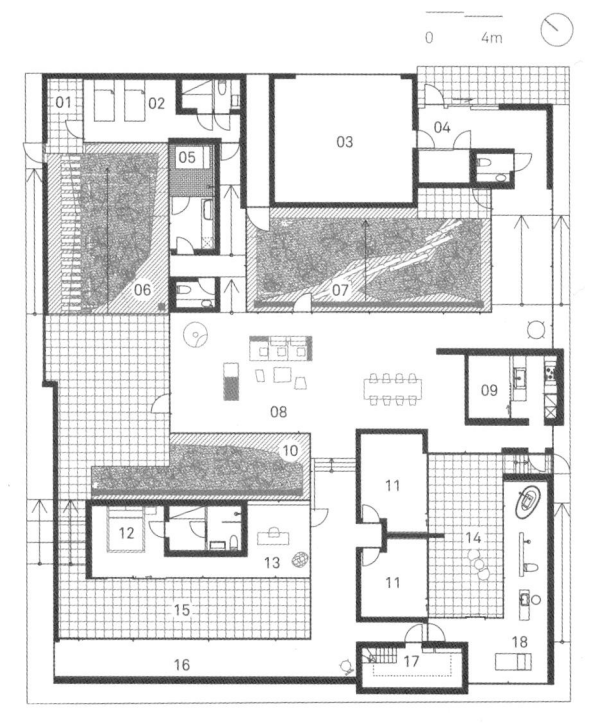

0 4m

Plan
01 Verandah
02 Guest room
03 Garage
04 Entrance
05 Main bathroom
06 Courtyard 5
07 Courtyard 1
08 Living room
09 Pantry
10 Courtyard 4
11 Bedroom
12 Main bedroom
13 Study room
14 Courtyard 2
15 Courtyard 3
16 Gallery
17 Storage
18 Bathroom

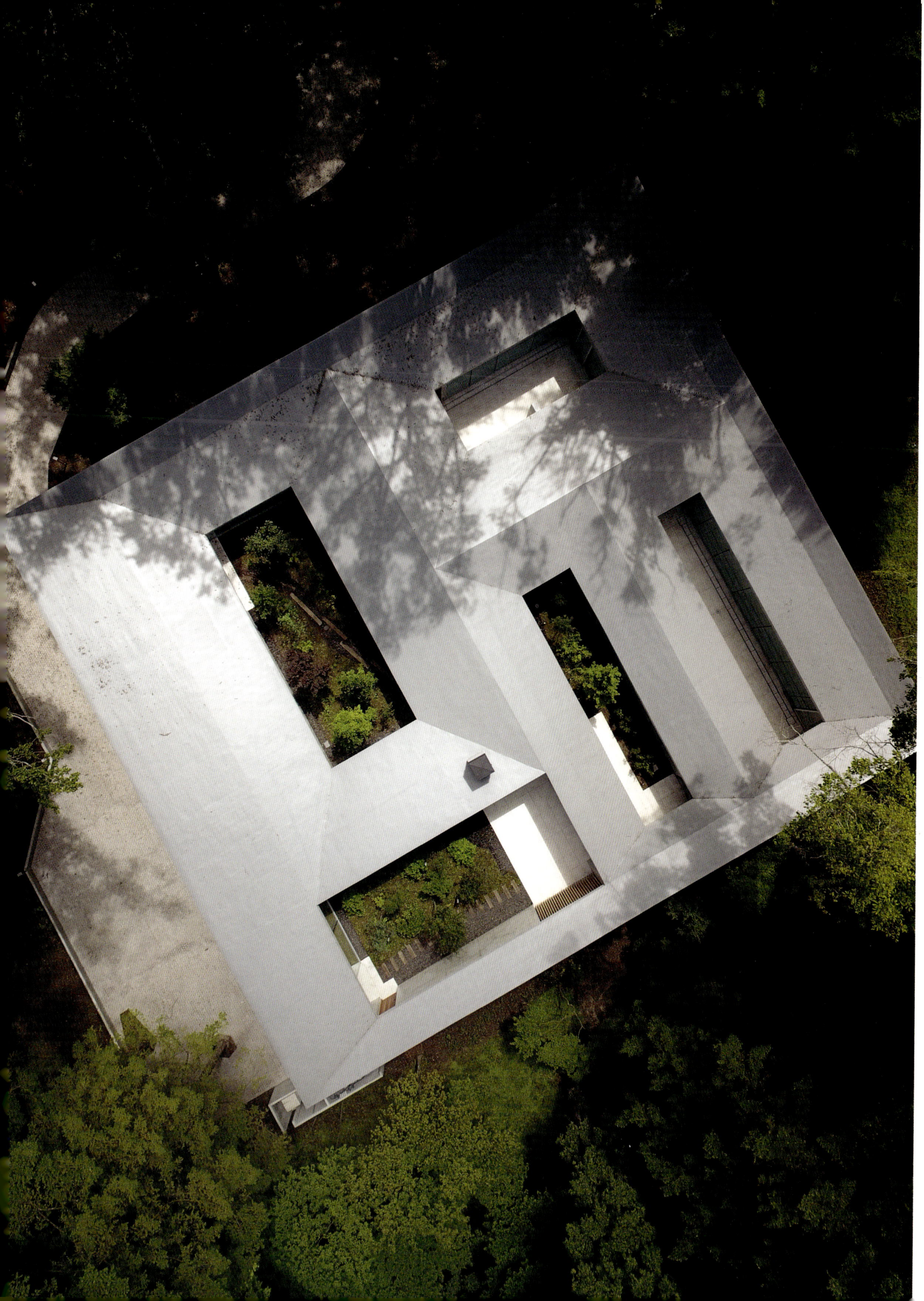

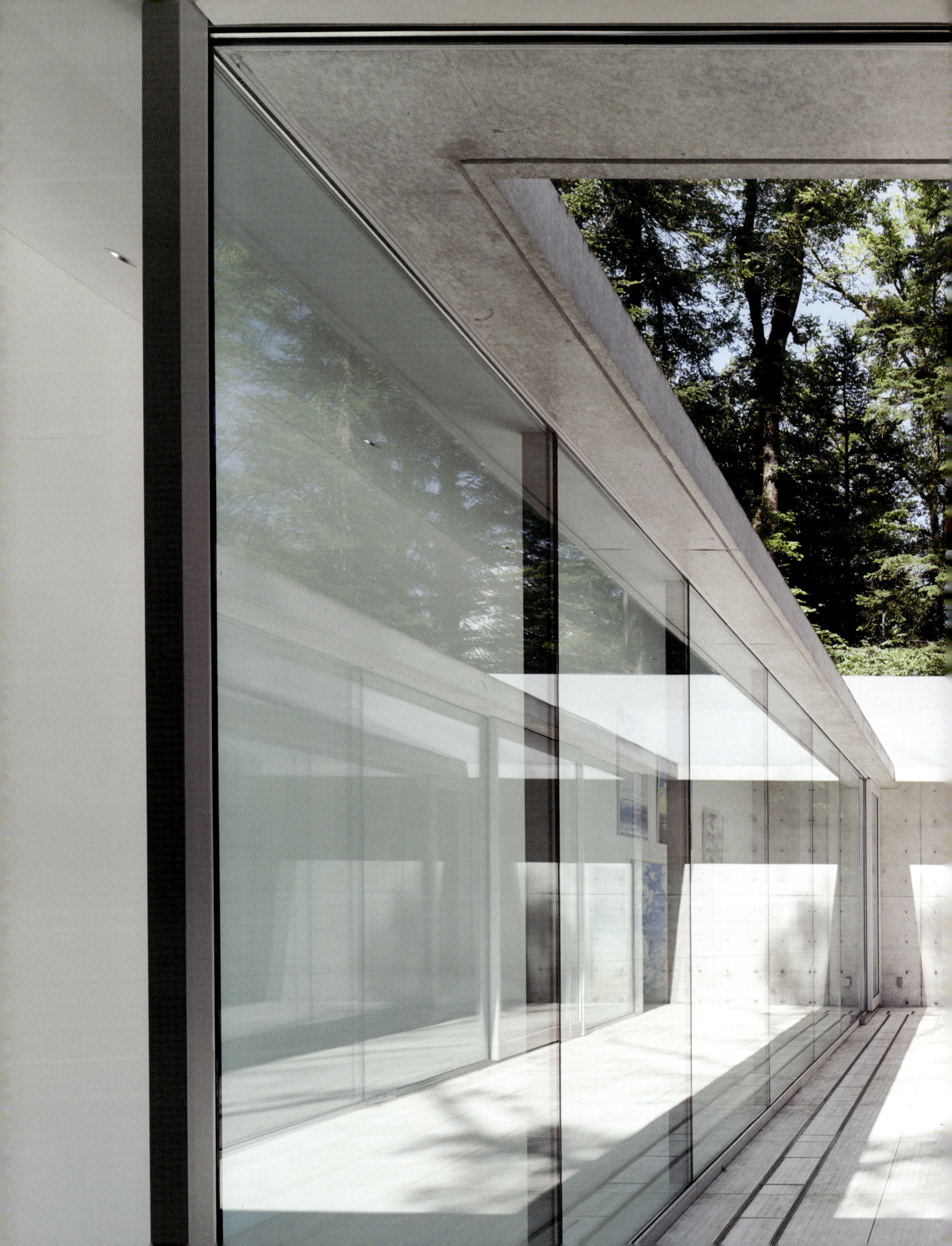

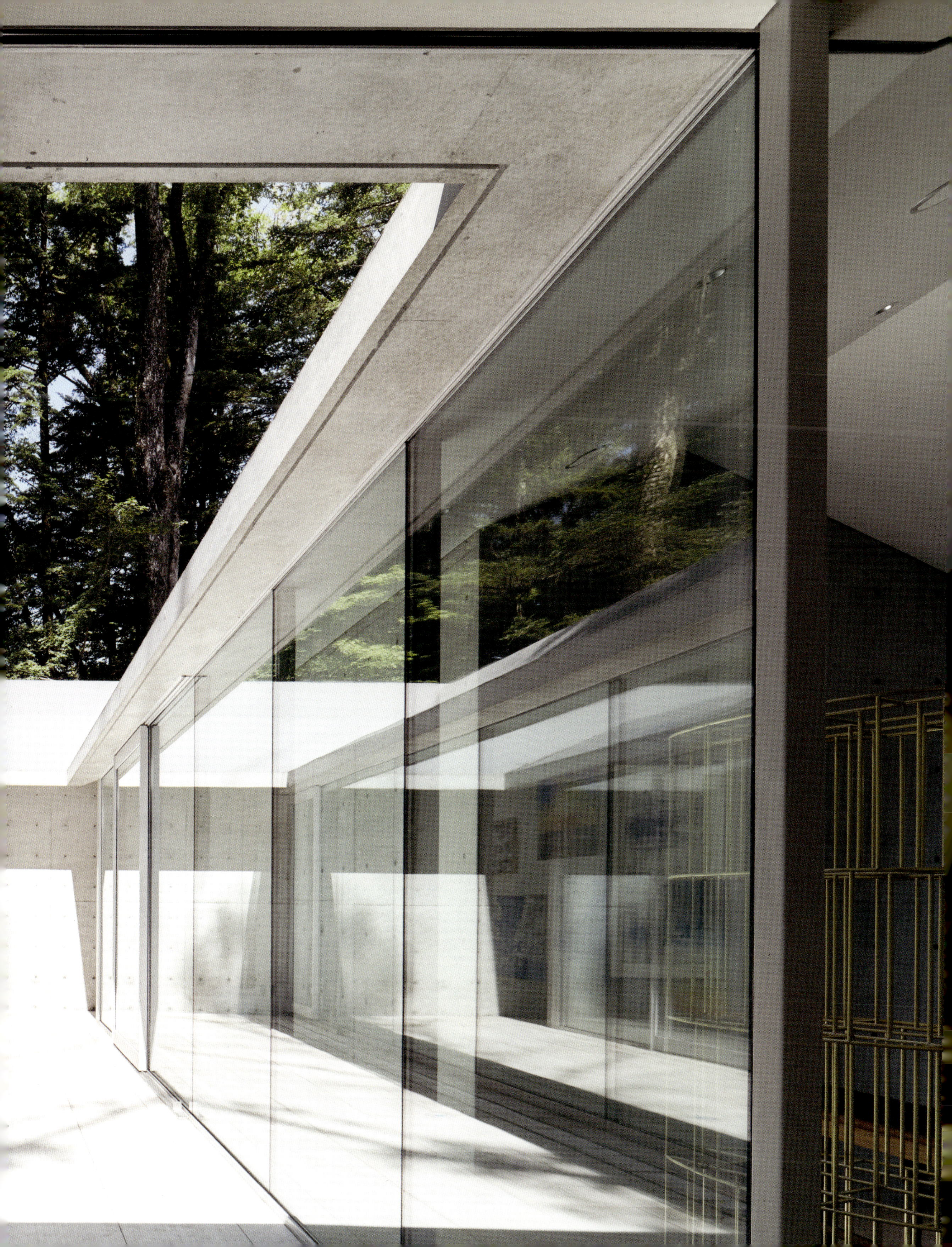

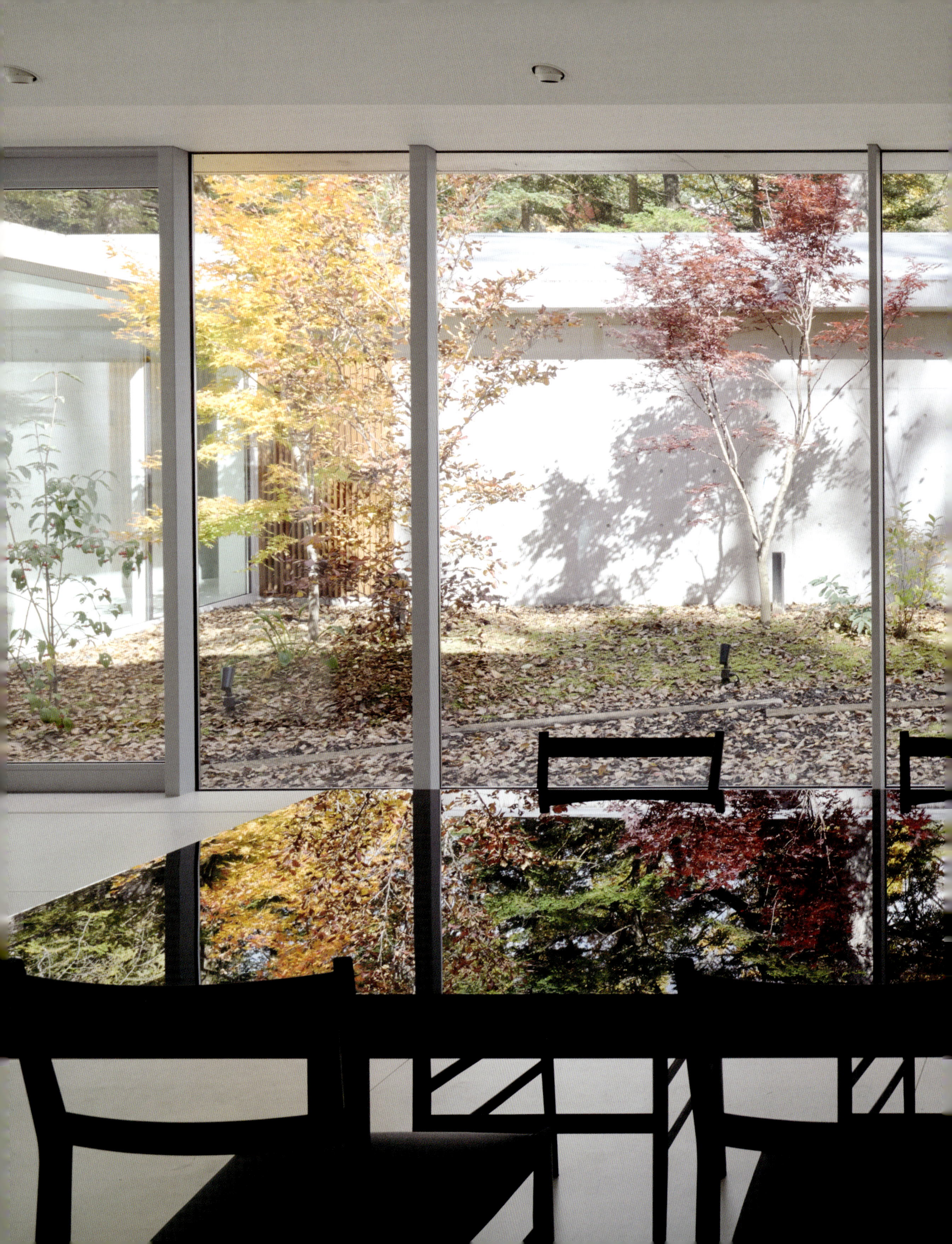

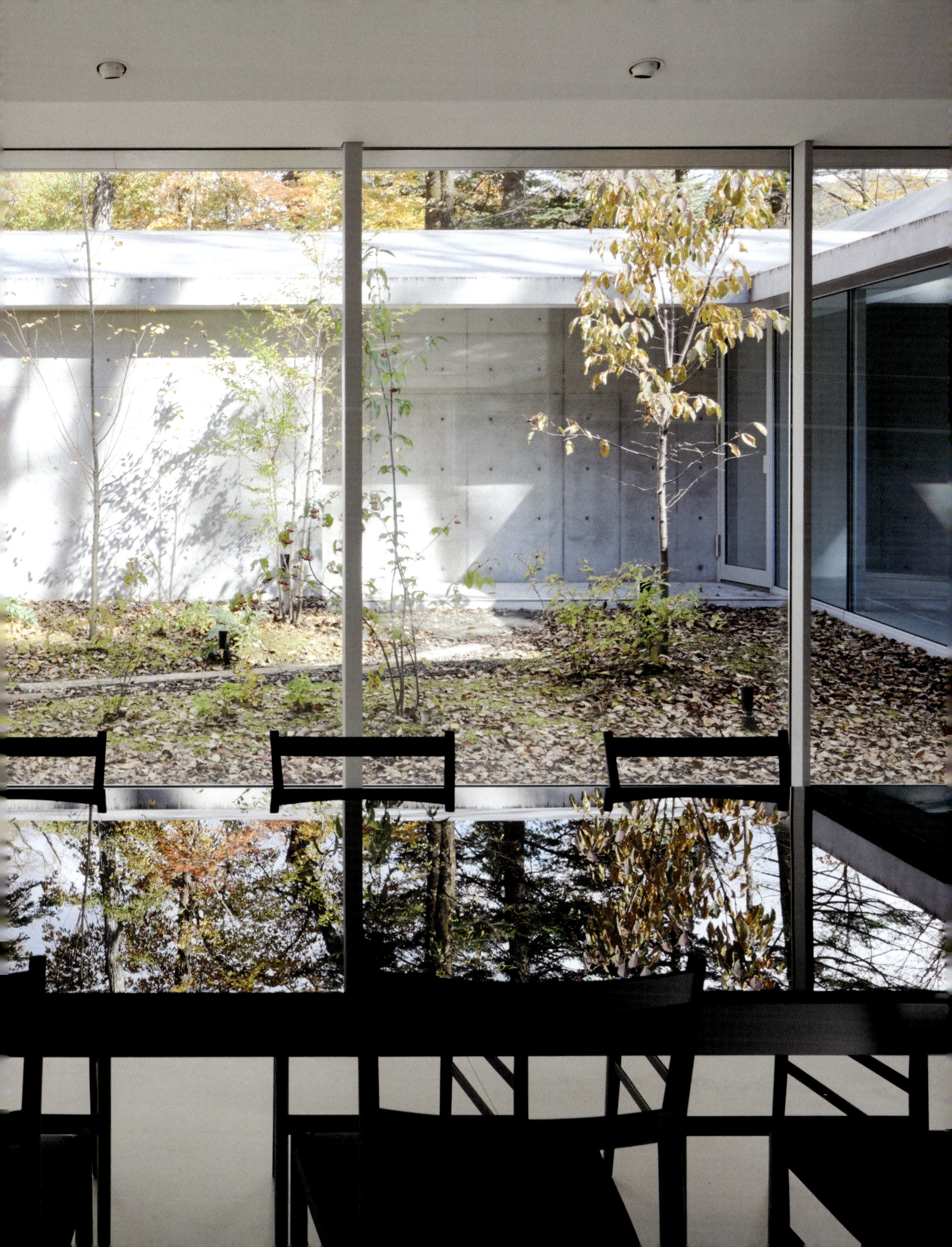

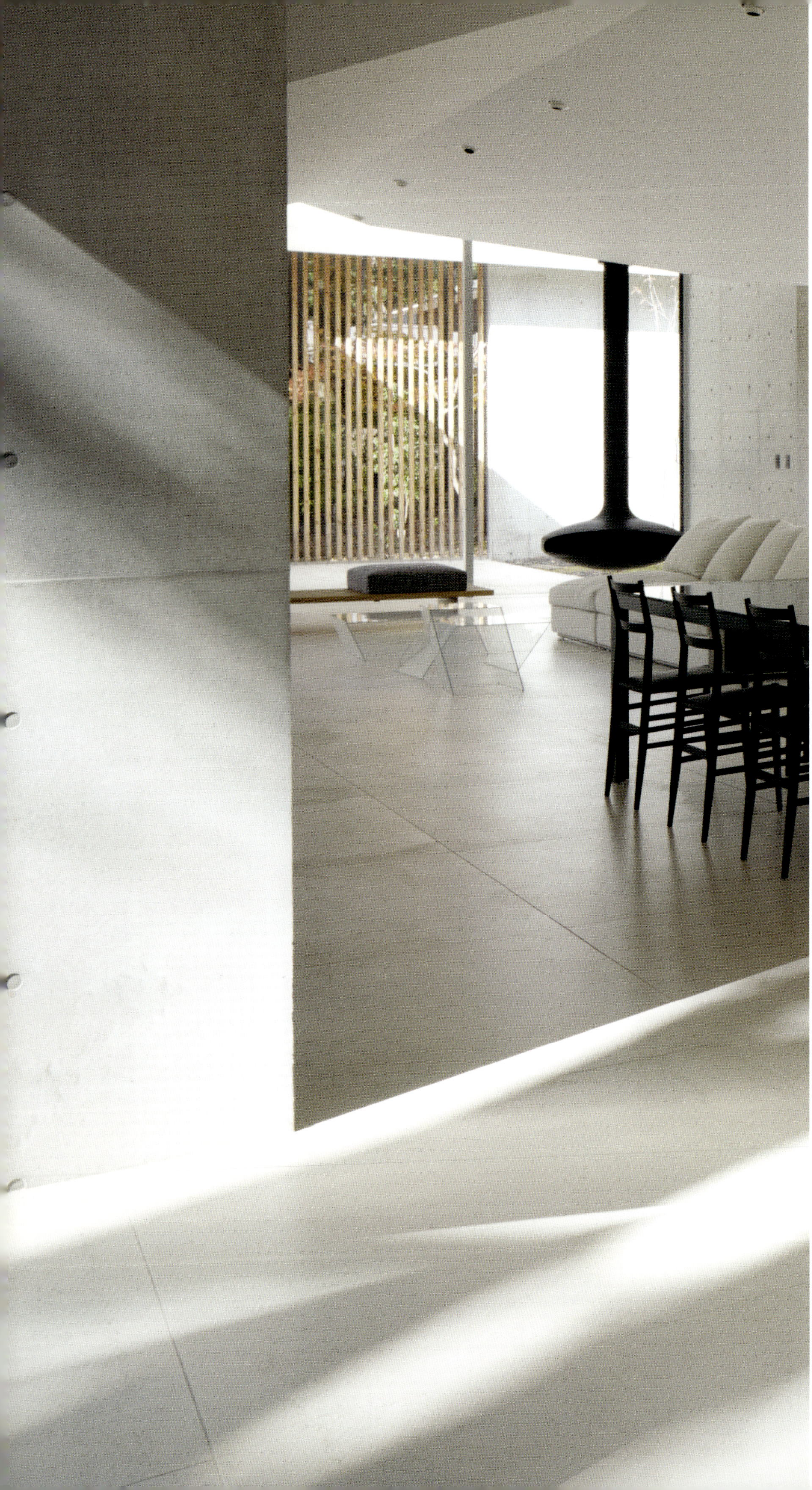

102—103

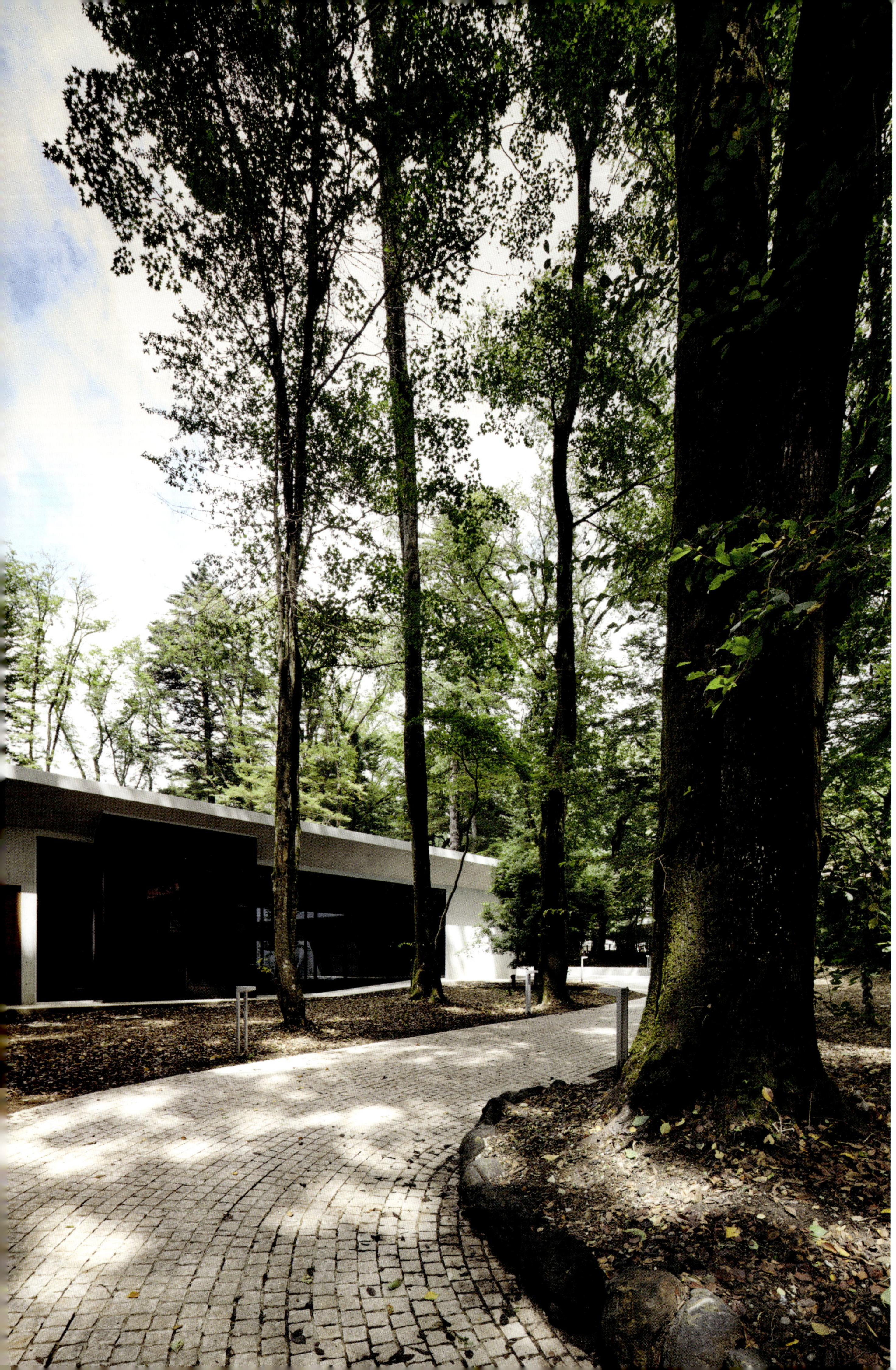

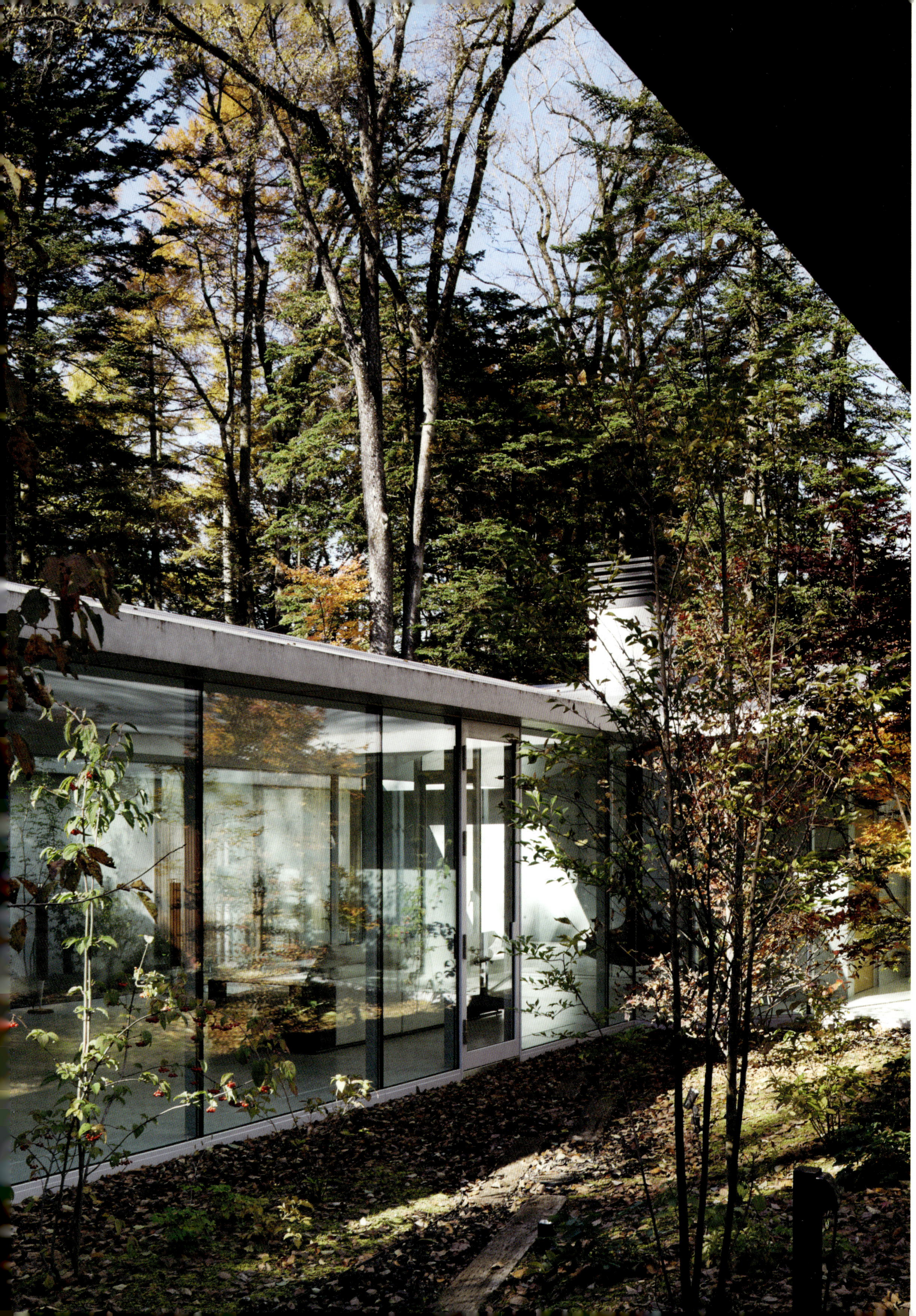

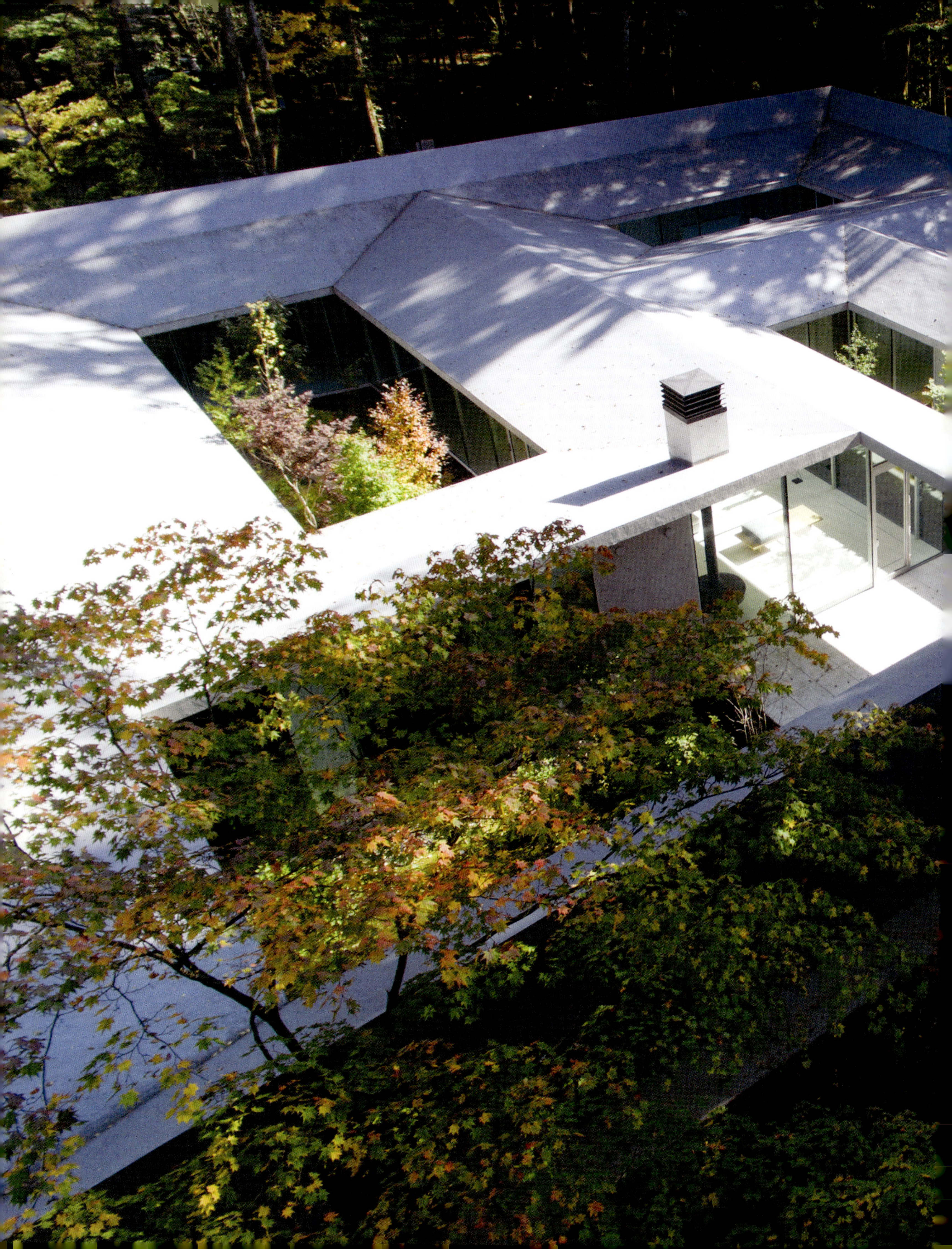

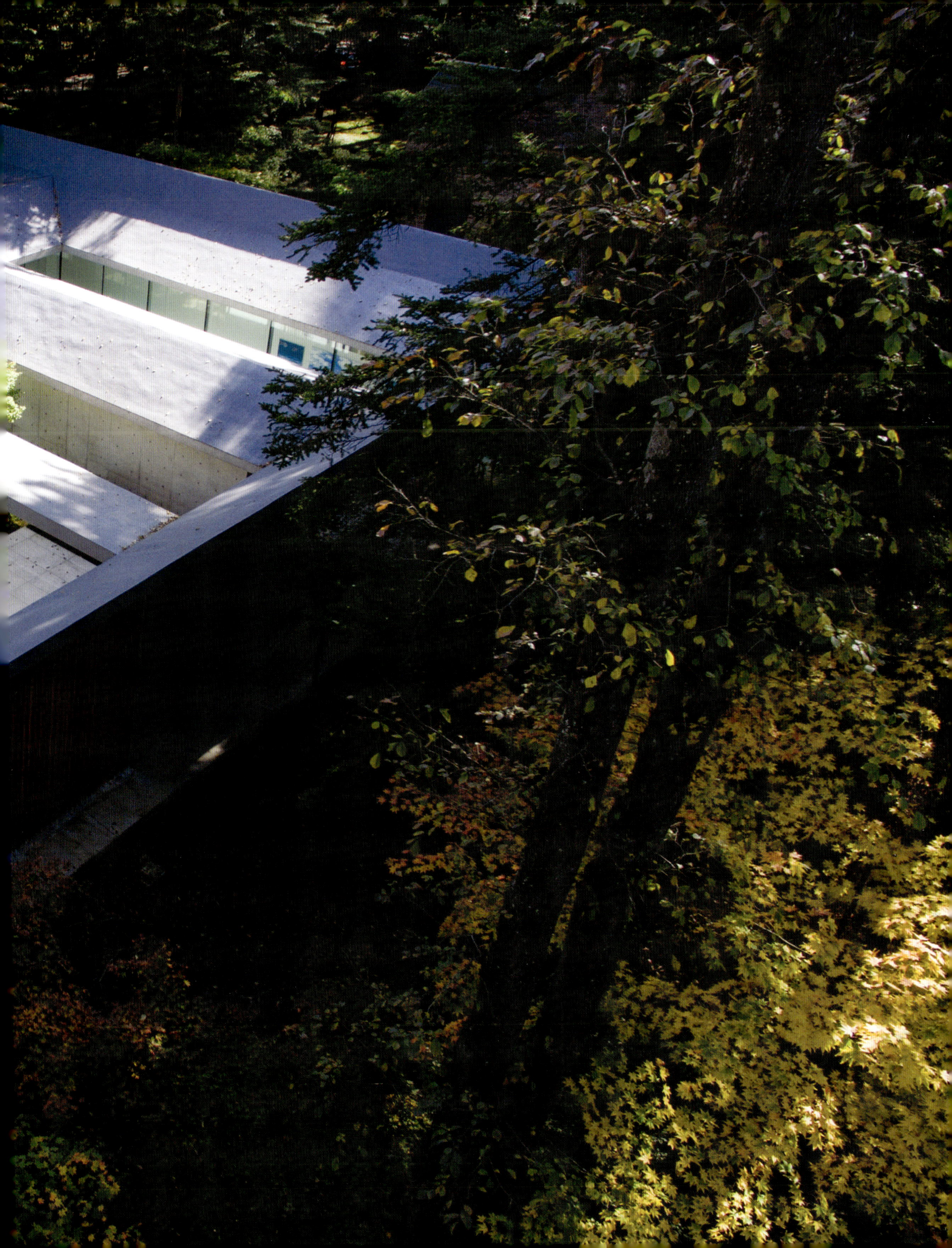

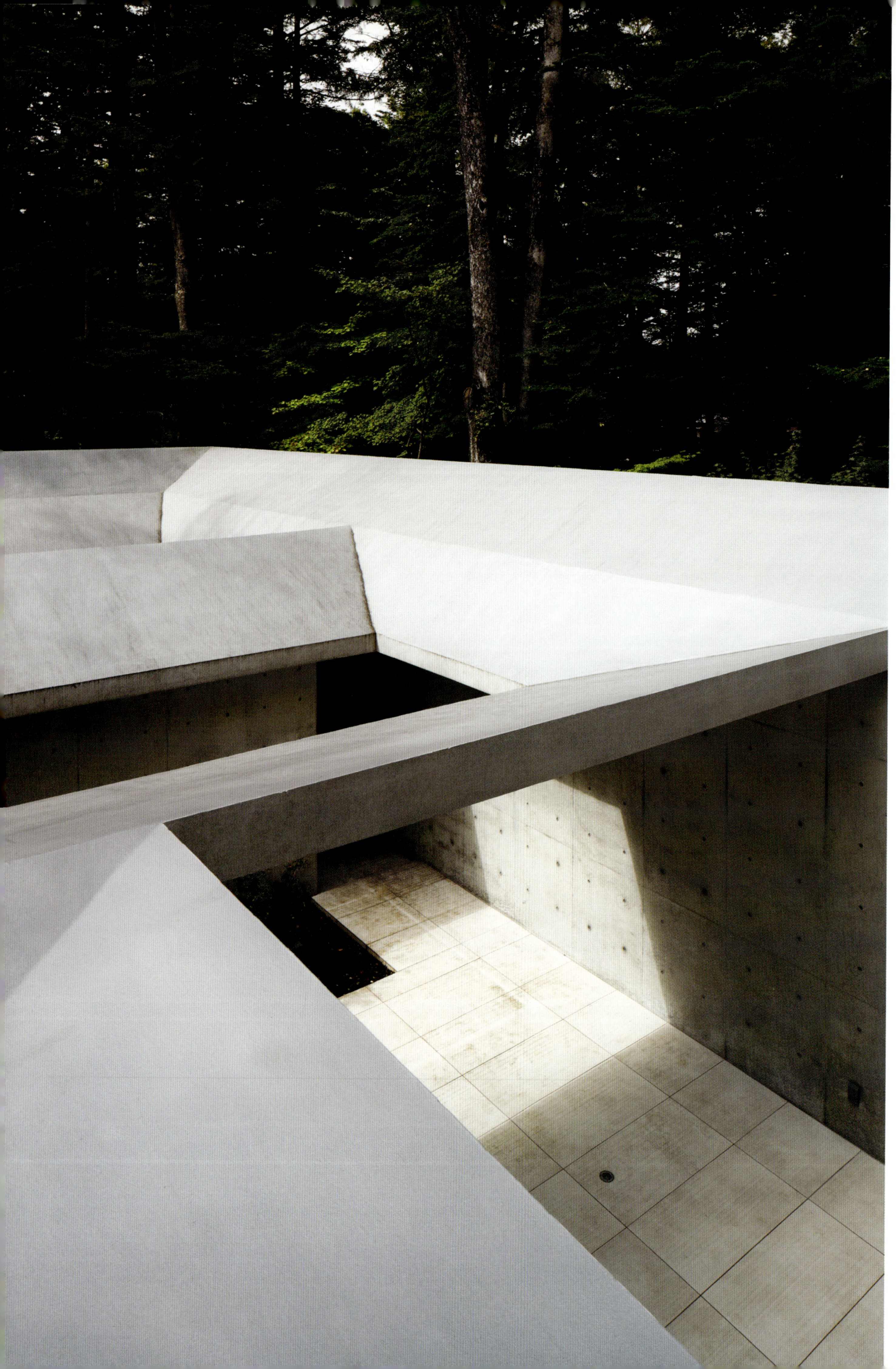

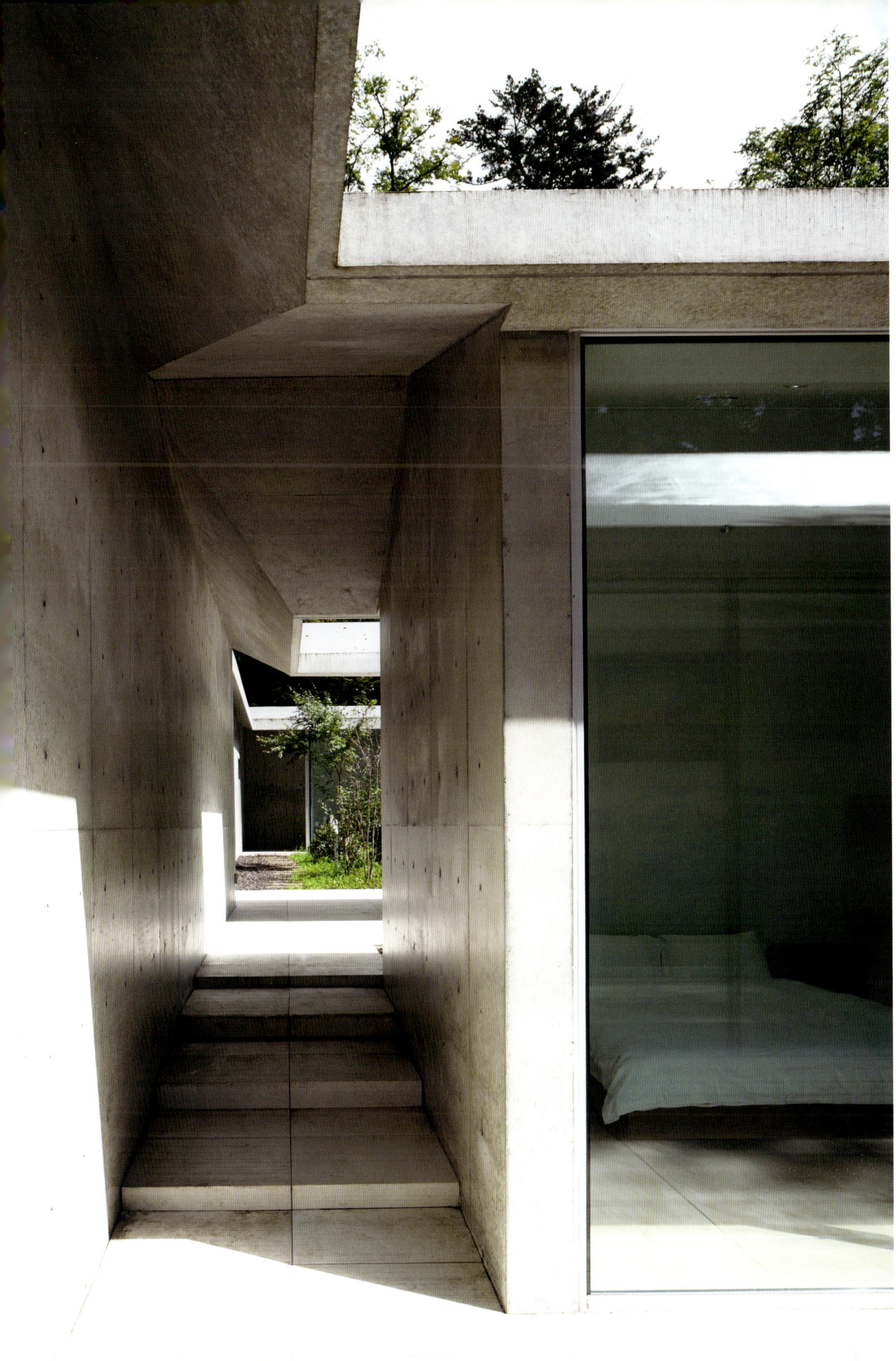

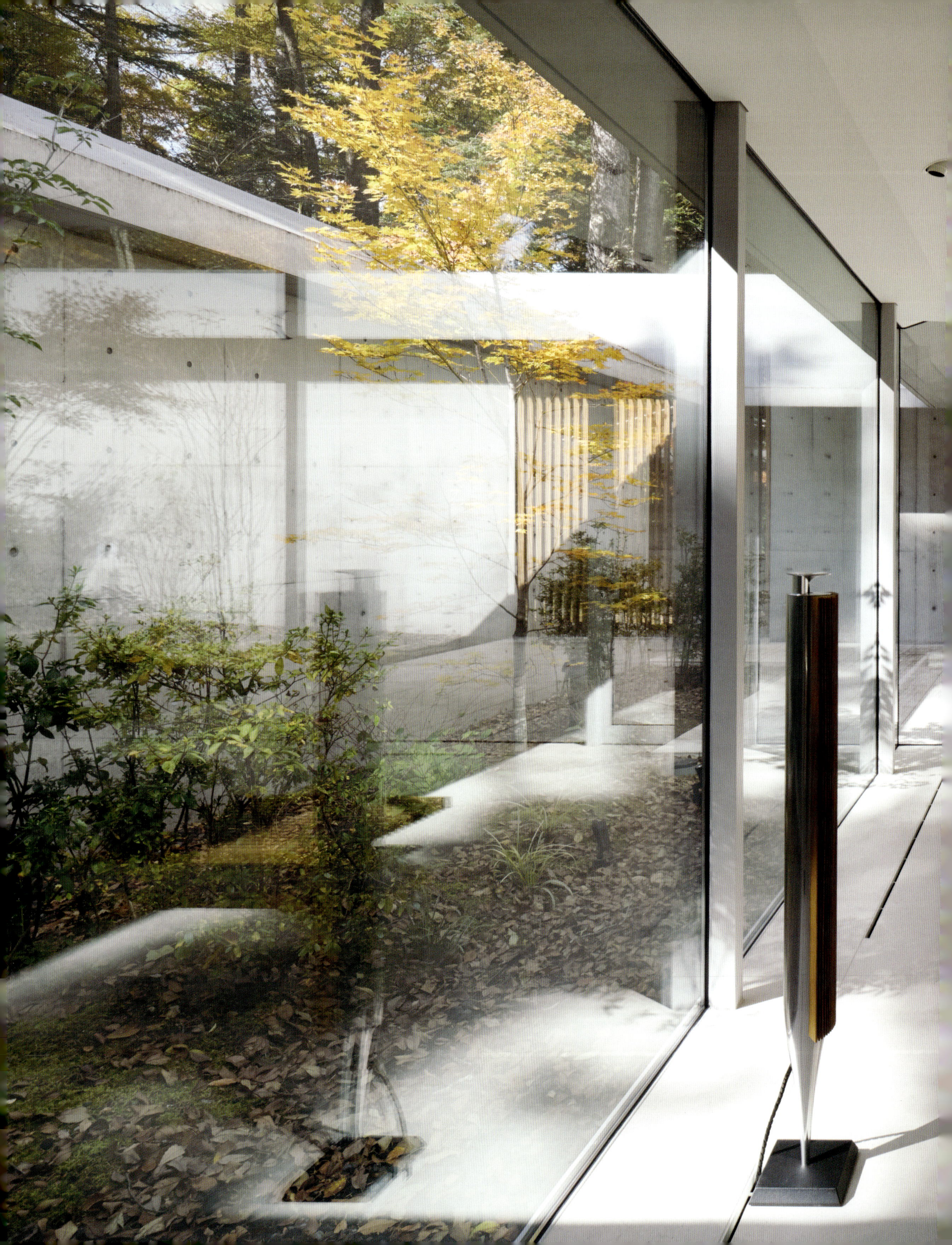

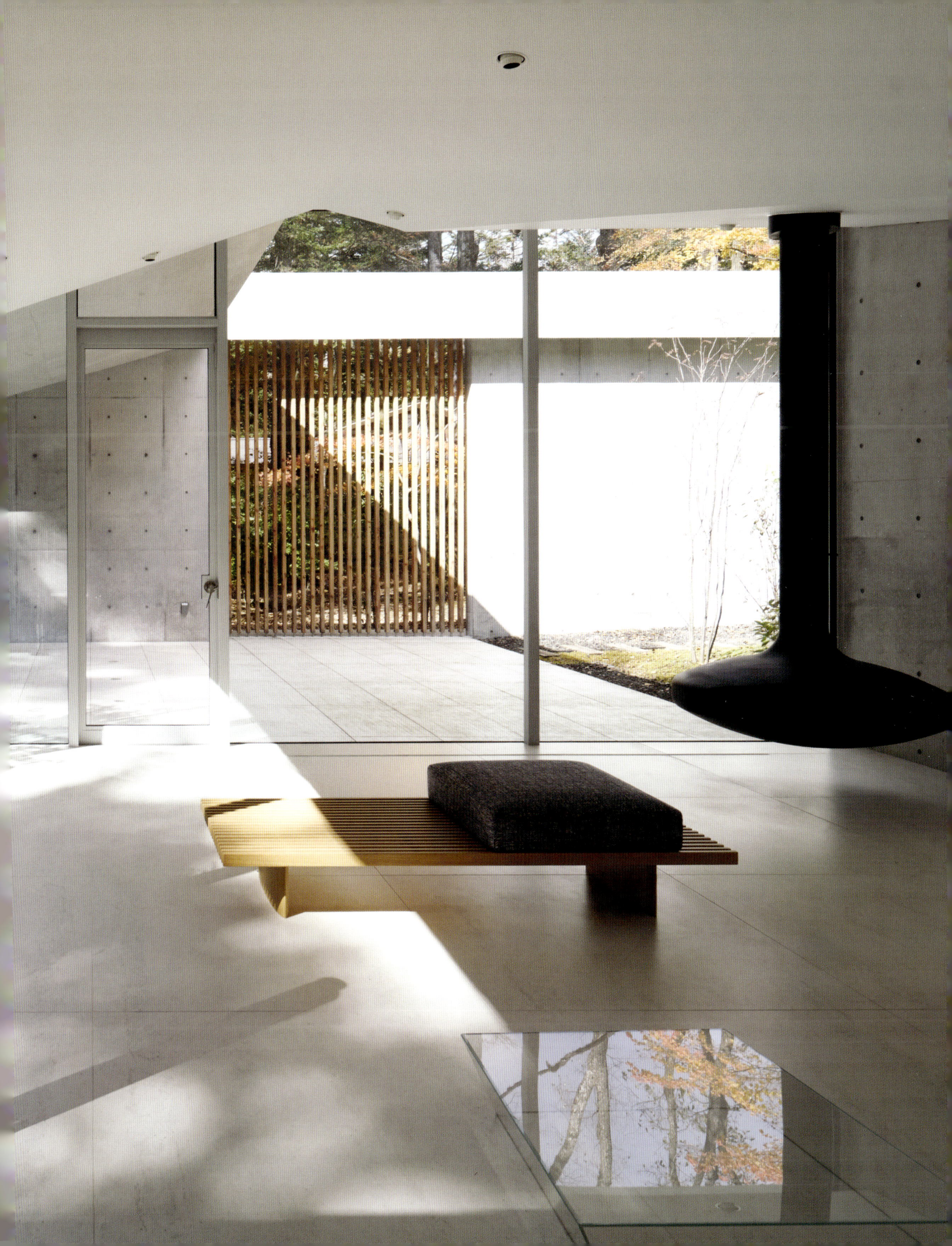

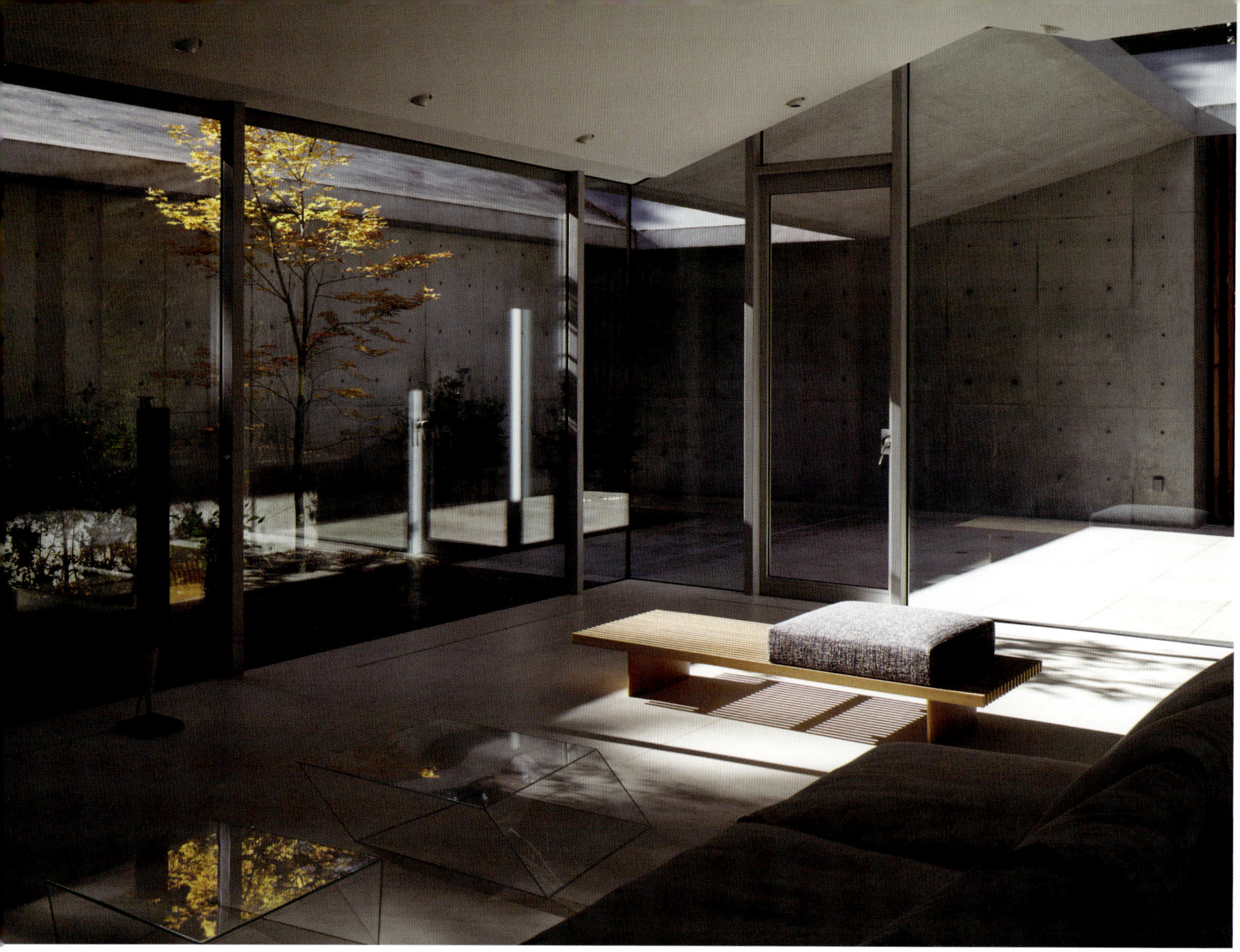

You wake up to the sunrise, see the reflections of nature and hear the singing of birds and rustle of leaves. Everything is moving within and around the house in harmonious complexity. The sun creates delicate and delightful phenomena, moving freely inside the house, entertaining and embracing the visitors as a perfect host. The sun rises and sets. The moon waxes and wanes. *Megumi Matsubara*

    Our architectural language expresses chance and movement. The interplay of light, wind, trees, even living creatures like birds, their reflections and shadows, are deliberately designed to be part of the space, as much as the human lives that occur within. *Megumi Matsubara*

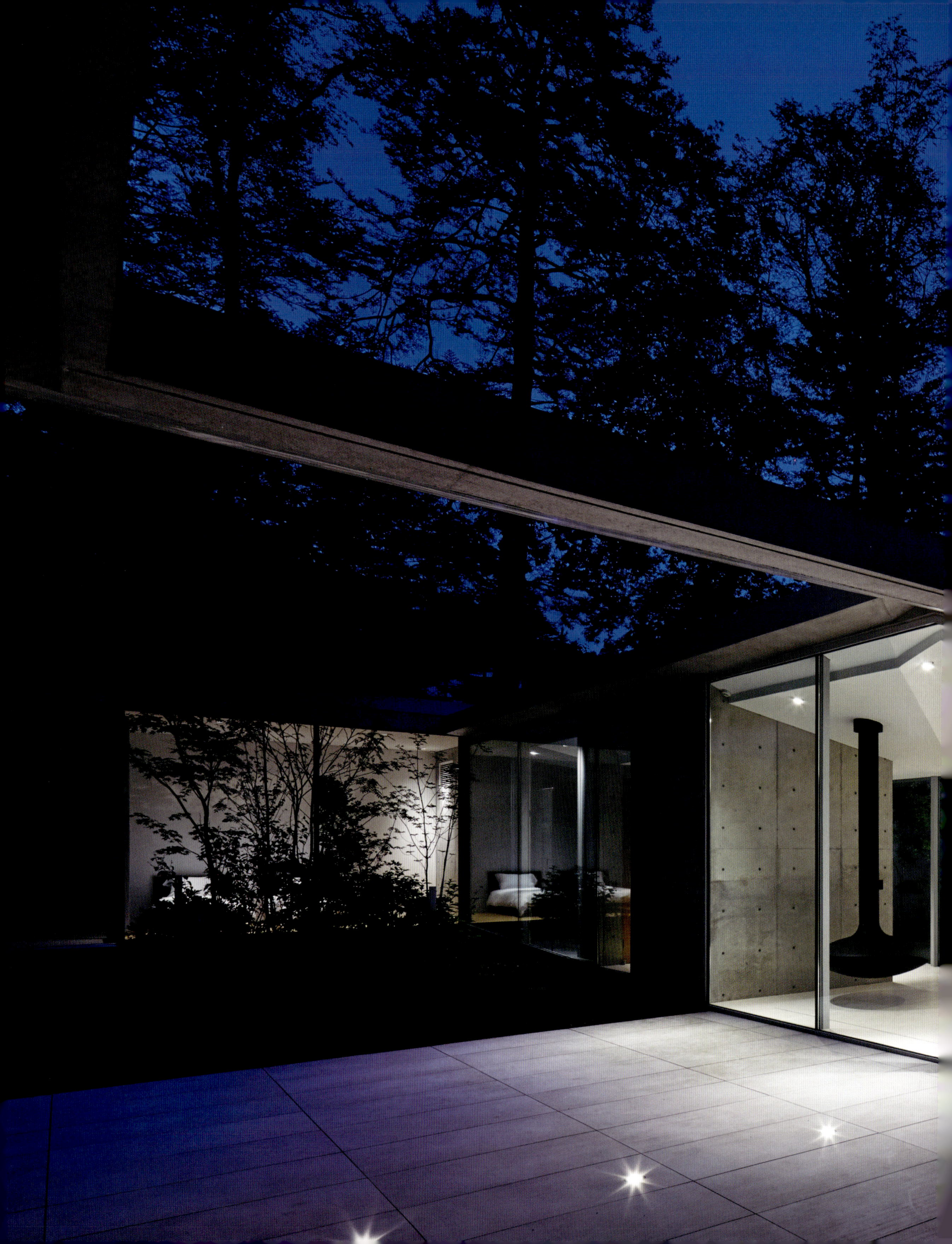

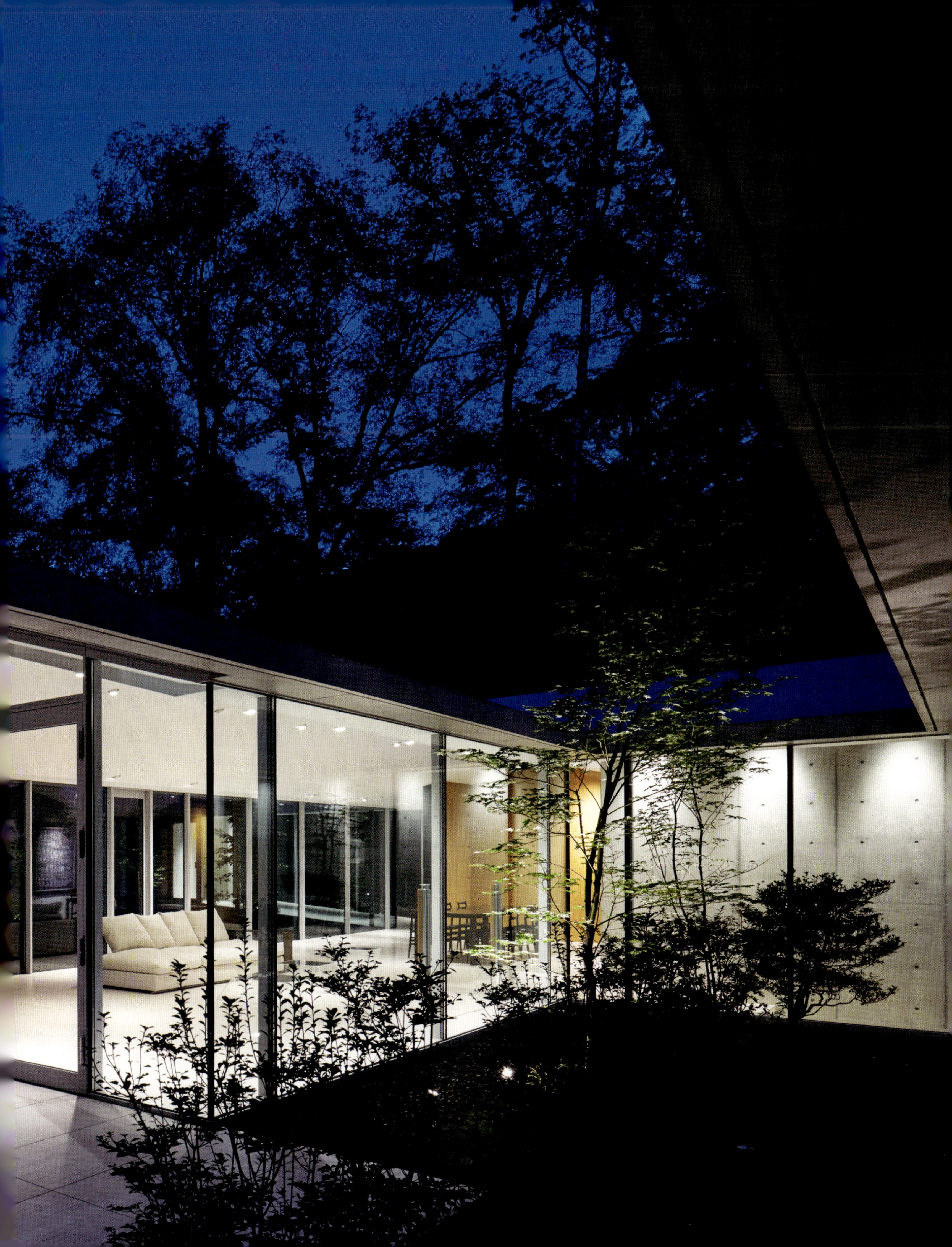

Photographs: Benjamin Benschneider and Dwight Eschliman

THE PIERRE

THE PIERRE
SAN JUAN ISLANDS, USA, 2011
TOM KUNDIG, OLSON KUNDIG ARCHITECTS

Tom Kundig's houses do unfamiliar and wonderful things. The Seattle-based architect eschews tasteful formalism and conventional assumptions about program, type, function, structure, enclosure, scale, proportion and ornament in favour of an industrial aesthetic that meshes tough materials – concrete and steel in the main – with inventive details to produce hypnotic buildings on dramatic sites, predominantly along the United States of America's Pacific Northwest.

Operable elements are a longstanding theme in Kundig's works, replete with walls and roofs that hinge, pivot and roll in ingenious ways. To control these movements he devises mechanical elements and hand-cranked mechanisms – 'gizmos', he calls them – such as levers, racks, gears, oversized hinges and wall-sized shutters that turn static elements into ones with dynamic movement, which directly connect the architecture to its surrounding landscape.

An admirer of the great Italian architect Carlo Scarpa, who once said he 'always dreamed of building a house with moveable stone walls; vertical planes which run on bearings and grooves', Kundig's is an architecture of rawness and refinement, in which details large and small are exquisitely designed and realised. One of the most striking examples of this is the kitchen island of Studio House (Seattle, 1998), a Chinese puzzle of in situ concrete counter tops and cabinet doors, cold rolled-steel storage units, specially designed cast-bronze fittings and stainless steel. The heavy cast-concrete cabinet doors swing on bronze rollers moving along in-floor steel rolling tracks.

The Brain (Seattle, 2002), for a video artist and film director, is a 404-cubic-metre double-height raw concrete box, slightly tapered to deflect noise reverberation, with a specially constructed and formed steel mezzanine, library and darkroom inserted along one of its walls. It features lights on motorised pulleys, a fireman's sliding pole and a low-level lookout for the client's dog. Studio Sitges (Spain, 2010), a work and living space for a photographer and his family, is a strikingly raw and powerful composition of board-marked concrete volumes and rusting steel. At Chicken Point Cabin (Northern Idaho, 2002), fronting a lake and forest, a large wheel turns gears to pivot a 9-metre x 6-metre window wall to make the interior dissolve into the expansiveness of the spectacular site just outside; while the Delta Shelter (Mazama, Washington, 2005) is a cabin on stilts on a flood plain, shuttered down on all sides by moveable 6-metre x 3-metre steel shutters operated by a simple hand crank.

This concrete and glass house, called The Pierre (French for stone), on Lopez Island in the San Juan group of islands in Washington, off the north-west tip of the United States, appears at first sight to burst from the rock outcrop into which it is wedged. Seen from above, its roof sown with grass, the house all but dissolves into the rocks and the landscape that surrounds it. In this wild setting, with expansive views out to the Salish Sea, Kundig created a weekend home for an art collector that works as a civilised shelter and protective vault for its owner's collections of art.

To set the house into the rocks, the outline of its footprint was first imposed onto the rocky surface and then gouged out with a combination of large drills, dynamite, hydraulic chippers and a selection of wire saws. The house structure of raw concrete and steel windows consists of a tall main space, 18.5 metres long, with a large kitchen at the back, the living and dining area overlooking the sea, a bedroom and sitting room, and a small guest room. Another guest room is tucked beneath the house at one end. A wood-clad storage box made from timber siding boards reclaimed from a house designed by Lionel Pries (1897–1968), a renowned architect, artist and educator of the Pacific Northwest, transitions from outside to inside and contains a utility shed, as well as a pantry and laundry concealed behind bookshelves.

The entry sequence is along a narrow path between the rock face, still bearing drill marks, and a wall of concrete with the tie holes left exposed. The impression is distinctly one of approaching the mouth of a cave. A small powder room just behind the main entrance has been carved entirely out of the rock, lit by a sky tube inserted into the top, directing a single shaft of light onto a sink of forged bronze. The materiality between rock and concrete extends throughout the house. In the main living space, the concrete fireplace incorporates a large rock, levelled and polished to serve as a hearth. Rock chips from the excavation were crushed and ground to make aggregate for the terrazzo floors of the dining area. The master bathroom is placed within a section of rock with enough marble-like qualities for it to be polished into a basin composed of water cascading through three polished pools in the existing stone.

Throughout, the rock protrudes into the house, contrasting with the luxurious textures of the furnishings. Interior and exterior fireplace hearths are carved out of existing stone; levelled on top, they are otherwise left raw. In the master bathroom, water cascades through three polished pools, like natural sinks in the existing stone. Off the main space, a powder room is carved out of the rock; a mirror set with a sky tube reflects natural light into the space. *Tom Kundig*

Kundig's is an architecture of rawness and refinement, in which details large and small are exquisitely designed and realised. In this wild setting, with expansive views out to the Salish Sea, Kundig created a weekend home for an art collector that works as a civilised shelter and protective vault for its owner's collections of art.

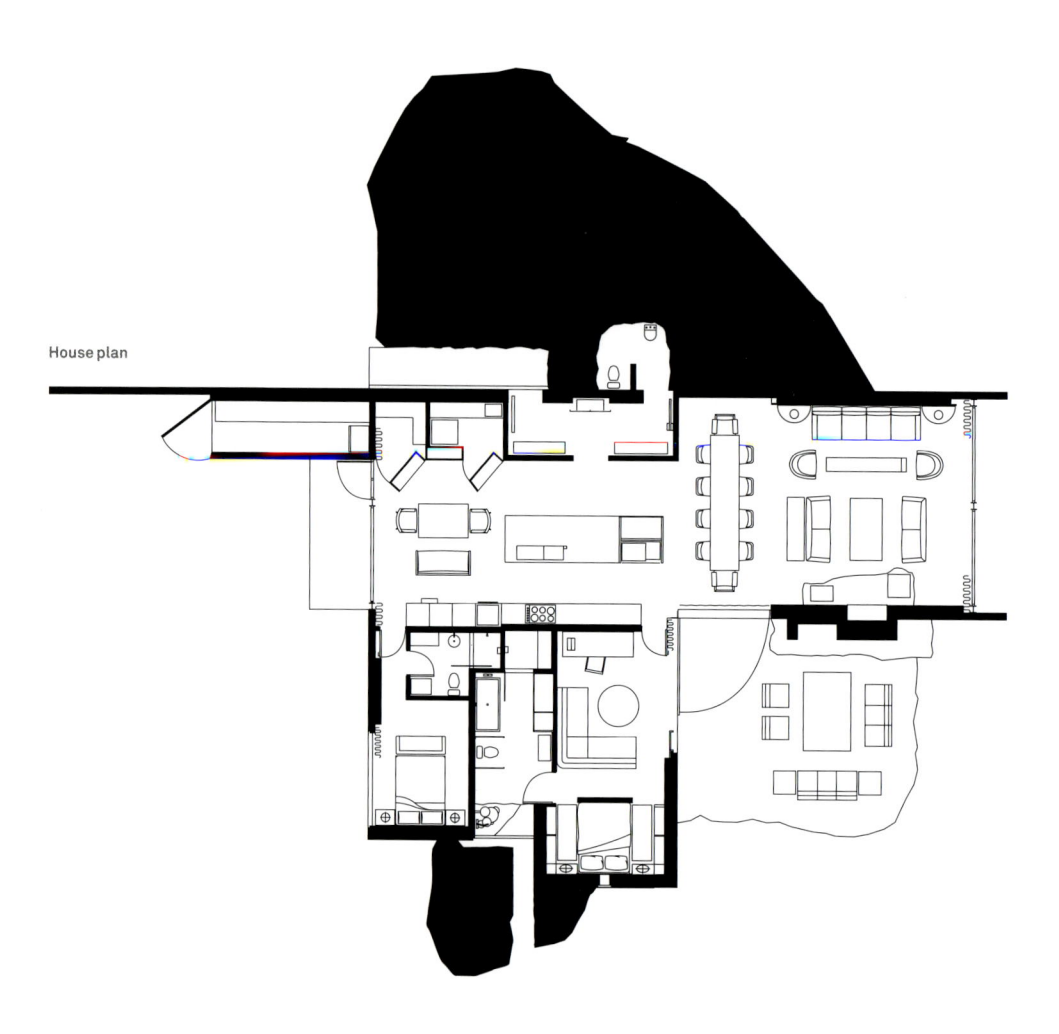

House plan

East–west section

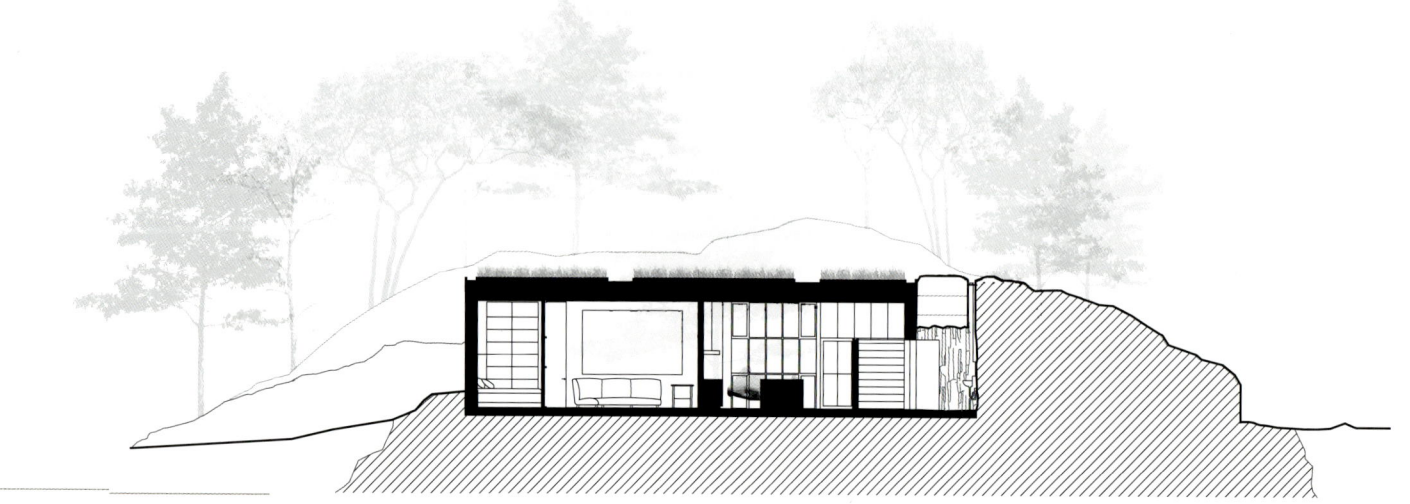

0   30'

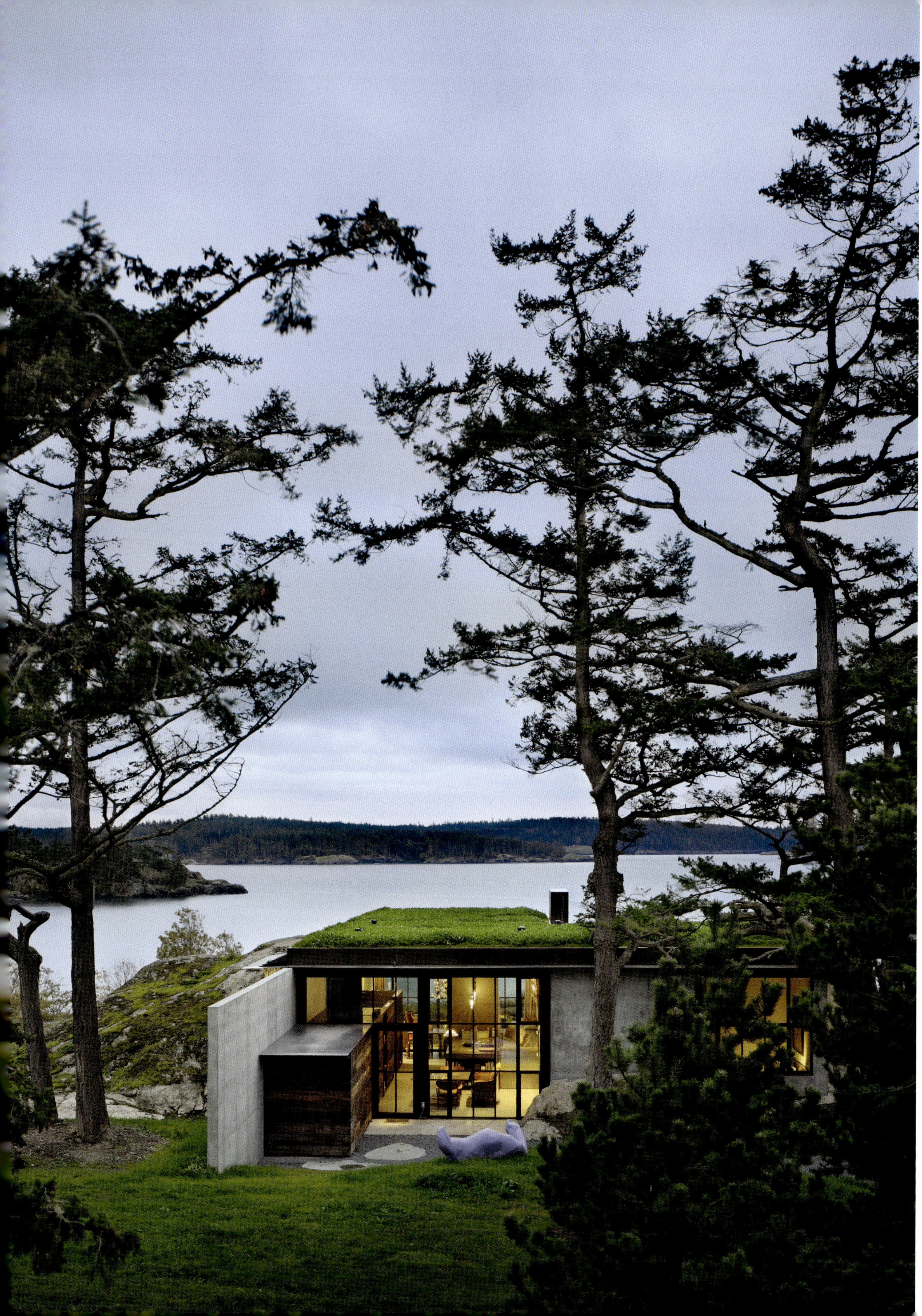

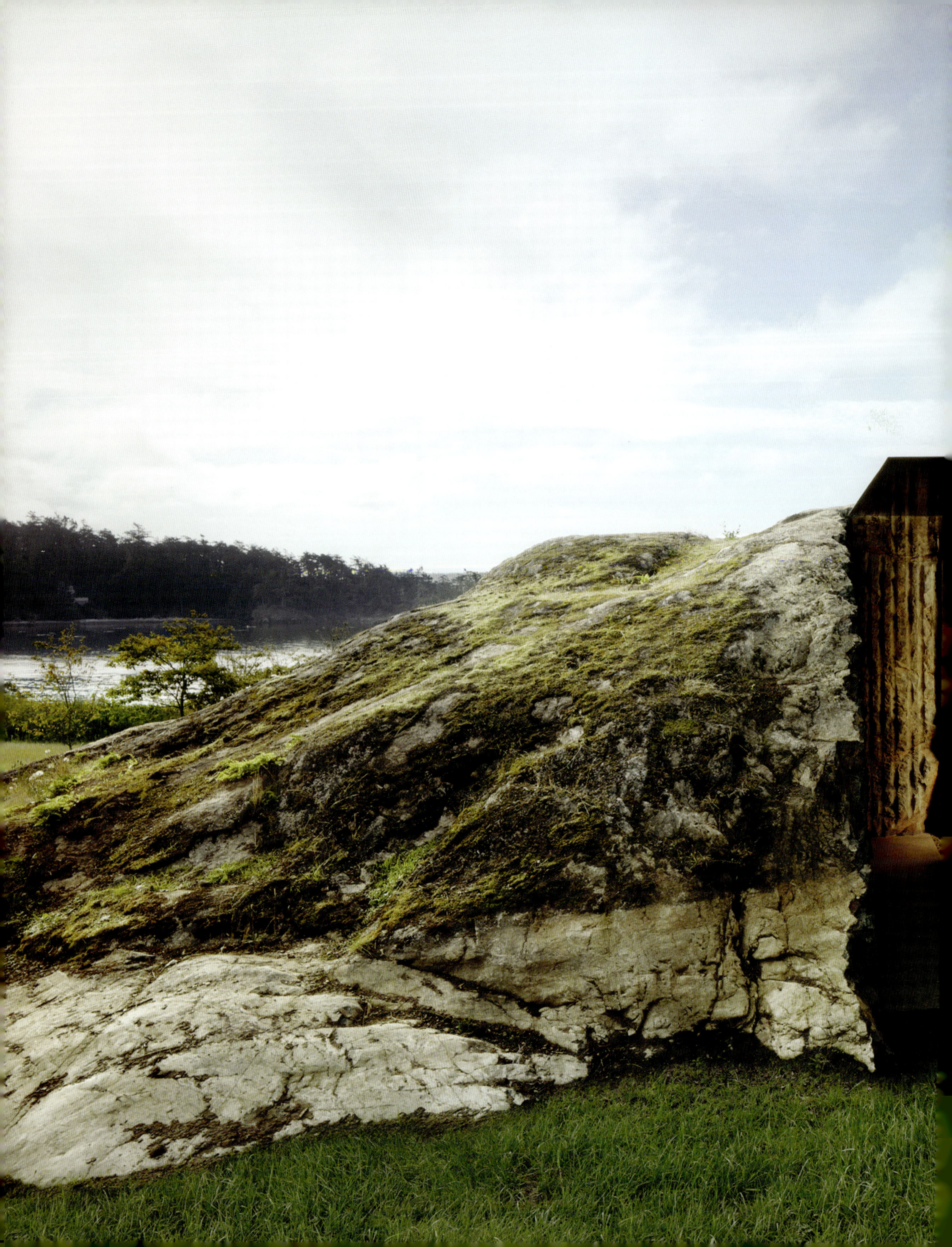

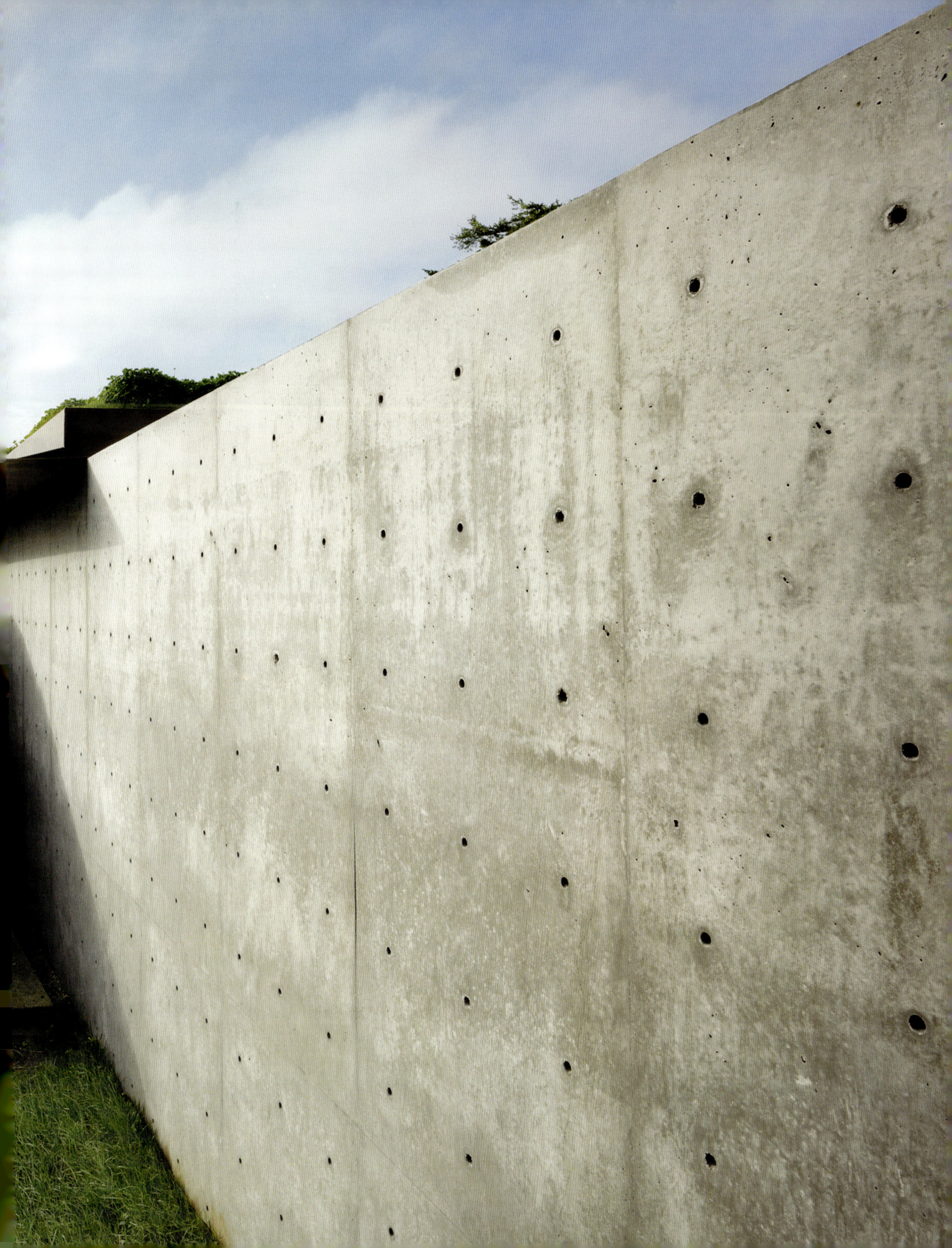

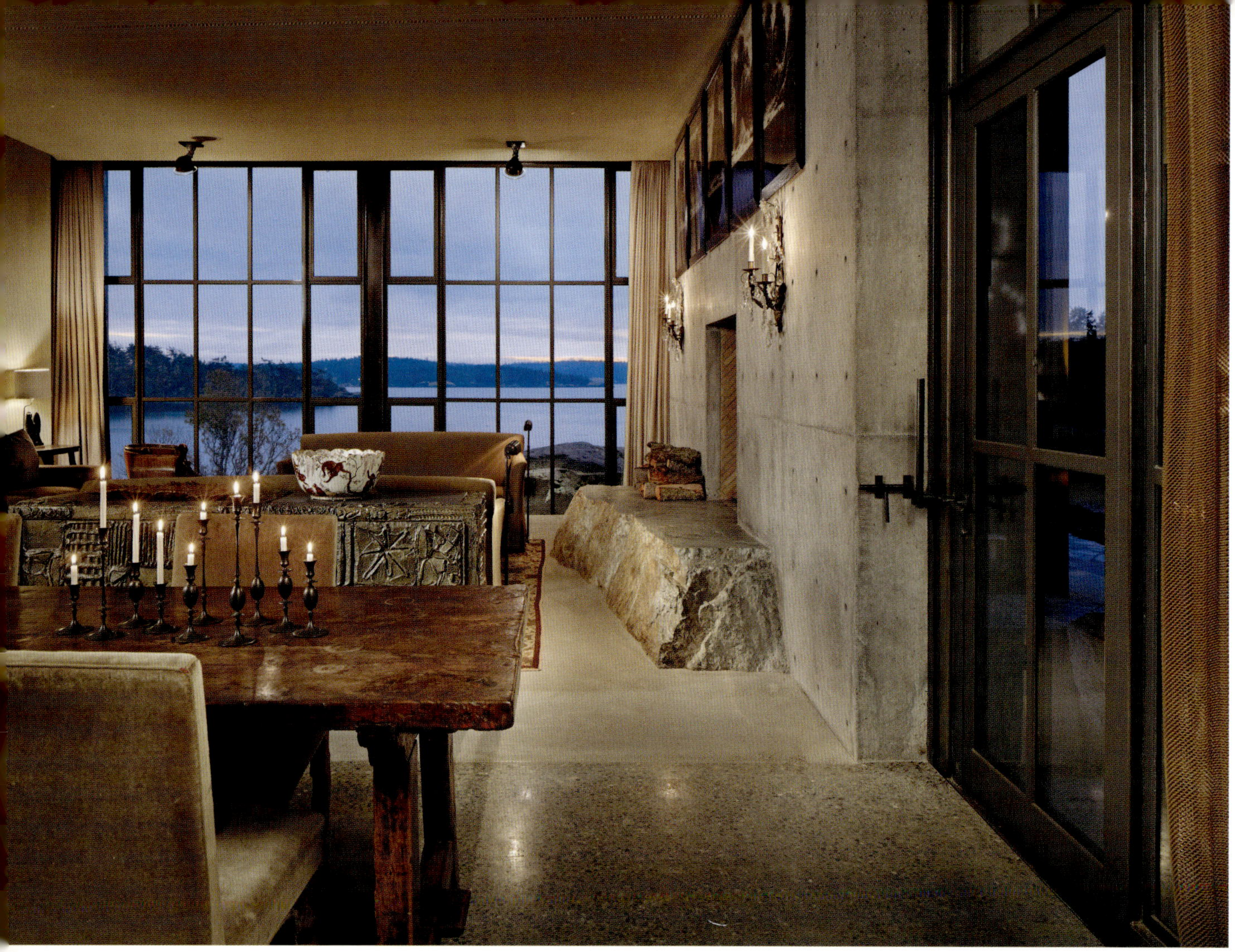

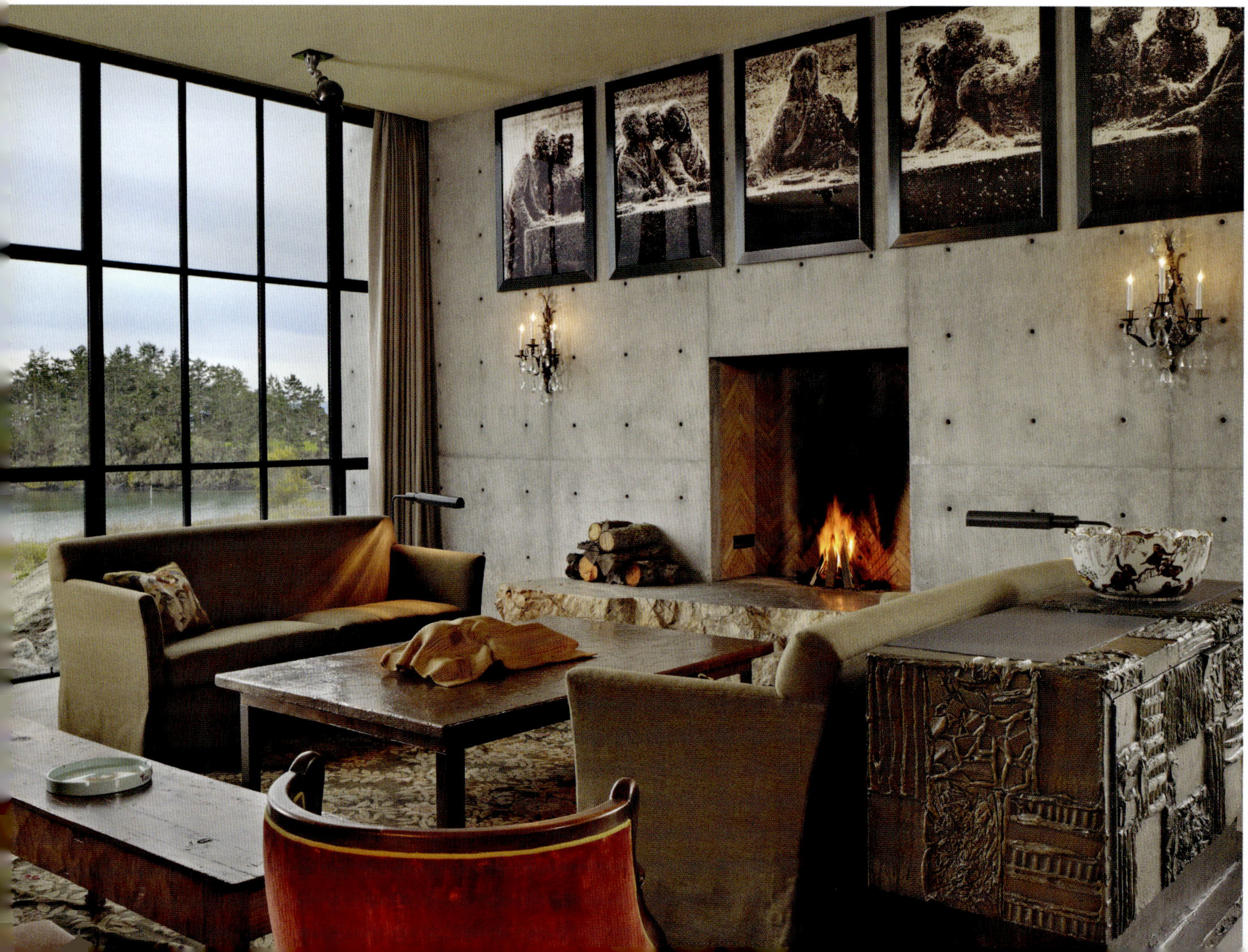

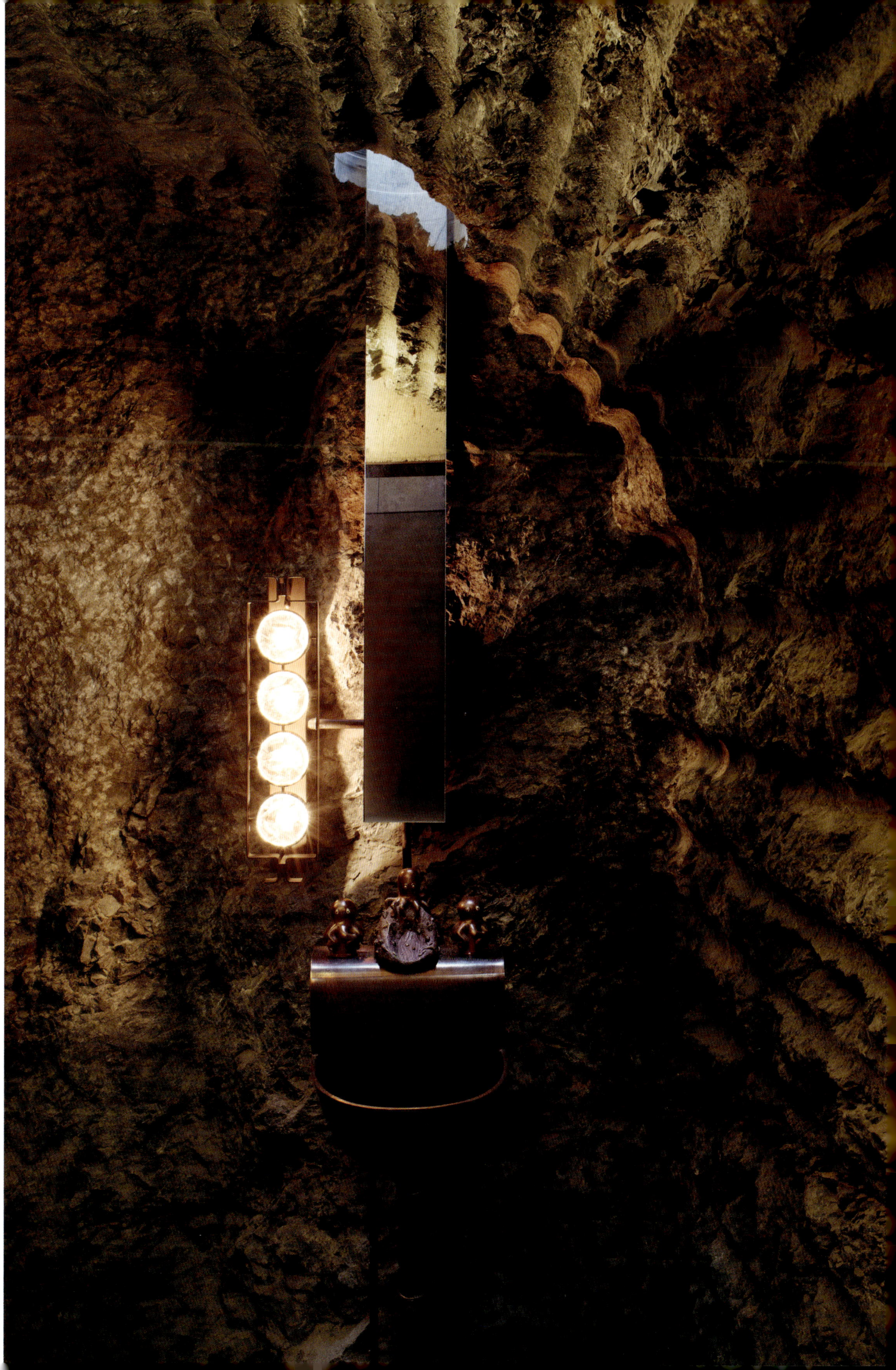

Photographs: Brett Boardman

LUNE DE SANG PAVILION

LUNE DE SANG PAVILION
NORTHERN NEW SOUTH WALES, AUSTRALIA, 2018
CHROFI

In November 2013, in a magazine piece about a Sydney couple's vision to transform a lantana- and camphor laurel-infested bushland in the hinterland behind Byron Bay into a future rainforest, sustainably grown and selectively harvested for the production of prized cabinet timbers, I waxed lyrical about the completion of 'two muscular buildings of in situ concrete, of minimal form, nestled into the hillsides, facing north, purposefully designed for permanence. Like the trees, these are structures that likely will remain in place for a hundred years and more. Only the fullness of time, the weathering and the ageing of the concrete and the maturing of the rainforest will see their vision realised.'

The sheds, designed to hold farm machinery, tools and the kinds of equipment and materials required for the running of such an operation, were remarkable for their singularity of form: one, a rhythm of eighteen concrete piers, supporting H-shaped concrete beams carrying the roof; the other, for materials handling and storage, a series of tapering, cantilevered concrete beams, 20 metres long, anchored into the slope of the hill, supported midway on a metre-deep concrete truss beam.

Now a residential pavilion, Lune de Sang, has been added to the property. Like the sheds, it was designed by the Sydney-based architectural practice CHROFI and it, too, has been designed for permanence. Sited uphill of the sheds, the pavilion sits along a ridge line and is defined by two large Moreton Bay fig trees and a tall palm. First impressions are of a large raking protective roof hovering over a glass enclosure, supported on a concrete post and beam structure. The 28-metre concrete beams – poured in situ, steel reinforced and with tie holes expressed – cantilever 7 metres at each end of the pavilion, creating a carport at one end and a shade canopy at the other, where a large irregular-shaped swimming pool spills into a stone moat. An adventure playground, a folly made from tree timbers collected on the property and bolted together, hides the pool plant.

The rectangular box serves as a large gathering space; a singular room in which to receive family and guests for social activities, cooking and dining, separated by a wall of blackbutt panelling from a bathroom, laundry, pantry and mudroom.

Like the sheds there is a distinct sense of permanence here, of reshaping the land, of inserting significant architecture in the landscape. Surrounded by lush tropical plantings, it is not difficult to imagine that in time the building will be all but reclaimed by the forest and, like an ancient ruin, rediscovered and made habitable again.

The simplicity of the pavilion is deceptive, for behind it, accessed through a cleverly concealed external timber door (you have to go outside to go inside), lies an entirely private domain for sleeping, bathing and relaxing. Here, the soaring raked ceiling of the public pavilion gives way to a low, flat roof of deep concrete beams; the geometry is disrupted, radiating and extending outwards to make a series of fluid spaces, cranked and separated by cabinetry. To one side, behind a wall of blackbutt, lies an open sleeping, bathing and dressing zone; to the other, a triangulated living and art space, the grid of concrete ribs stretched and extended to a point to make a shade canopy hung with a series of colourful hammocks swaying in the breeze, embraced by stone retaining walls and lushly planted gardens.

The lower ceilings, the disrupted grid of concrete ribs, the close views out to retaining walls of large blocks of basalt stone, the deep roof overhangs and the tangible evidence of the house and roof anchored to the site, all contribute to a pervasive sense of calm and intimacy; the space, concealed behind mounded earth, rock and subtropical plantings, feels unassailable.

The pavilion is part of a suite of structures on the Lune de Sang site, including the two working sheds, a guesthouse, a new general manager's residence, and two more work sheds, one of which is an artist's studio, also designed by CHROFI.

Site plan
01 Shed 1
02 Shed 2
03 Pavilion
04 Log cabin
05 Guest house
06 Caretaker

0   200m

Roof plan

House plan

0   10m

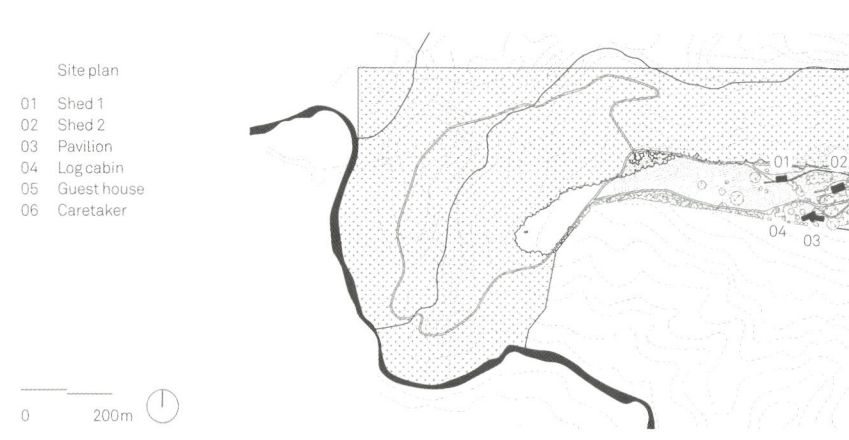

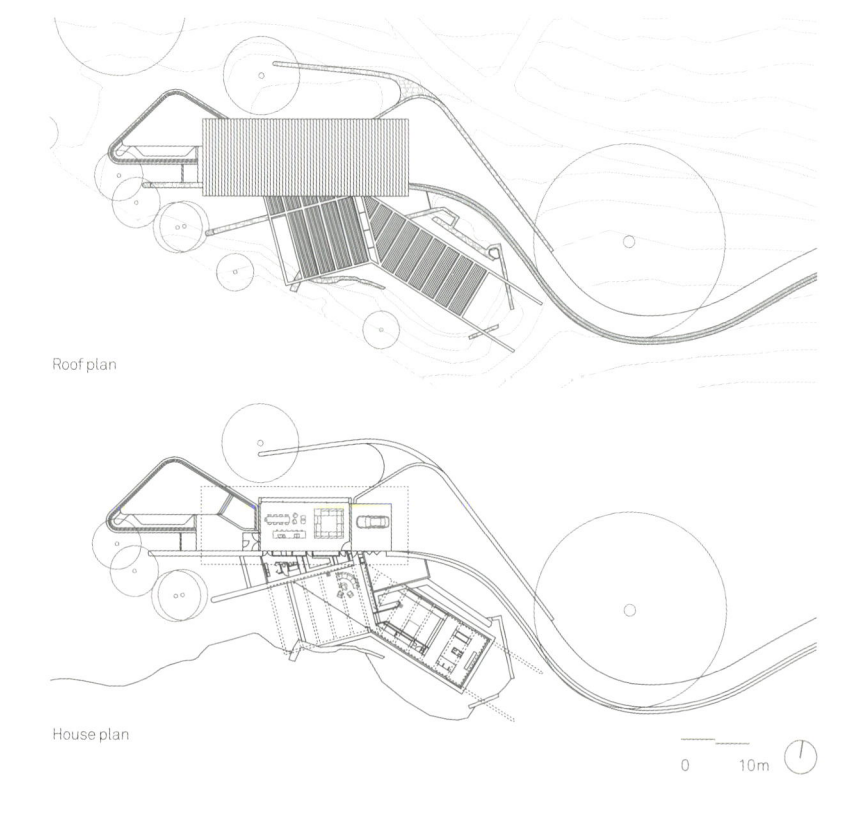

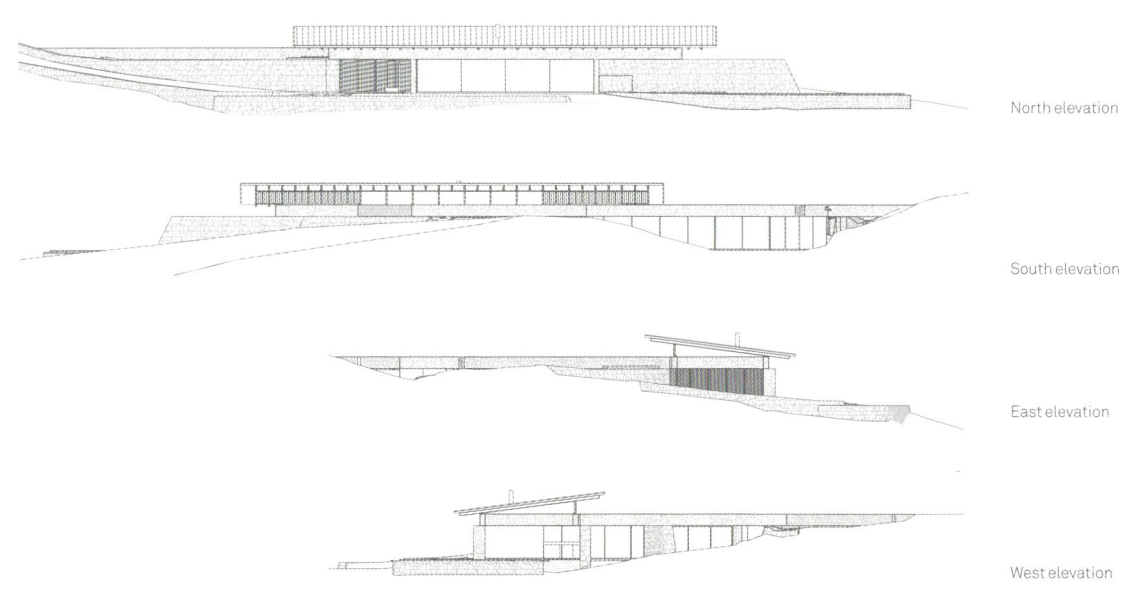

North elevation

South elevation

East elevation

West elevation

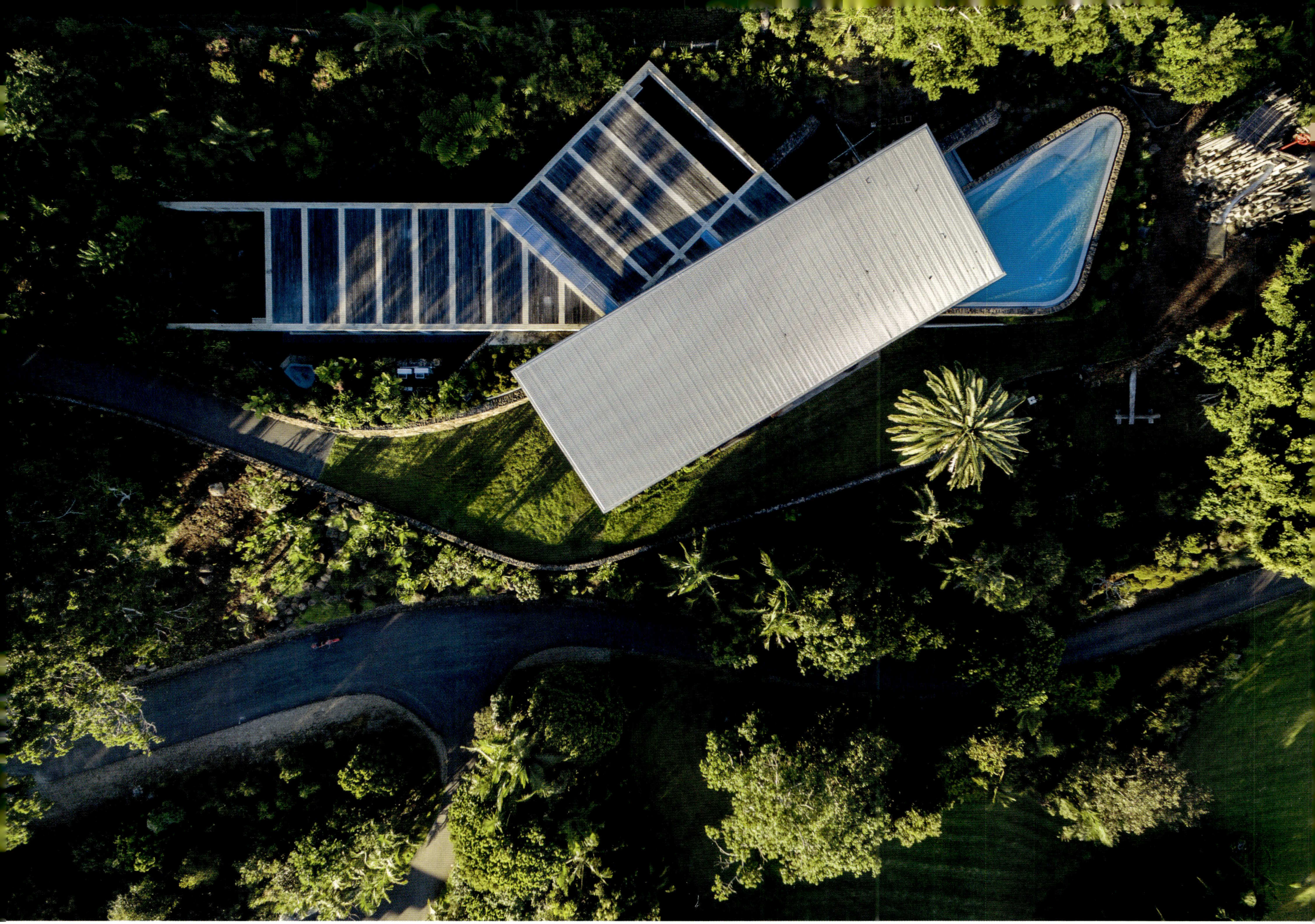

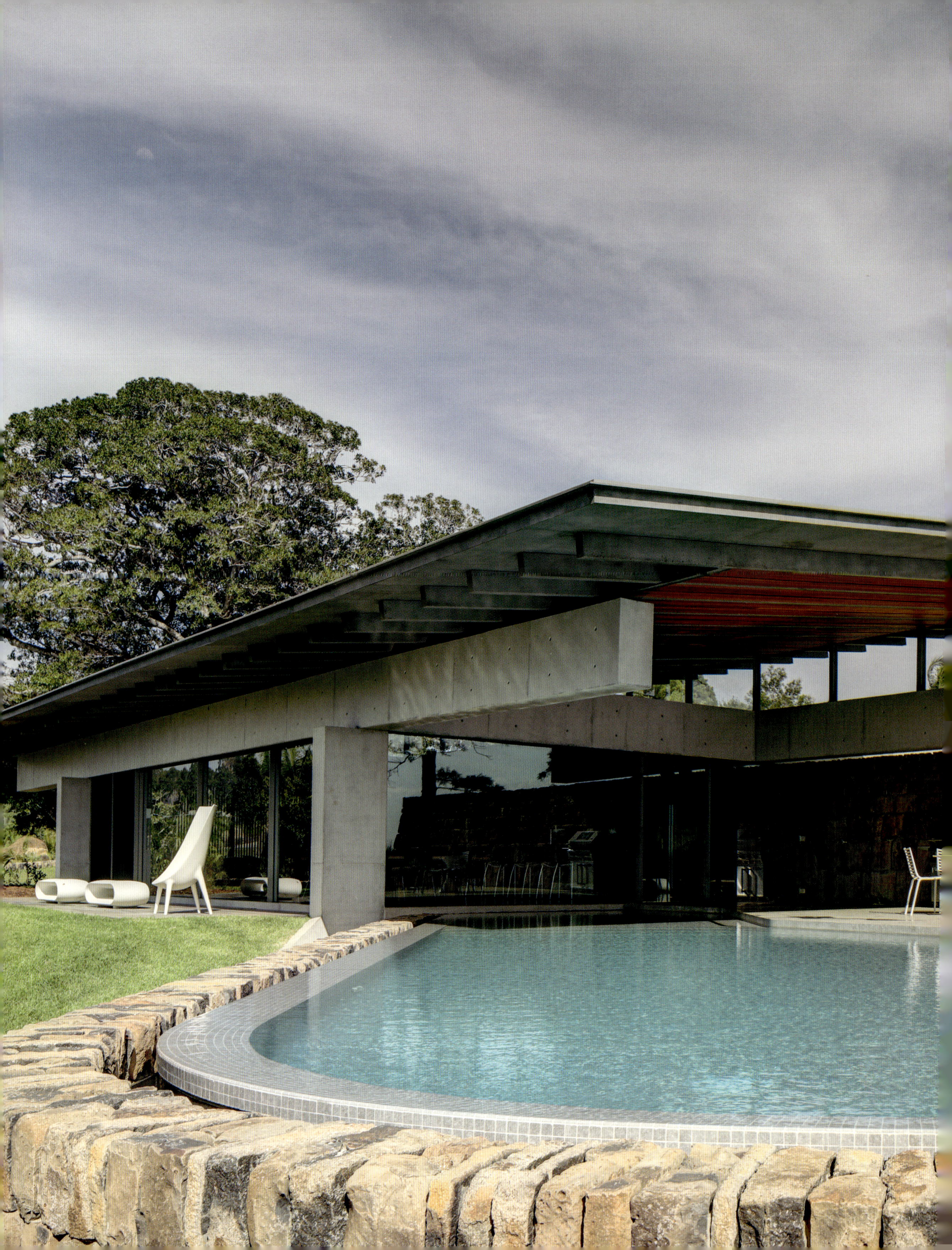

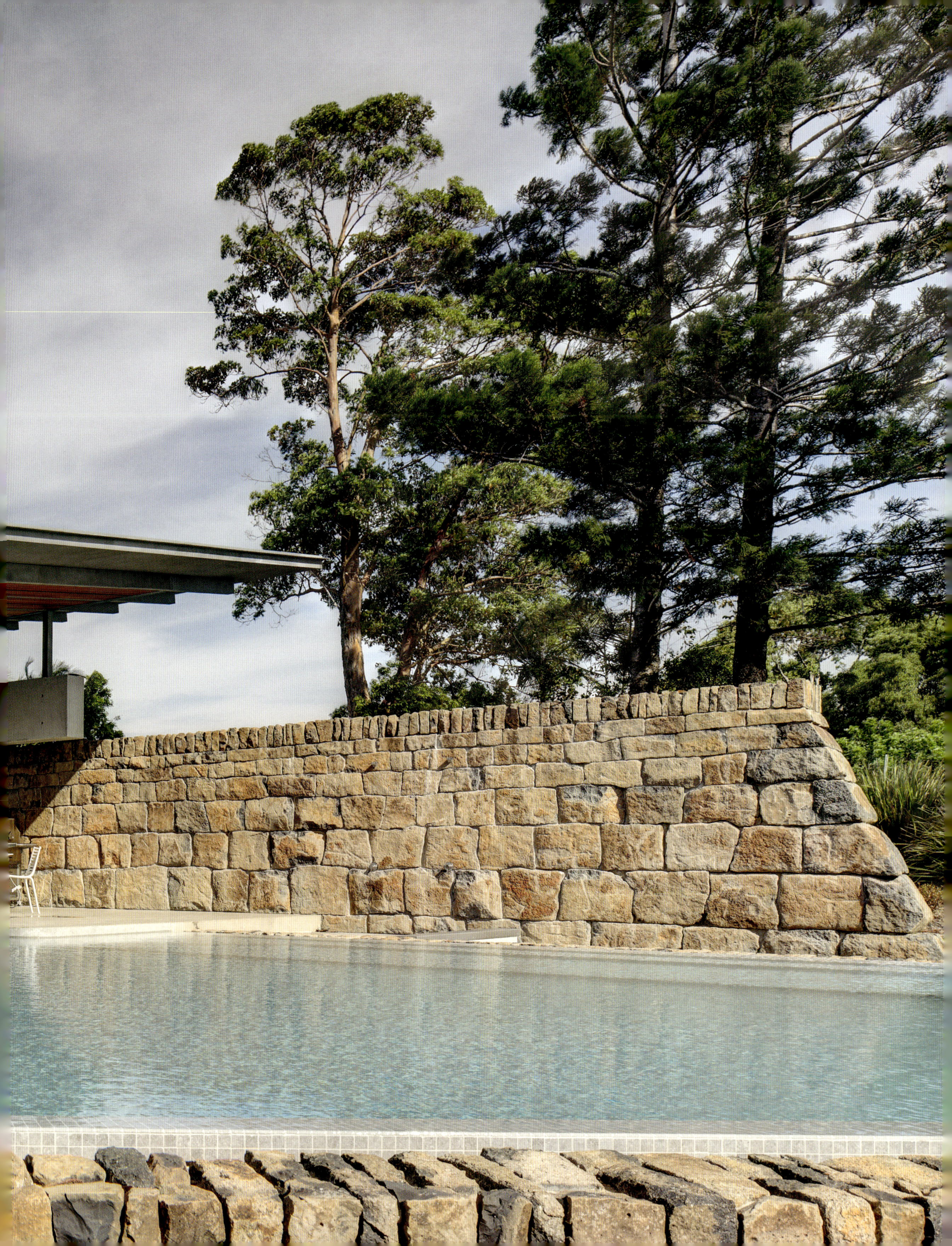

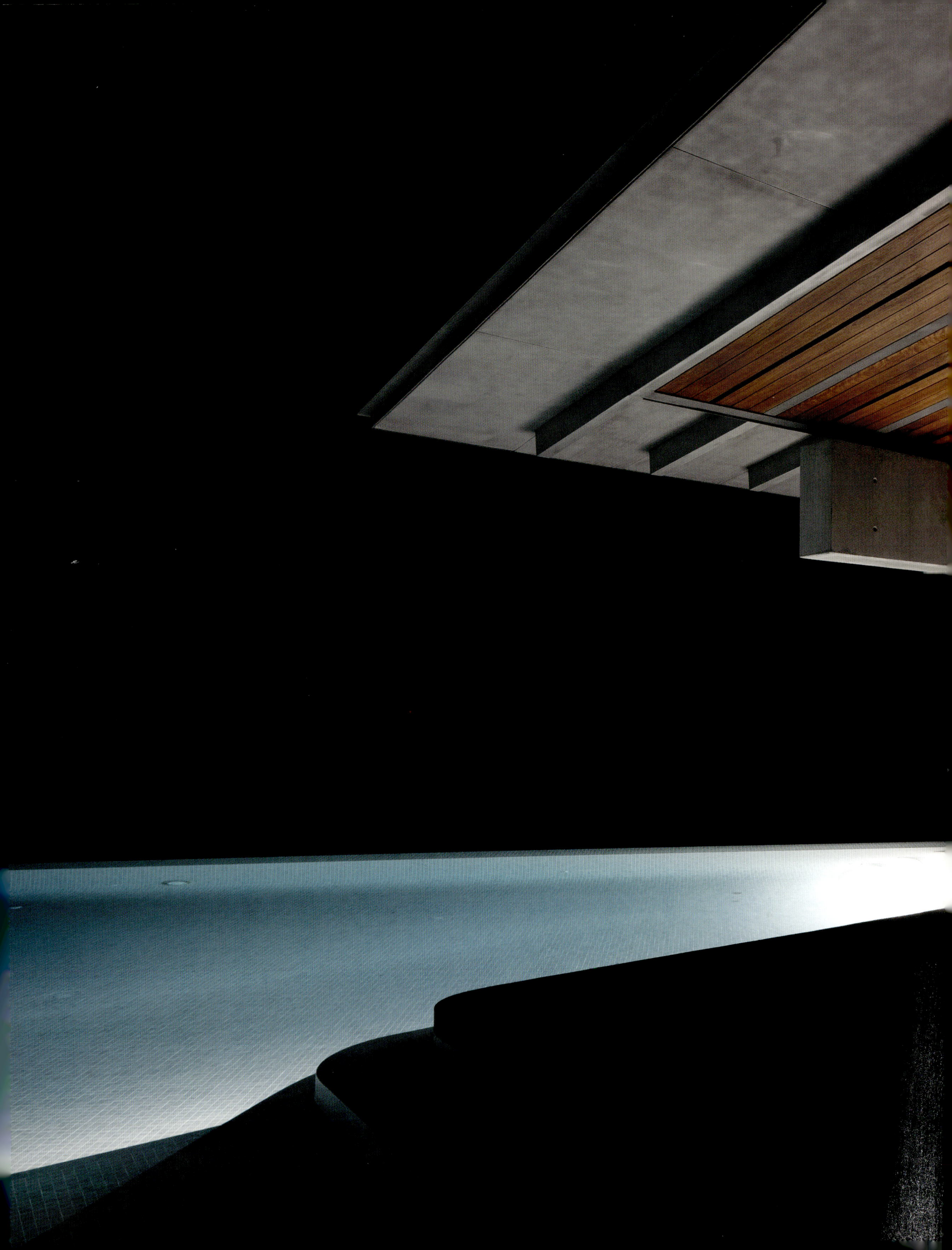

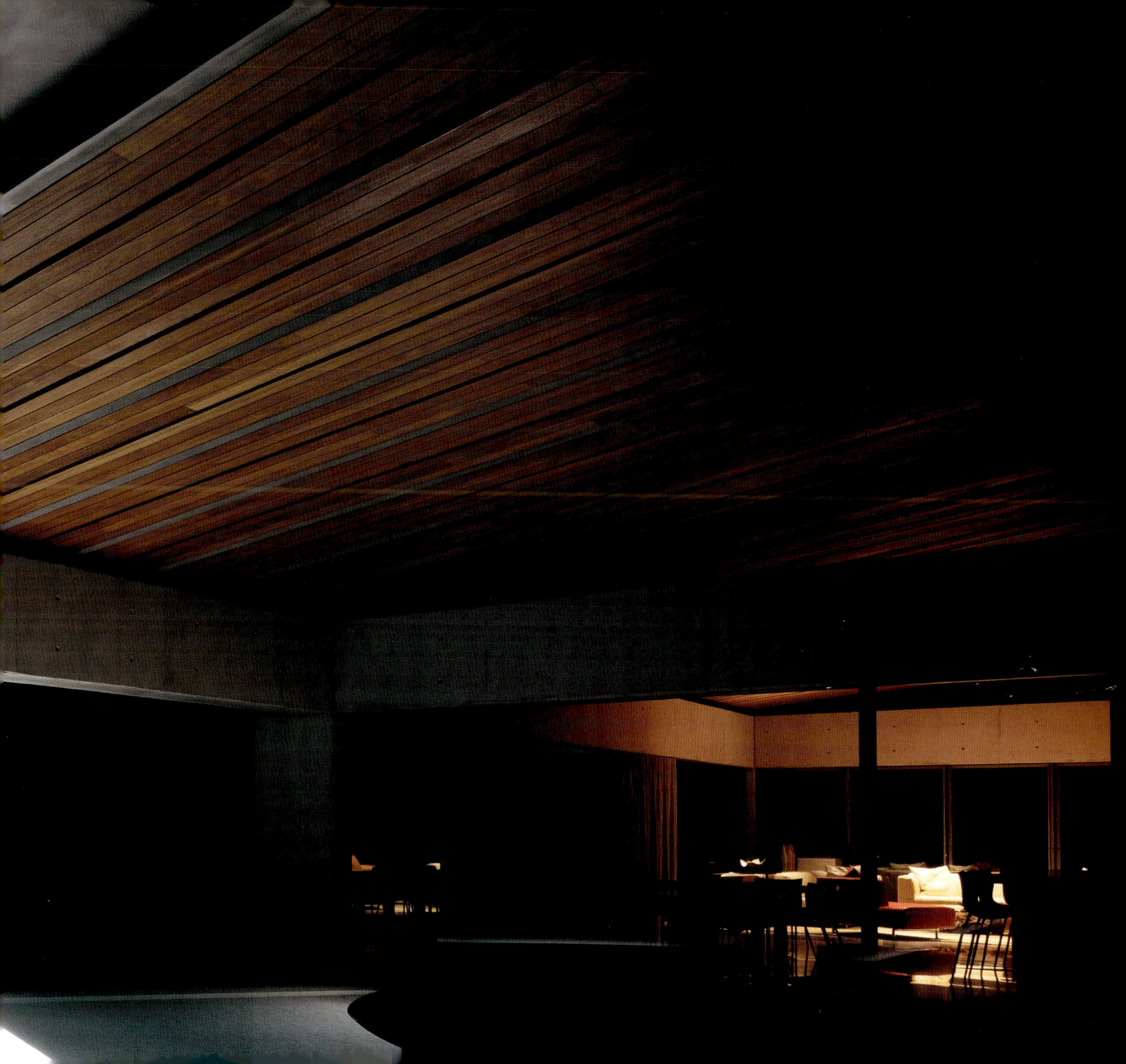

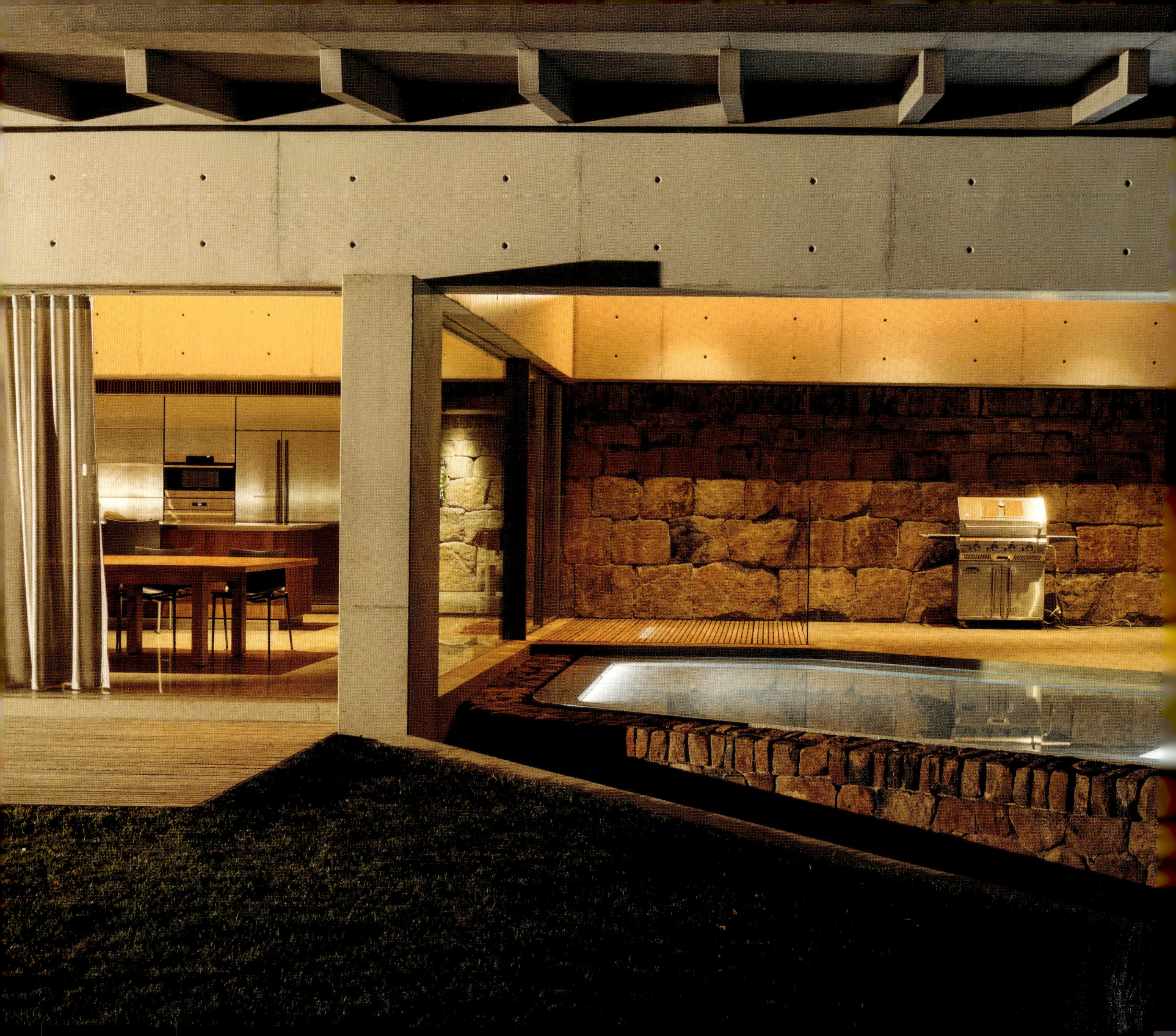

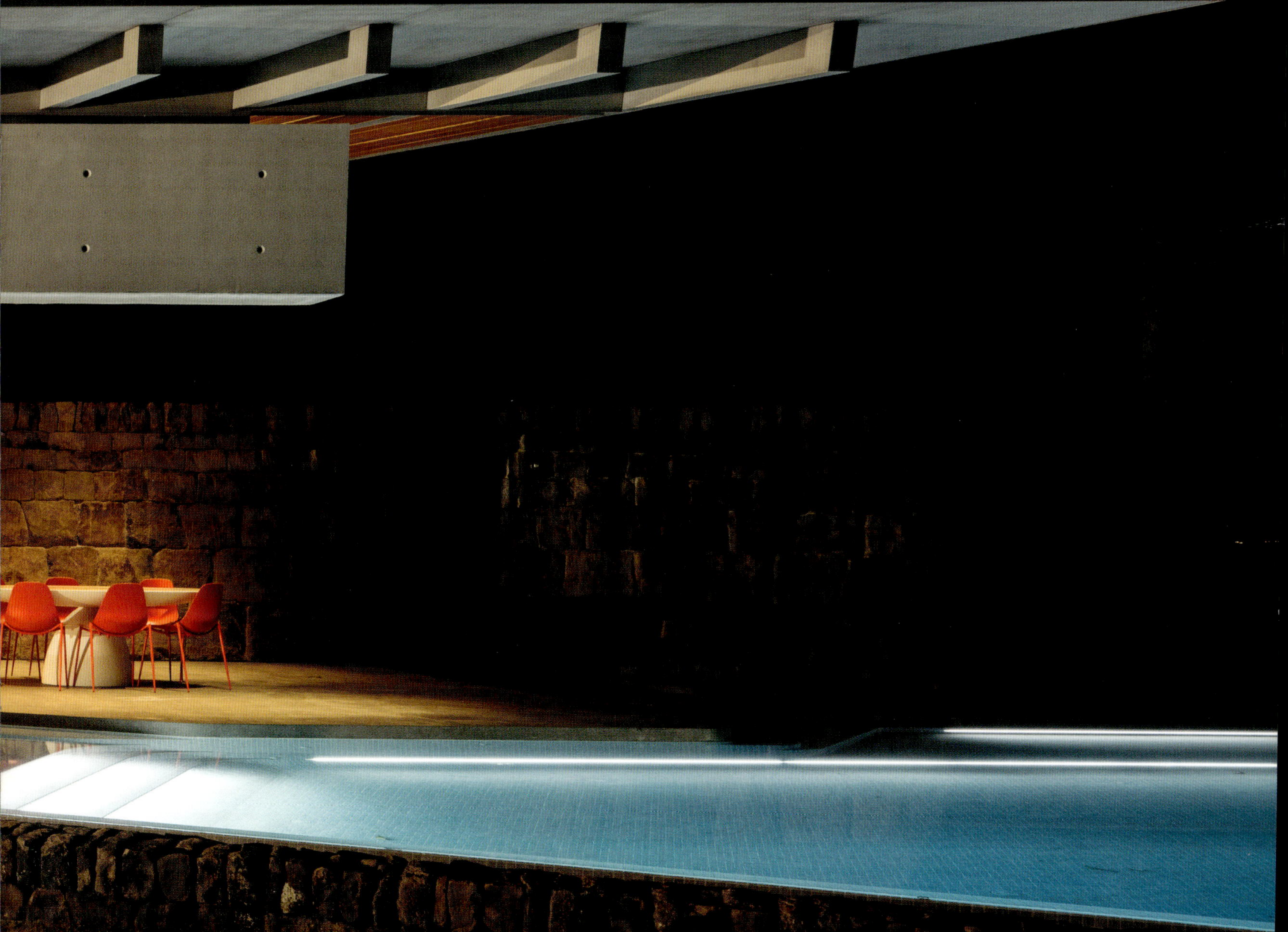

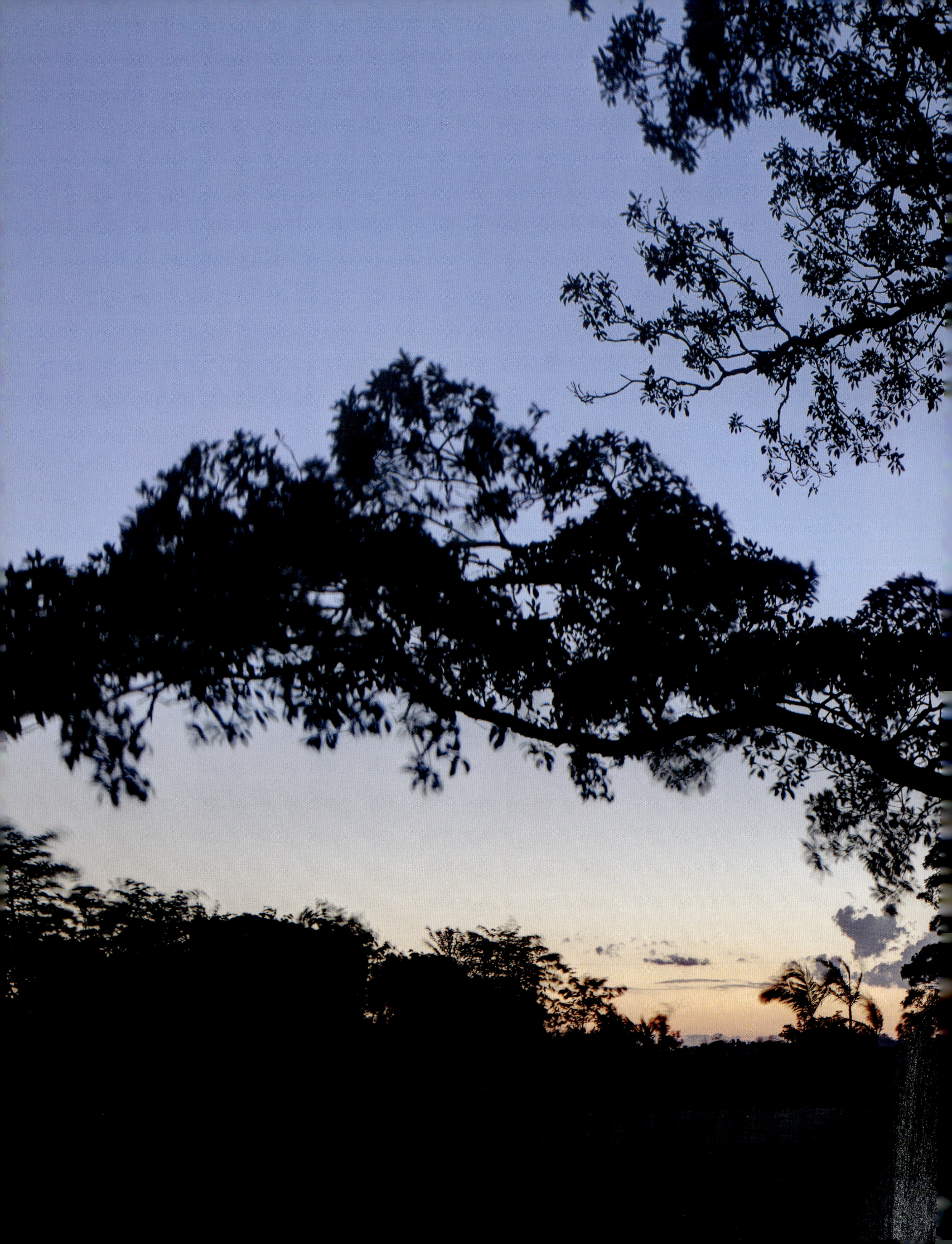

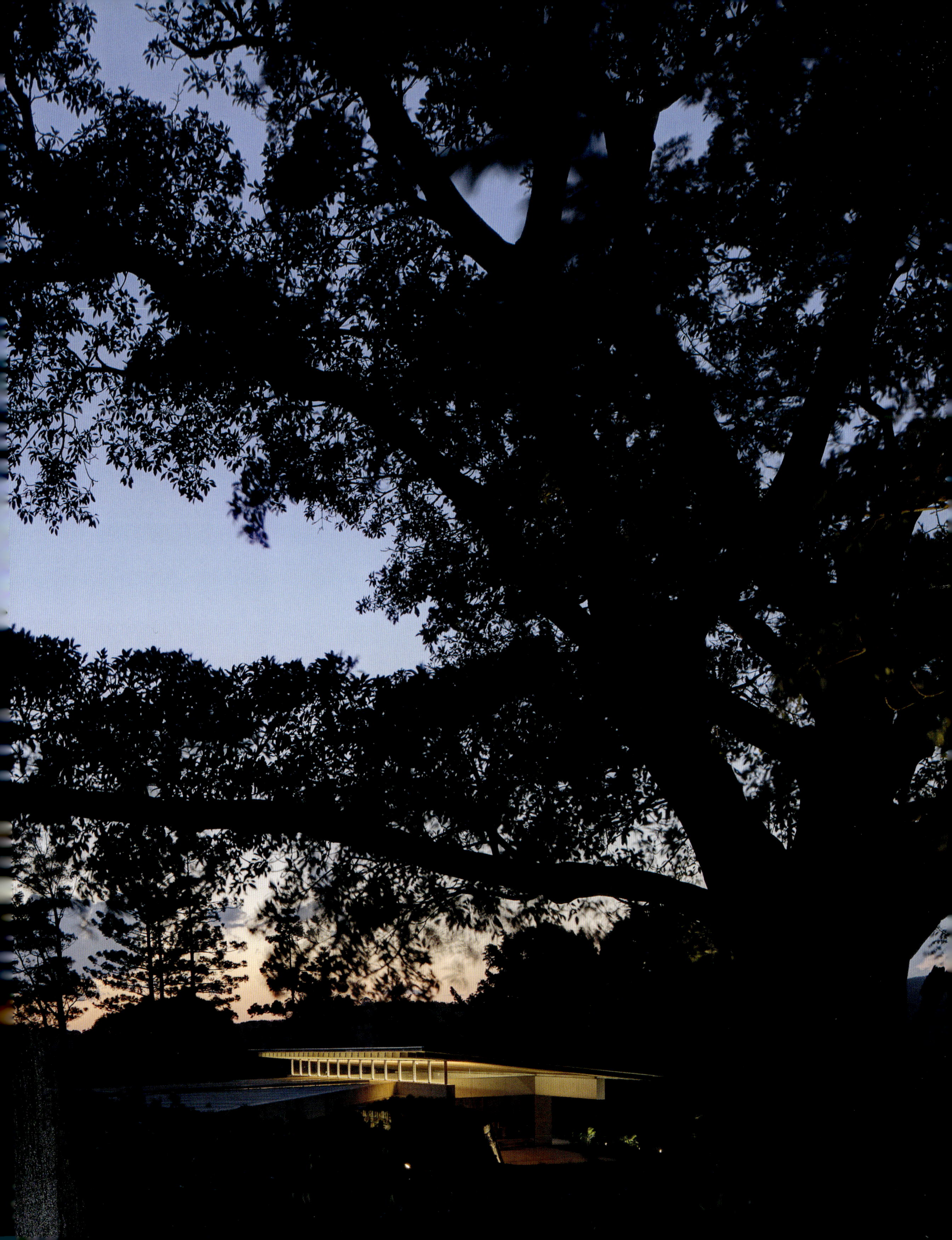

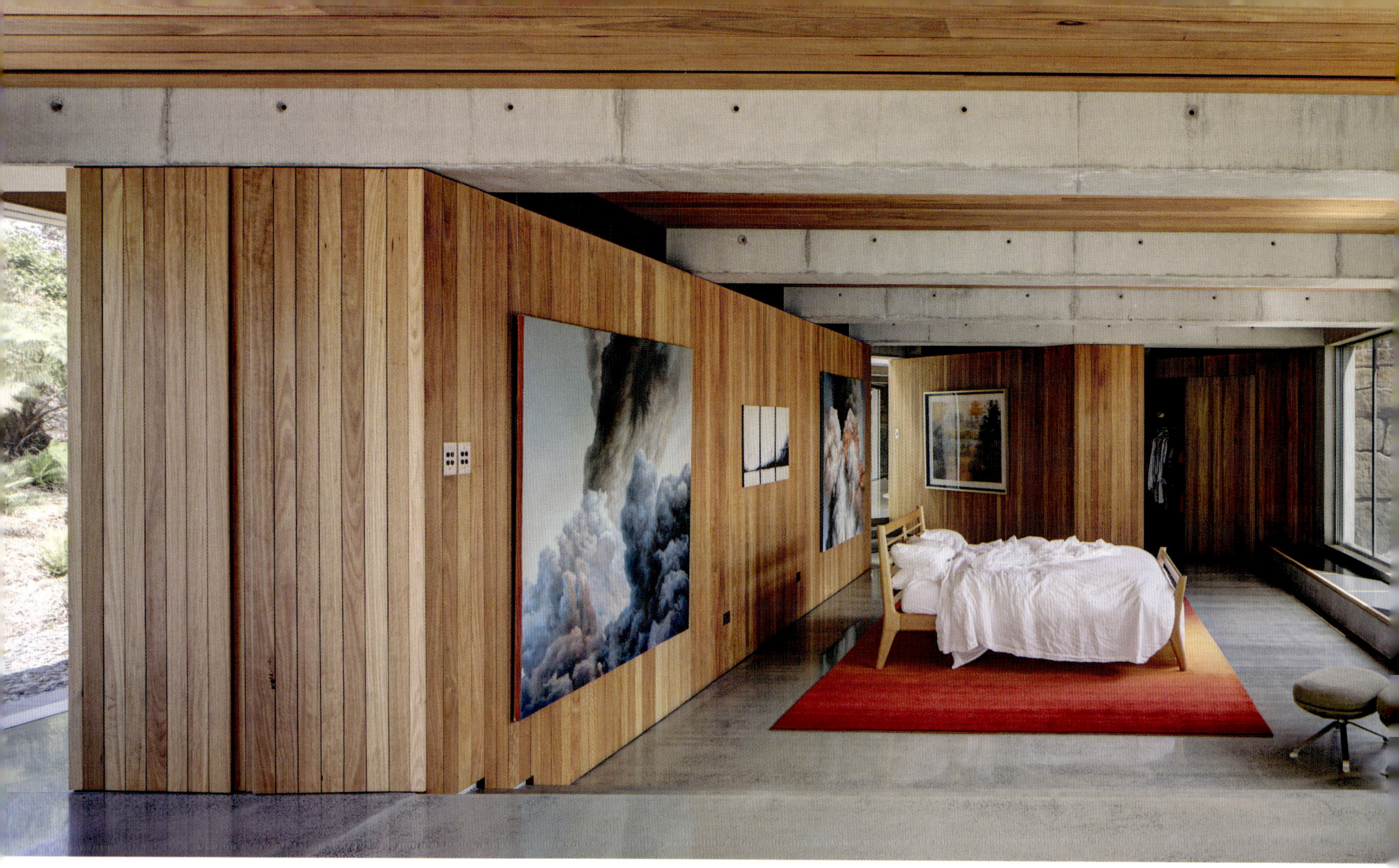

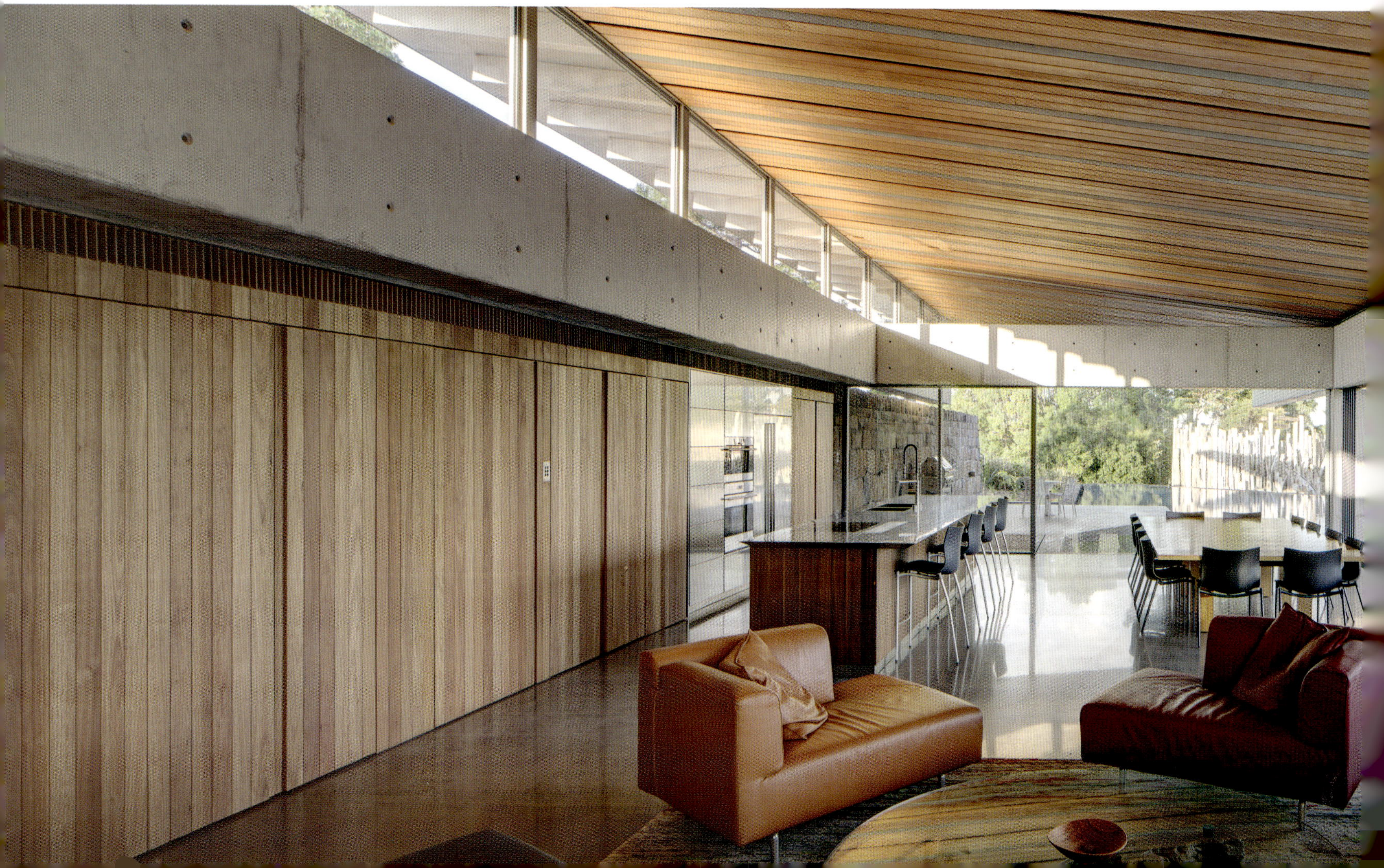

We sought materials that would mature over time...
we settled on concrete and stone: concrete as both a precise,
modern, abstract material but also ancient in its quality...
stone as a direct link back to the underlying geology of the
region. *John Choi, CHROFI*

    The rainforest's unhurried growth influenced our approach
for inserting architecture in the site, with all the buildings being
designed to respond to the notion of a 300-year life cycle.
The buildings were conceived as site-ordering devices; concrete
and stone elements that stitch and structure spatial relationships on the land. *John Choi, CHROFI*

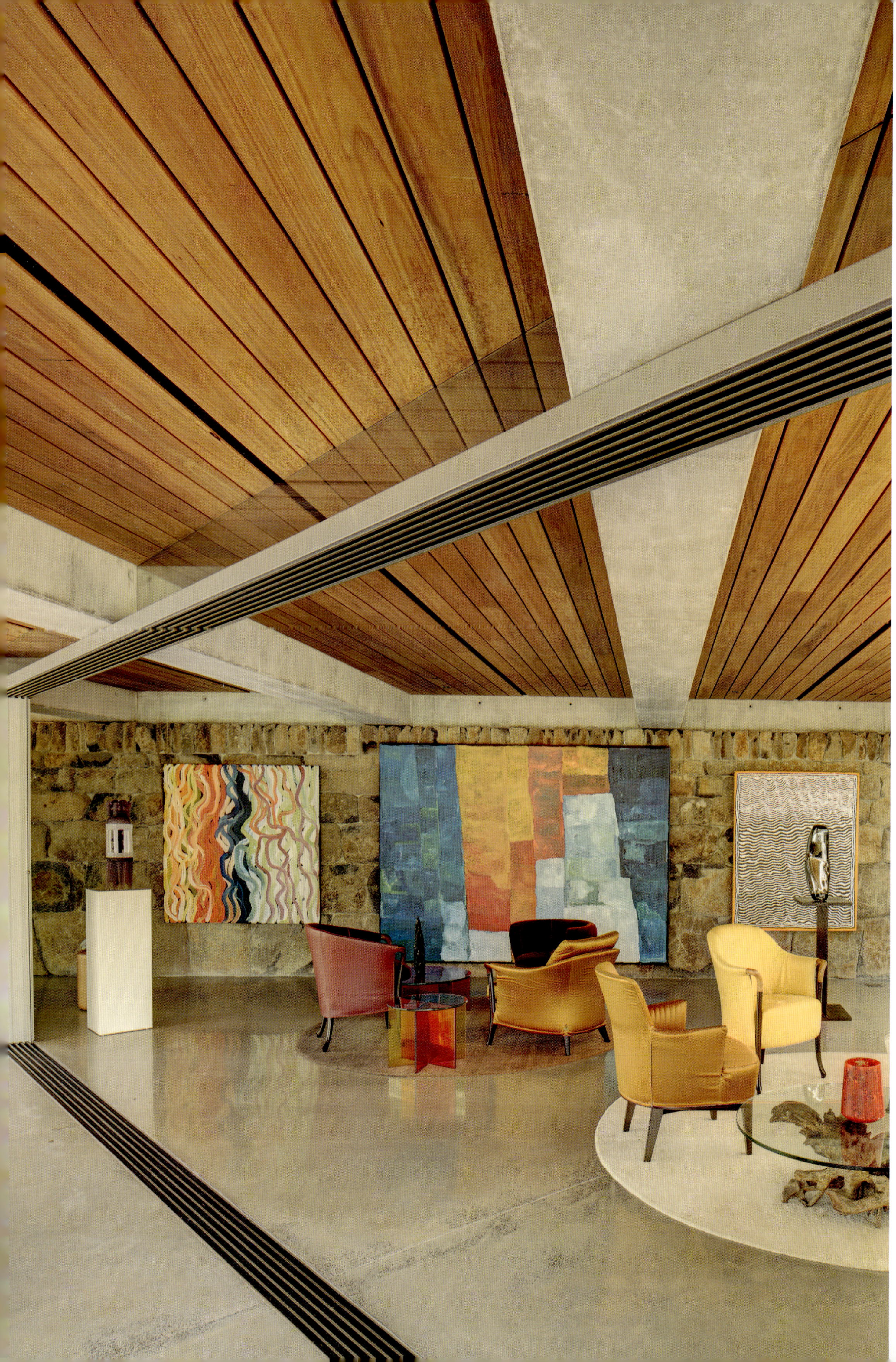

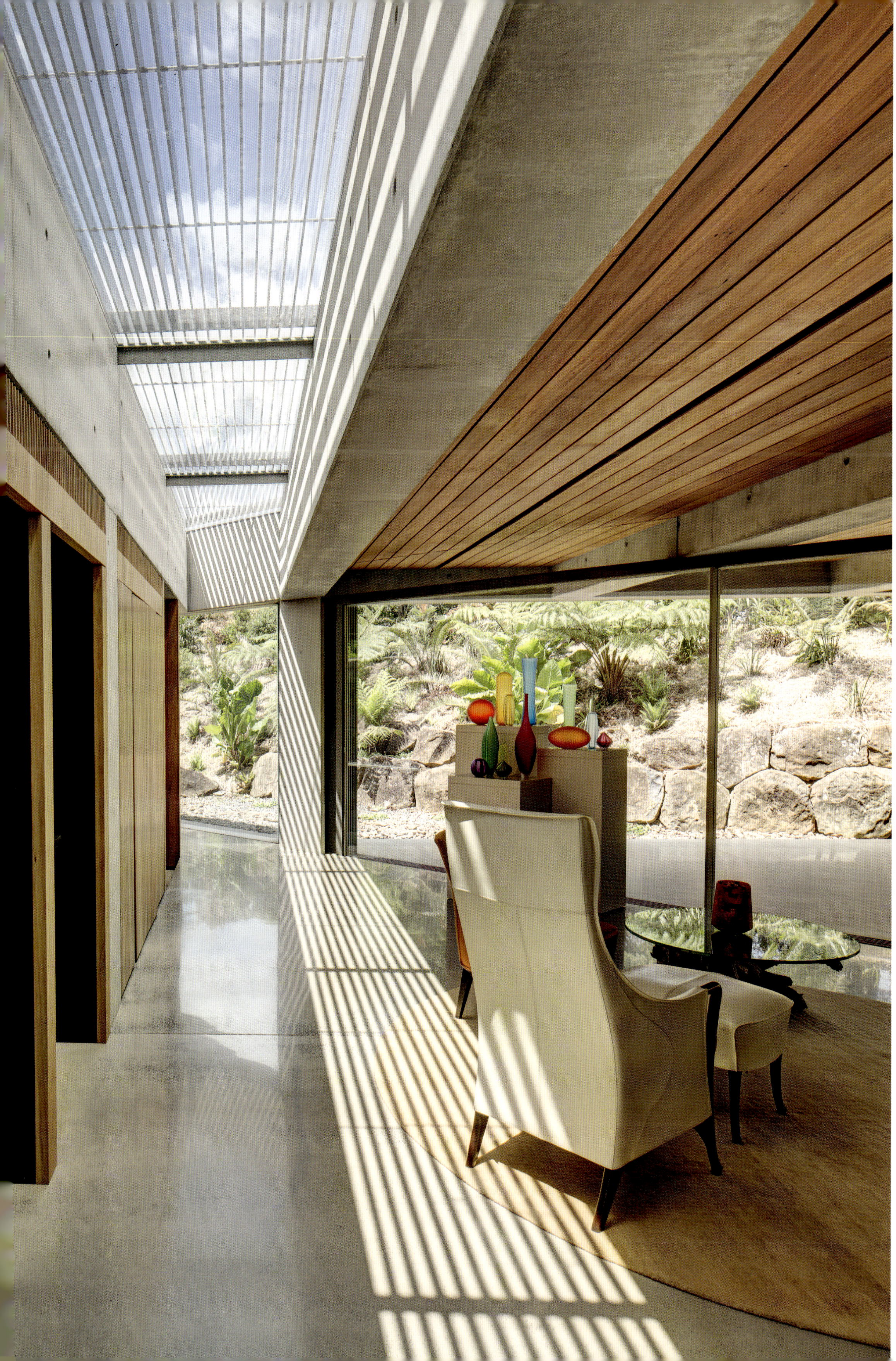

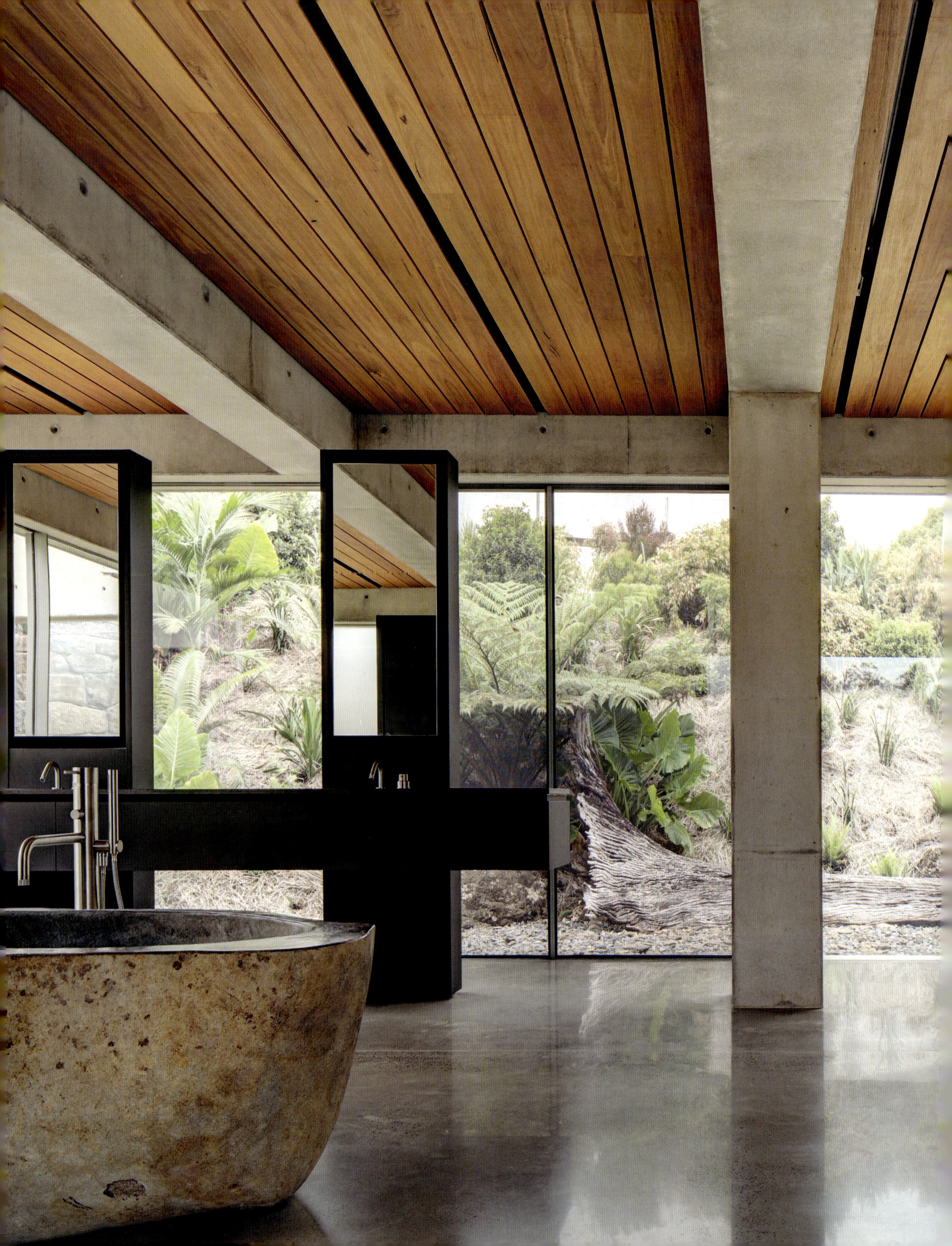

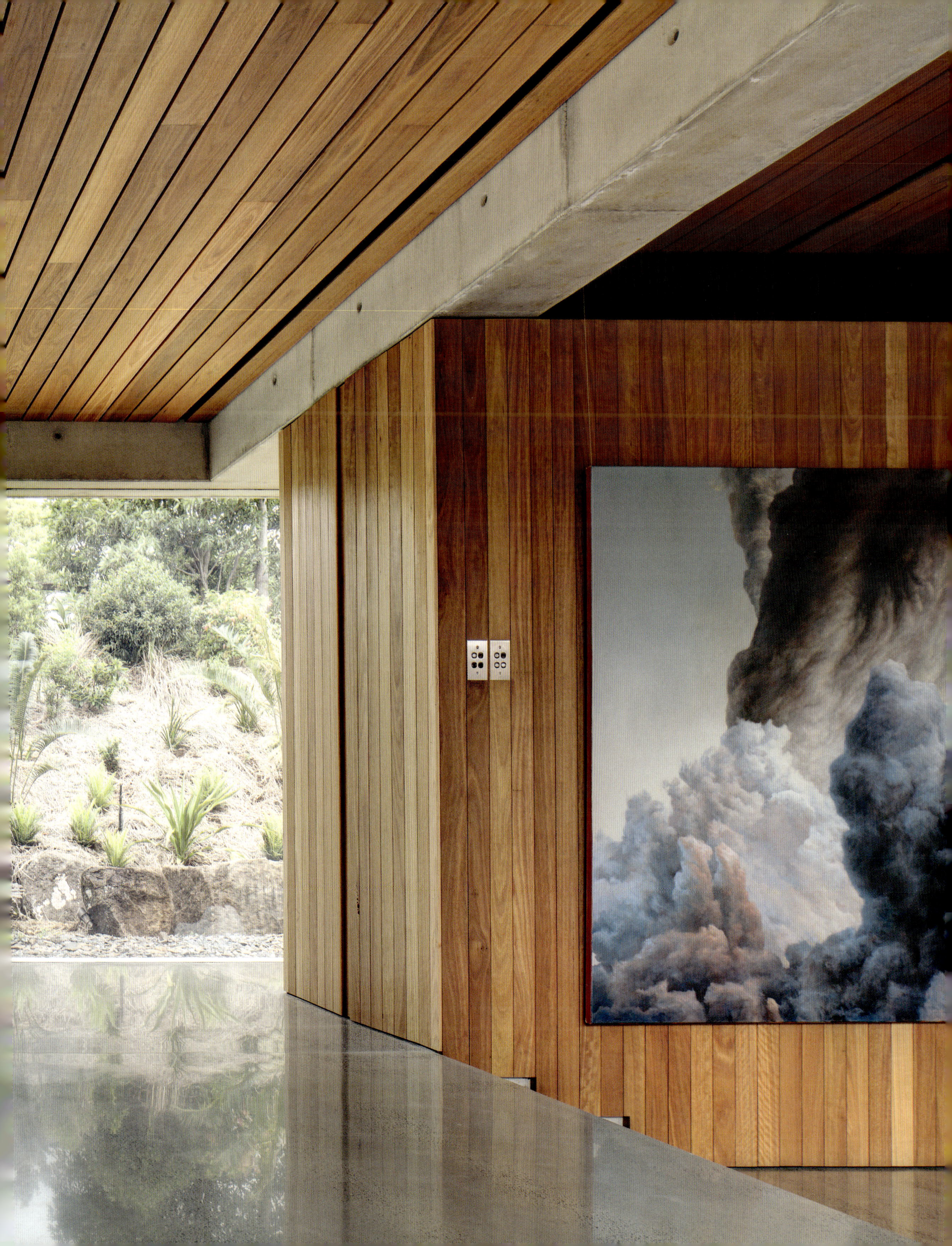

146

Photographs: David Roche, copyright © Judith Neilson

INDIGO SLAM

INDIGO SLAM
SYDNEY, AUSTRALIA, 2016
SMART DESIGN STUDIO

This extraordinary house, for a Sydney gallery owner and art collector, is as fine an example of the use of concrete in architecture as you are likely to see in Australia today. Located in Chippendale, at the edge of the Sydney central business district opposite the newly completed Central Park and in sight of Jean Nouvel's One Central Park apartment towers, the house is a striking combination of complex concrete forms, steel and glass.

While it is likely that the exterior won't be to everyone's liking – its scale and form fly in the face of conventional notions of domesticity – it has already become a landmark house on the Sydney landscape. Extravagant and sculptural, Indigo Slam is an exercise in curve and counter-curve, purposefully designed to manipulate light and views and privacy, the concrete facade alive to the changes wrought by light, shade, sun and cloud.

The exterior language is one of peeling and folding planes of concrete – like paper cut-outs in a pop-up book – to create shade, a balcony and a spectacular light scoop in one. It required a year's work to make and place the plywood formwork to produce the near-flawless curves and planes of in situ concrete that make the facade.

The mastery in this house, designed by Smart Design Studio, however, rests with its interior, in the manipulation of light and scale and materials. Complex shifts of scale, together with a refined control of views balanced with privacy, make each and every space a delight to inhabit. The deft choreography of these elements creates an experience of calm and serenity, with an almost monastic quality that is not apparent from the lively exterior. Step past the remotely operated patterned steel entrance and massive front door of aluminium, brass and glass and you find yourself in a surprisingly modest semicircular vestibule, its low ceiling acting as a prelude to the drama awaiting beyond. From here, at the end of a small entry, the house explodes into a spectacular hall and grand stair that rises for four flights to a height of 14 metres. Frank Lloyd Wright used compression and release in his architecture to dramatic effect in works such as the Robie House in Chicago; at Indigo Slam (named after the title of a Robert Crais crime novel) it is breathtaking. The palette is restrained: unadorned white waxed render over concrete and floors of sand-coloured bricks, also waxed to a light sheen.

The drama comes from the play of natural light cascading from the vaulted ceilings. The sense of calm is palpable and if you didn't know this was Sydney, you could be forgiven for thinking of a grand house in Spain, a sun-drenched palazzo in Sicily or the city of Porto in Portugal, home to some of Álvaro Siza's most important buildings, from whose work the interiors of this house seem to have drawn much inspiration.

A reception hall to one side, with a dining table for sixty-four guests, is designed to cater for large numbers and receptions. This is a semipublic space, supported by a commercial kitchen, store, coolroom and a basement-level, brick-vaulted cellar. A landing halfway along the stairs leads to a suite of private bedrooms and bathrooms reached by a glass bridge to one side, and to a terrace and guest apartment, also struck in folds of in situ concrete, on the other, looking into a small landscaped courtyard below. At the top of the stair you step into a sequence of living, dining and kitchen spaces, lit in large part by natural light flowing over vaulted ceilings from the concealed light scoop. What's remarkable is that in spite of the grand scale, the private zones of the house are modest and rational in plan.

The brief was for Indigo Slam to last 100 years. Finishes are pared back: floors are brick-paved; walls are of set render; and fittings are simple. Materials were selected to wear and endure, with operable elements operated mechanically rather than manually. These include oversized vertical timber blinds that turn and retract by means of hanging chains and awning windows operated by geared winders. Exposed brass armatures for these moving parts lend a finely grained detail to the interior.

The project aspires to an exemplary level of environmentally sustainable design, with natural lighting, cross-ventilation, rainwater harvesting and adherence to passive solar design principles reducing the energy and water load of the building. Geothermal heating and cooling have also been incorporated into the design and solar hot water and photovoltaic cells populate the roof. Indigo Slam adds to the reinvention of Chippendale as one of Sydney's artistic and cultural hubs.

0 4m

North elevation

South elevation

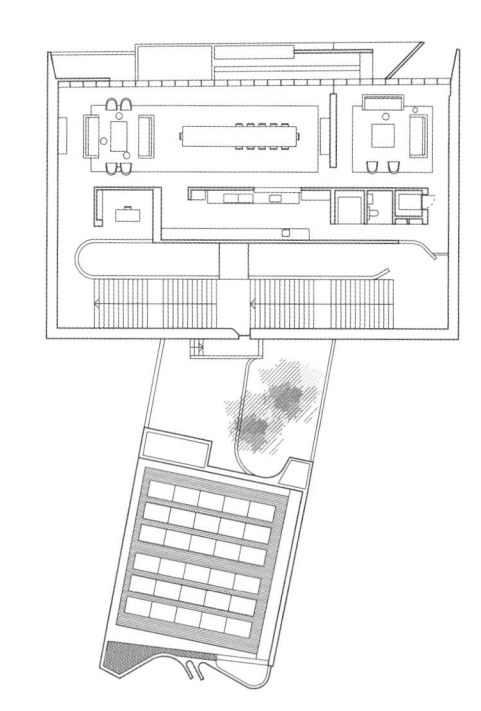

Section

Second floor

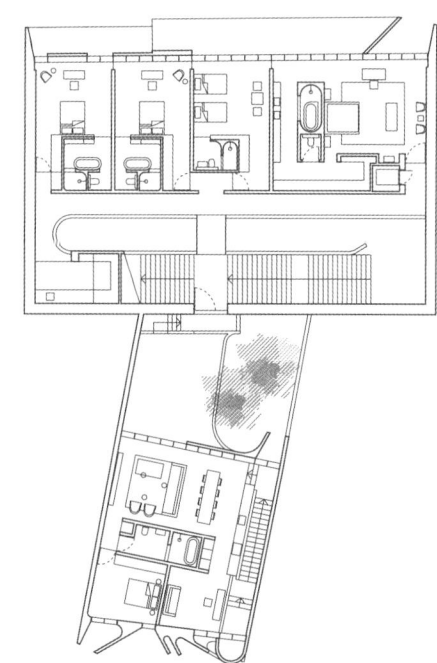

First floor

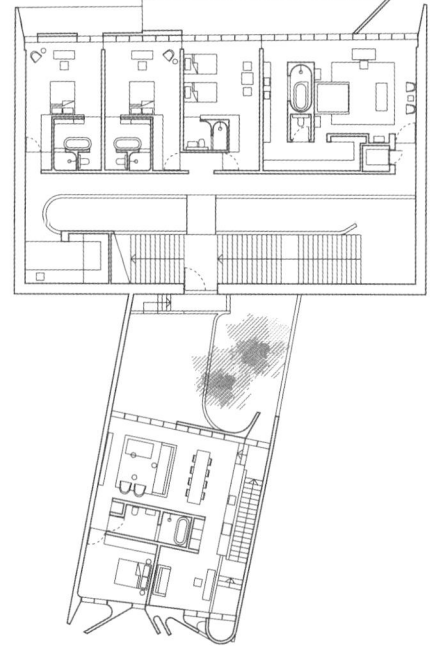

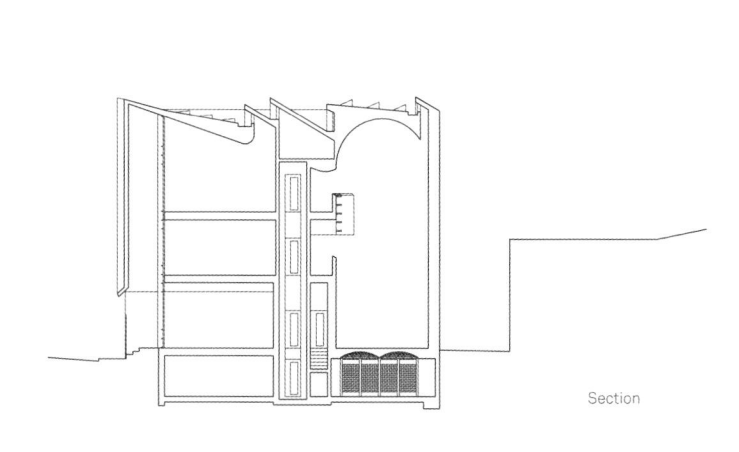

Ground floor

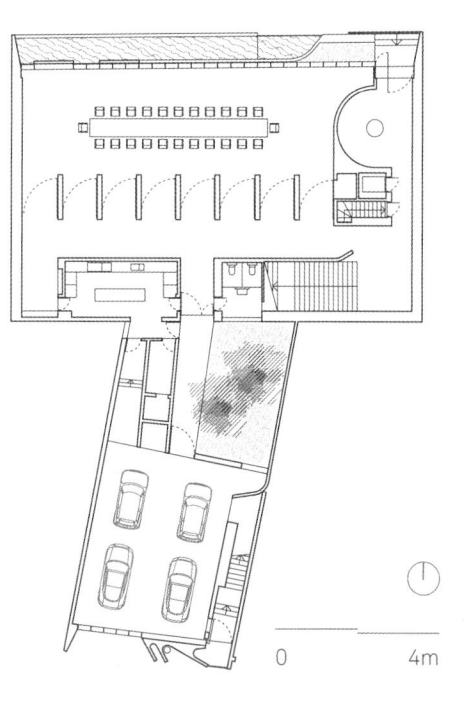

0 4m

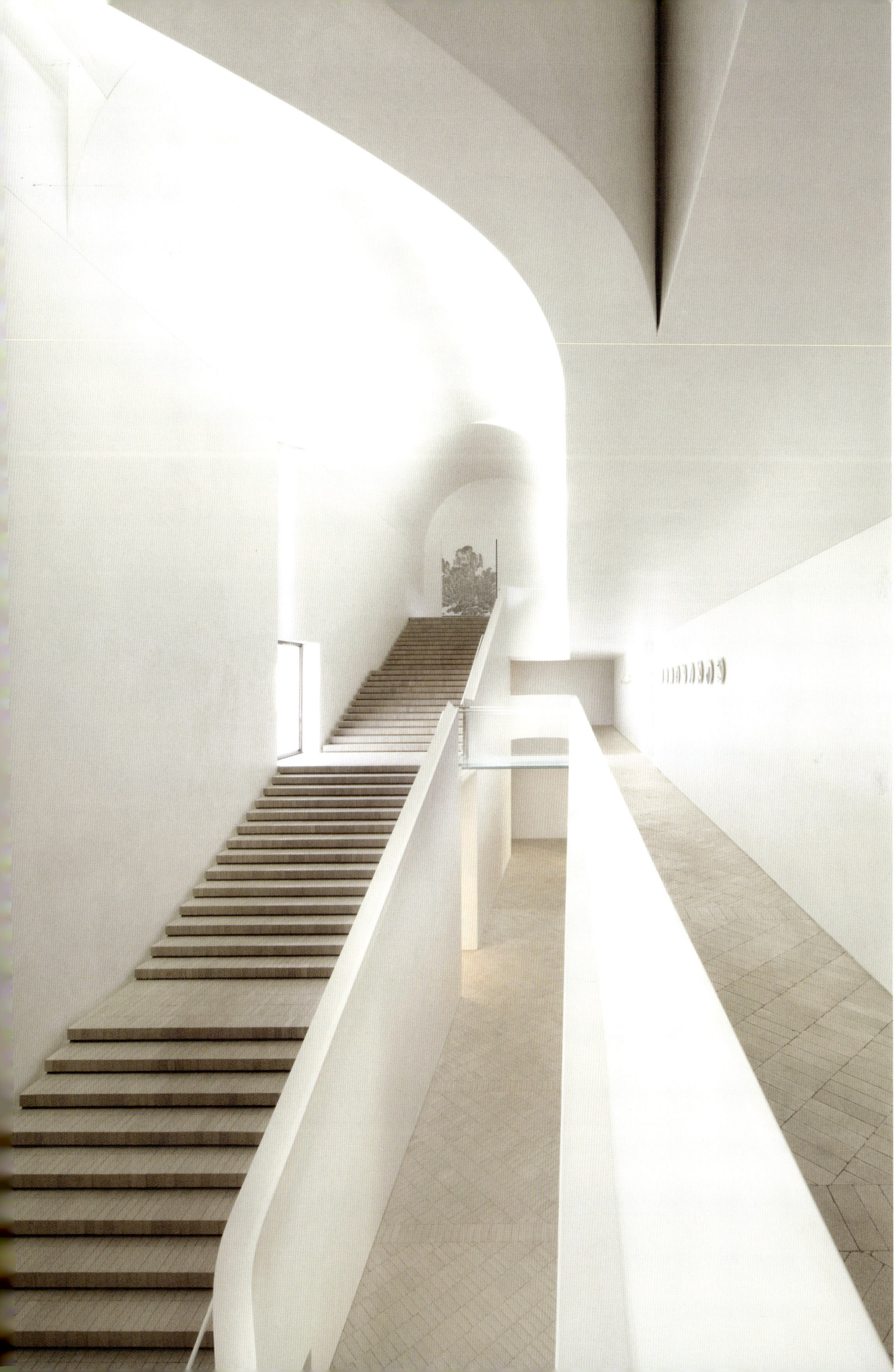

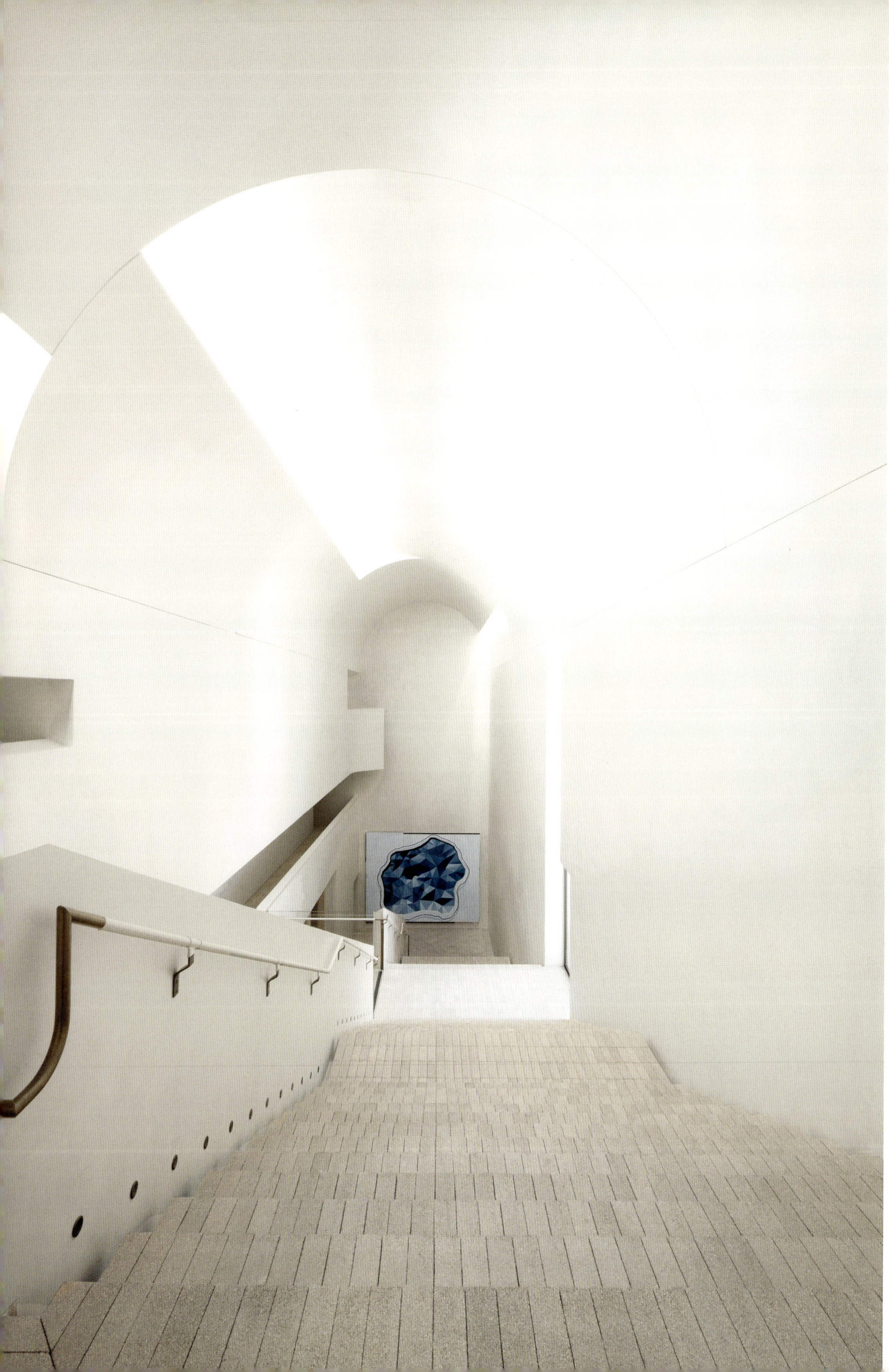

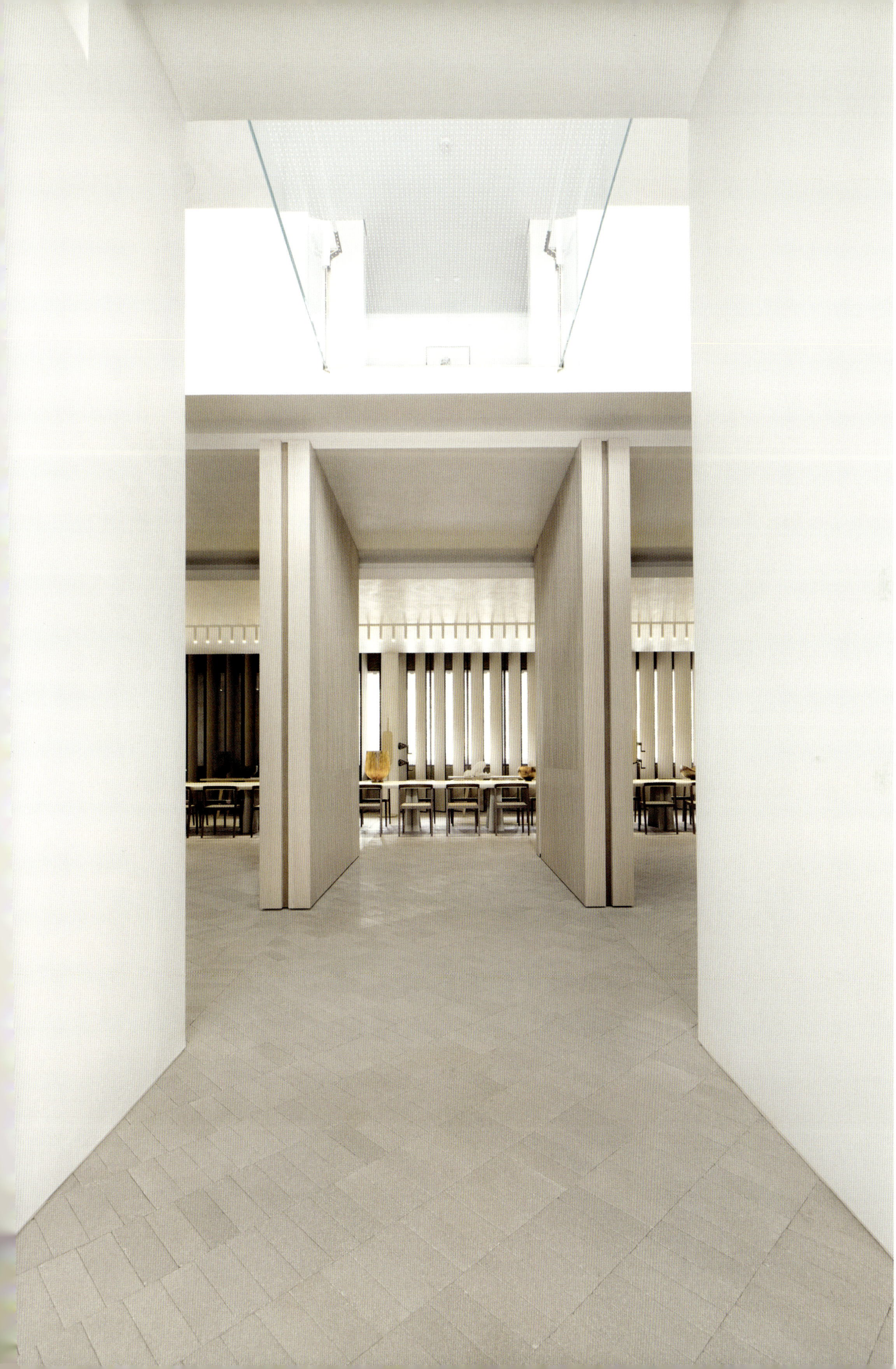

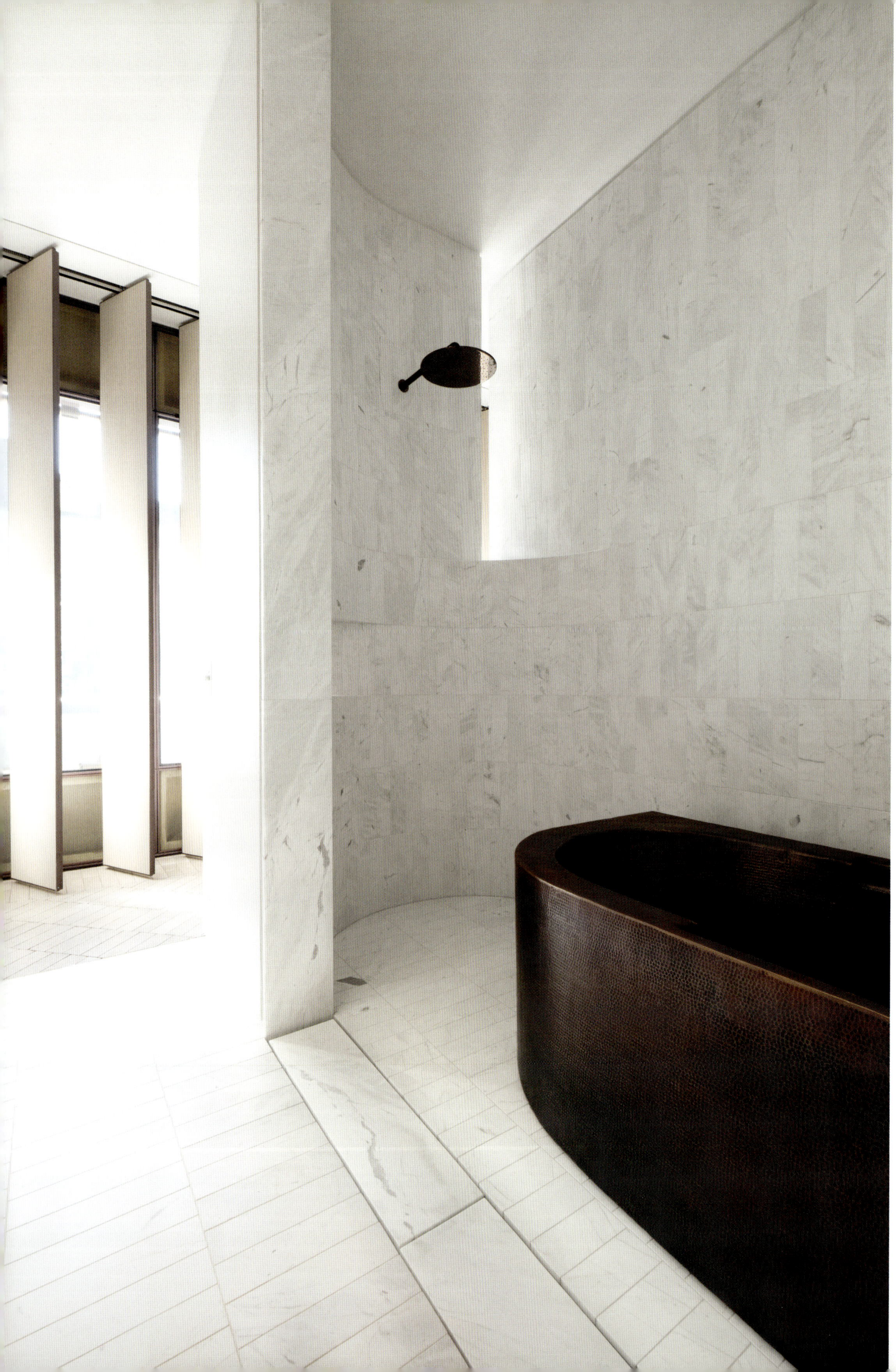

154 — 155

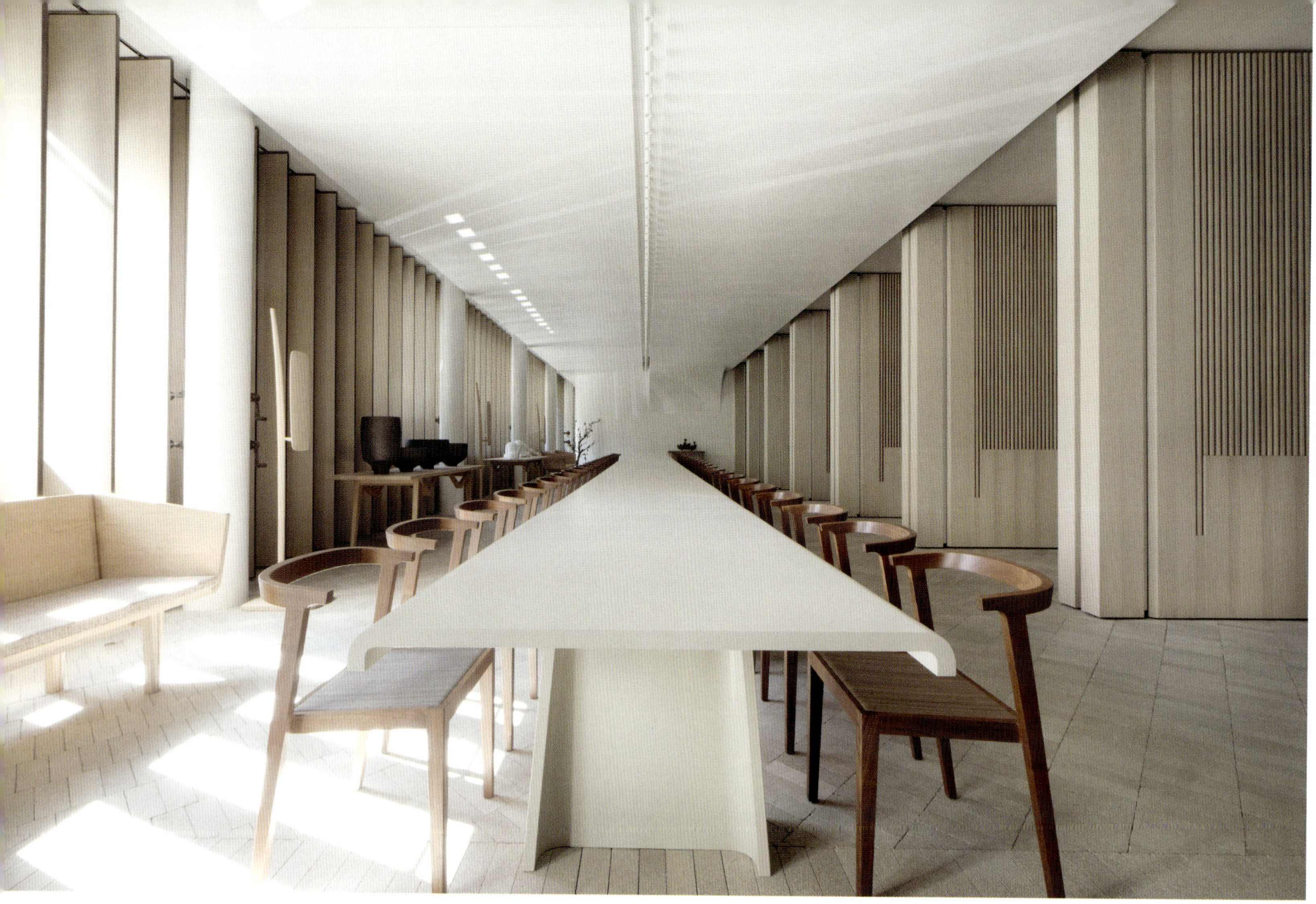

Extravagant and sculptural, Indigo Slam is an exercise in curve and counter-curve, purposefully designed to manipulate light and views and privacy, the concrete facade alive to the changes wrought by light, shade, sun and cloud. The exterior language is one of peeling and folding planes of concrete – like paper cut-outs in a pop-up book – to create shade, a balcony and a spectacular light scoop in one.

Finishes are pared back: floors are brick-paved; walls are of set render; and fittings are simple. Materials were selected to wear and endure, with operable elements operated mechanically rather than manually. These include oversized vertical timber blinds that turn and retract by means of hanging chains and awning windows operated by geared winders. Exposed brass armatures for these moving parts lend a finely grained detail to the interior.

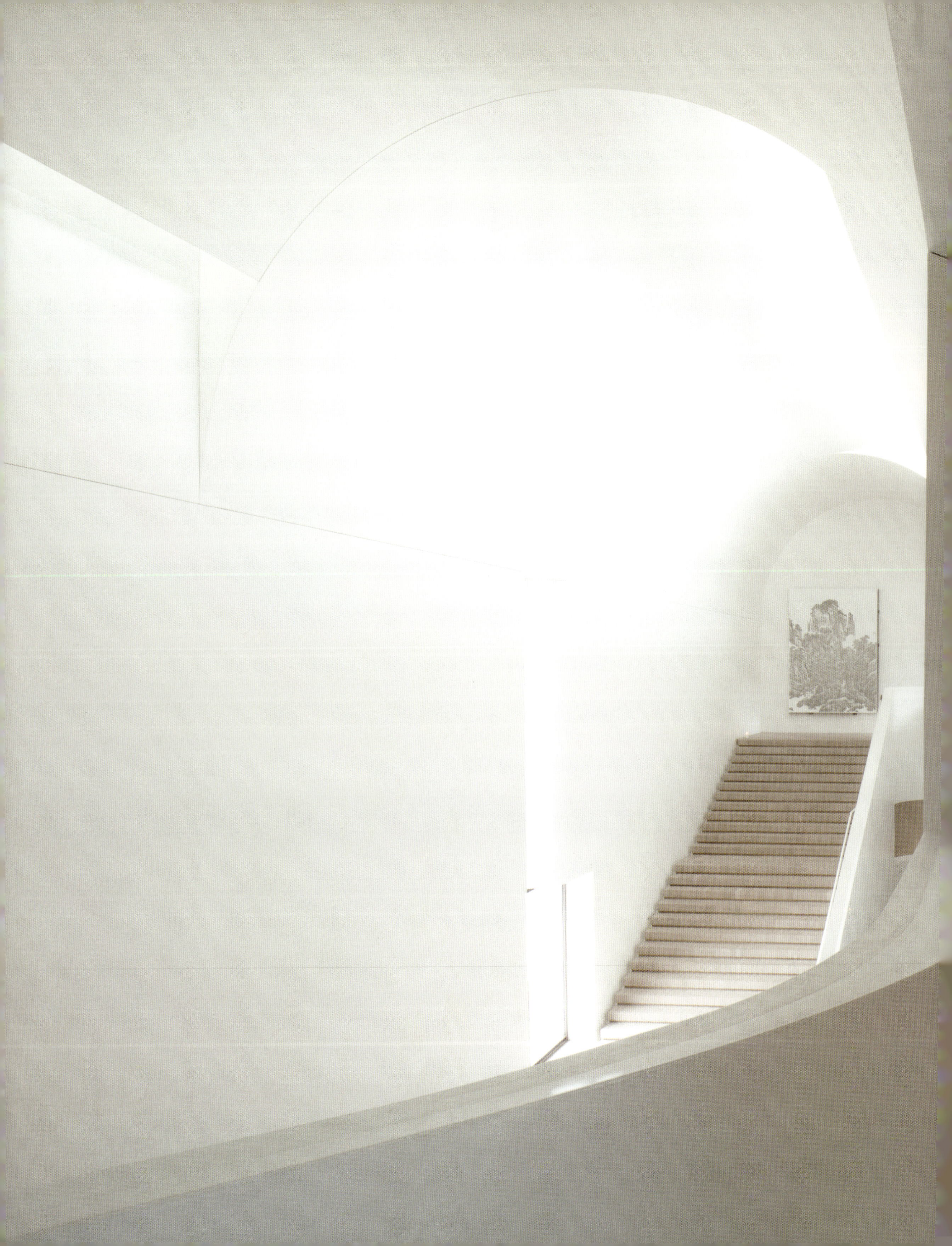

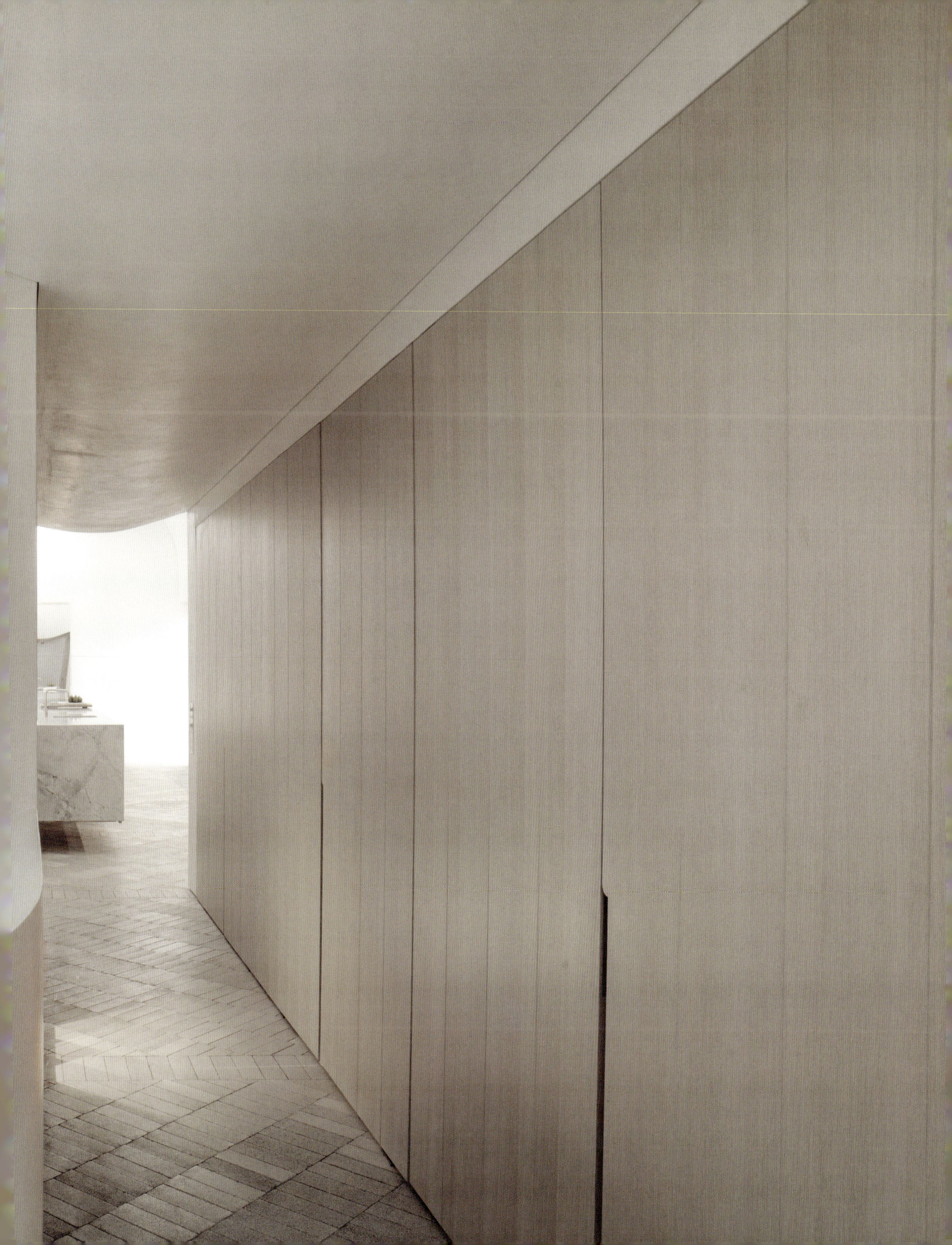

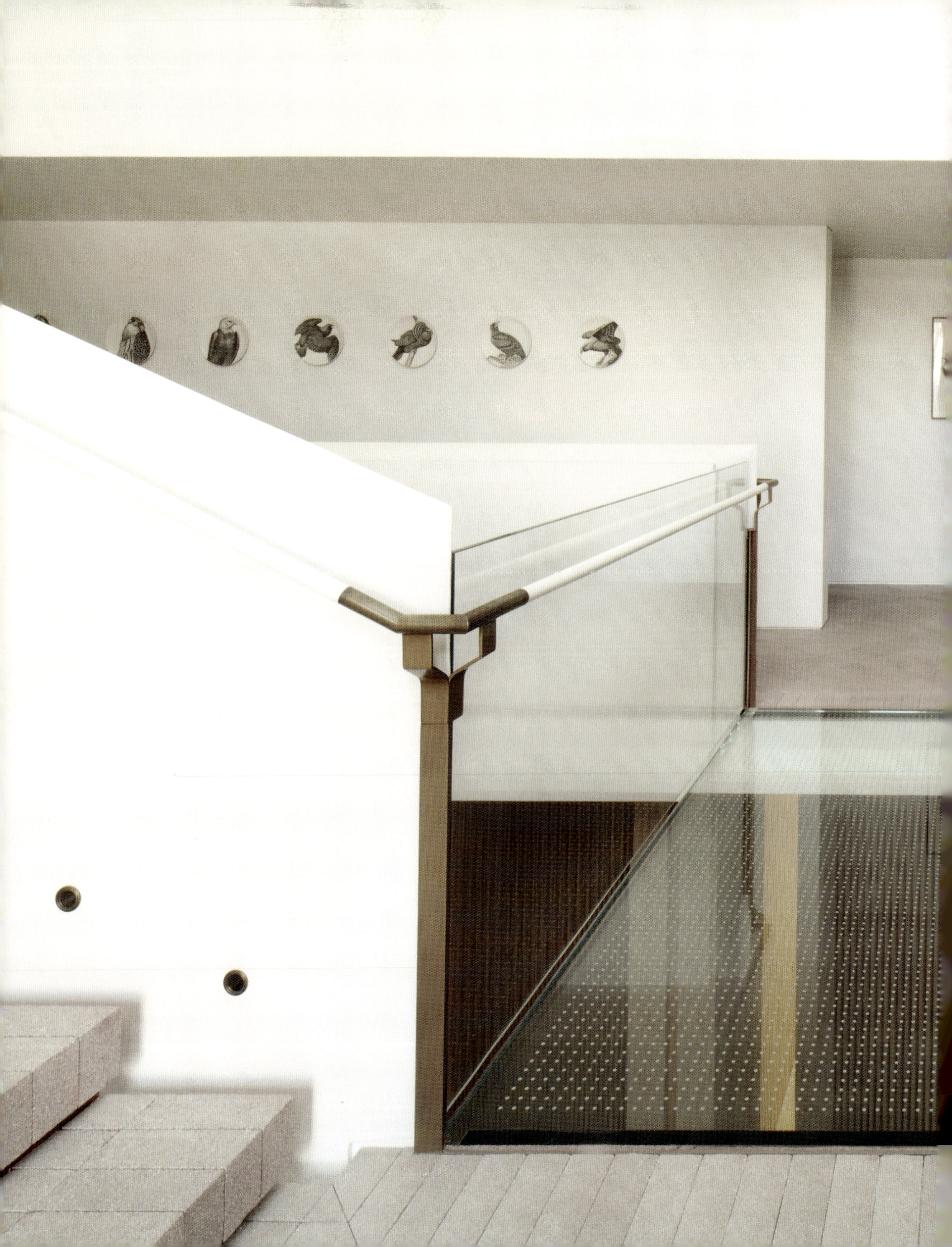

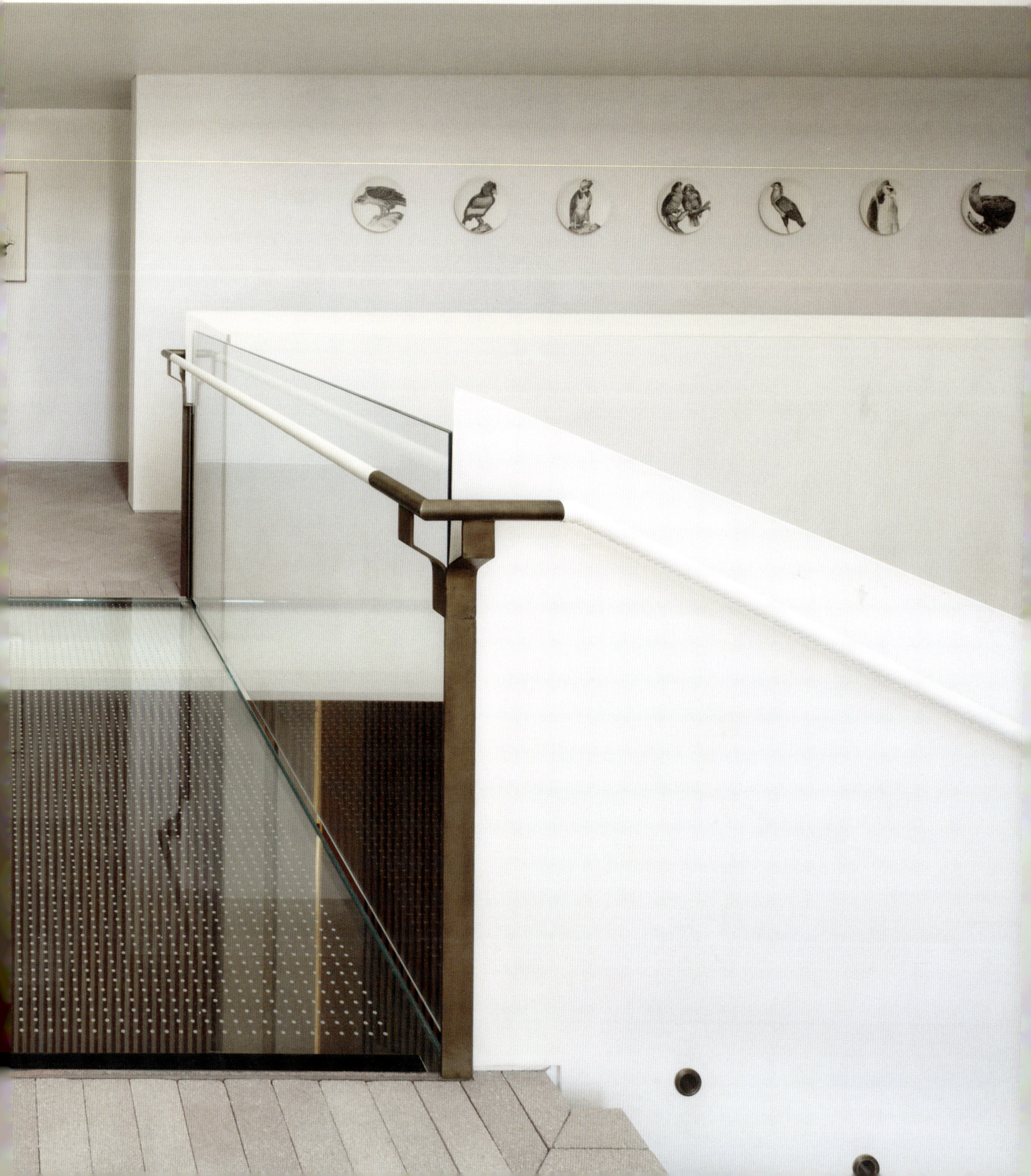

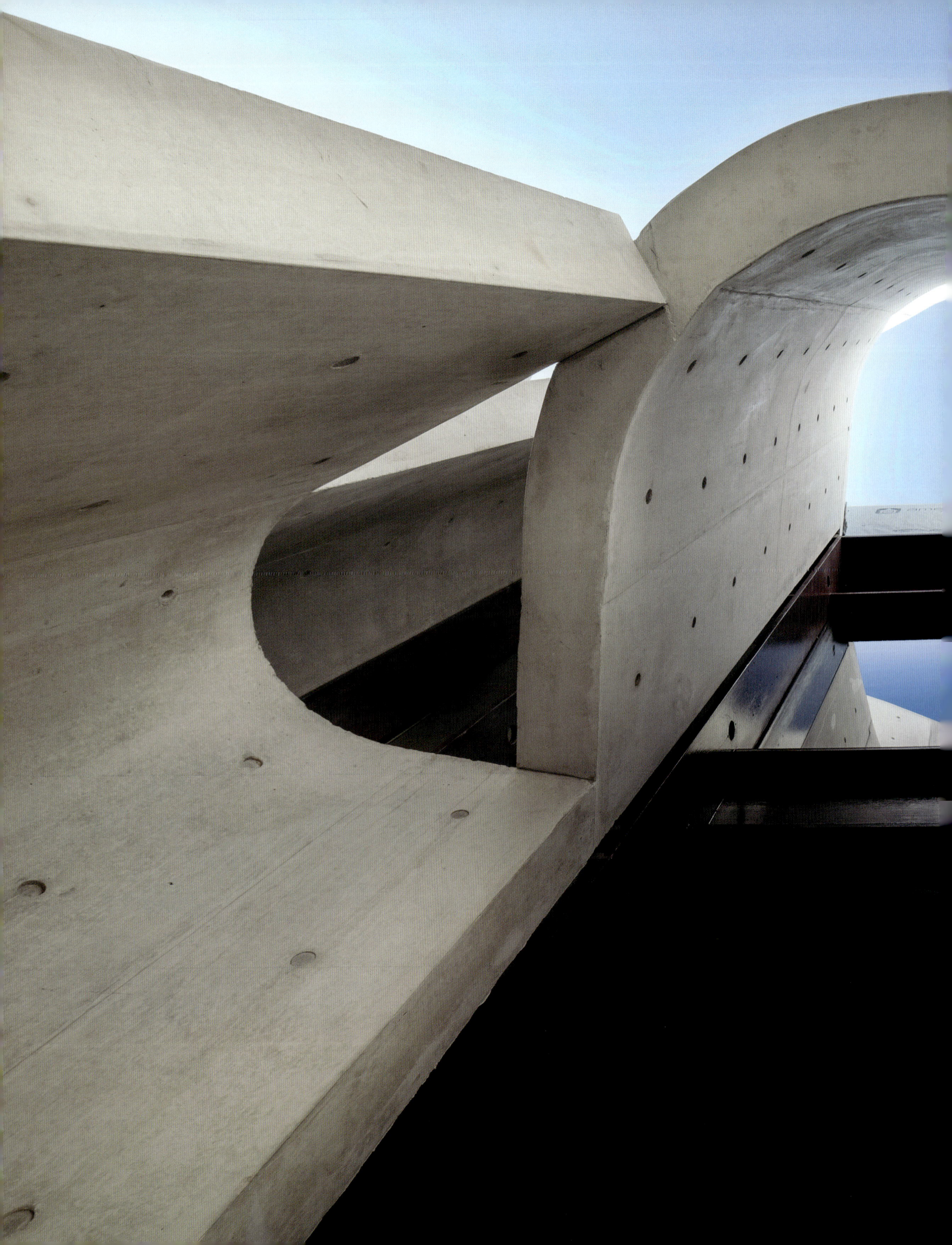

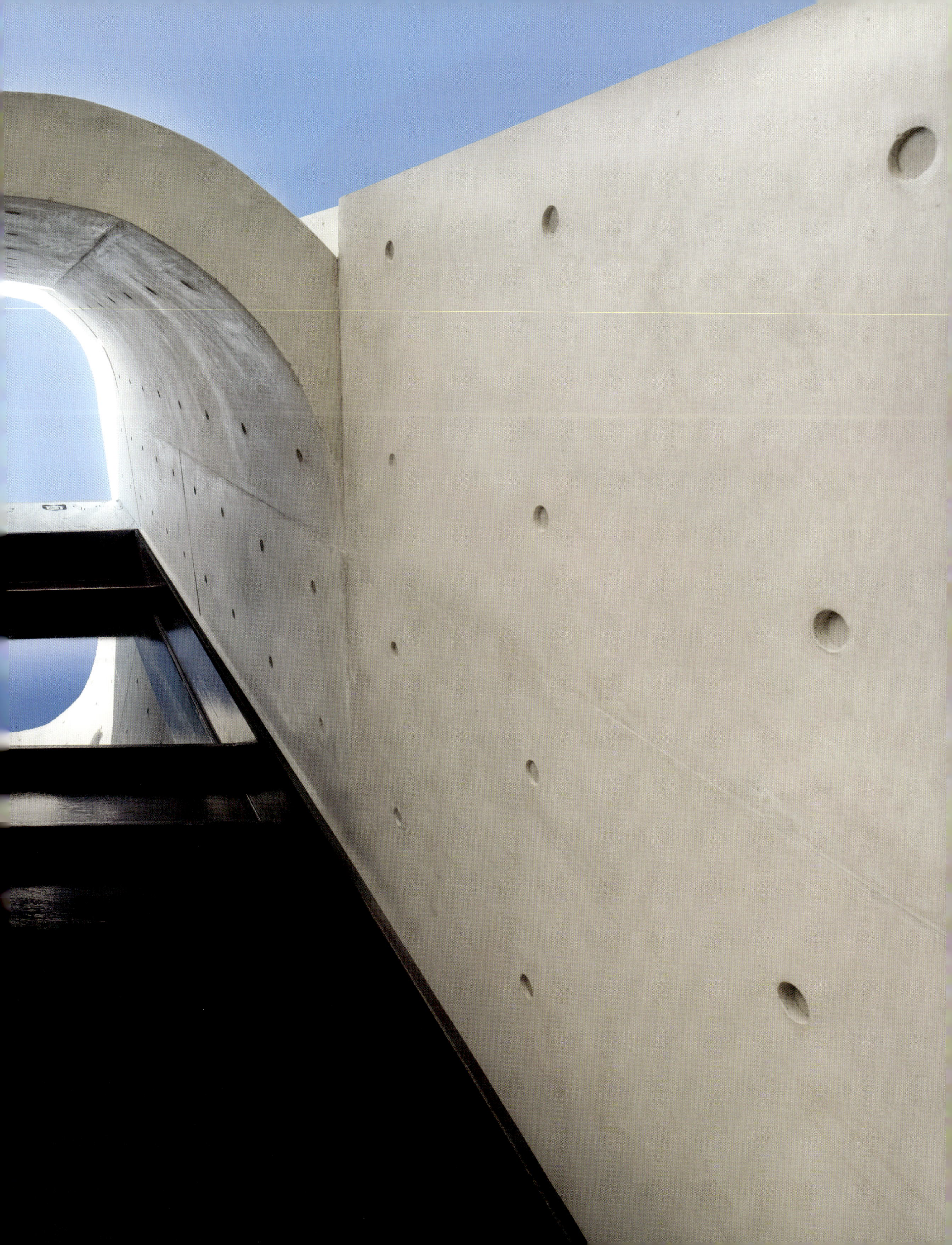

164

Photographs: Michael Nicholson

INVISIBLE HOUSE

INVISIBLE HOUSE
BLUE MOUNTAINS, AUSTRALIA, 2012
PETER STUTCHBURY ARCHITECTURE

The site is spectacular: a narrow scar carved into the side of an escarpment on an old sheep farm at the edge of the Blue Mountains, looking out over the majestic Kanimbla Valley, near the Jenolan Caves west of Sydney, 1200 metres above sea level with views that go on forever. From here, standing at the edge, you can almost look pairs of wedge-tailed eagles in the eye as they soar over the valley floor deep below. Winds, when they blow, are ferocious; summer heat can be harsh; and temperatures in winter are often sub-zero, with windchill factors of up to 14 degrees below, and it snows sometimes, too.

It is here, in these extreme conditions, that architect Peter Stutchbury has located this house for a film director. Made mostly of raw, poured in situ concrete, the house hunkers down just below the brow of the escarpment, all but invisible on approach across a stony terrain save for what looks like a line of rusting steel boxes popping out of the ground along the ridge line. The boxes, with slots cut into them like Ned Kelly's mask, contain bedrooms at one end and serve as lanterns to draw light into the northern end of the house at the other. Approached obliquely from above, along a descending, stepped entry sequence, the house is best read as a long, sheltering plane of concrete, on top of and under which is an arrangement of living, dining and kitchen zones, bedrooms, an artist's studio, a plant room, services and more.

But this is no ordinary concrete roof, for it runs 50 metres, the entire length of the house, in a series of undulations, with a dramatic cantilever of some 3.6 metres, hovering over what seems at first a retaining wall of concrete, the space between the top of the wall and underside of the roof in-filled by a band of strip glass filtering light into the house. There are echoes in the floating slab of Hugh Buhrich's own house at Castlecrag, Sydney (1972), with its waving, sinusoidal roof of copper floating lightly over a band of glass above a concrete beam. Only here, in the Blue Mountains, Stutchbury flattens out the roof along one edge, where the big views are to be had, to make a tapering cantilever to shelter the house from the harsh western sun.

The concrete wall gathers and ties together all the elements of this relentlessly rigorous work of architecture. Step inside and the wall transforms on one side into a long, wide gallery for the display of art, while an opposing wall, made from mauve-pink sandstone quarried locally, dry-stacked precisely and of sharp angles and shafts, offers tantalising glimpses into other parts of the house.

A concrete post and beam system is employed as both an organising device and to frame walls of glass that open the house almost entirely to summer breezes and views over the blue-green valley just beyond the boundaries of the building. To the north, the concrete wall extends past the house to enclose, with the help of an embankment, a sheltered north-facing courtyard accessed directly through sliding walls of glass. A central courtyard, with a deep fire pit for large logs of firewood, is enclosed by the projecting walls of the living zone at one end and a sleeping zone at the other, partially protected by the cantilevering concrete plates of the roof overhead. Interiors are robust and minimal, as you'd expect of a dwelling designed by Stutchbury. The living zone of the house is remarkable for tall undulating ceilings of wood battens reminiscent of the houses of Finnish architect Alvar Aalto. The roof of the house has been conceived as a 'tank' for water when there is rain, and to act variously as a firefighting source, a thermal device and an aid for the 'invisibility' of the house by casting reflections of sky and bush as you approach the building over the brow of the hill. Upstairs, within the rusted Ned Kelly boxes, entire walls slide away to open bedrooms and bathrooms to the elements.

A geothermal system comprising a 60-metre pipe embedded 3 metres underground, where temperatures are constant all year round, has been installed, with warm air pumped into the house, ensuring that internal temperatures never drop below 10 degrees. It works in conjunction with an under-floor hydronic heating system.

East elevation

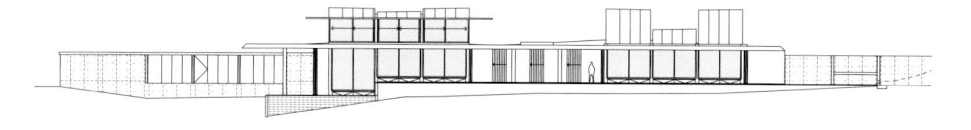

West elevation

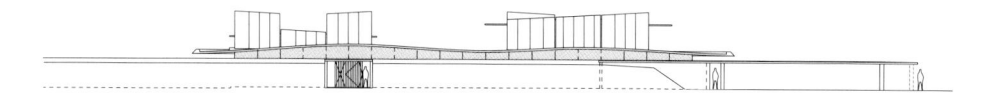

South elevation

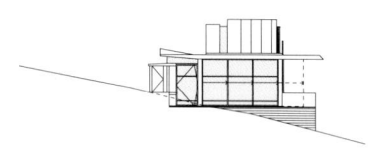

North elevation

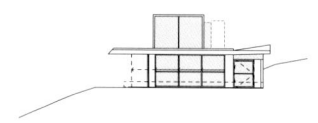

0   50m

Floor plan

01 Void
02 Bedroom
03 Ensuite
04 Barbecue
05 Terrace
06 Living
07 Dining
08 Kitchen
09 Pantry
10 Bathroom
11 Study
12 Gallery
13 Art studio
14 Entry
15 Laundry
16 Garage

First floor plan

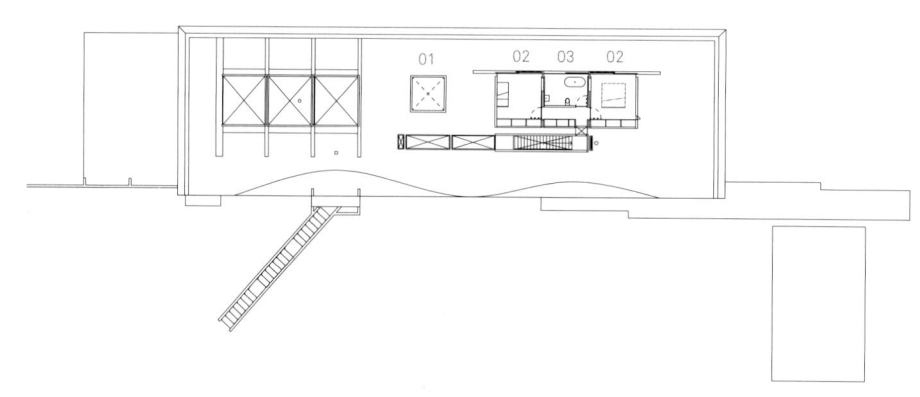

Ground floor plan

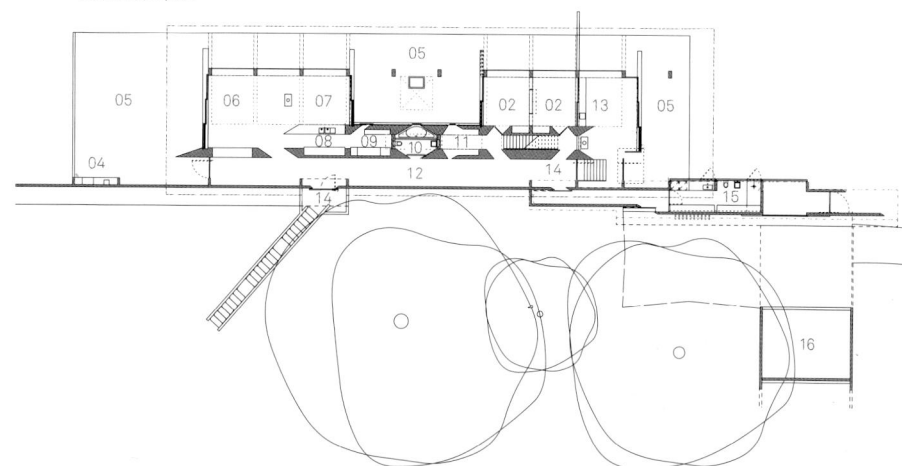

0   10m

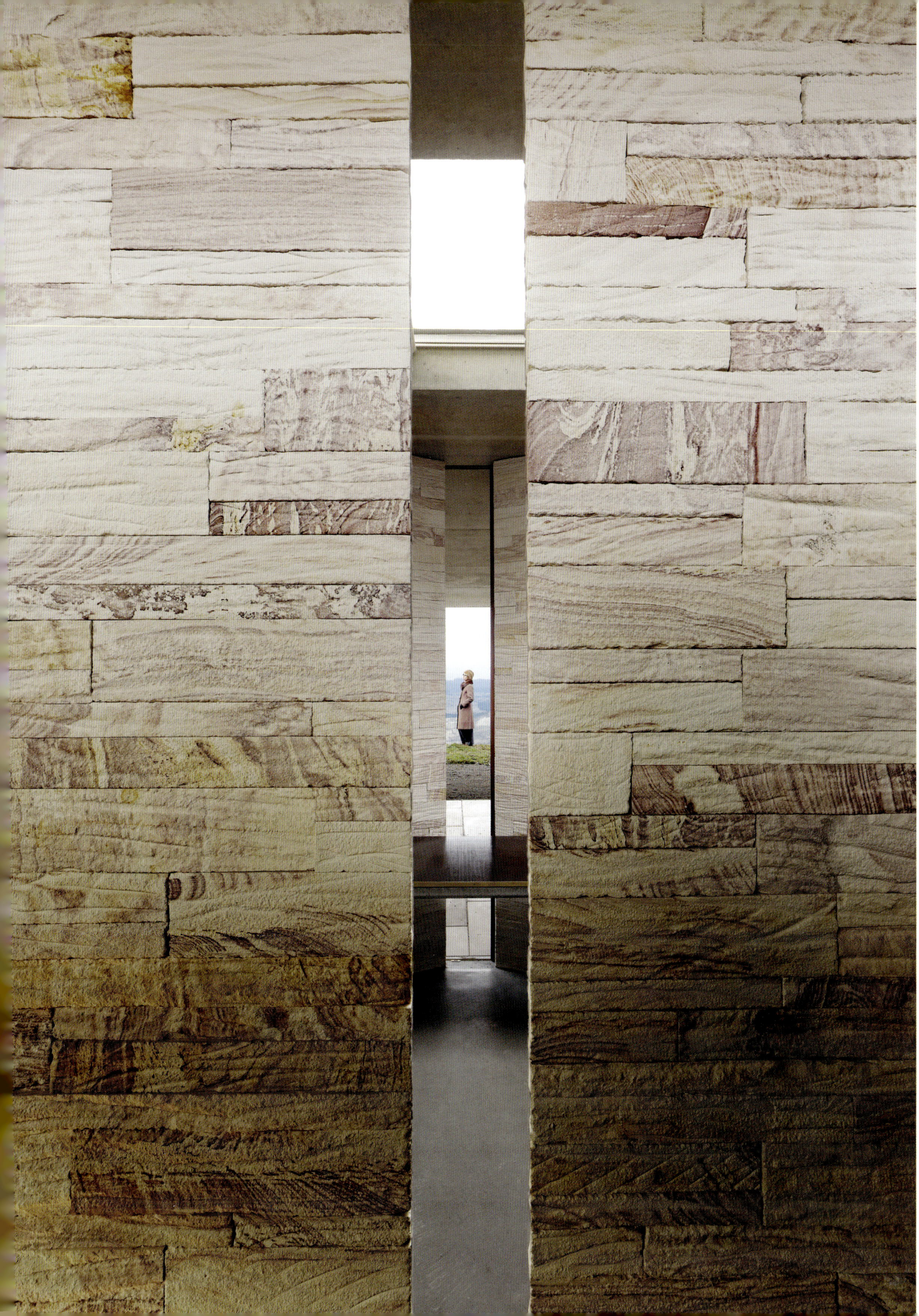

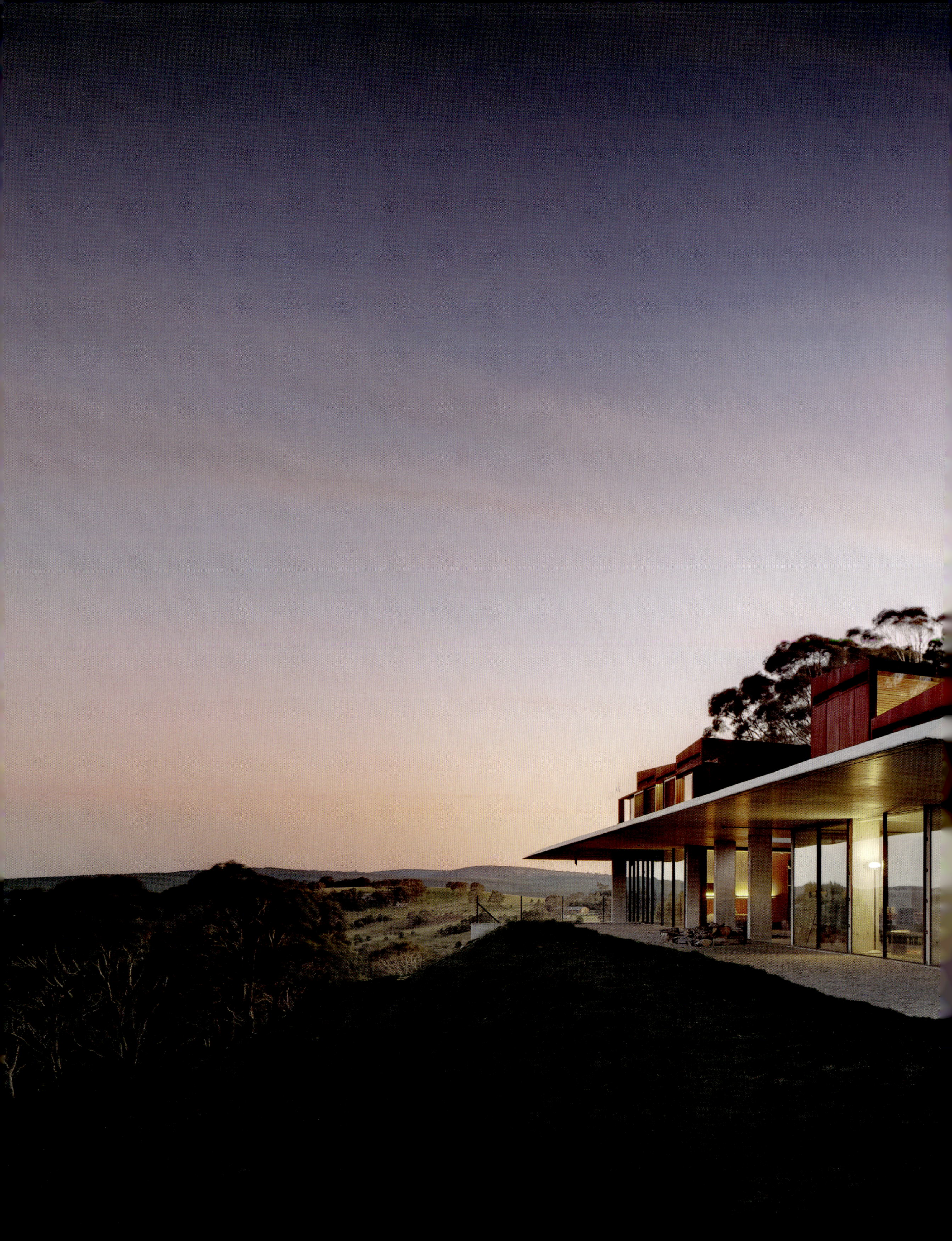

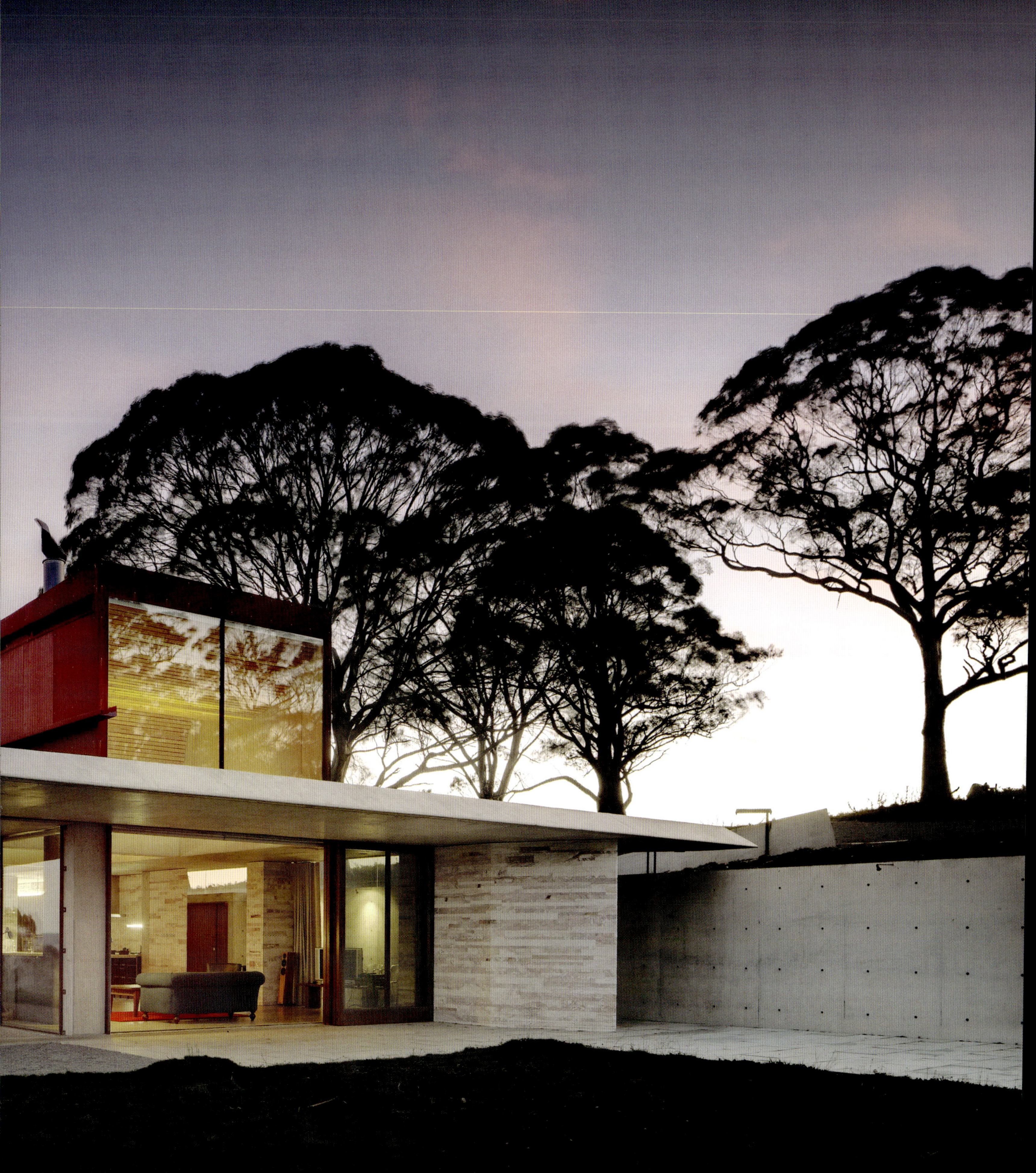

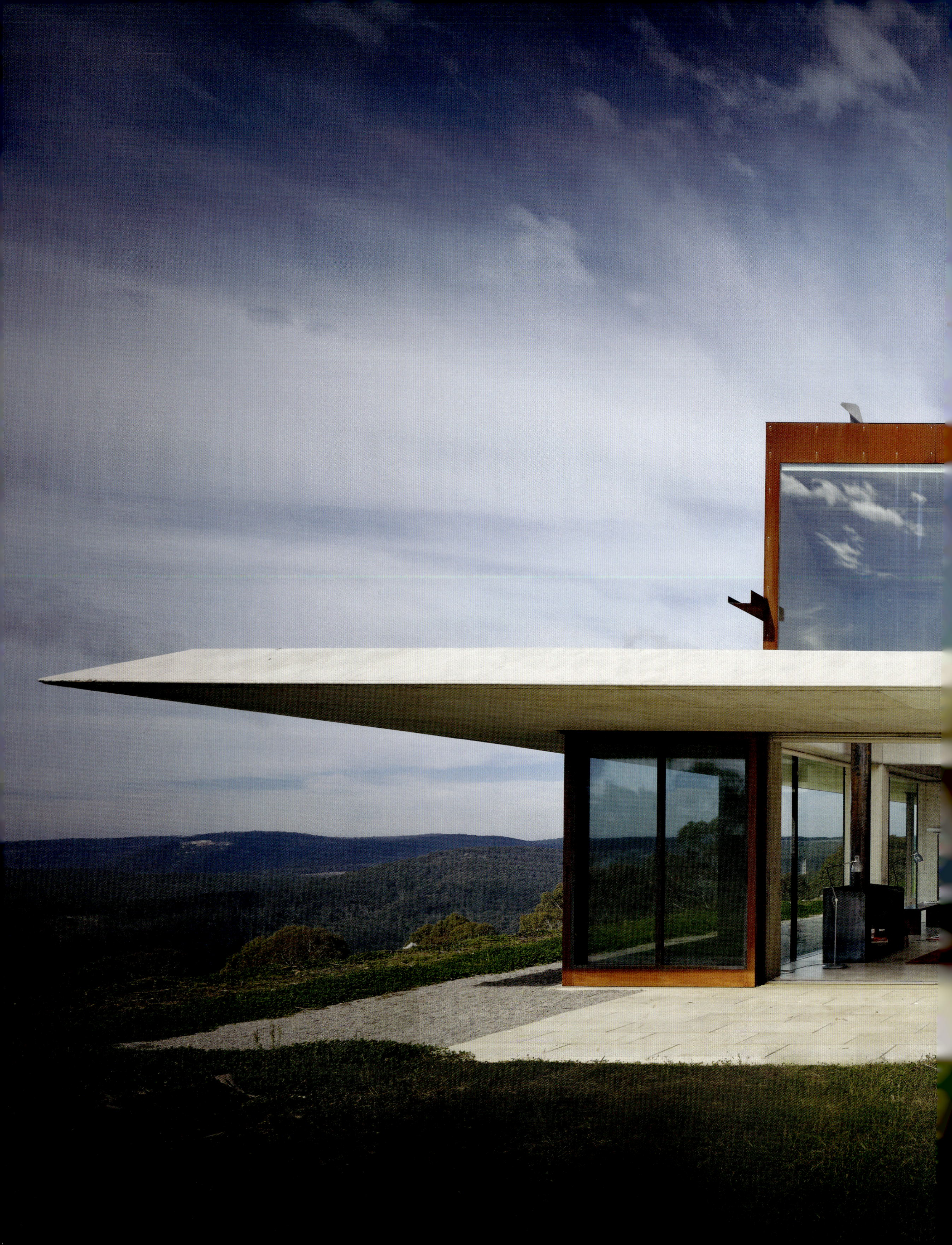

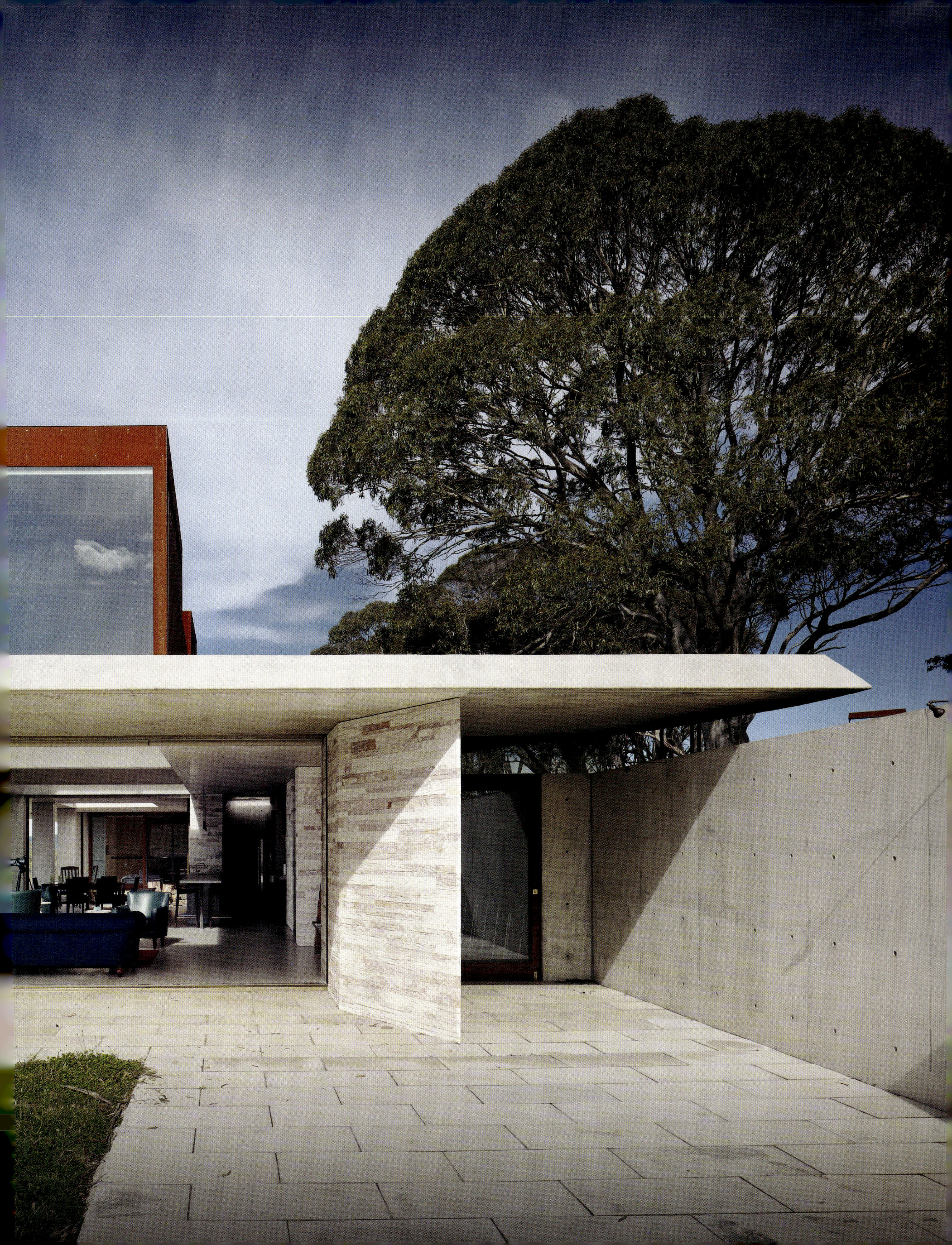

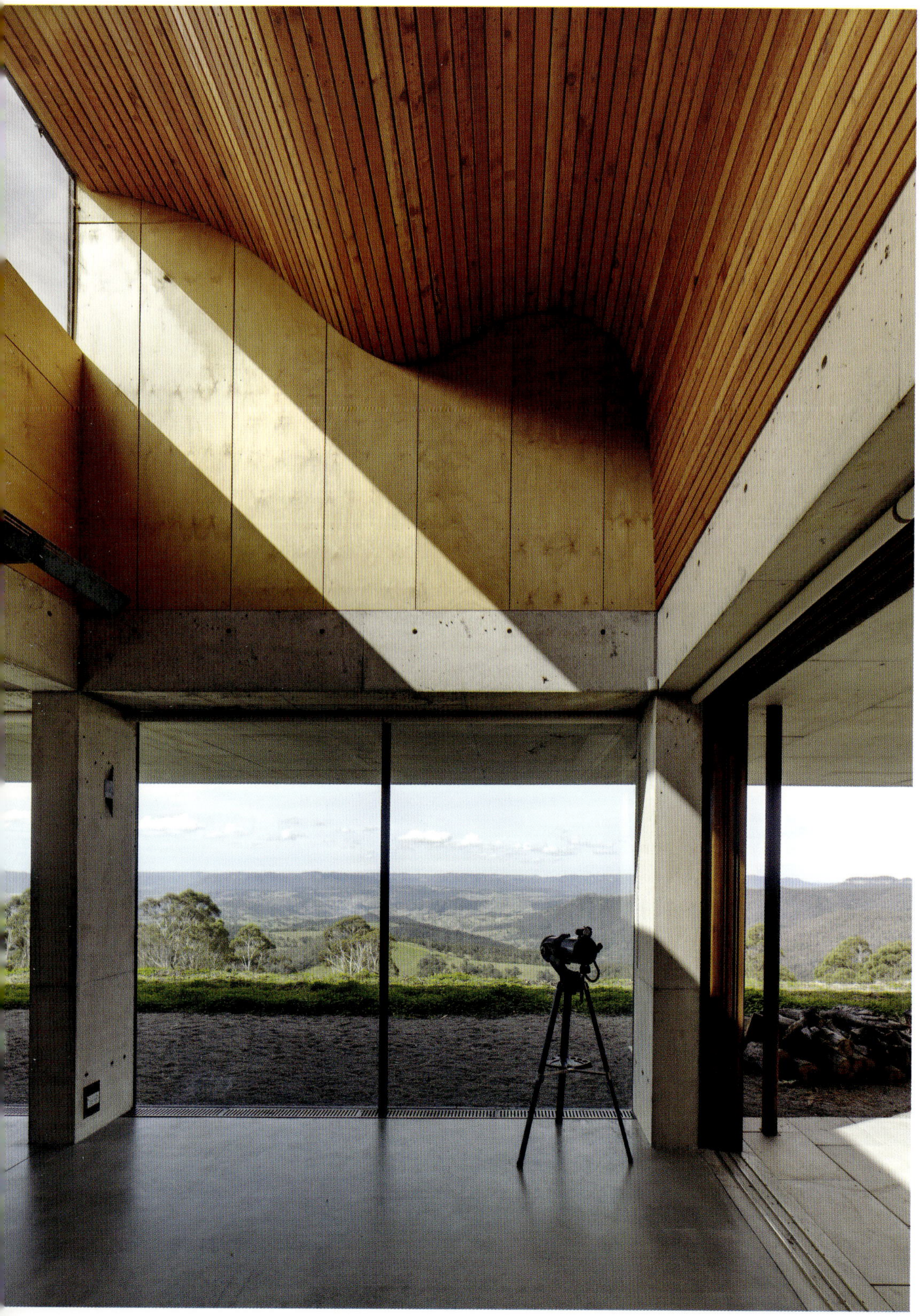

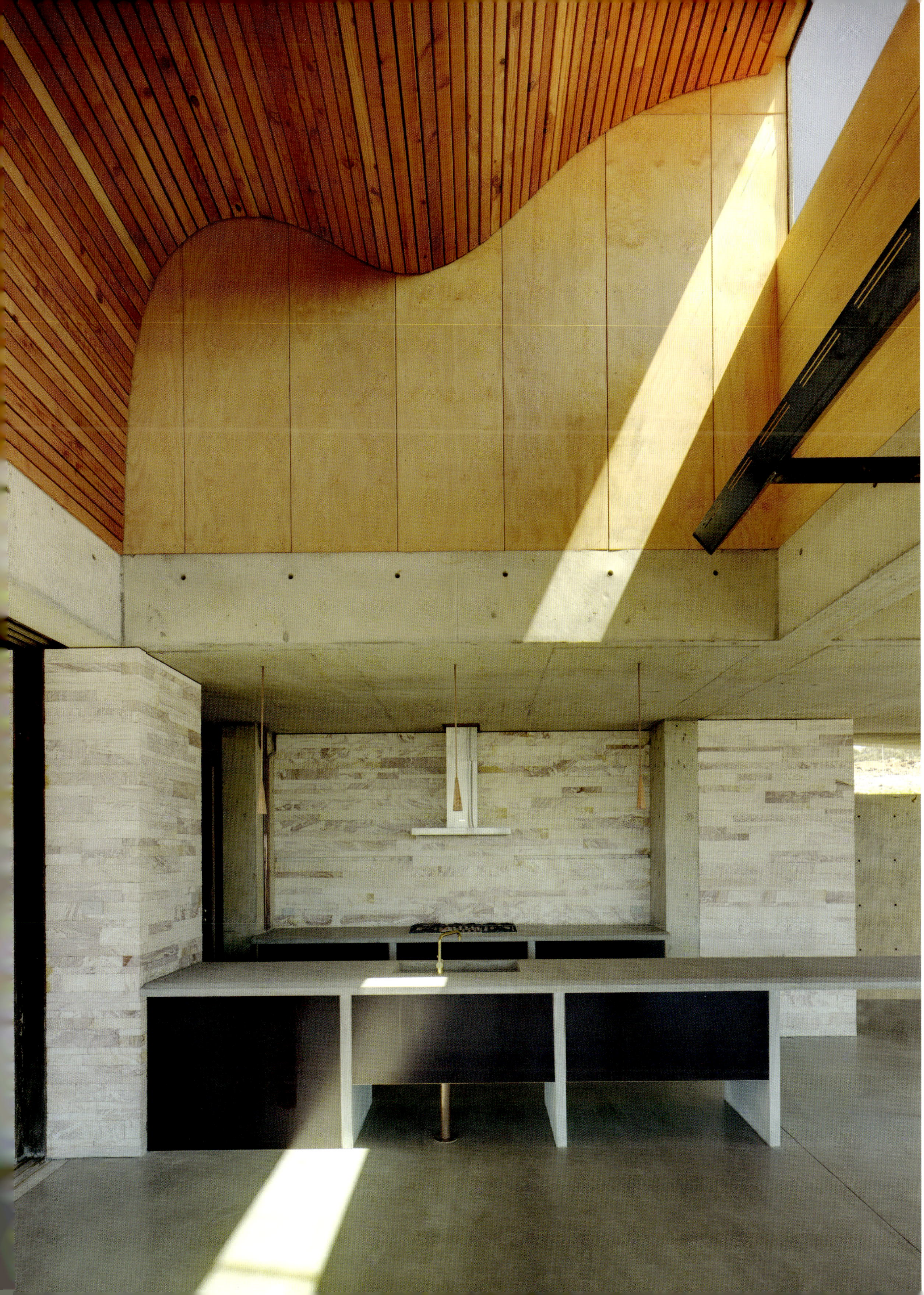

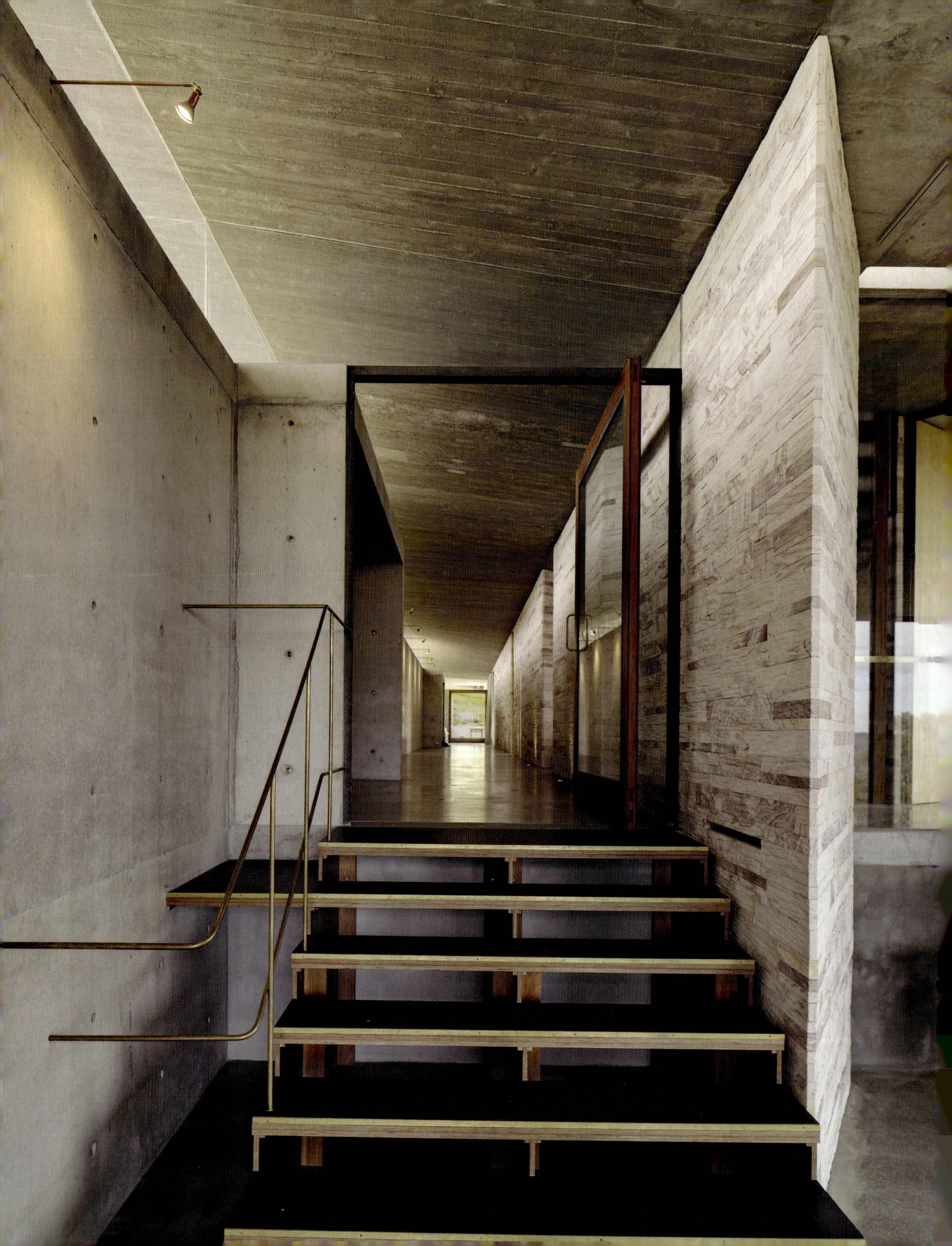

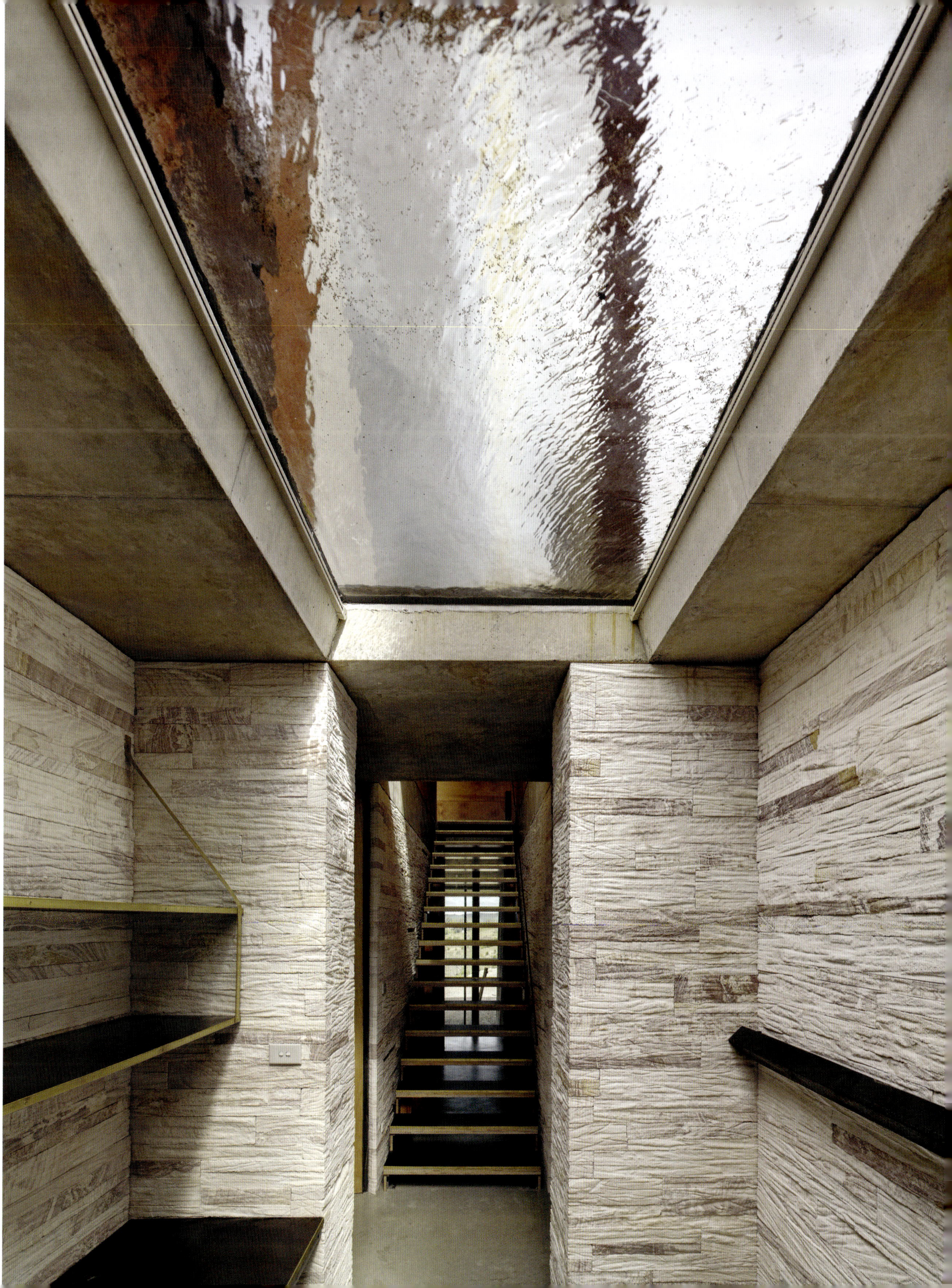

Invisible House is located on the western edge of the Blue Mountains, as it slopes gradually to the west and the desert. Situated as it is, exposure is a constant. Daylong sun, the blistering cold winds both up the valley and across the range, and hot winds from the west across thousands of kilometres of desert hit the site like a furnace in summer. The design of the house could not ignore these elements. *Peter Stutchbury*

In designing for this site we did not direct our thoughts to a gesture but rather studied the surrounds, both immediate and distant. It was from these studies that we found a sculptural form that although foreign was not of a different order to this place. The building represents an interpretation of all the factors that accumulate to form a story of belonging. Invisible House can be there and it cannot. If the roof, with water, reflects the sky, this building will never be found – until it is discovered. *Peter Stutchbury*

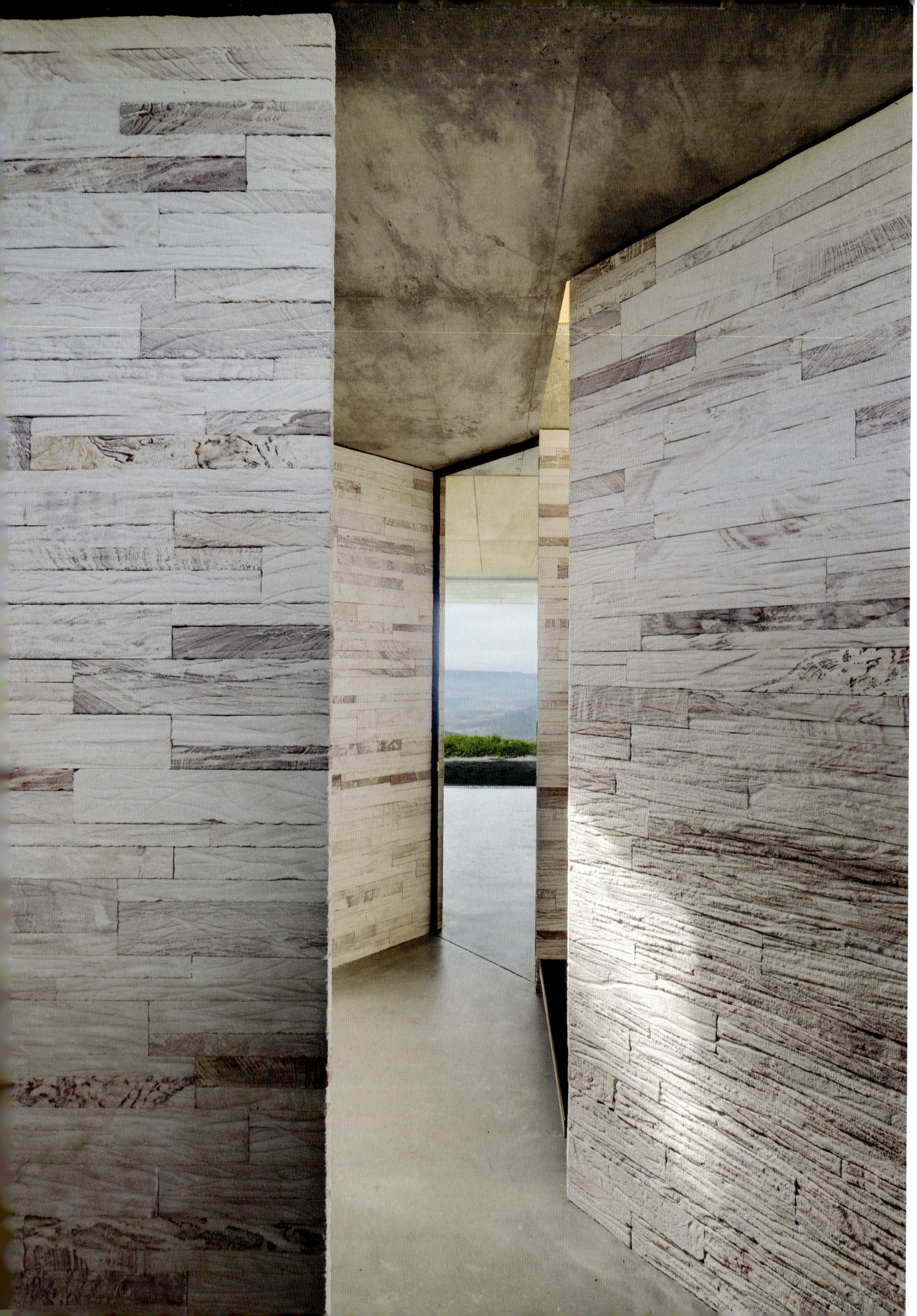

180

Photographs: Brett Boardman and Tom Ferguson

TAMARAMA HOUSE

TAMARAMA HOUSE
SYDNEY, AUSTRALIA, 2017
DURBACH BLOCK JAGGERS

Shoehorned into a steep site between a block of brick flats and a mundane house, this house at Tamarama, Sydney, is exceptional. Set above the Bondi to Coogee coastal walk, the house comes as a breath of fresh air on an overcrowded street of garage fronts and over-the-top mansions jostling for views of the breathtaking waters and headlands spread before them.

Made from sculpted in situ concrete, it is a house of remarkable detail, of overlapping geometries, of fineness and robustness – restrained, modest and grand all in the same breath. It is a feast for the eye. Attempts to take it in on a single visit are almost impossible. From the compressed entry down to the swimming pool, concealed behind a concrete wall, with the coastal walk just beyond, the visitor is taken on a rollercoaster journey of masterful, purposeful and sequential manipulation of space and volume.

It is an extraordinary piece of invention, architectural delight and craftsmanship, and everywhere the hand of its architect, Neil Durbach, a principal at Durbach Block Jaggers, is evident. It is no secret that Durbach is an ardent fan of the architecture of Le Corbusier, the pioneering Franco–Swiss architect. Corbusian touches grace much of Durbach's architecture, and it is no different here at Tamarama: the free-form bas-relief encrusted on the underside of the entry canopy; the slender steel pilotis carrying massive loads; the random arrangement of tiny windows glazed in red, yellow, blue and white, casting splashes of coloured light into the entry hall; and a slanted funnel-shaped oculus are all unmistakable references to Le Corbusier.

Handed a spectacular but south-facing site, Durbach and his team took the radical approach of digging the house in and setting it back several metres from the street, creating in the process a lush, subtropical courtyard garden – full-grown palms, frangipani and more – both as a buffer from the bustle of the street above and to allow much desired northern light to penetrate into the building. Direct sunlight enters the house in myriad other ways: from little windows in unexpected places, to large skylights and portholes that bring the sun in directly from above, to long bands of strip glass 'floating' across the top of the double-height room. It comes in, too, reflected from strategically placed mirrors in dark corners of the house.

The program is straightforward: bedrooms are located on the upper entry level (the only routine move of the plan), while the tall living room acts as a piano nobile in the truest sense, with its subtropical, north-facing sunken garden at one end and the pellucid sea at the other. Below the piano nobile is a double-height space, with guest bedroom and study on the mezzanine, and lounge and den on the lowest level, spilling out to another garden and the swimming pool. A concrete spiral stair encased in a black sheet-steel cylinder connects all the levels of the house. There's a lift if you don't feel energetic.

The overlapping geometries of the form and the dual garden arrangement of the plan respond to the difficulties of the site in an expert manner. Central to this is the sunken front garden facing the street. Sheltered from wild weather, it acts as both a place of repose and respite, and a balanced juxtaposition to the expanse of ocean on the south side. This is a house, too, of remarkable detail: animated, impossibly thin steel handrails; folded sheet steel; and sculpted, textured board-patterned concrete. The ply-sheet formwork has been placed this way and that to produce a patchwork texture on curving walls in the lower levels, while elegant frames in deep reveals show the massiveness of the concrete walls. The restrained palette of materials – in situ concrete, oak and glass – works seamlessly to convey at once a sense of casualness and grandeur. Tamarama House stands as a modest, brilliant white concrete cube amid the ugliness of its suburban environment.

0 25m

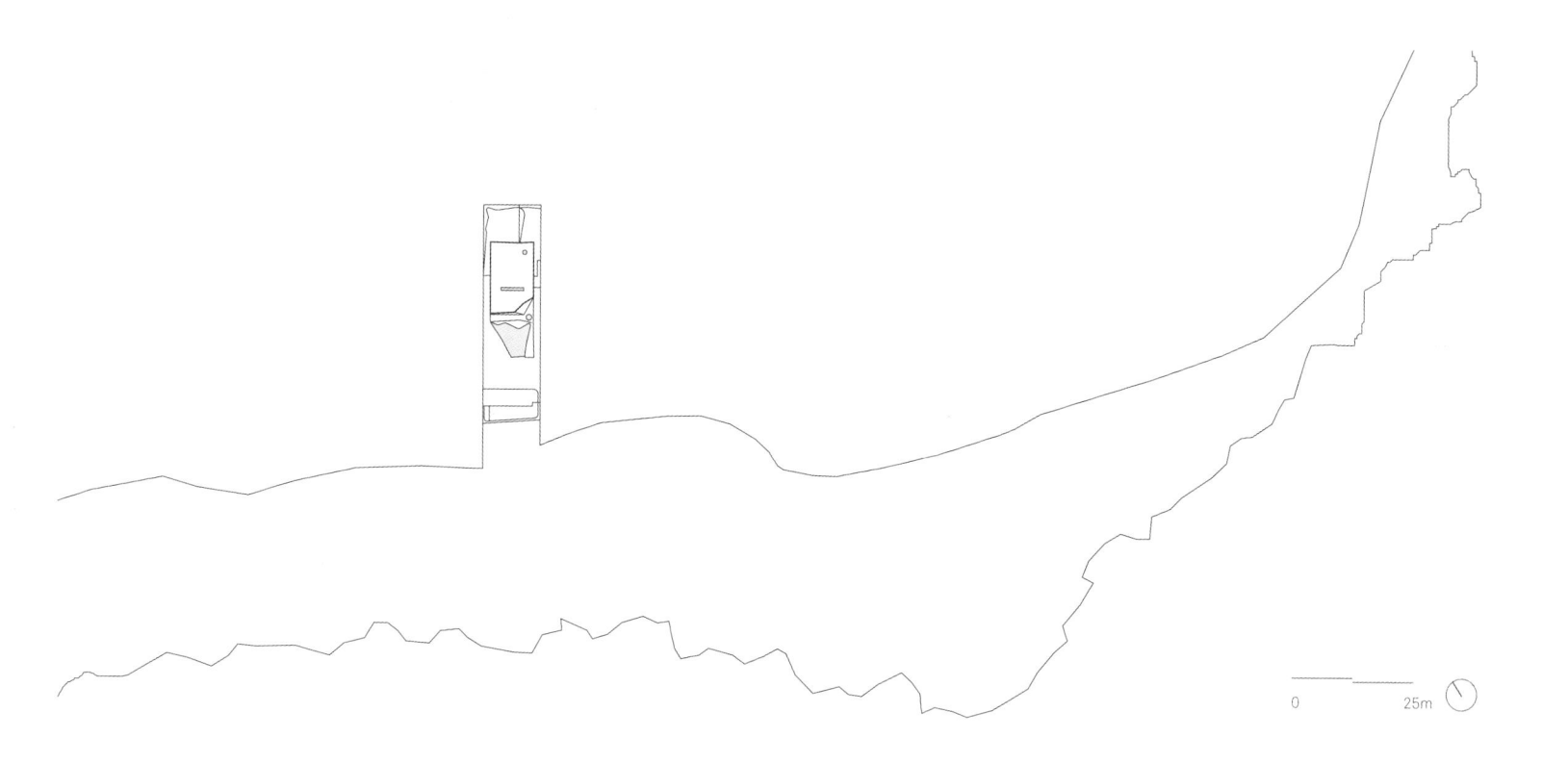

South elevation

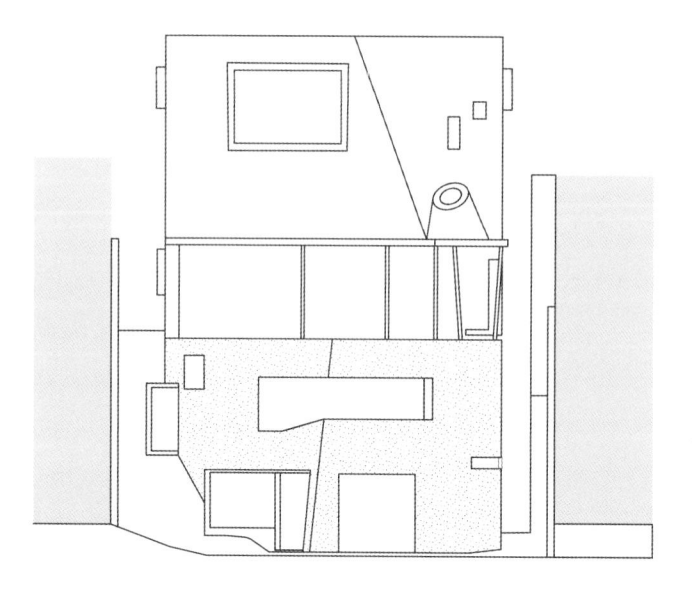

Lower ground floor
Mezzanine

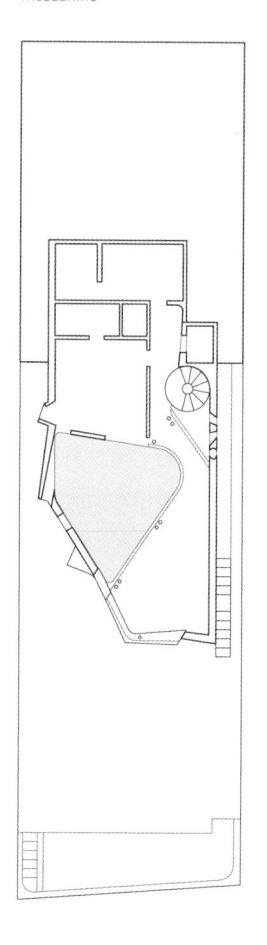

Ground floor
Mezzanine

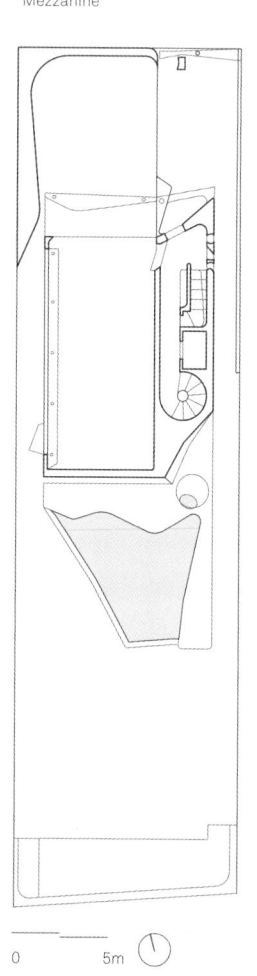

North elevation

0 5m

0 5m

184 — 185

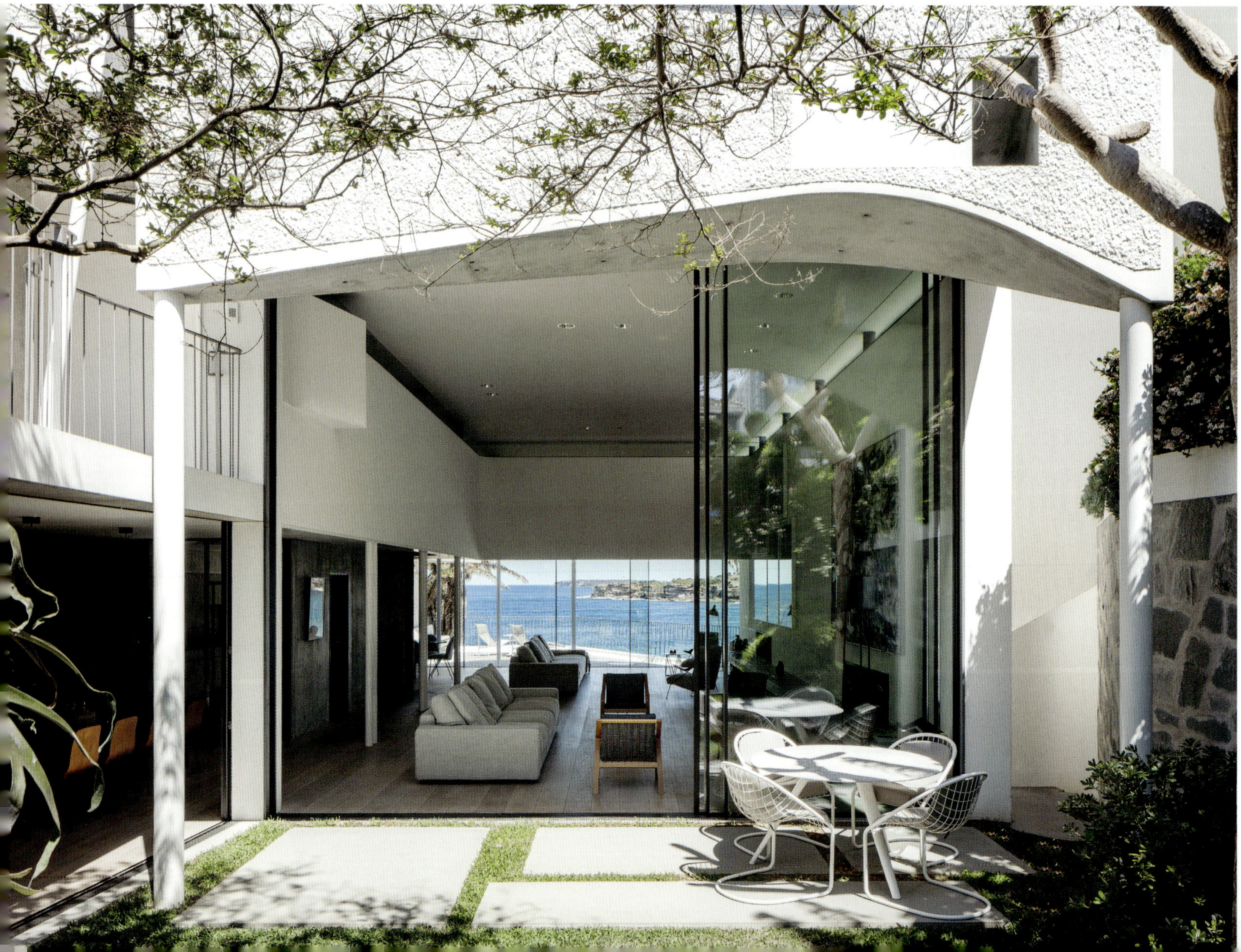

The compressed gridded upper floor of this house gives way to the calming linear piano nobile, which in turn gives way to the soft buoyancy of the lower ground-centric space that opens onto the pool garden and the headland walk just beyond. In a highly congested area, the idea of setting the house as far back as possible off the street to create a sunny, wind-free garden court was no longer just not sensible, it was thought preposterous. And the clients understood and encouraged this. From the street, the house is deliberately demure; from the rock edge, its shifted carved cubes of chalk echo the eroded cliffs nearby. *Neil Durbach*

Louis Kahn once observed that there is a house…and then there is a home; and you should be designing a house, not a home. Because a house is independent of particulars, it belongs to architecture, whereas a home is personal and momentary. It is specific and belongs to the architect and the client. But perhaps the sense of domestic delight, the feeling of beauty, comes from the friction, the rubbing together, of patterns and particulars. *Neil Durbach*

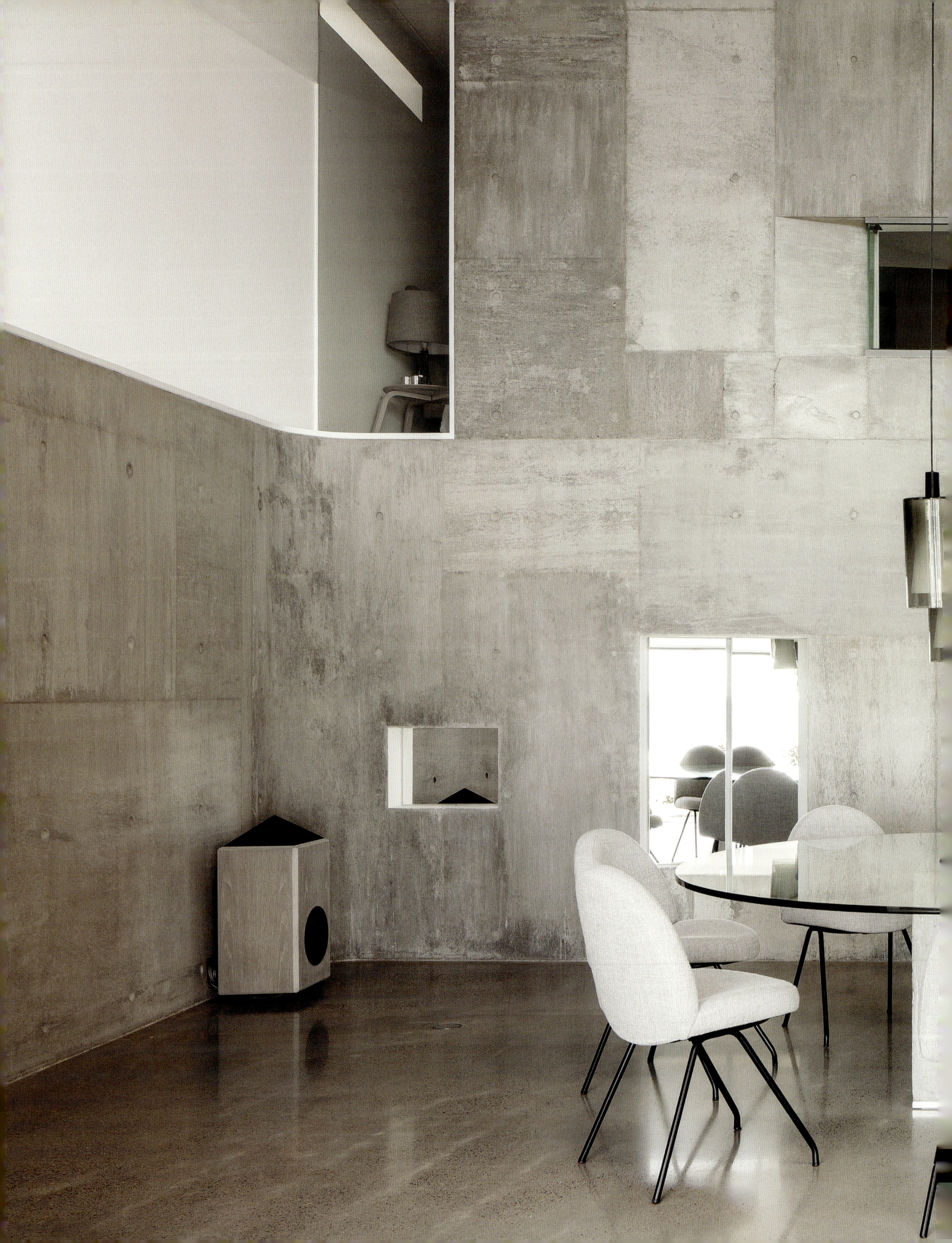

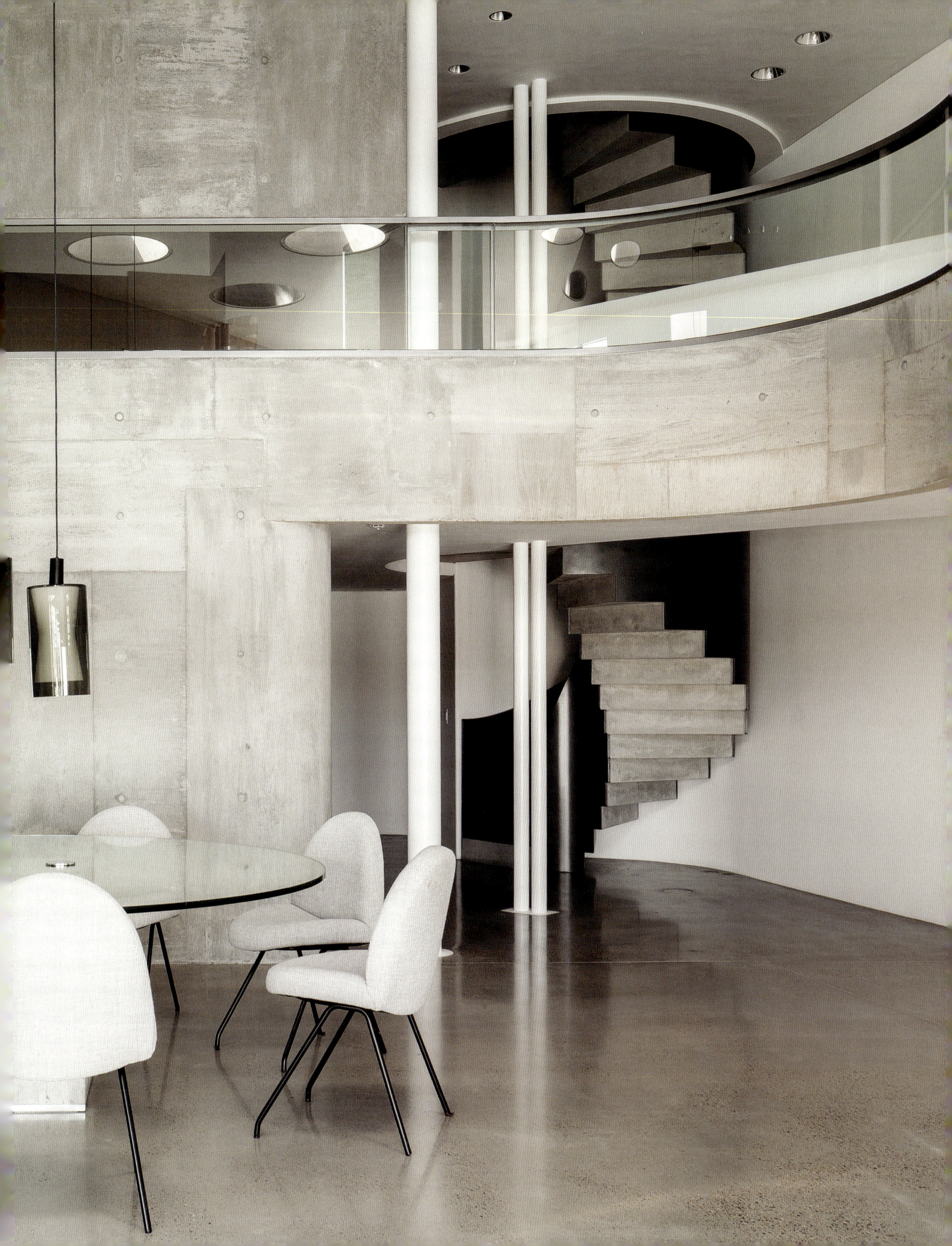

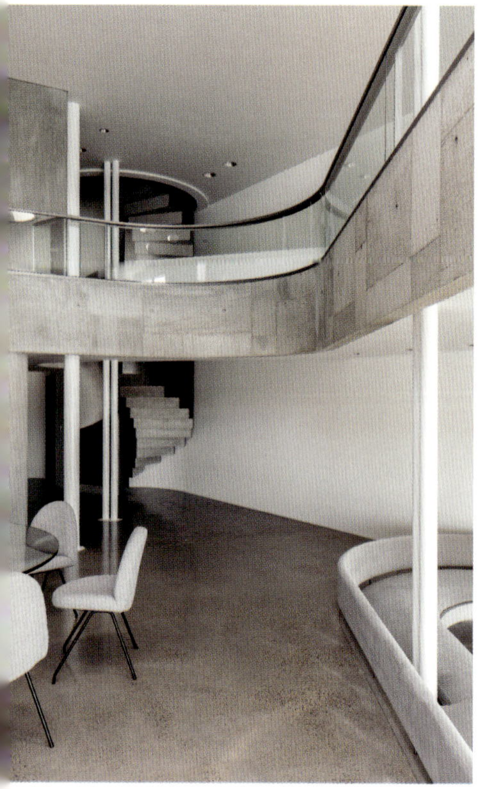

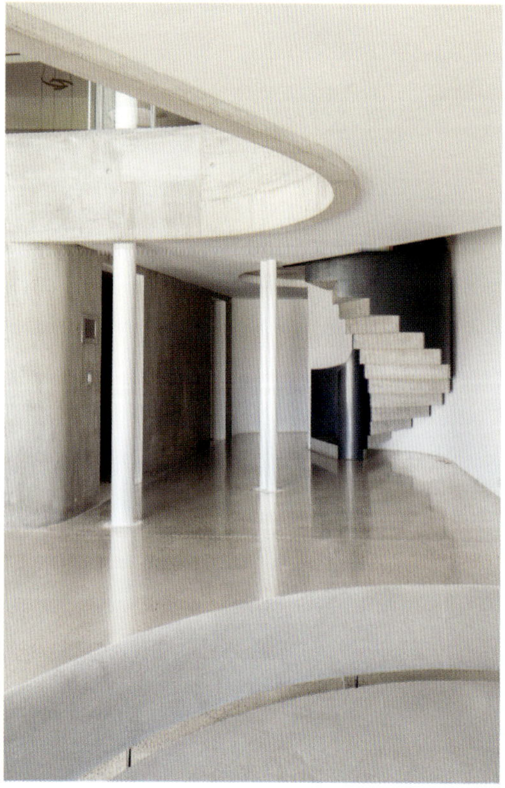

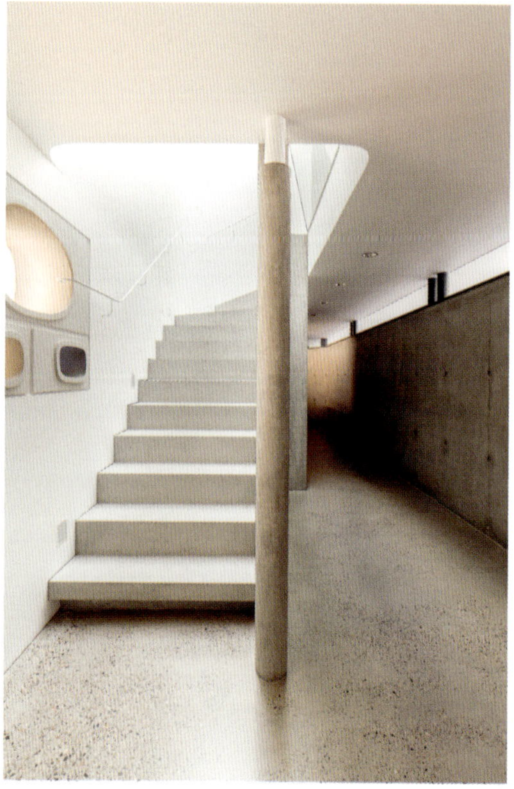

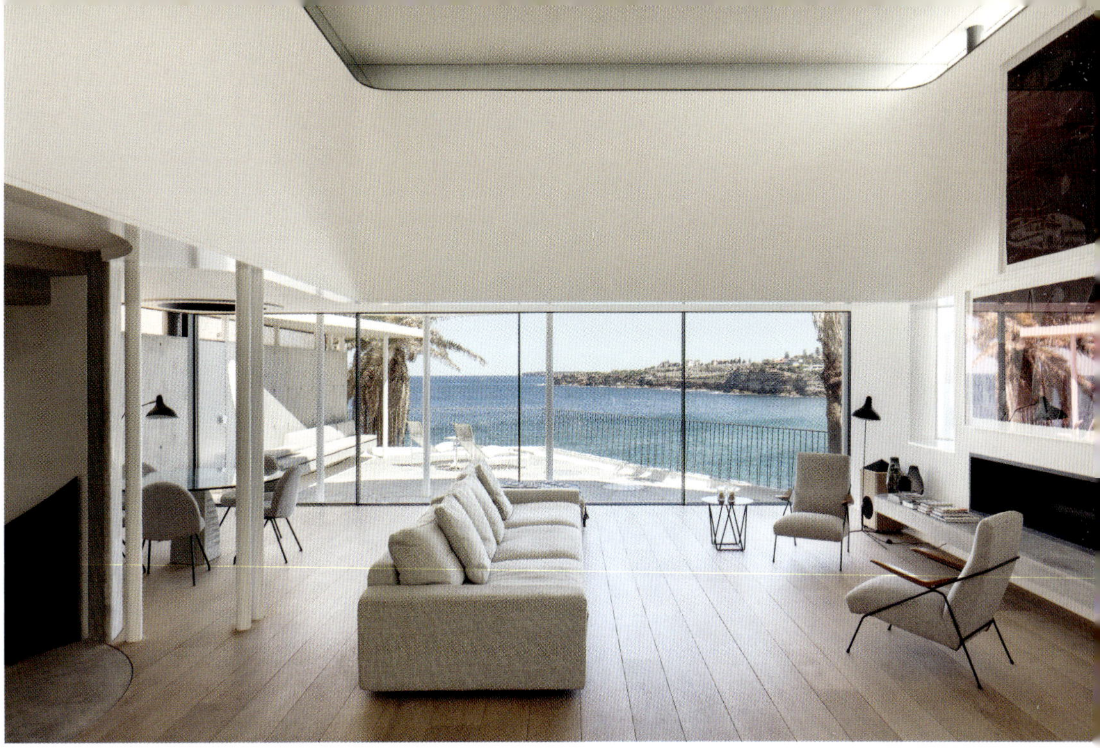
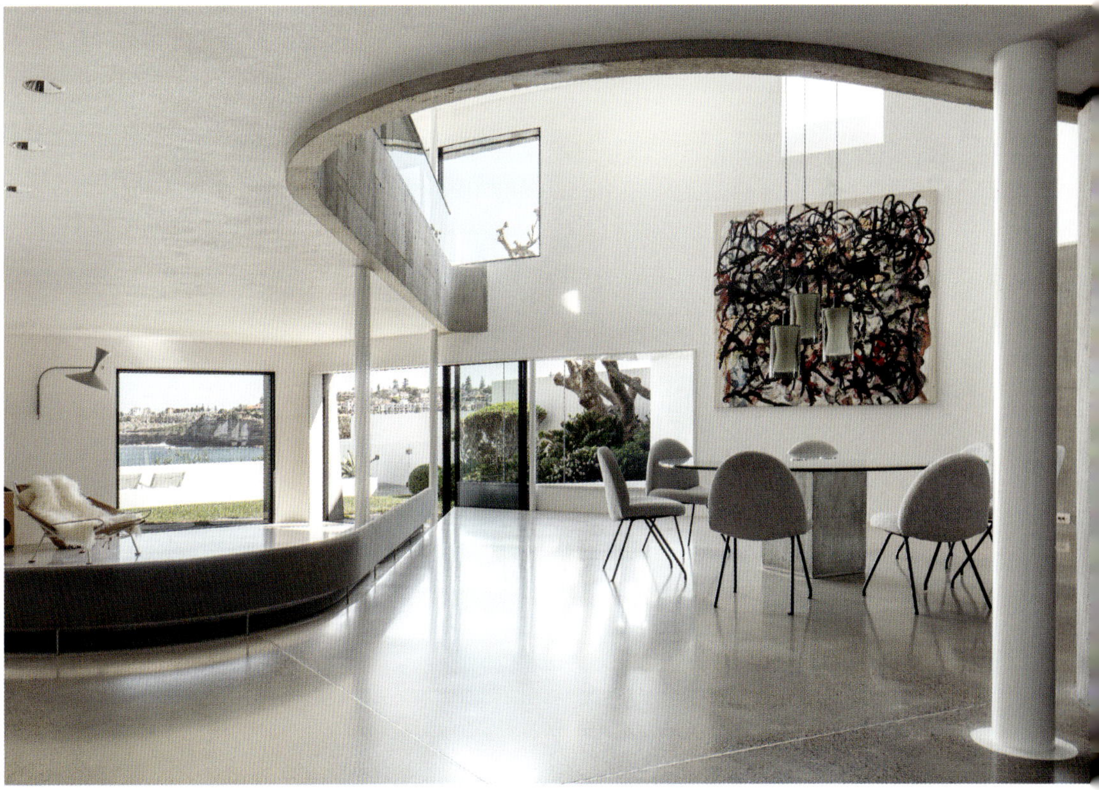
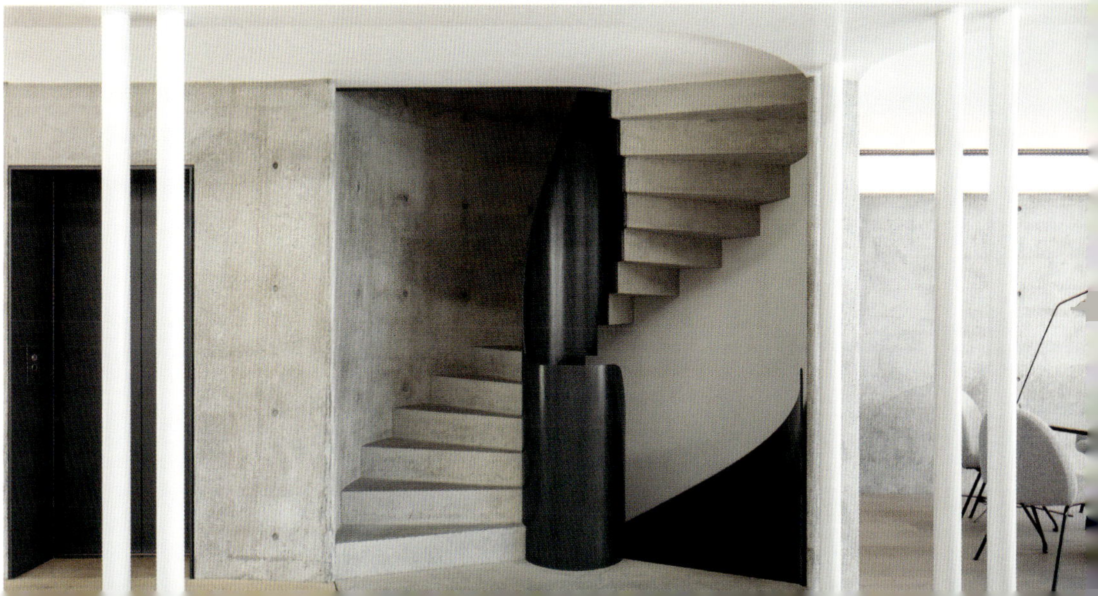

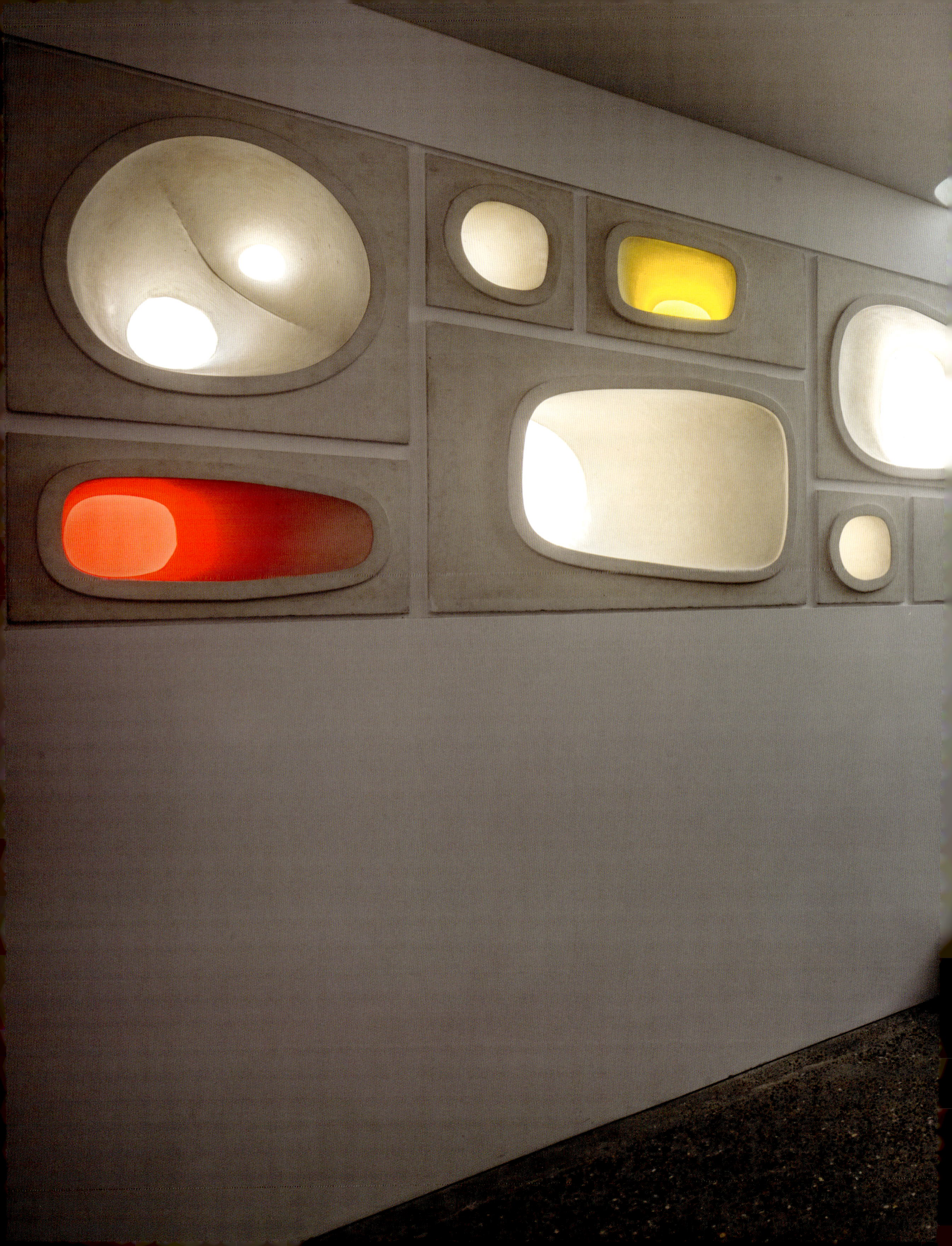

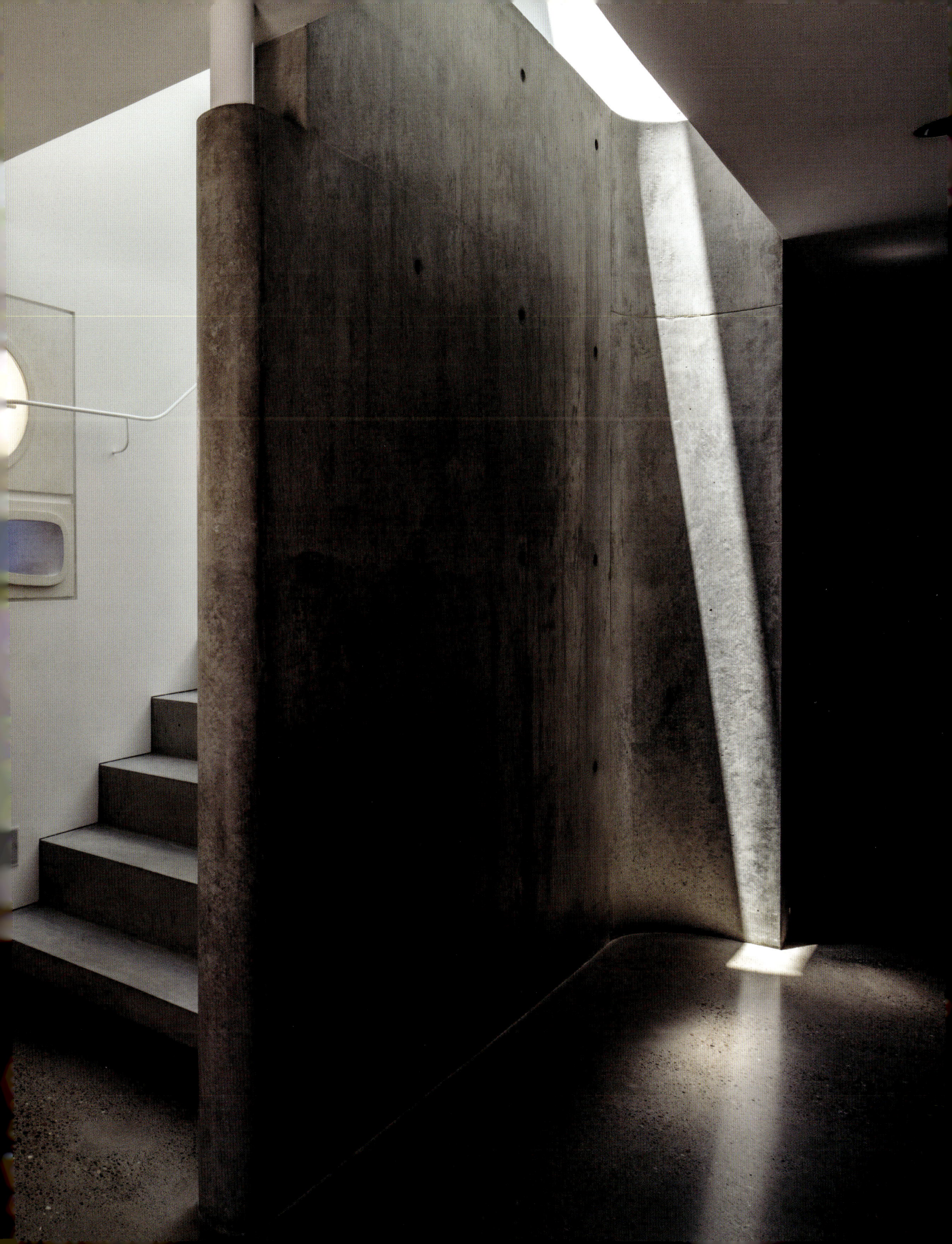

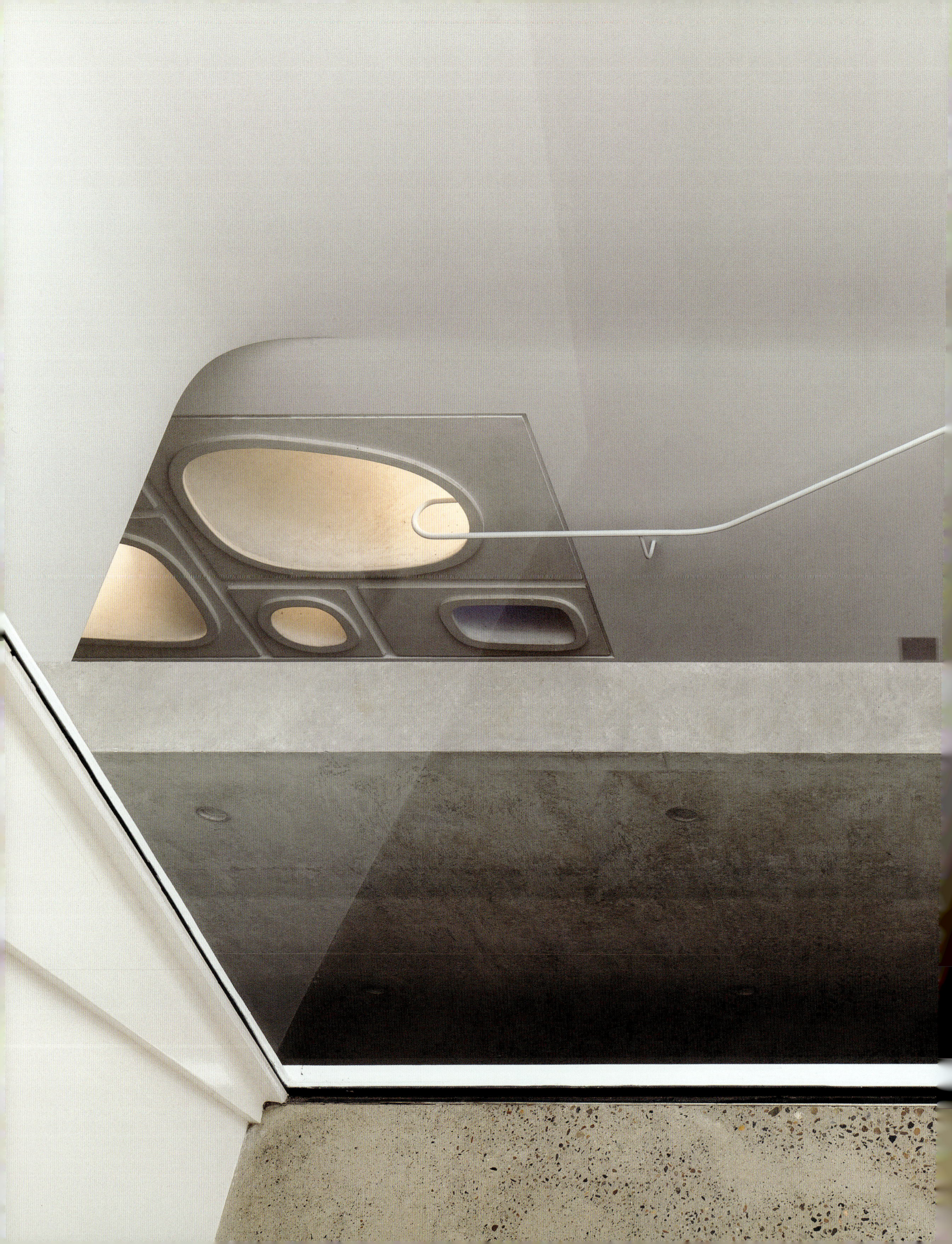

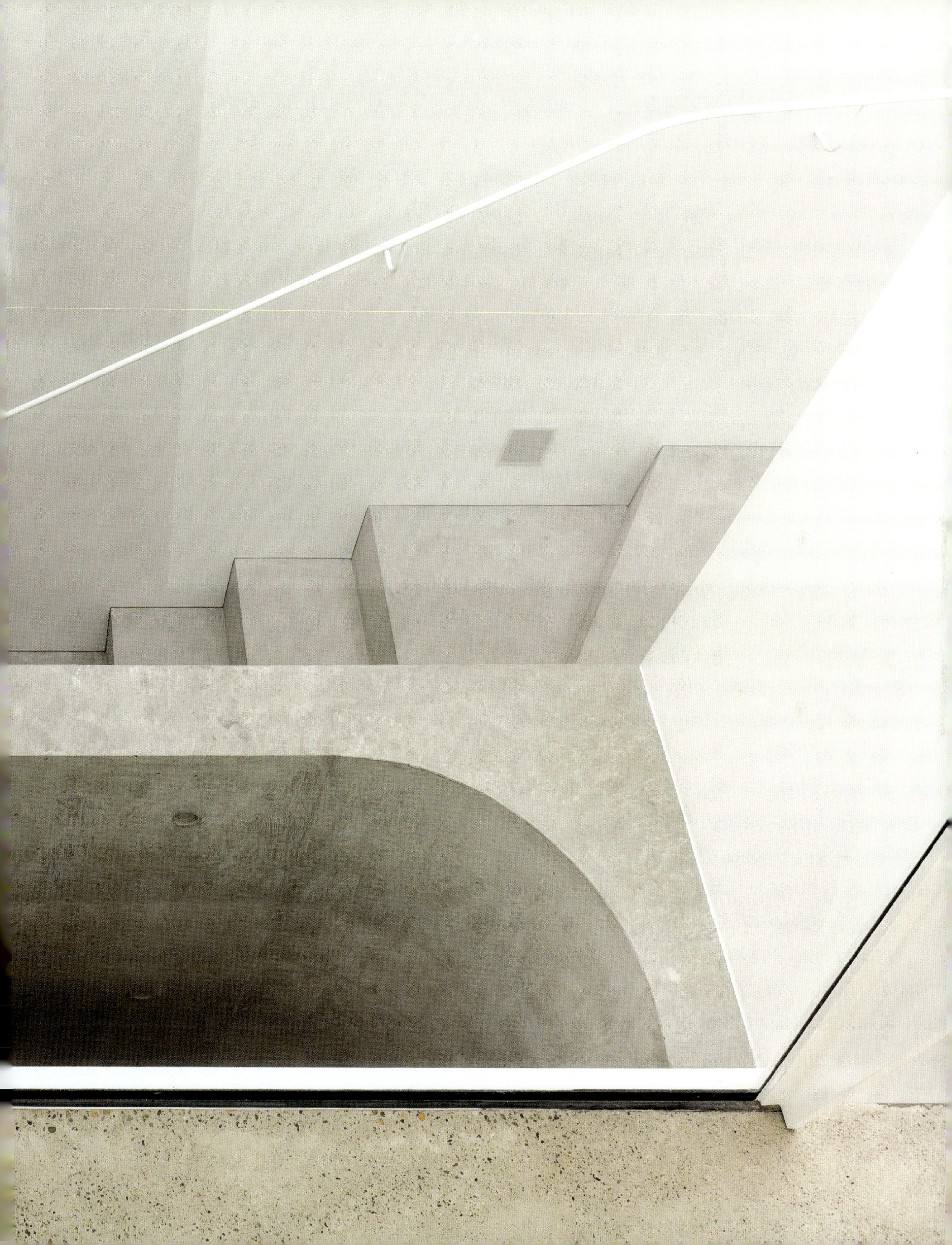

Photographs: Brett Boardman

196

BALMORAL HOUSE

BALMORAL HOUSE
SYDNEY, AUSTRALIA, 2015
CLINTON MURRAY AND POLLY HARBISON

The siting for this house at Balmoral, in Sydney's northern suburbs, is spectacular. Perched on the side of a steep block, it looks over Balmoral Beach, the historic Bathers Pavilion and out over Sydney Harbour National Park, right through to The Heads at the harbour entrance. The fall from the top to the bottom of the site, on a sloping bend in the road, is some 12 metres.

At the heart of its design, by architects Clinton Murray and Polly Harbison, was a strong desire to give the house sculptural form, as a reflection of its owners' abiding interest in art, in particular early 20th-century European cubist art, and to take advantage of the arresting site. A sculpture by Isamu Noguchi, a study on the interplay between solid and void, was pivotal during early design deliberations.

The house, then, is an assembly of concrete cubes, piled one atop the other, turned this way and that, each box positioned to consider aspect, frame views, to take in sun or exclude it altogether. The boxes are monolithic; in some places concrete walls are 60 centimetres deep. Some are anchored firmly into the site, while others appear to launch out from the cliff face.

The placement of each box has been carefully considered, too. The uppermost box, for instance, containing the main sleeping zone with a study and living area, is angled so as to capture views toward the harbour and a headland of native Australian bush – water and bush land, after all, are constants here – and turned so as to project out over the street, creating a canopy over the front door in the process.

Another of the concrete cubes, containing the main living area, spans two lower boxes, resting gingerly on one and sitting on large rubber pads on the other, as a bridge between the main part of the house below and a music recital room, while at the same time creating a framed vista from the street out towards the water. It is a deft touch; where others might have turned the building's back to the street, here passers-by are invited to stop, linger and take in the view through to the water, with landscaped gardens and some precisely placed sculptures in the foreground. From inside this living room, dominated by a transfixing ceiling painted ultramarine – as close to International Klein Blue as the architects could achieve – the aspect is a full-on panoramic view of the harbour and out towards The Heads. Generally, though, the temptation to open the house out completely to the mighty views over Balmoral Beach has been resisted.

In contrast to the colossal nature of the concrete cubes, the interior of the house has been used to display the owners' extensive collection of art and sculpture. Soft grey, exposed concrete walls form the background on which much of the art is displayed. Concrete edges and cut out openings are expressed and unencumbered. Glass meets concrete free of frame, head or sill. Views into, through and out of the house are carefully framed. Timber joinery and timber-clad walls add warmth throughout the house and serve to divide spaces. Cavities in the deep walls conceal blinds and help shade large sheets of glass. Entry into the house is at mid-level and a stair, also used to display sculpture, takes you up or down to a suite of bedrooms and another living room.

In a programmatic twist, the recital room is a stand-alone concrete bunker, accessed independently of the house across a covered court set below street level, beneath the 'bridge', and used for receptions and music performances. A sculpture by Antony Gormley, famous for his *Angel of the North* at Gateshead in the north of England, dominates this outdoor space. The room doubles as an art store and games room when not used for recitals. A series of concrete beams step down to a swimming pool, which is all that remains of a previous house on the site.

Floor plan

01 Entry
02 Living
03 Kitchen
04 Bedroom
05 Gym
06 Garage
07 Utility
08 Terrace
09 Study
10 Pool

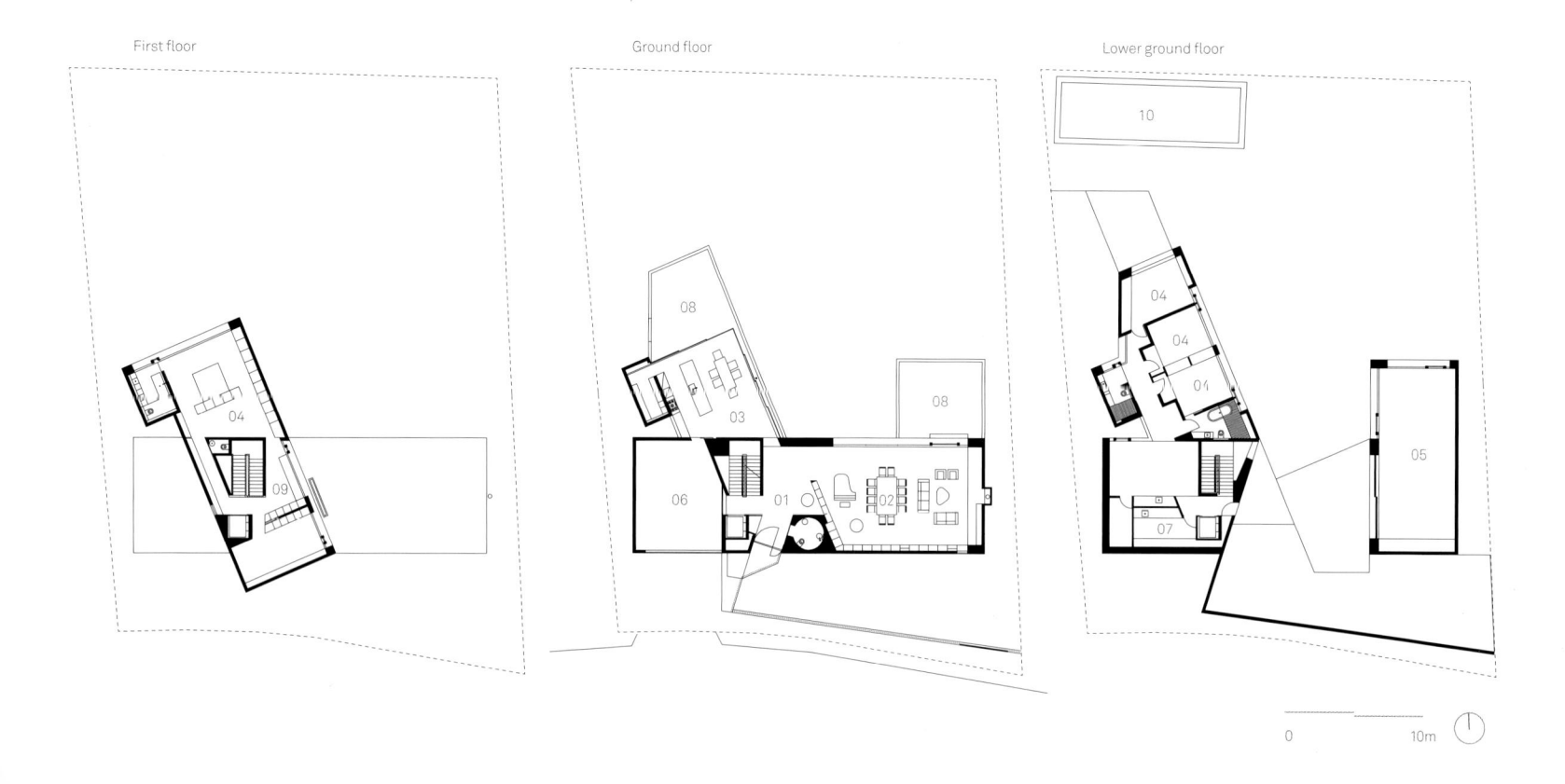

First floor

Ground floor

Lower ground floor

0   10m

We were influenced by an early work from the hand of Isamu Noguchi, a sculpture that is a play on solid and void. Given our clients' passion for art, this core idea of a house as sculpture became the mantra for detailed design decisions. The carving and contorting continued until we had reached the nirvana between form and function. *Clinton Murray*

    Considered, crafted and cropped, parts of the house welcome the sun and other parts exclude it. Parts are buried into the hill, other parts are pushed out into the elements. *Clinton Murray*

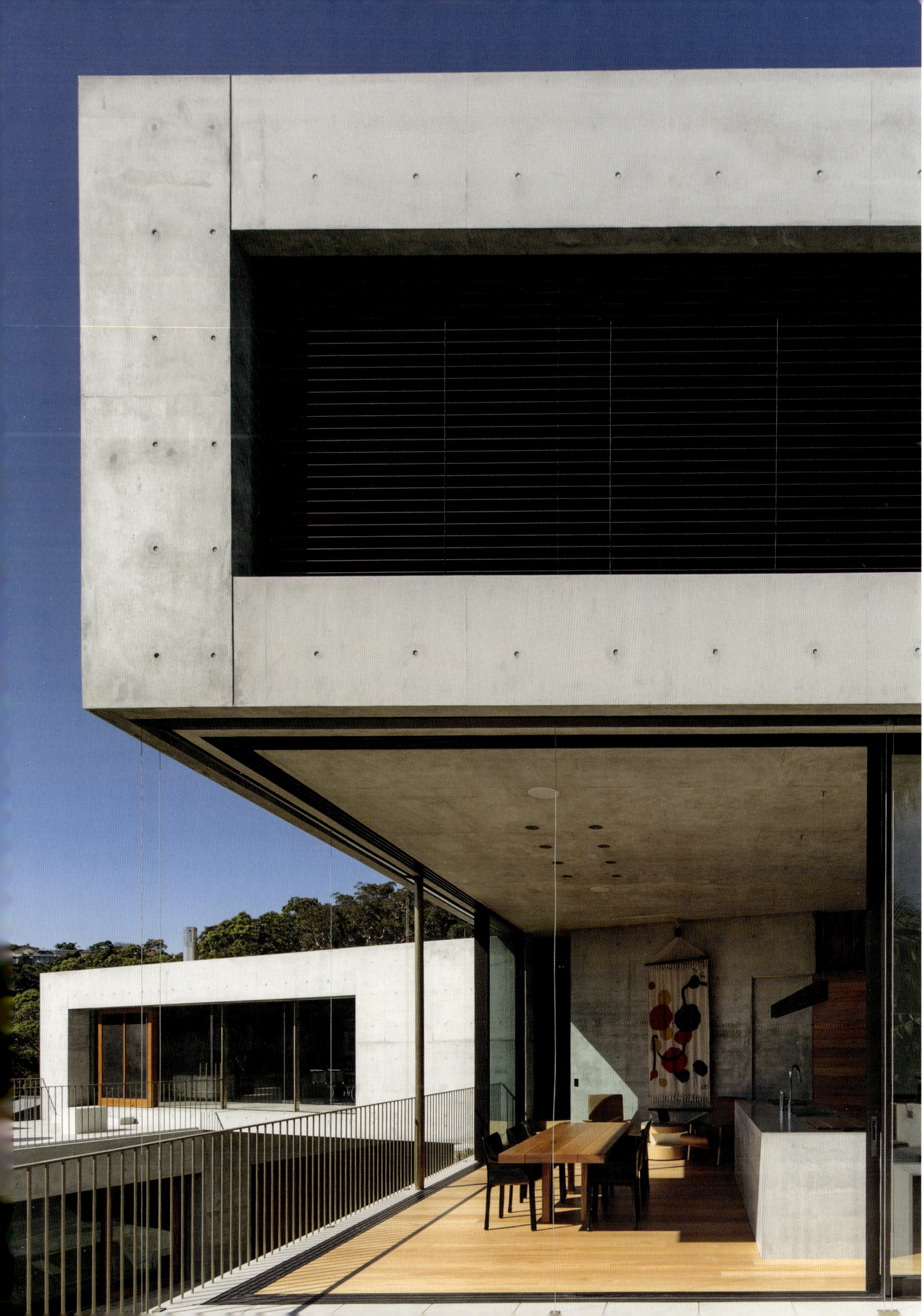

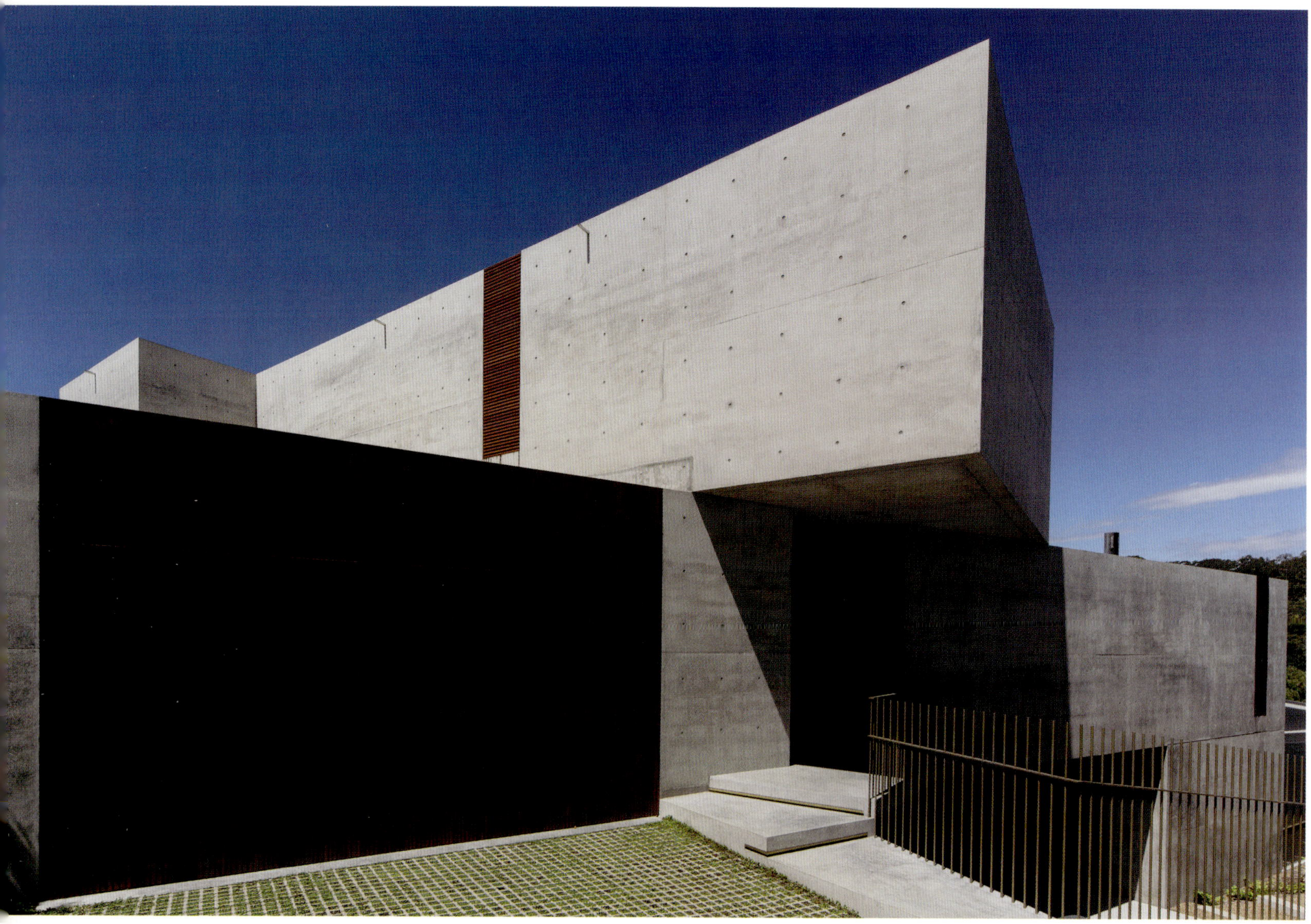

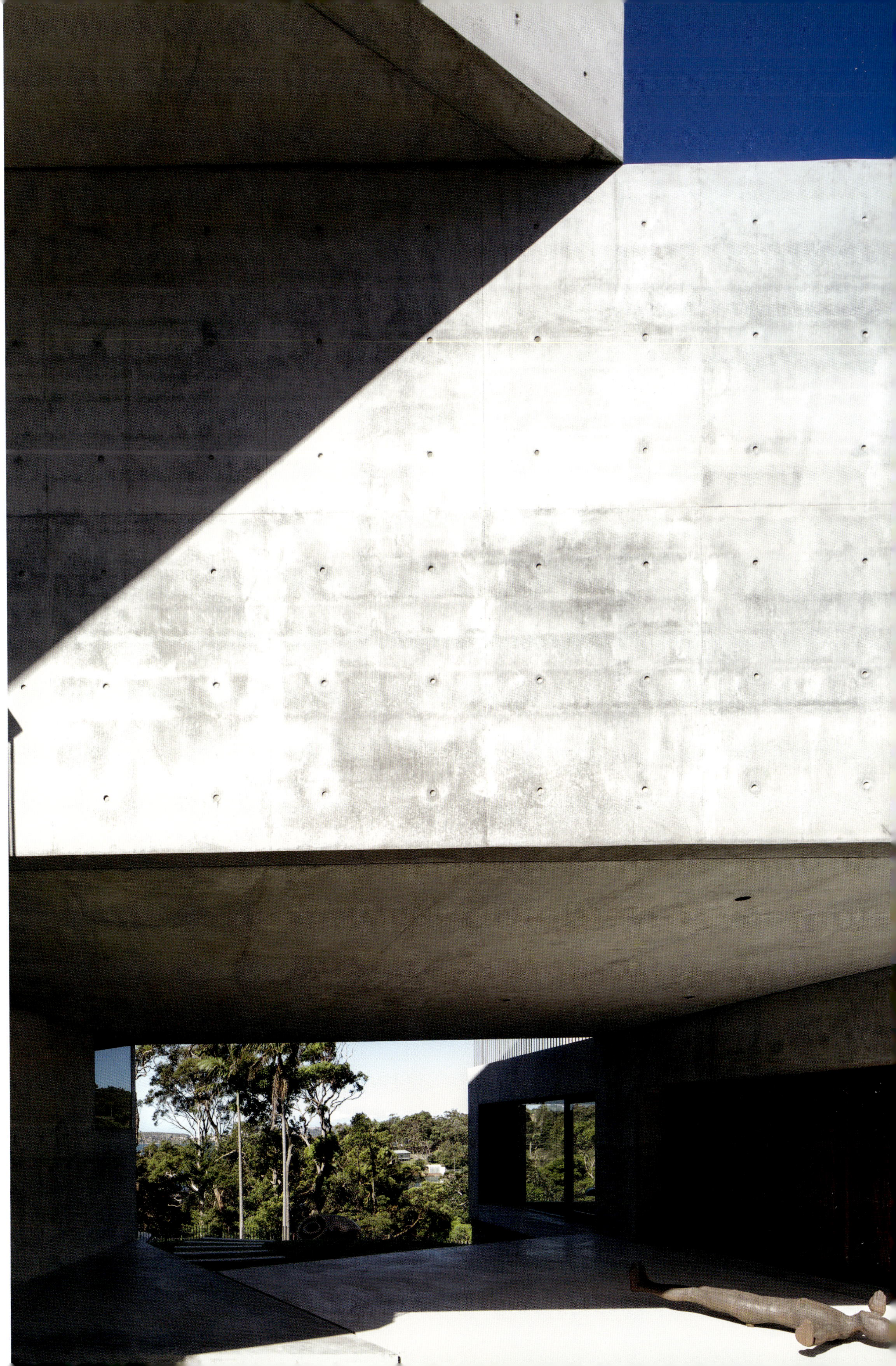

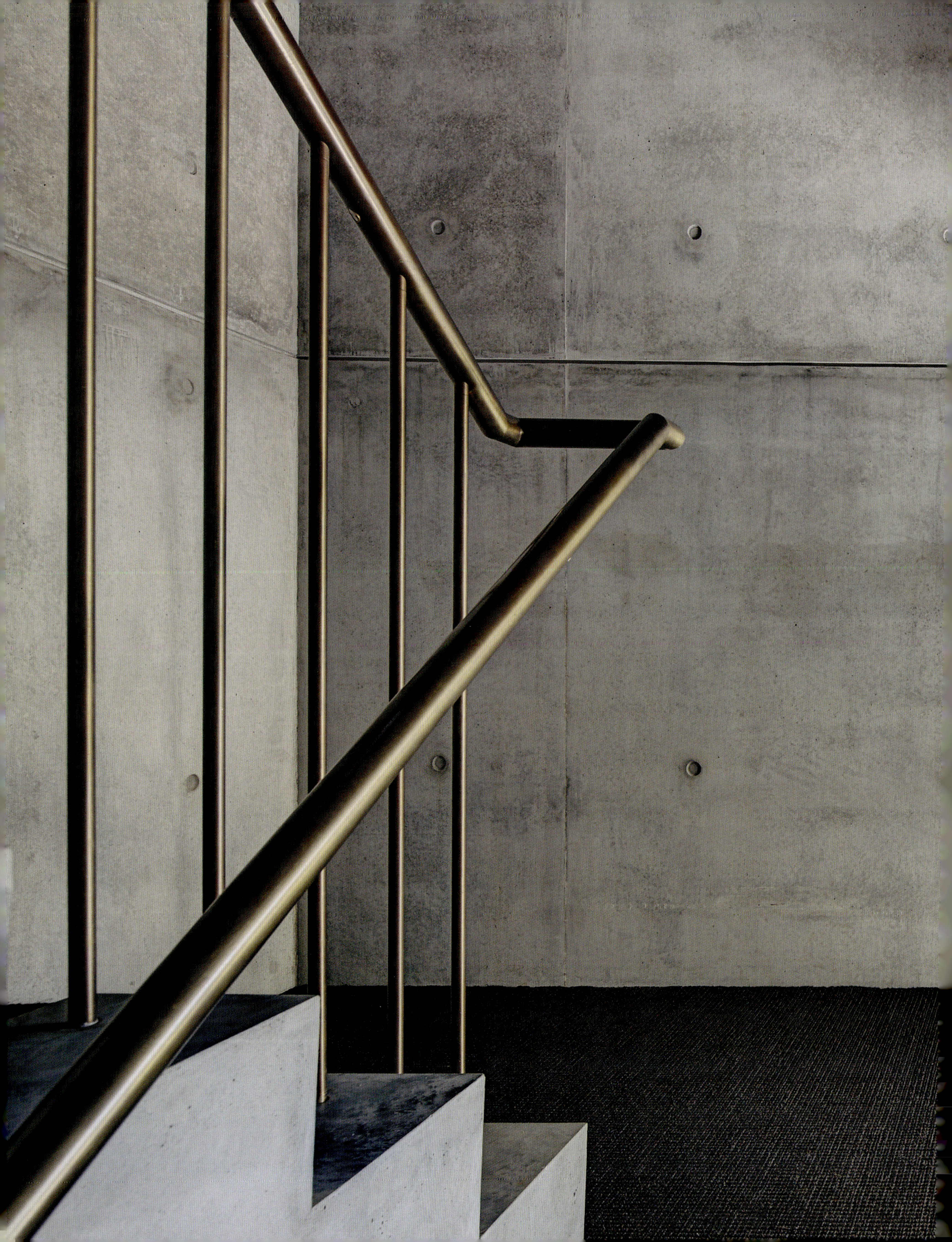

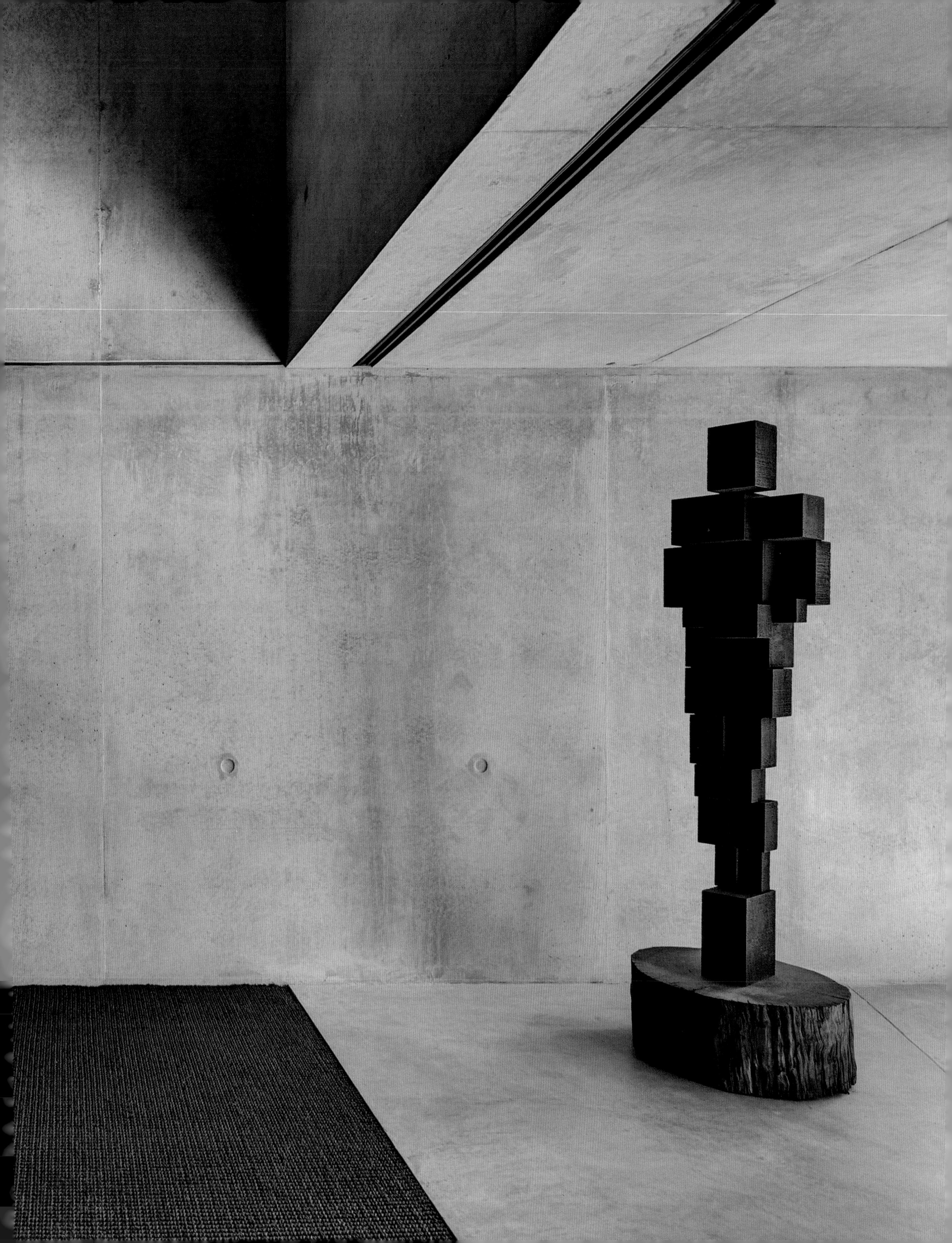

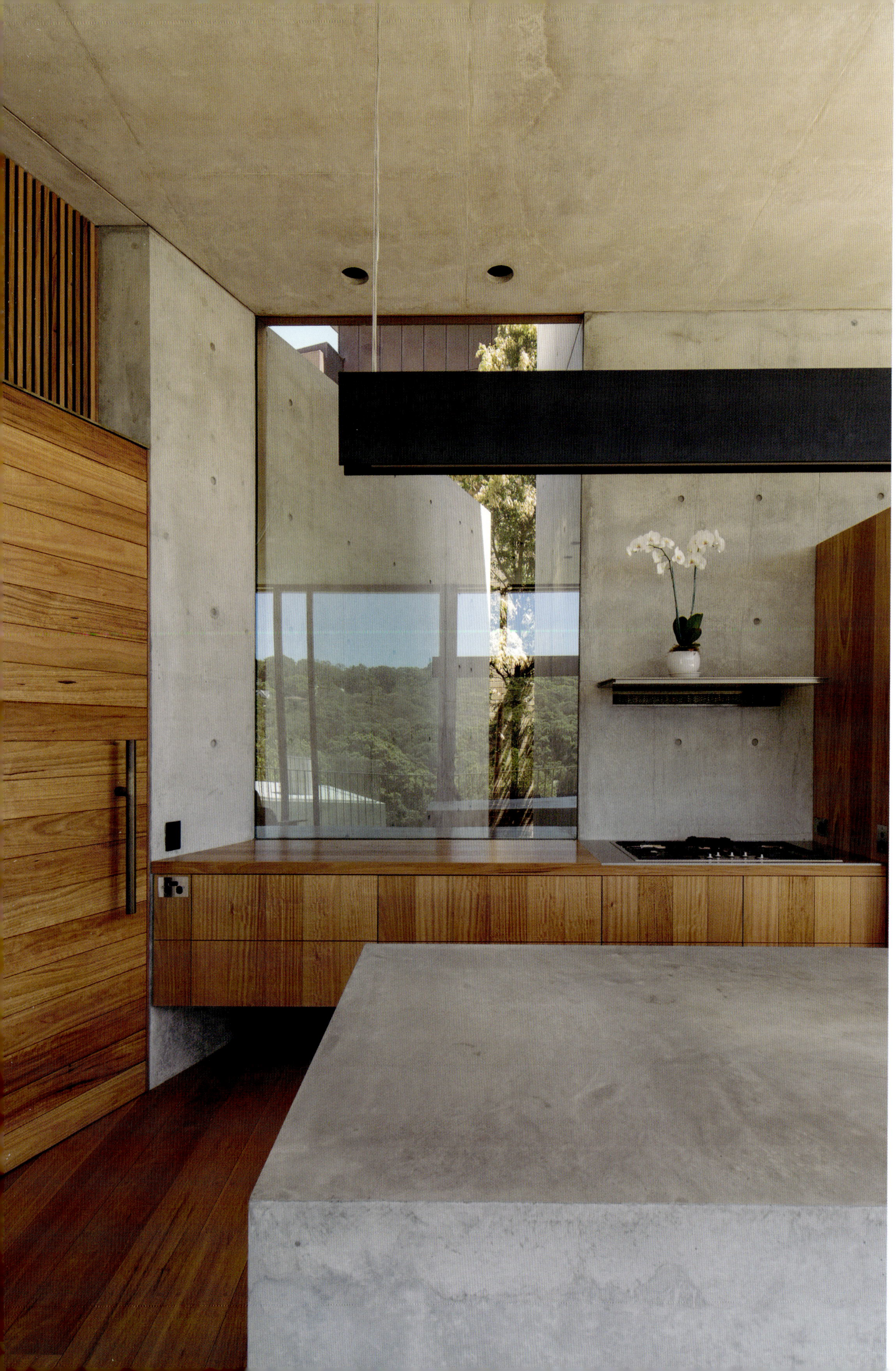

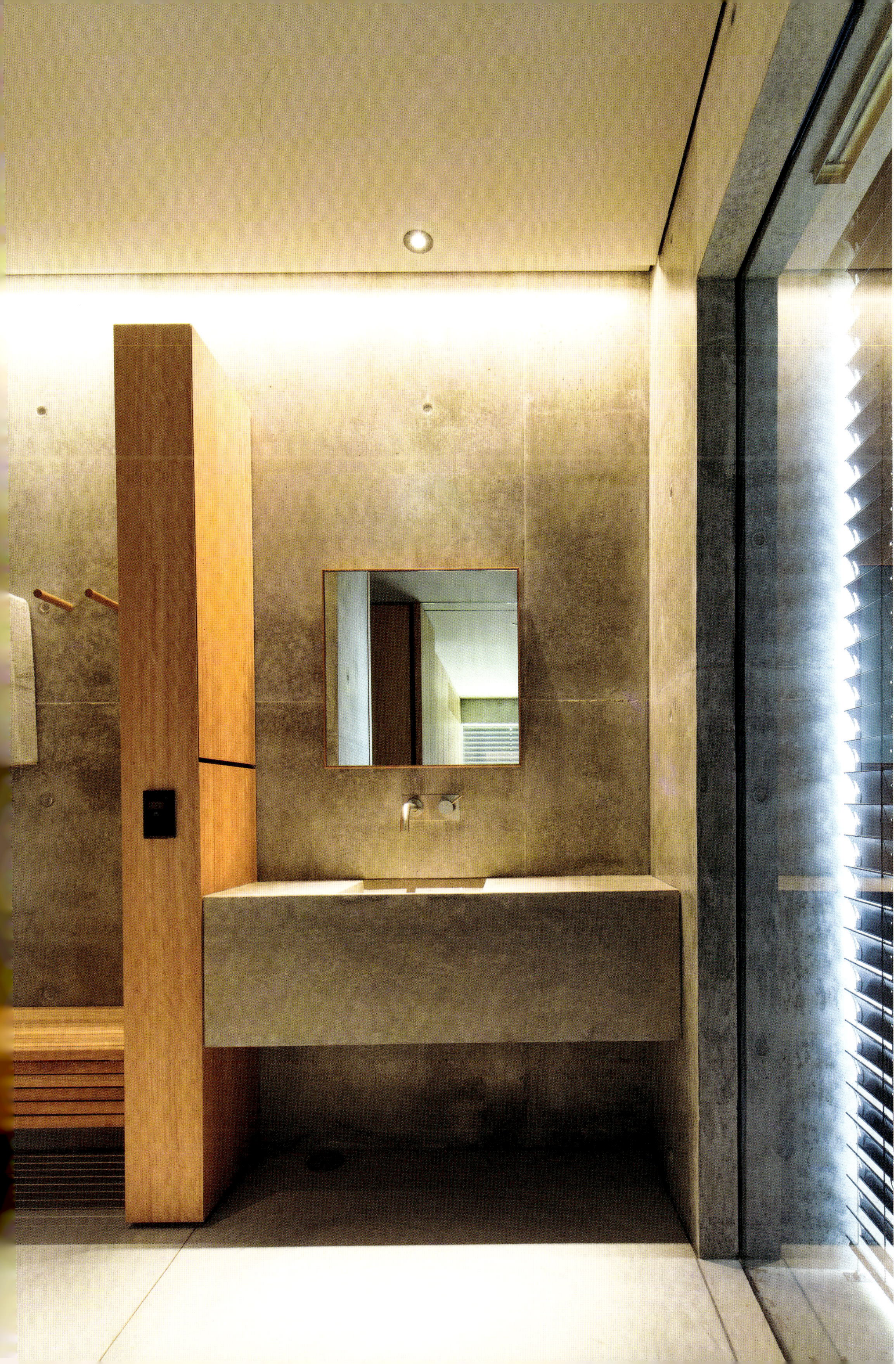

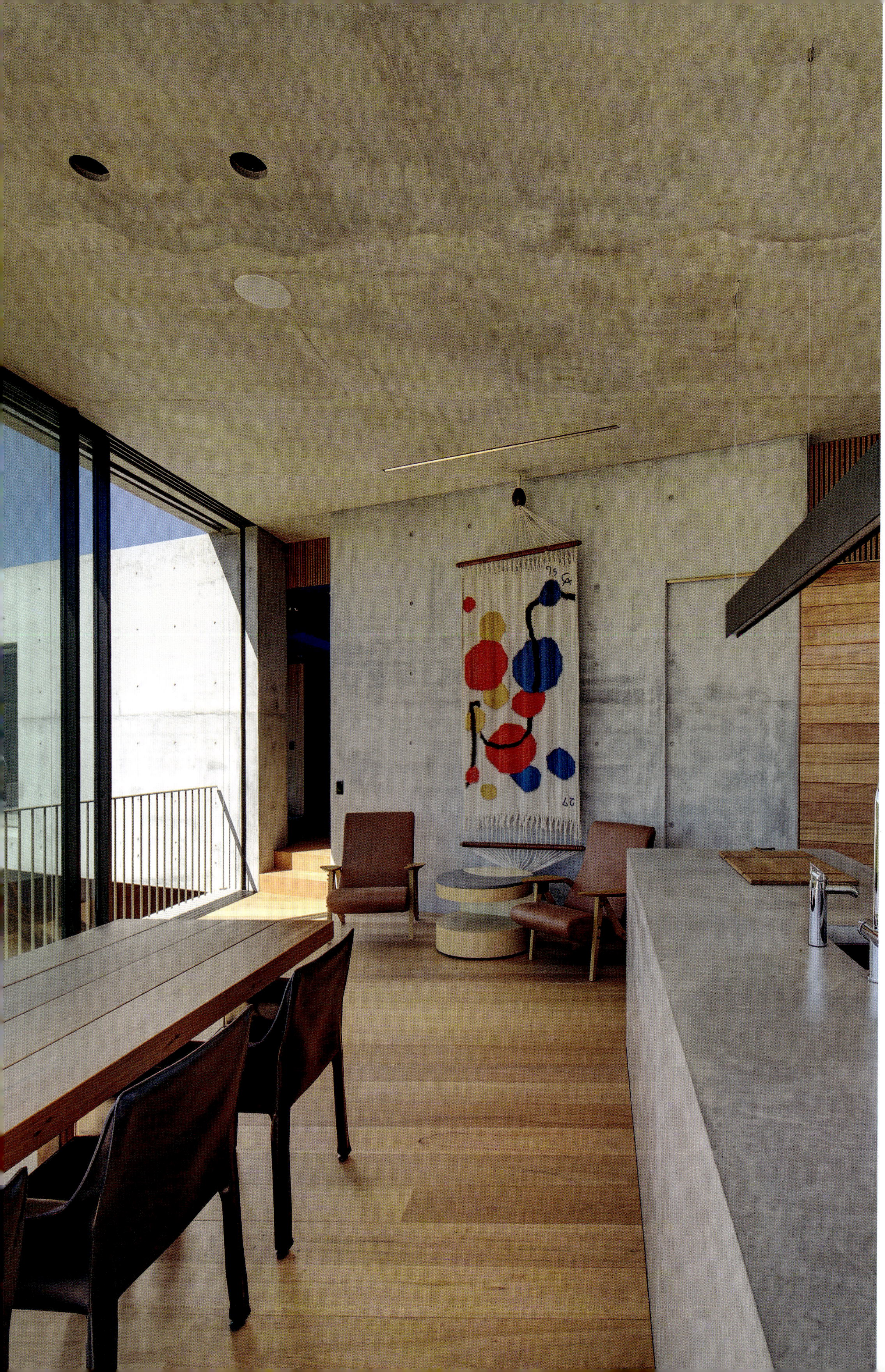

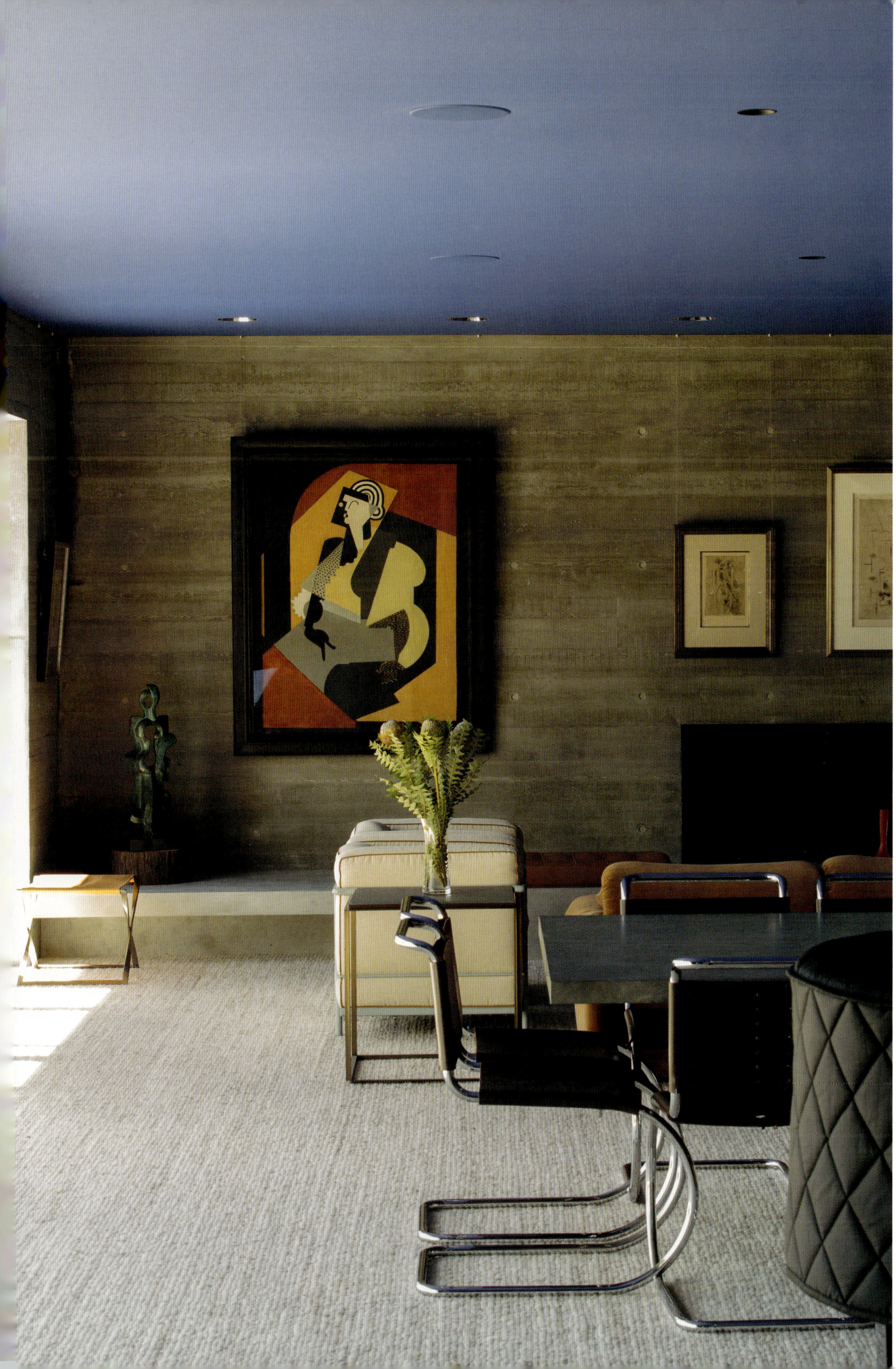

Photographs: Åke E:son Lindman

210

SUMMERHOUSE

SUMMERHOUSE
LAGNÖ, SWEDEN, 2012
THAM & VIDEGÅRD ARKITEKTER

For many years now, Swedish architects Bolle Tham and Martin Videgård have sought to redefine traditional Swedish building typologies by stripping them to their core; which is precisely what they have done here with this summer vacation house in Lagnö, on the northern shore of the island of Värmdö, looking out across the Stockholm archipelago.

The house stands on bedrock of granite, between forest and sea, flanked on all sides by large stands of spruce, pine and birch trees. In a departure from the typical rustic timber houses and boat sheds found along this part of the Swedish coast, the architects chose to explore a different sensibility.

'We wanted to search for a way to design the house as an integral part of the landscape, in which the weight and colour of the materials could be seen to rise from the archipelago's natural granite bedrock,' Tham says.

In a contrast-filled reinterpretation of classic Swedish coastal cabins, they placed a linear multi-gabled building containing a main house and guesthouse facing the sea, the two connected by a glazed single-gabled pavilion, which serves as open shelter, entry sequence and a clear divider between the two dwellings.

While the house's multi-gabled roof line might appear familiar and intelligible at a distance, closer inspection reveals a new typology altogether: instead of the typical wooden structure you'd expect, the house is in fact constructed of in situ concrete. It was a first for the pair, who saw it as a challenge, given the Scandinavian climate.

The house is divided into two volumes set side by side as a rectilinear bar on the landscape, where the forest opens out into the bay. Approached from the north, the entrance presents itself as an opening between the larger and smaller volumes, drawing the visitor towards light and water. From the south, facing the sea, the house reads as a series of roofs of varying heights, pleated and folded as a silhouette against its backdrop of forest and sky.

From a distance the gables could easily be mistaken for a row of boathouses lining the edge of the coast. The pleated profile of the roofs is reflected inside the main house with a series of pitched ceilings of varying heights that help establish living and dining areas without the need for intrusive dividing walls. 'The roofs are the key architectural feature that hold together the character of both interior and exterior space,' Tham says. 'In contrast to the typical timber boat house, the concrete, which was cast in situ against plywood boards, adds a soft grain and worn quality to the exposed surfaces.'

Where the south is open to sunshine and views – it opens onto a terrace and pool with a series of large sliding glazed doors – the northern facade, facing the forest inland, reads as a near-impenetrable wall of folded concrete panels, save for a solitary square window inserted into one of the gabled facades. This side of the house contains cell-sized bedrooms, which are largely lit by operable skylights inserted into the folds of the roof line. The lack of windows here draws the eye to the entry space beneath the glazed gable. Sliding panels of ash wood separate the sleeping quarters from the living zones.

As you move through to the large living area running the length of the main house, the archipelago, the sea and the spectacular landscape effectively explode before you through the large glazed openings facing south. Martin Videgård has described the movement through the house as 'a sequence of layers gradually opening towards the archipelago and the sun'. The guesthouse comprises a living zone and loft bedroom. Floors throughout are of polished concrete, counterpointed by white walls and fittings of ash wood. A detached sauna block, also of in situ concrete, is located close to the beach and pier. This is a deceptively simple house, finely tuned and crisply detailed to appear as if to grow from the natural bedrock on which it stands.

South facade

0 10m

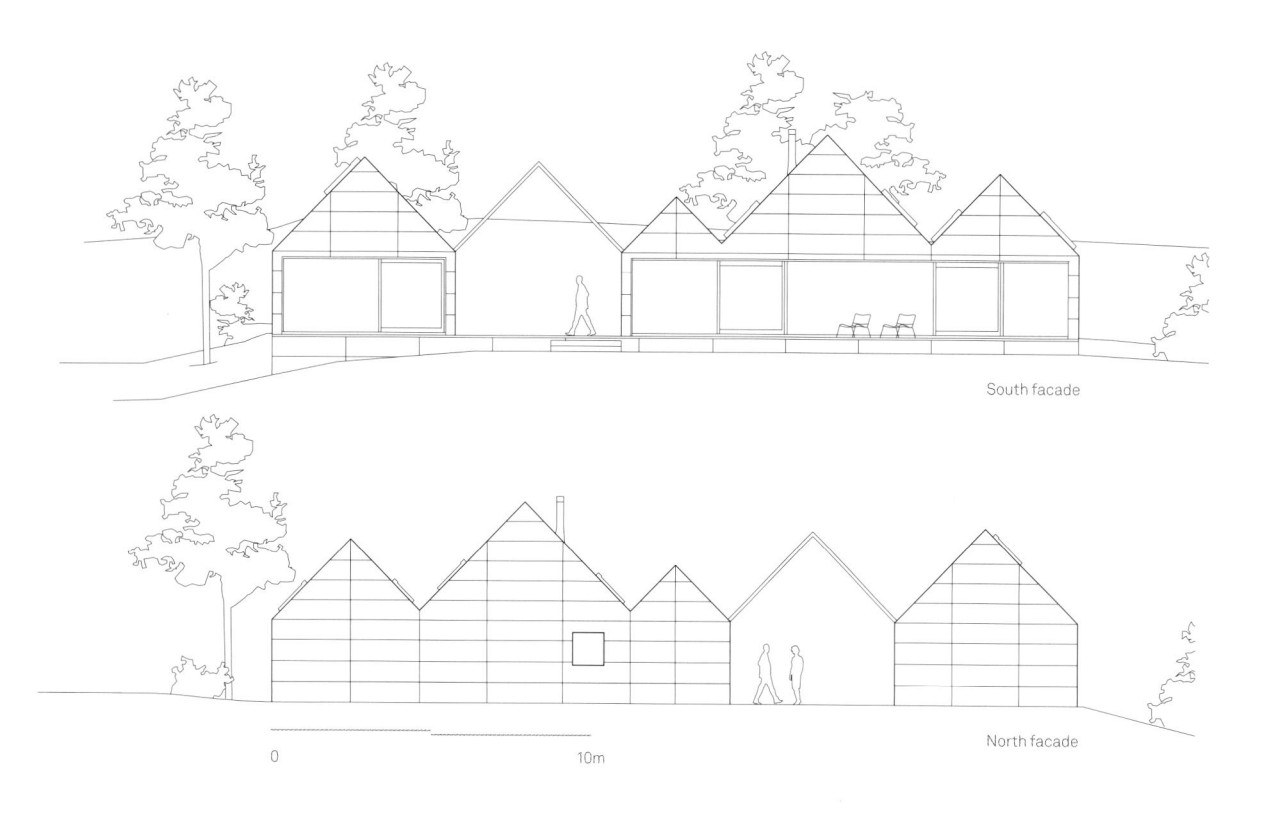

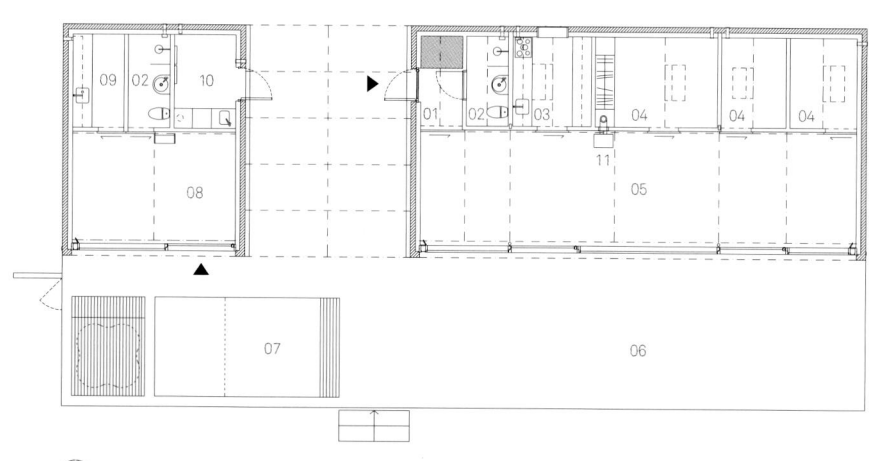

North facade

Cross-section a

Cross-section b

Floor plan

01 Entrance
02 WC/shower
03 Kitchen
04 Bedroom
05 Family/dining
06 Terrace
07 Pool
08 Guest studio
09 Pantry
10 Laundry/equipment room
11 Wood stove

0 10m

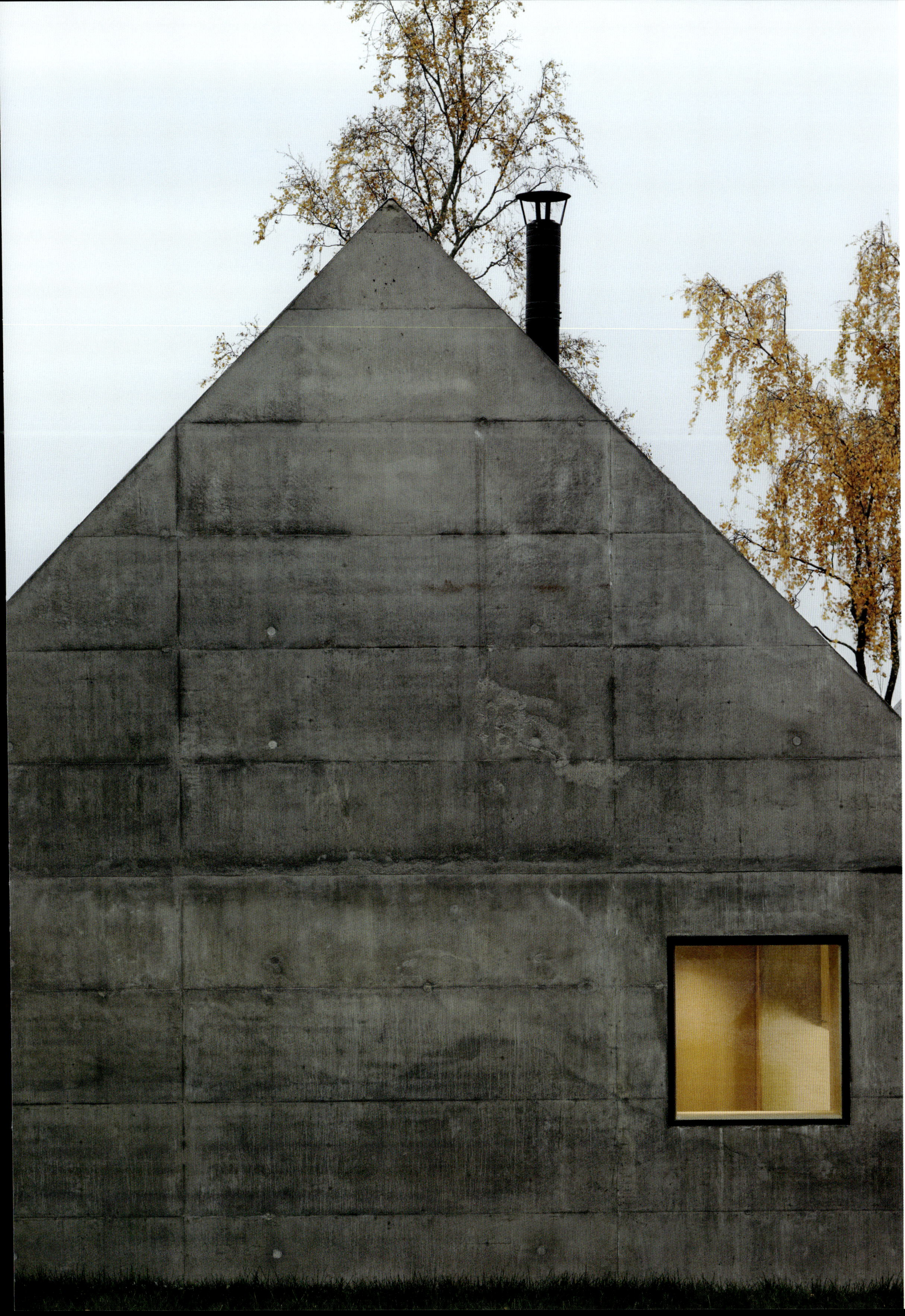

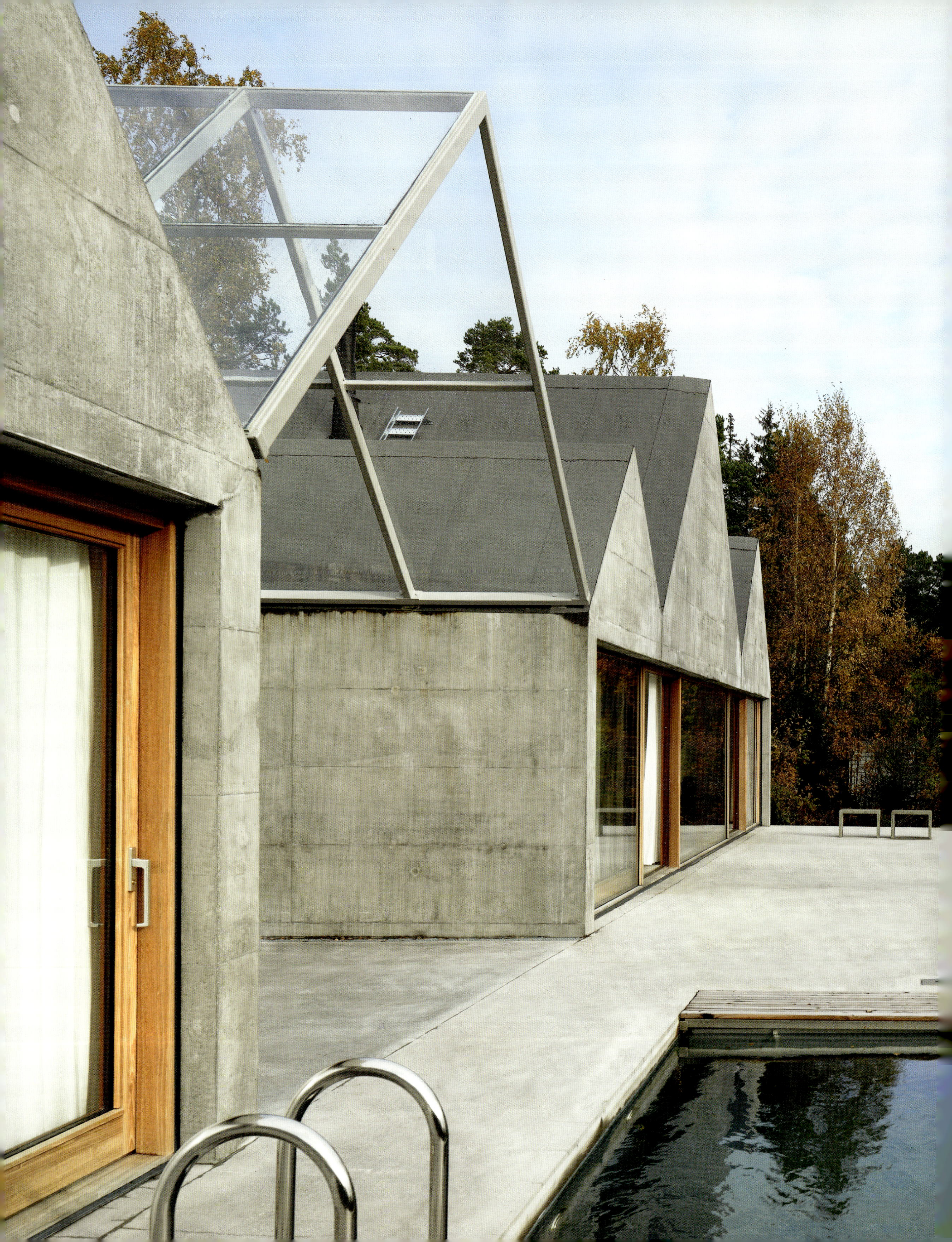

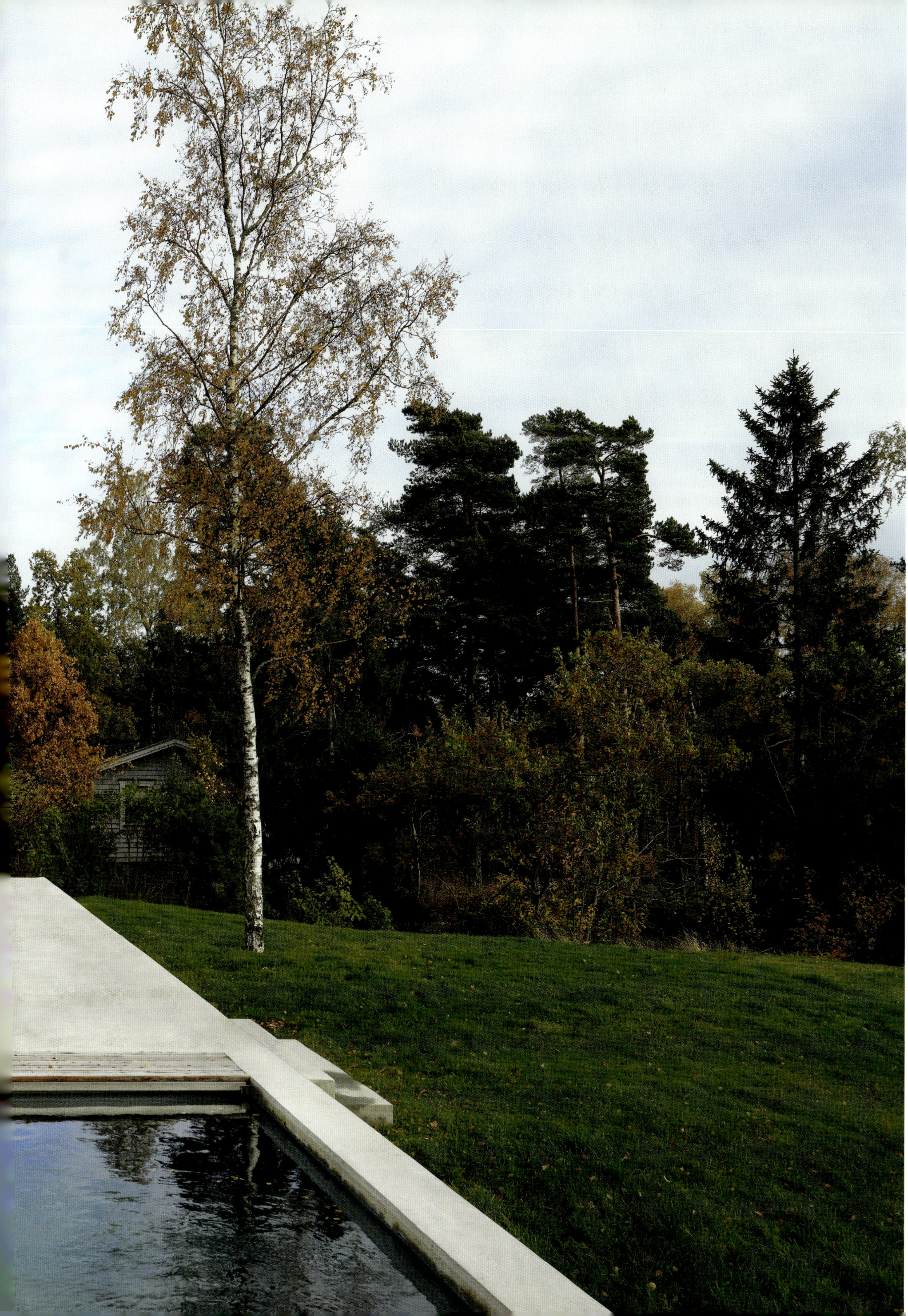

The setting is the Stockholm archipelago, with natural ground sloping gently down to the sea in the south, mostly open with a few trees and bushes. Unlike other projects we have worked on, located on more isolated islands in the archipelago without car access from the mainland, this site was relatively easy to reach, even for heavy transport vehicles. This, together with our client's desire for a maintenance-free house, inspired us to search for a way to design the house as an integral part of nature, where the concrete's weight and colour could connect with the archipelago's granite bedrock. *Bolle Tham and Martin Videgård*

A deceptively simple house, finely tuned and crisply detailed to appear as if to grow from the natural bedrock on which it stands...the concrete, cast in situ against plywood boards, adds a soft grain and worn quality to the exposed surfaces.

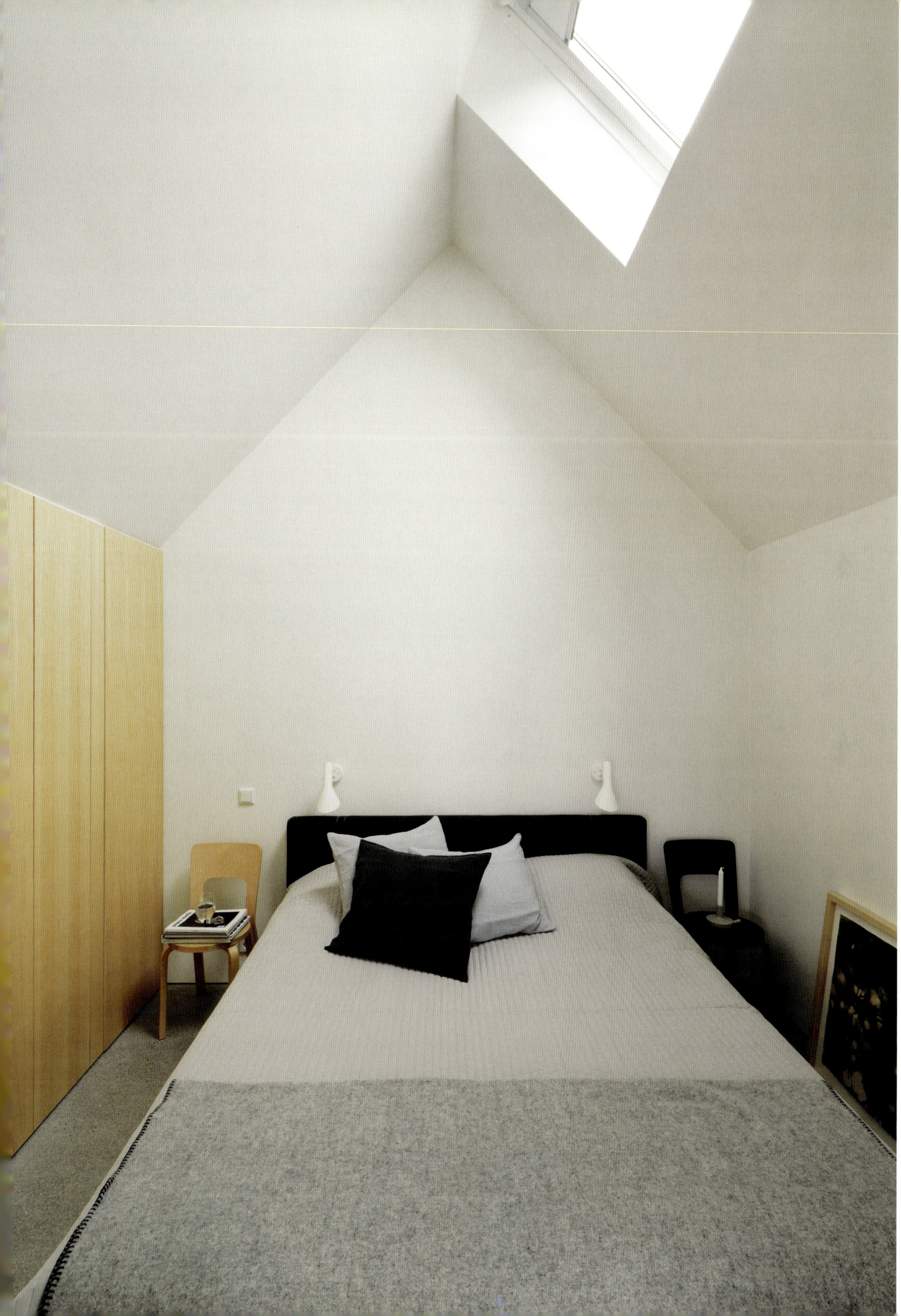

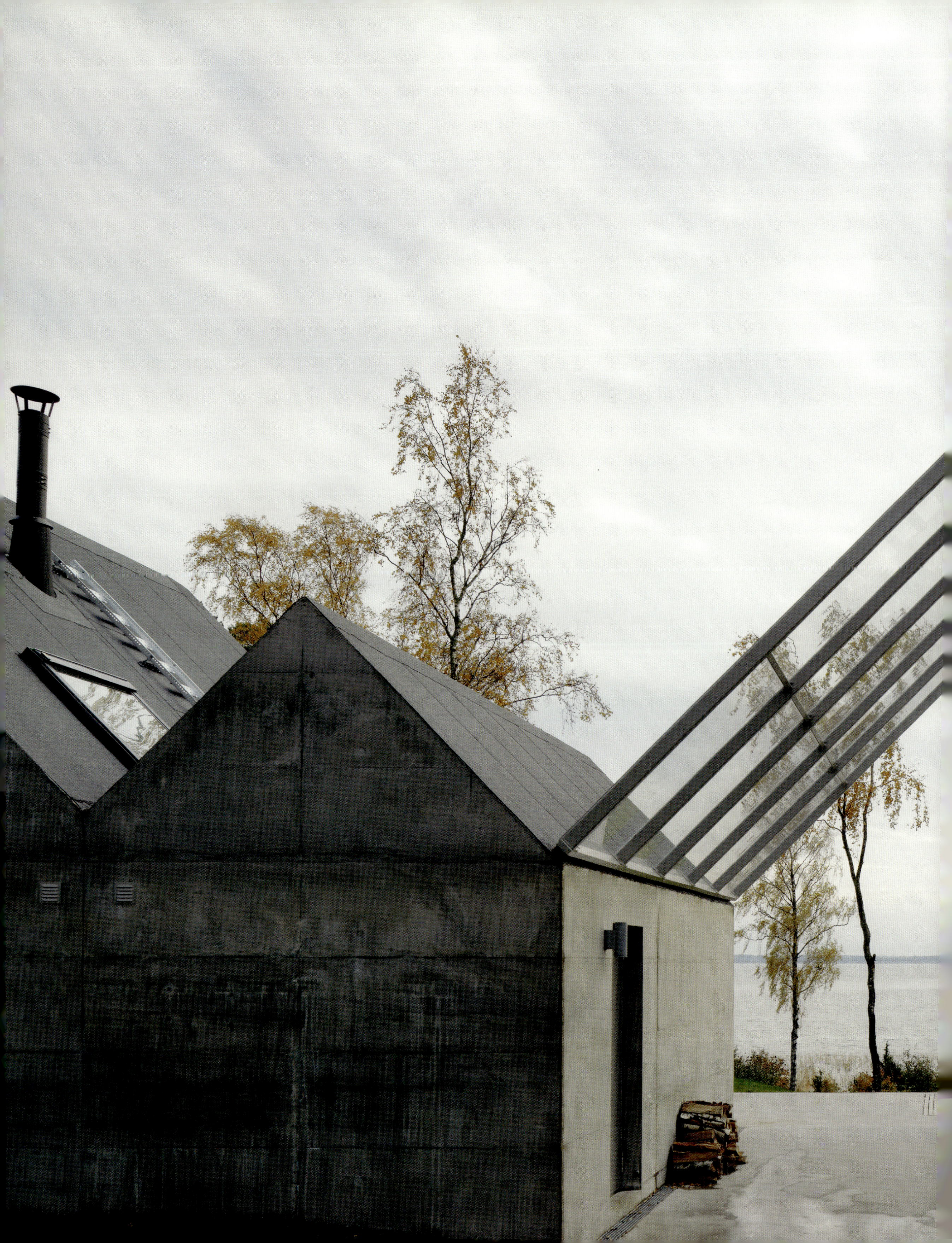

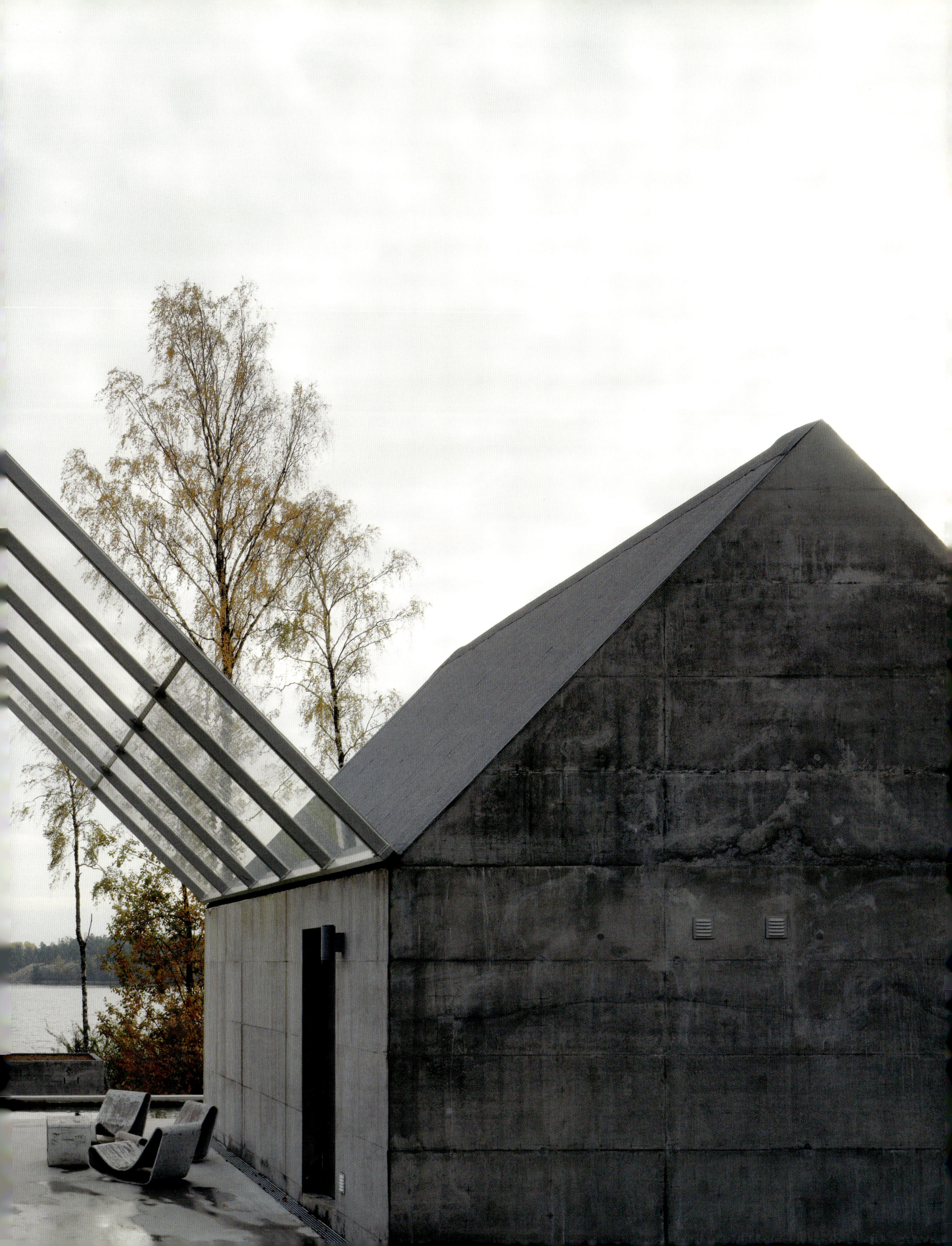

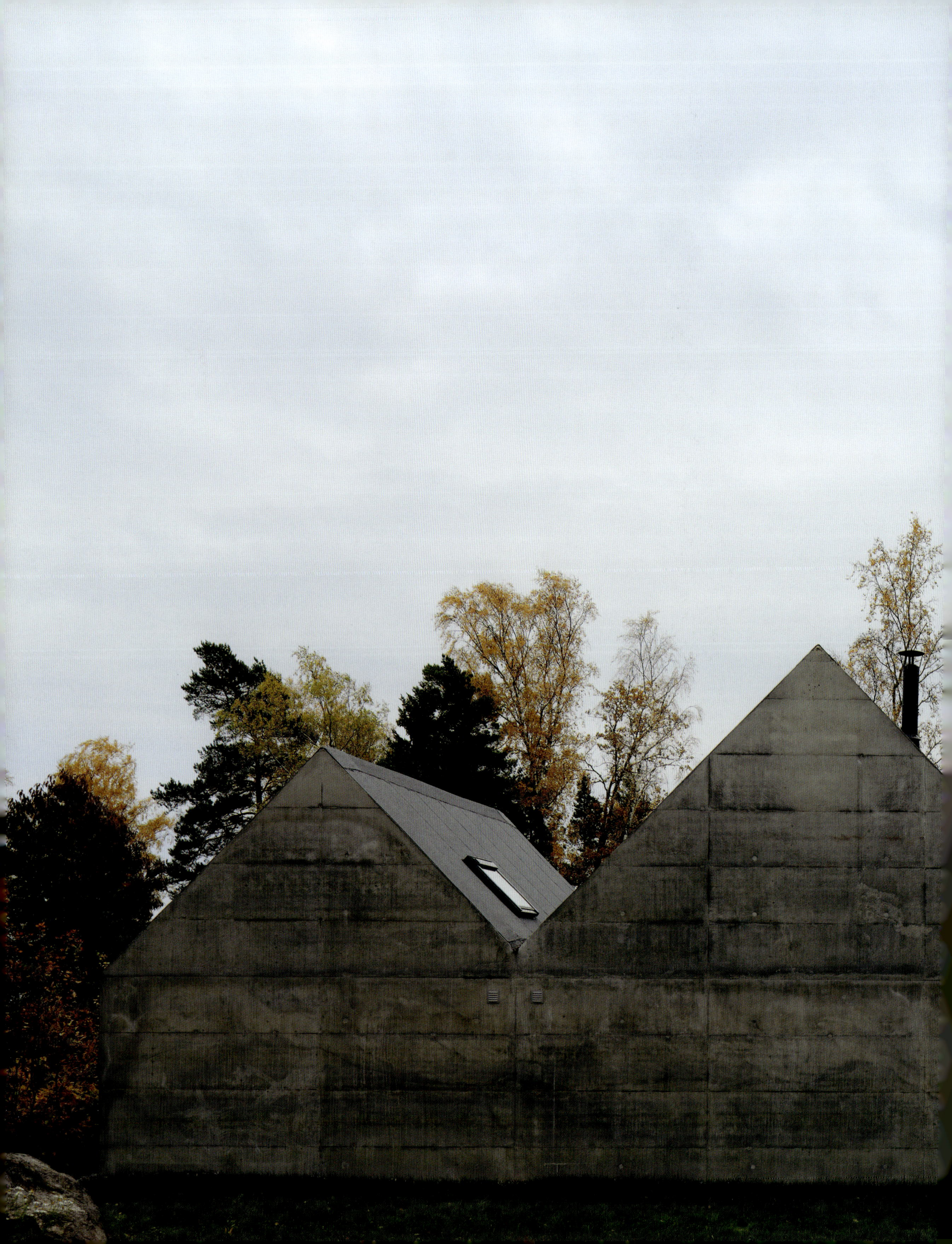

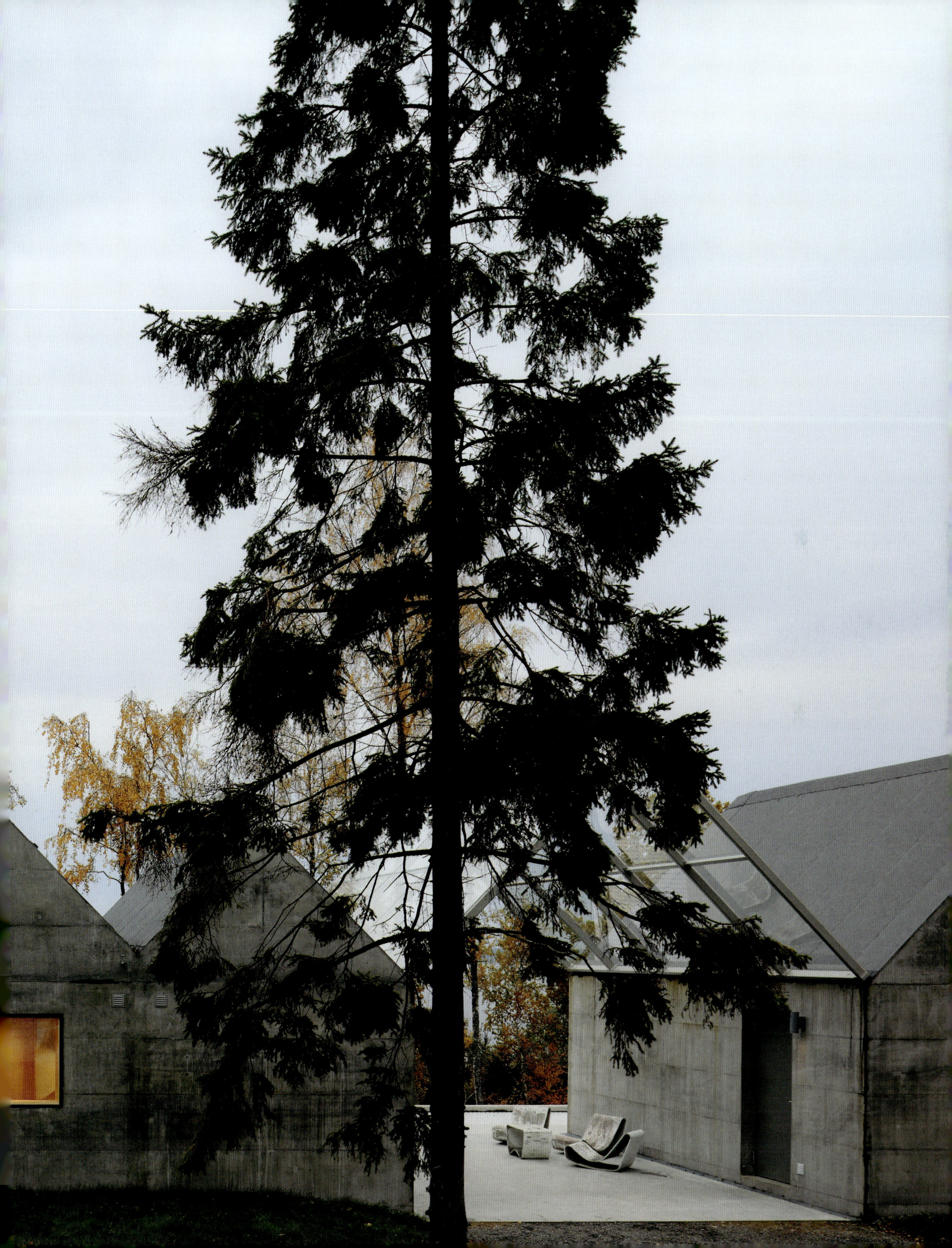

224

Photographs: John Gollings

ELWOOD HOUSE

ELWOOD HOUSE
MELBOURNE, AUSTRALIA, 2017
ARM ARCHITECTURE

Houses are more than mere shelter; more than ways to temper heat and cold, keep out wind and rain. At their best, they are art. Art that at once expresses the spirit of a particular time and transcends it. This house, in bayside Melbourne, has no physical street presence. It hides behind a steel screen, as a continuation of a bold two-storey, red steel facade for a speculative townhouse development along a streetscape of sedate, post–World War I homes and flats.

When you consider that it comes from ARM Architecture, perhaps Melbourne's most unconventional architectural office, it is hardly surprising. ARM's stock-in-trade is to keep the observer destabilised and engaged. Constantly. And so it is here at Elwood by Port Phillip Bay.

Made almost entirely of silky white concrete and glass, the house appears as a mix of several types of architecture. The most obvious seems a deliberate reference to the Underground Car Park at the University of Melbourne, with its hyperbolic concrete shells raised on a forest of mushroom-shaped piers. There are echoes, too, of Spanish architect Josep Lluis Sert's urban courtyard houses in Spain and of his own house at Cambridge in Massachusetts. Touches of the Moorish gardens at the Alhambra, in Spain, of brightly coloured tiles, water features and shade plants, can be seen in the main walled courtyard, as well as in the long entry sequence from the street. And, in a nod to its beachside location, a cluster of bright-red painted plywood 'beach boxes' – a tiny village, if you will – appears to have been dropped onto its roof.

Architect Ian McDougall says ideas for the house originated while working on ARM's redevelopment of Melbourne's Shrine of Remembrance. 'That project juxtaposed the tomb-like monument in parklands from the 1920s with new subterranean galleries. This underworld was created by excavation and gaining access to vaults made by massive brick foundation piers that support the neoclassical memorial. It was here that the sense of an archaic but fundamental architectural experience was reawakened. The striking spatial experience, that of being in a vault, has a profound "underneath-ness" and containment, a sense of habitation that is deep and innate. This experience has been lost under the conventions of modernism, of minimalism and continuous space. This house tries to connect Gottfried Semper's hearth/mound and August Schmarsow's corporeal space, to capture a profound spatial type through material and mass.'

The house is on two levels: the ground floor accommodates living, a main bedroom suite and a ceramics studio; the upper floor provides two bedrooms, a bathroom and an open study at the top of the stair. The two levels are contradictory: concrete and open plan at ground, timber and attic-like on the first floor. At ground, the sense is one of inhabiting a concrete bunker or vault, the mass of the deep concrete walls sliced through and glazed to north and east, to look out onto the tessellated Moorish courtyard with its star-shaped planter of glazed bricks, a bubbling, red-tiled water feature and lush plantings. Climb upstairs and you get the feeling of stepping into a loft – flimsy, low-ceilinged and richly wallpapered, more akin to climbing into a roof space.

The ground floor is dramatic and evocative, a cavernous vaulted space intersected by a small forest of flared concrete piers – twelve in total – each cast in specially made fibreglass forms, their finished texture almost impossibly smooth, defying the temptation to reach out and stroke them. There is no sense of formal structure here, rather the feeling of being inside one continuous space encompassing living, dining and a kitchen tucked in under the stair, flowing into an open bedroom made private by an undulating, sheer fabric curtain on a metal track, leading to the ceramics studio.

The dance of concrete pillars appears random, however, each pillar has been carefully positioned under picturesque rules, articulating and subdividing the space rather than gridding it. They have been placed both to take structural loads and to draw the eye unimpeded towards the courtyard just beyond the walls of glass and to a more formal garden area to one side. The resultant space is open and expansive, but not empty; the columns, a seemingly scattered presence. 'The attempt was to produce a house that is simultaneously primal and elaborate; to some extent a decorated cave-house,' McDougall says.

Entry from the street is behind a red steel screen, along a narrow black-and-white zigzag tiled courtyard with two flared 'trees' of reinforcing steel, similar to those used in the concrete piers, to carry climbing plants, and a water feature leading to a bronze door and a small vestibule beyond. The client's eclectic collection of art is displayed to great and interesting effect on one wall of the house.

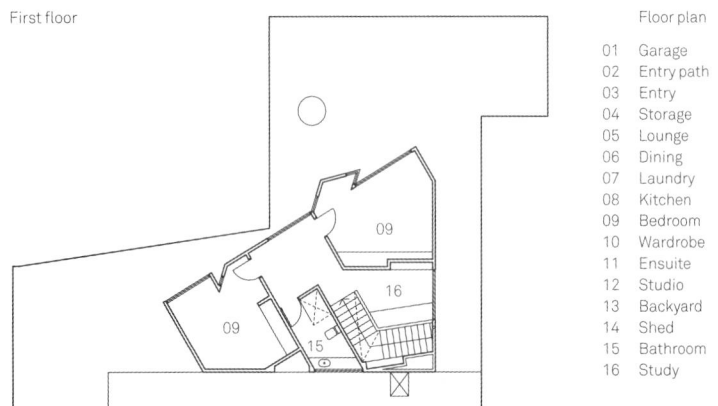

East elevation

North elevation

0   4m

First floor

Ground floor

Floor plan

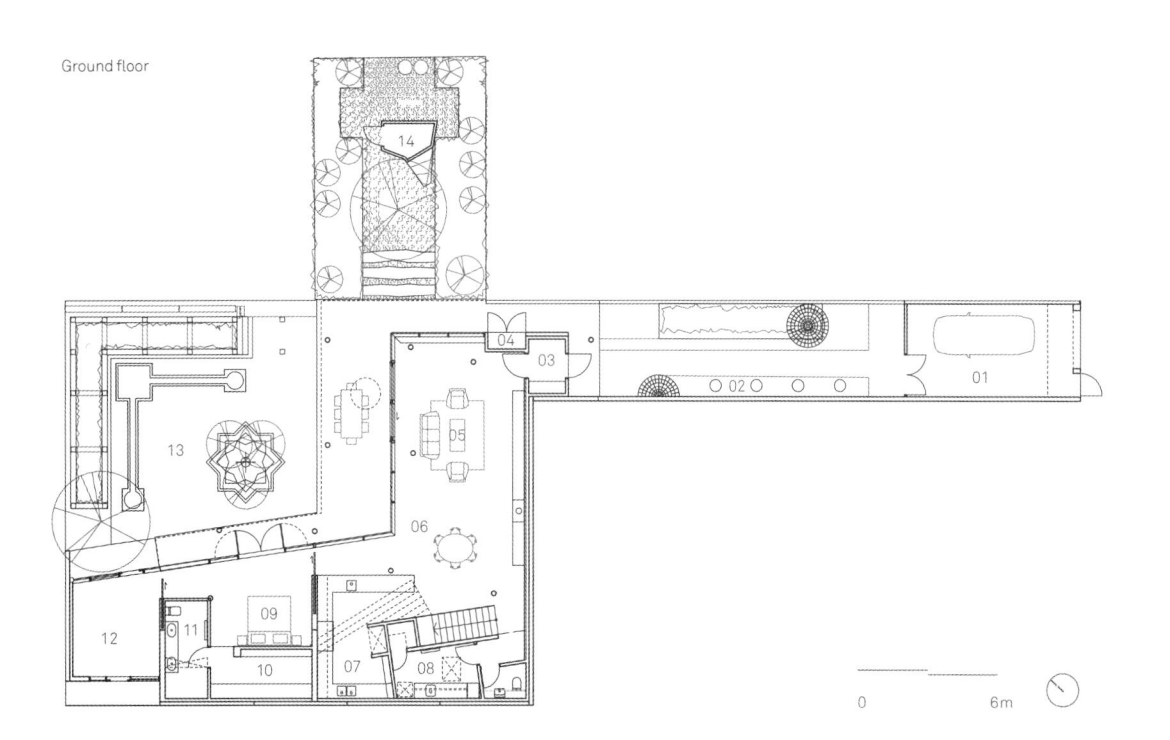

01 Garage
02 Entry path
03 Entry
04 Storage
05 Lounge
06 Dining
07 Laundry
08 Kitchen
09 Bedroom
10 Wardrobe
11 Ensuite
12 Studio
13 Backyard
14 Shed
15 Bathroom
16 Study

0   6m

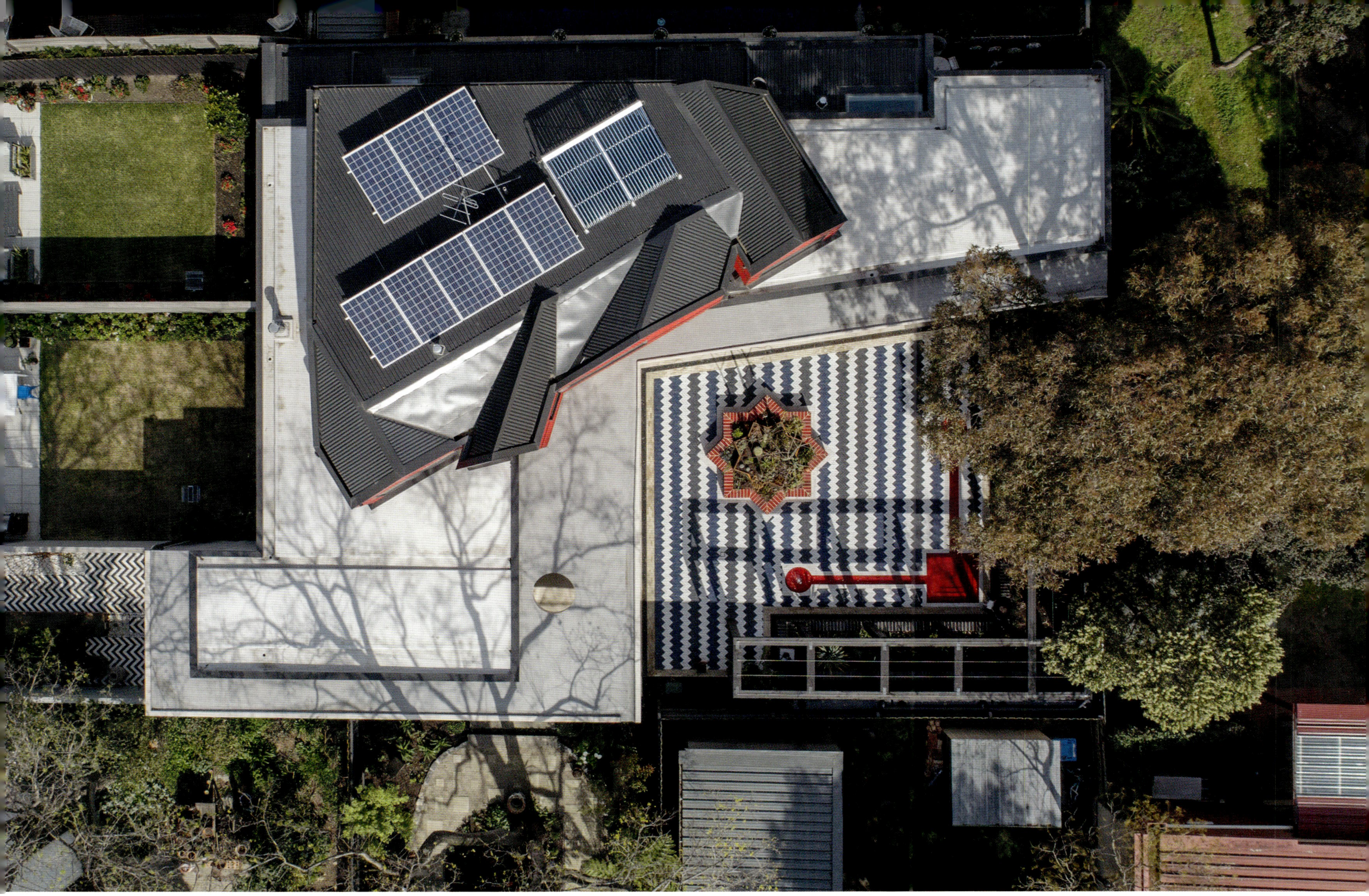

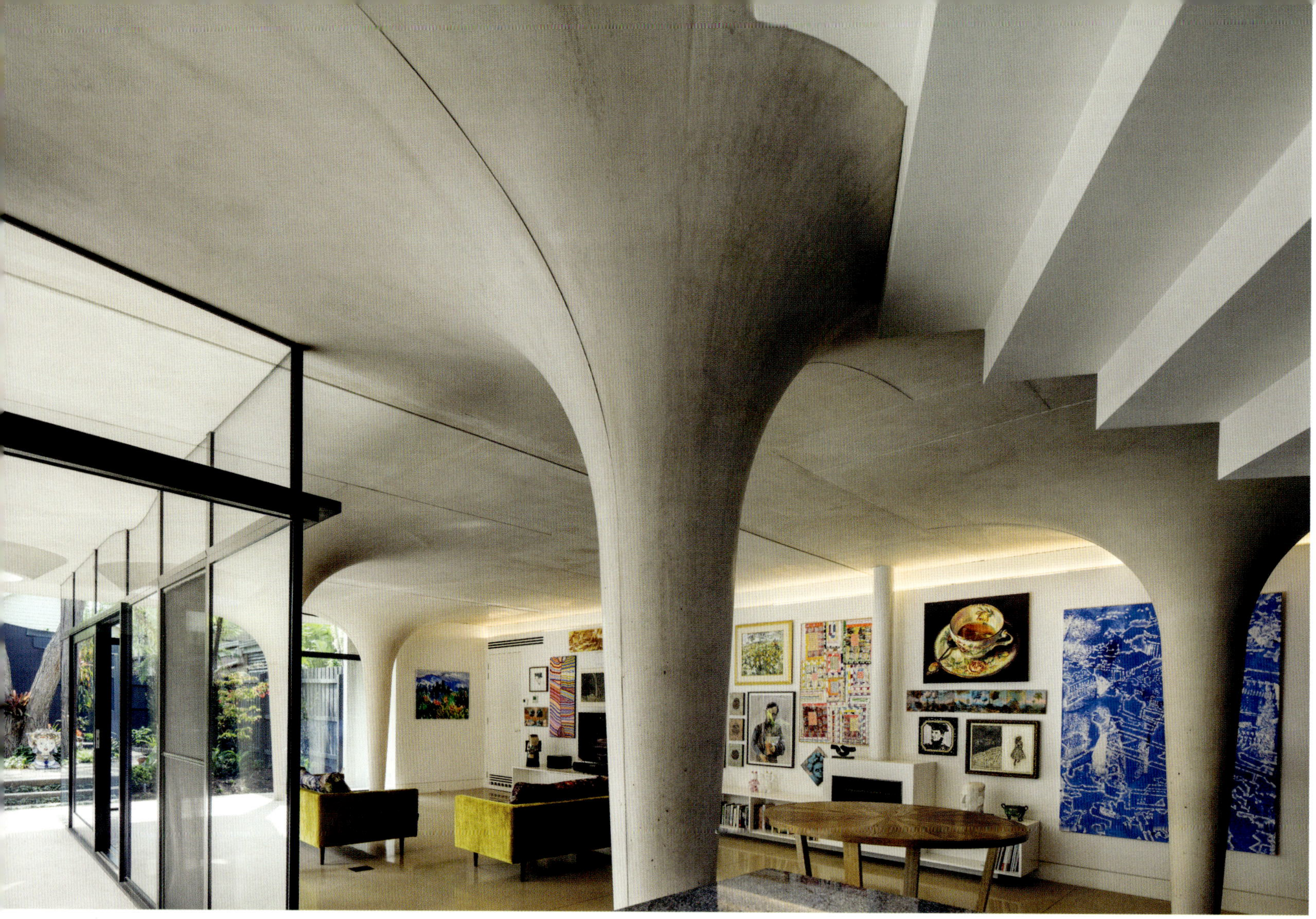

The modernist understands that such continuity of space, such flow, such notion of space as a field, was core to the condition of modernity: freedom, equality, rationality, even alienation. There is a convention that modernism 'discovered space'. But in fact, it is conceivable that modernism erased space. *Ian McDougall*

A cavernous vaulted space raised on a small forest of flared silky white concrete piers, each cast in fibreglass forms, each carefully positioned both to take structural loads and to draw the eye unimpeded toward the courtyard…the sense is one of inhabiting a concrete bunker.

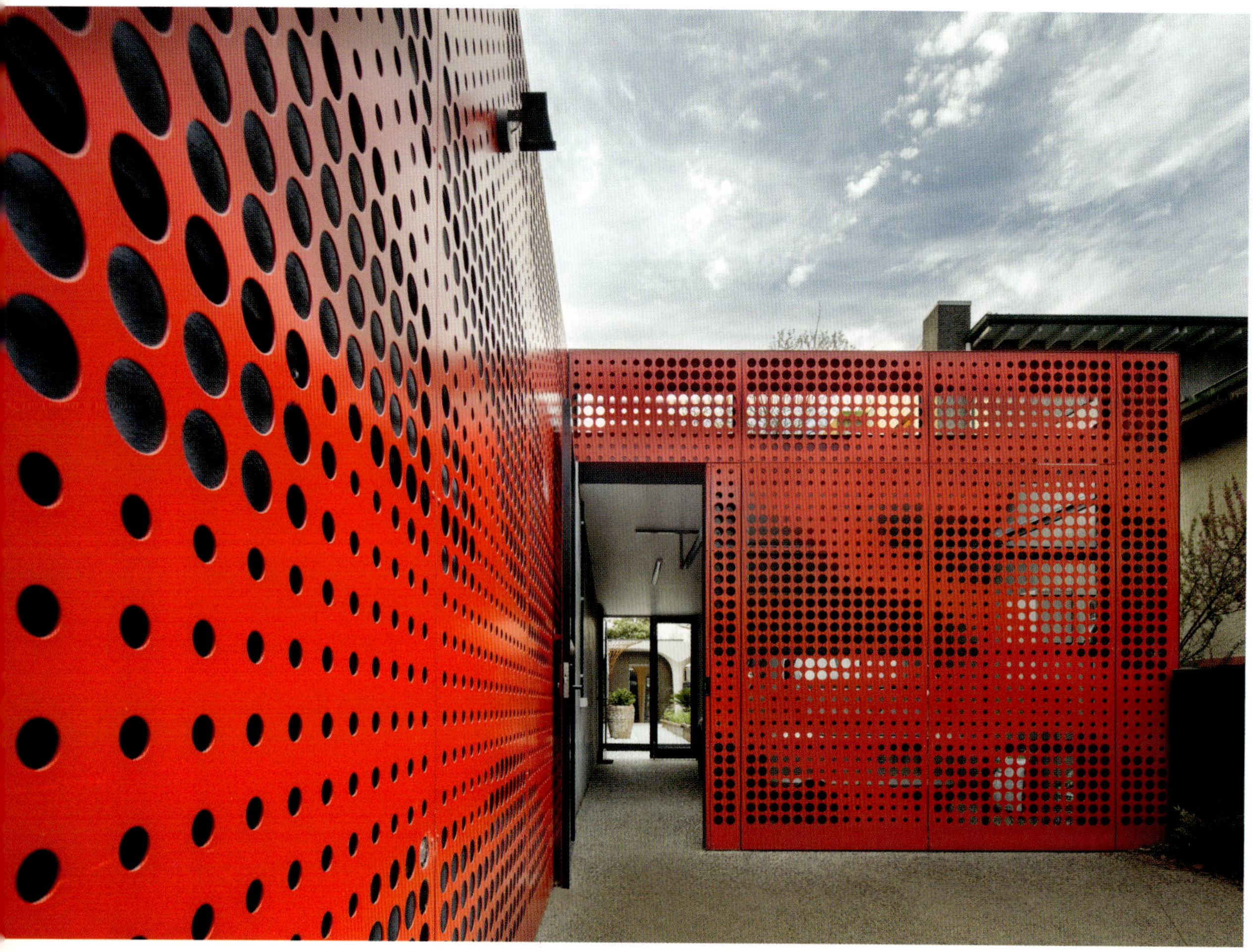

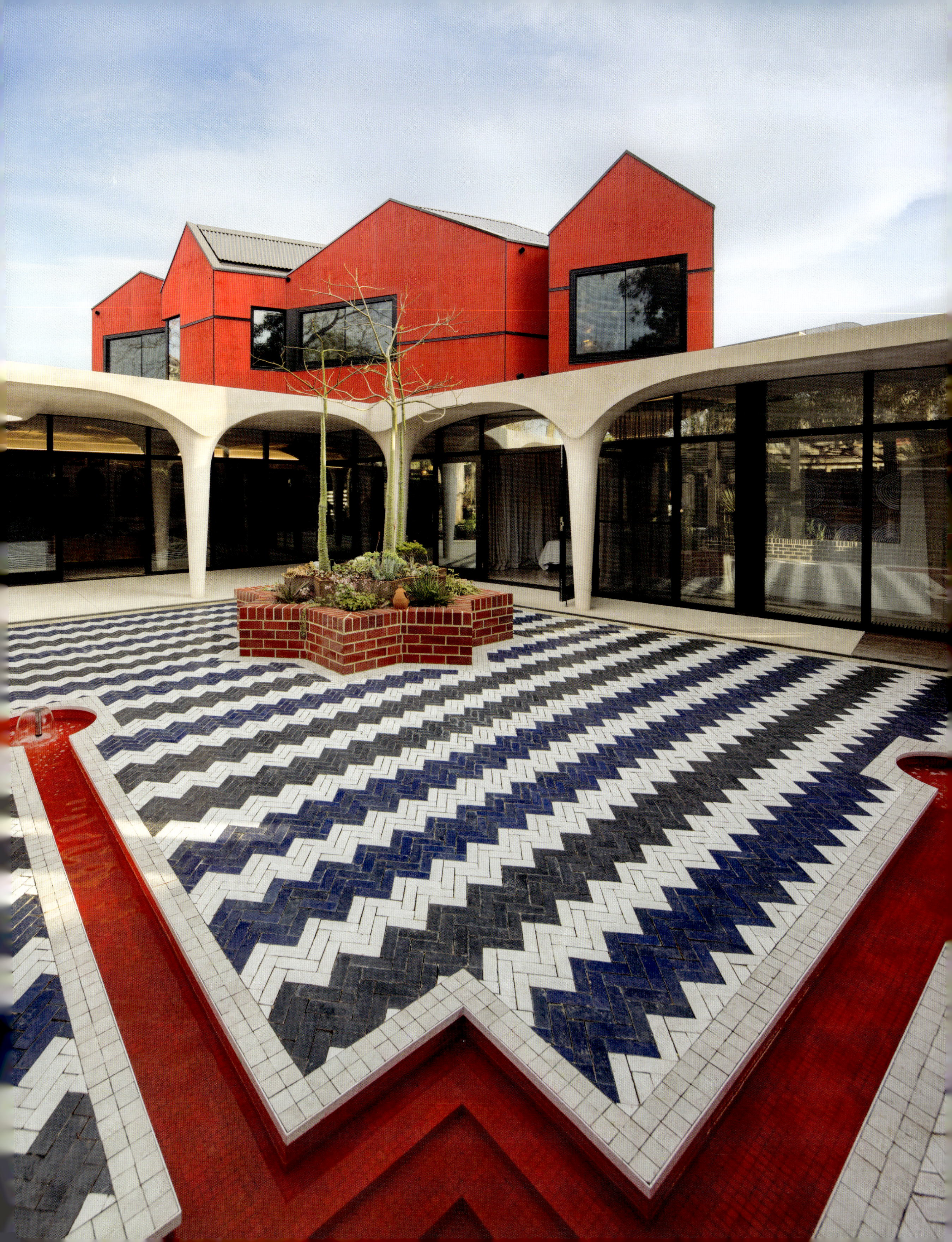

234

SMALL HOUSE

SMALL HOUSE
SYDNEY, AUSTRALIA, 2010
DOMENIC ALVARO ARCHITECT

This house in Surry Hills, Sydney, takes its cue from the small houses crammed into miniscule sites in cities such as Tokyo and Kyoto. In particular, it is inspired by Japanese architect Waro Kishi's House in Nipponbashi, Osaka (1990–92), on a site just 2.5 metres wide, which rises three levels to a dining room and open-air terrace. In Sydney, Domenic Alvaro has also designed a vertical house that climbs to a rooftop garden. Only here the site is a 7-metre x 6-metre near-square patch, barely big enough to park two cars, on the corner of a little back street at the edge of the city's CBD.

Where Kishi's sliver is a house of steel and glass, Alvaro's is a four-storey tower of pre-cast concrete that explores ideas for single-dwelling living on almost impossibly small sites formerly occupied by tiny workers' cottages or leftover micro sites deemed too small to build on. For Alvaro, a design principal at Woods Bagot Architects in Sydney, his determination to live in the inner city became an investigation into how to design and build decent architecture for the kind of money that wouldn't buy a poky two-bedroom apartment on the edge of cities like Sydney and Melbourne. Small House was completed for A$650,000, including all associated council fees and road closure costs due to restricted crane access. 'It was in part a reaction to over-inflated costs of apartments in the Sydney inner city, and in part necessity, because it was my budget!' Alvaro says.

It became, too, an exploration into the use of precast concrete 'to achieve a result which erases the sense of individual panels...to make the building feel monolithic'. The outcome is impressive architecture. The presence of the house hits the observer like a breath of fresh air amid the grunge of cottages and light-industrial buildings that surround it. Small House rises as if squeezed up and out of the ground: four levels – five if you include the rooftop garden – of minimalist design that dazzles the moment you step on the cantilevered stairs that carry you three flights up and through the house.

The zoning is clear enough: parking, utility and store on the ground; sleeping and bathing on level one; living or more sleeping on level two; and kitchen, dining and living on level three; all topped by a densely planted roof garden. Light is drawn into the house through large windows facing the street. And as you climb, the views get bigger and better: first you look directly onto the cottages opposite, then over rooftops, and finally across the treetops of Hyde Park and the Sydney skyline. Finishes are spare, with white-painted concrete walls, black stone floors, oak cabinetry and glass-screen walls. There is no overhead lighting save for lighting of art works. Otherwise, all lighting is provided by freestanding lights, chosen to double as sculptural elements. The stair void rising up one side of the house acts as a funnel, drawing air through each level of the house.

The trick in the successful cost management of the project was all in meticulous planning. The restricted nature of the site led Alvaro to consider prefabrication as the preferred method of construction. 'One of the key issues with conventional building on such a small site is the cost of the builder's preliminaries,' Alvaro says. 'Scaffolding was prohibitive, so we looked to using high-quality prefabricated concrete panels to reduce costs, even though road closure costs amounted to over A$3,000 a day.'

The precast panels, each 7 metres x 3.4 metres with a step joint, were stacked and erected in four days and the entire structure was built and completed in three weeks, including footings, floor plates, underpinning of neighbouring properties, installation of windows and the roof. All the panels were manufactured locally, using existing moulds at the precaster's plant. The concrete mix included recycled materials like slag and fly ash. Off-white cement was used to lighten the appearance of the finished panels.

Speculating about his design for the Nipponbashi house, Kishi cited Le Corbusier's Beistegui House in Paris, facing the Champs Elysées, which was planned to be topped by a penthouse 'which puts the observer at the same height as the Arc de Triomphe. At the same time, however, the observer finds himself in an elevated outdoor space that appears to be at ground level. In other words, the building creates in the observer both the sensation of a privileged view and a unique feeling of being afloat. That, I think, is the precious quality that was made possible by the modern concept of space, or more specifically the roof garden.' In the Small House, Alvaro has achieved a similar feat.

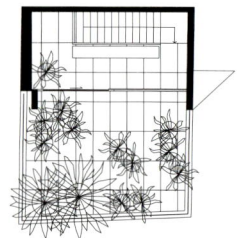

Roof terrace

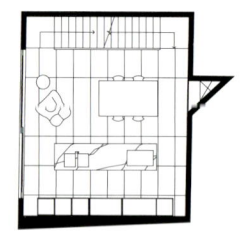

Kitchen

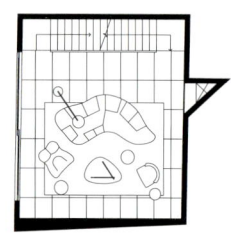

Living

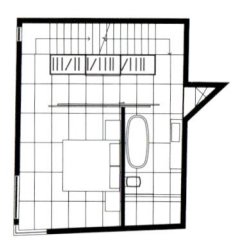

Bedroom/bathroom

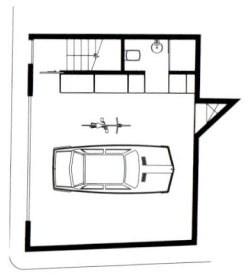

Garage

Section
South elevation
West elevation

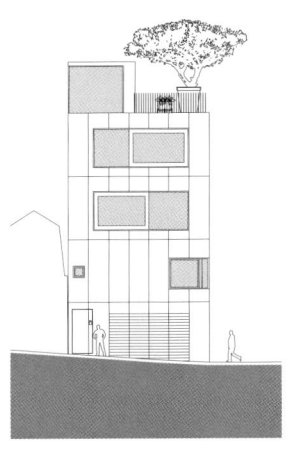

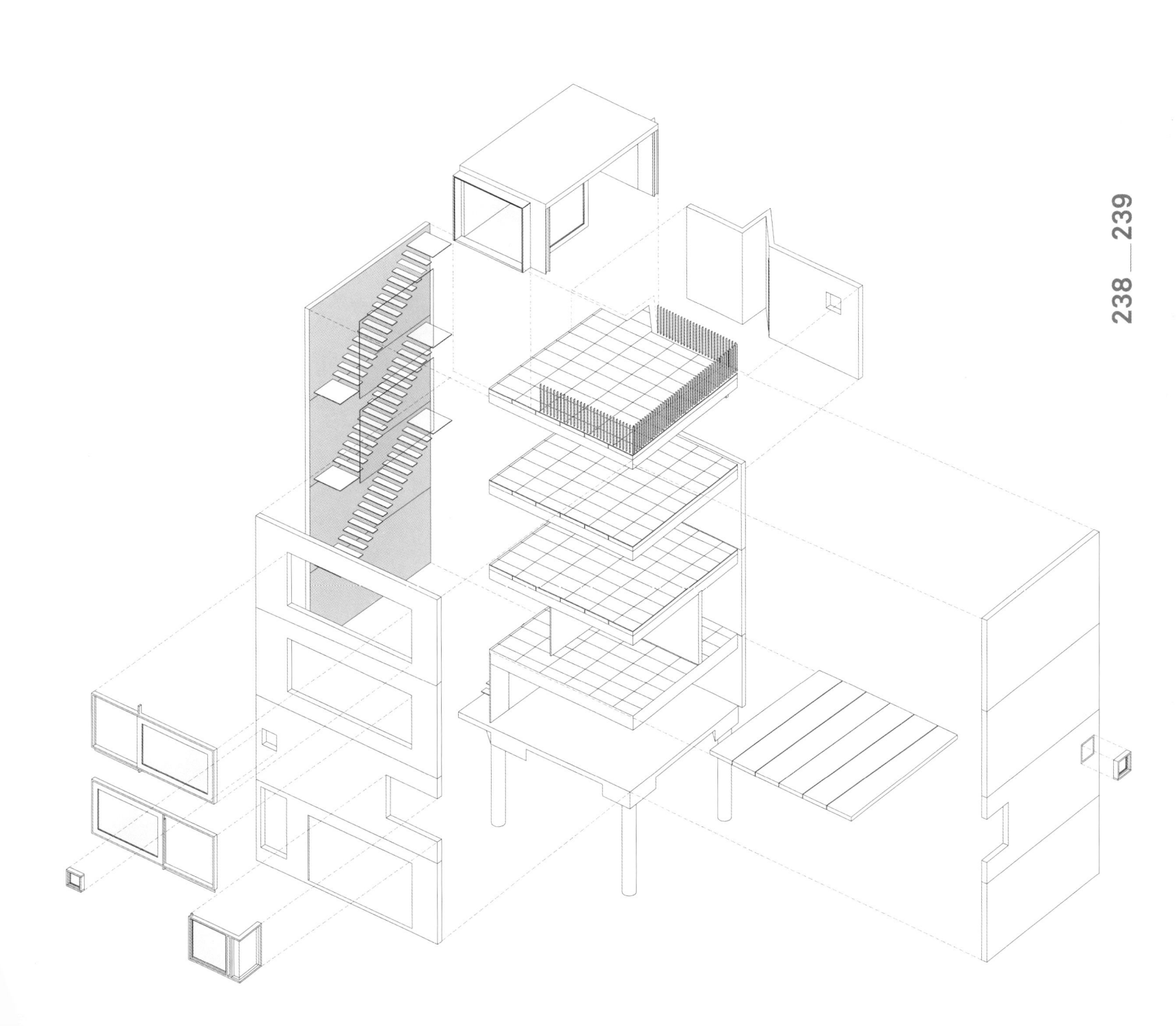

01 Garage
02 Bedroom
03 Bathroom
04 Living
05 Kitchen
06 Roof terrace

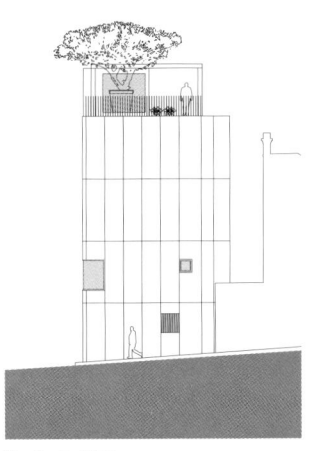

238_239

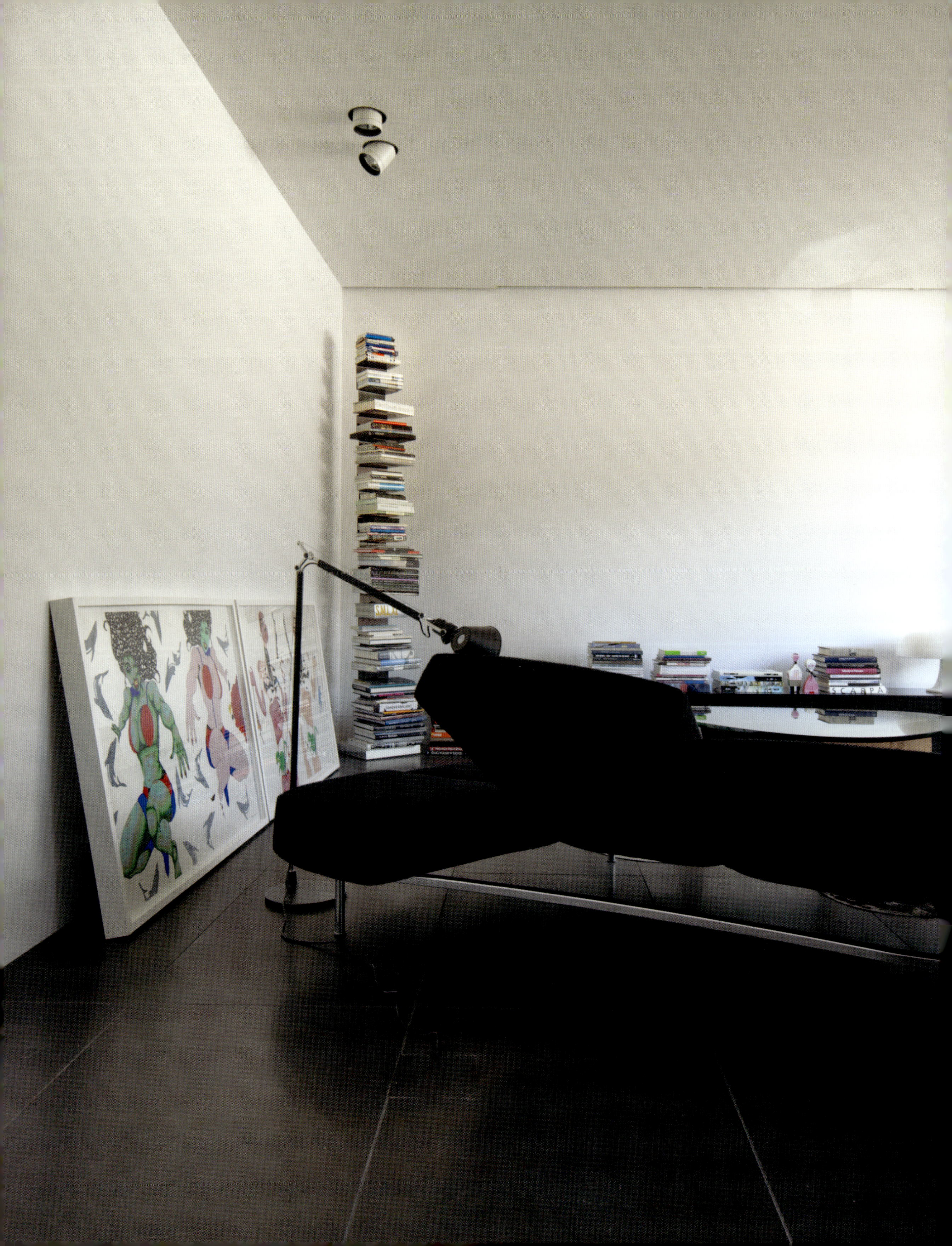

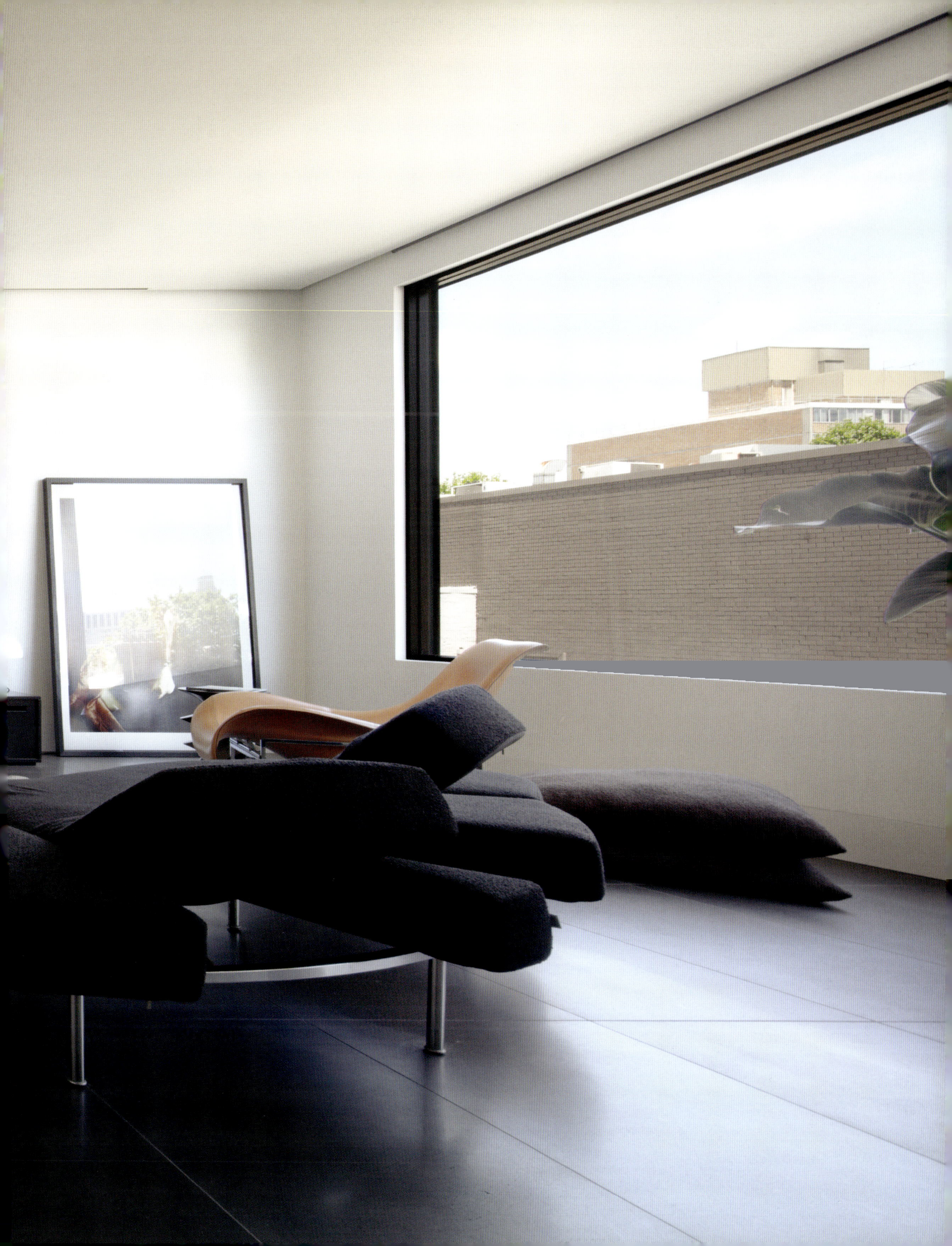

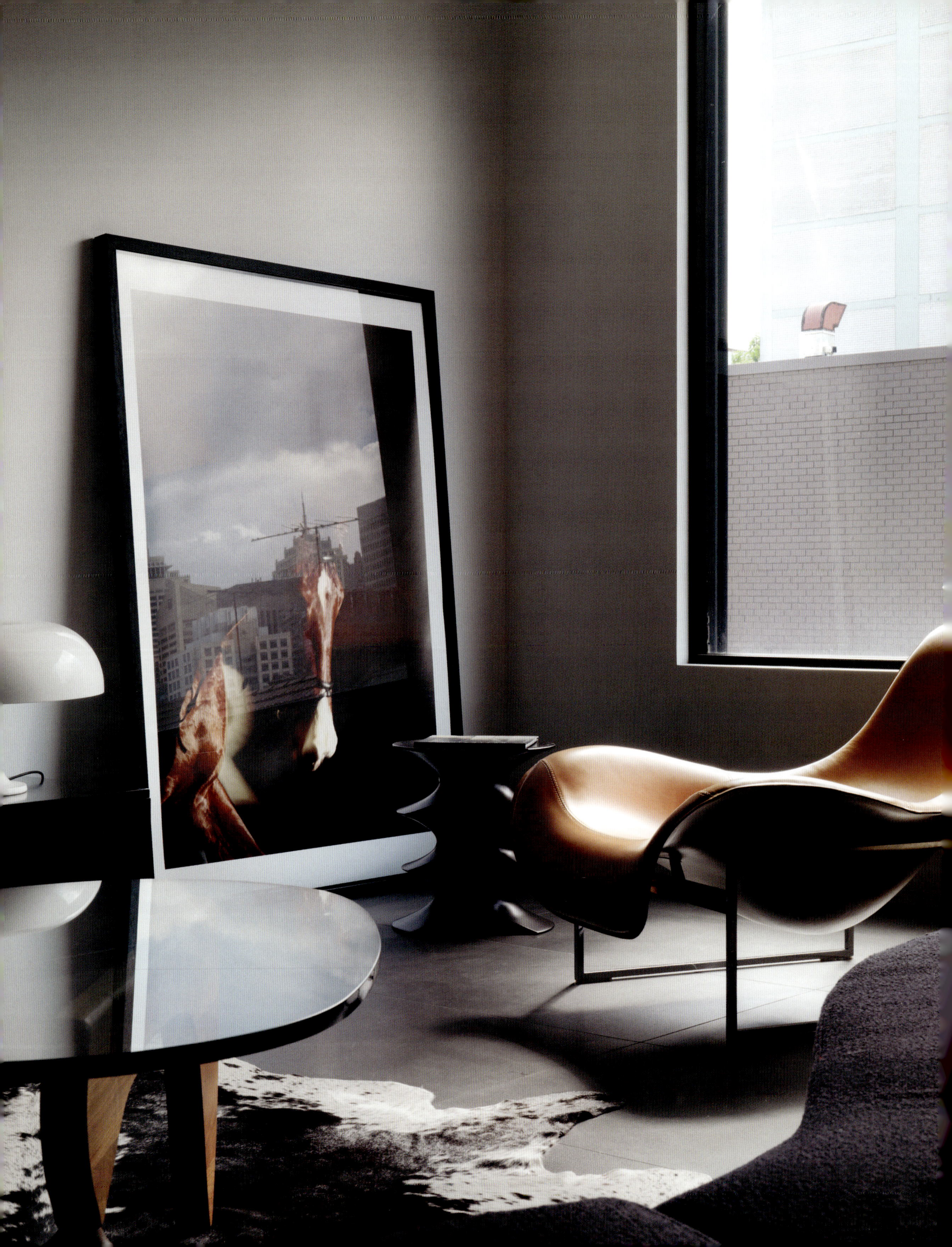

The site is so small it can fit into the garage of a typical sprawling suburban home. An exercise in urban consolidation, Small House proposes to build upwards rather than outwards by assigning multiple uses to single spaces, with flexibility for change in the future. *Domenic Alvaro*

With an eco-conscious spirit in mind, innovation was required for the construction, based upon a model of prefabrication. The two basic ideas were a structure with no columns to make effective use of the limited land area, and to achieve a final result which erased the sense of individual panels, in effect to make the building feel monolithic. *Domenic Alvaro*

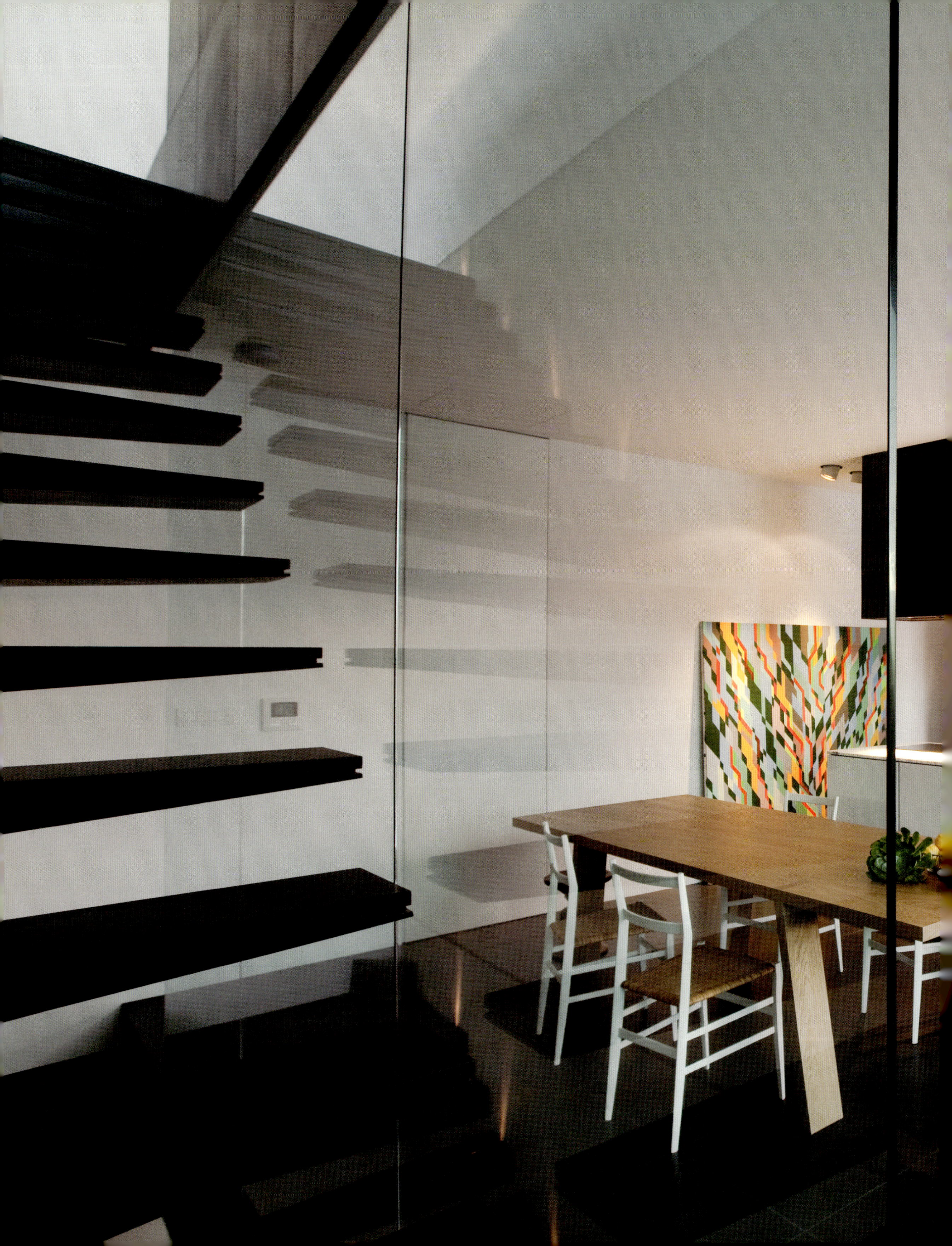

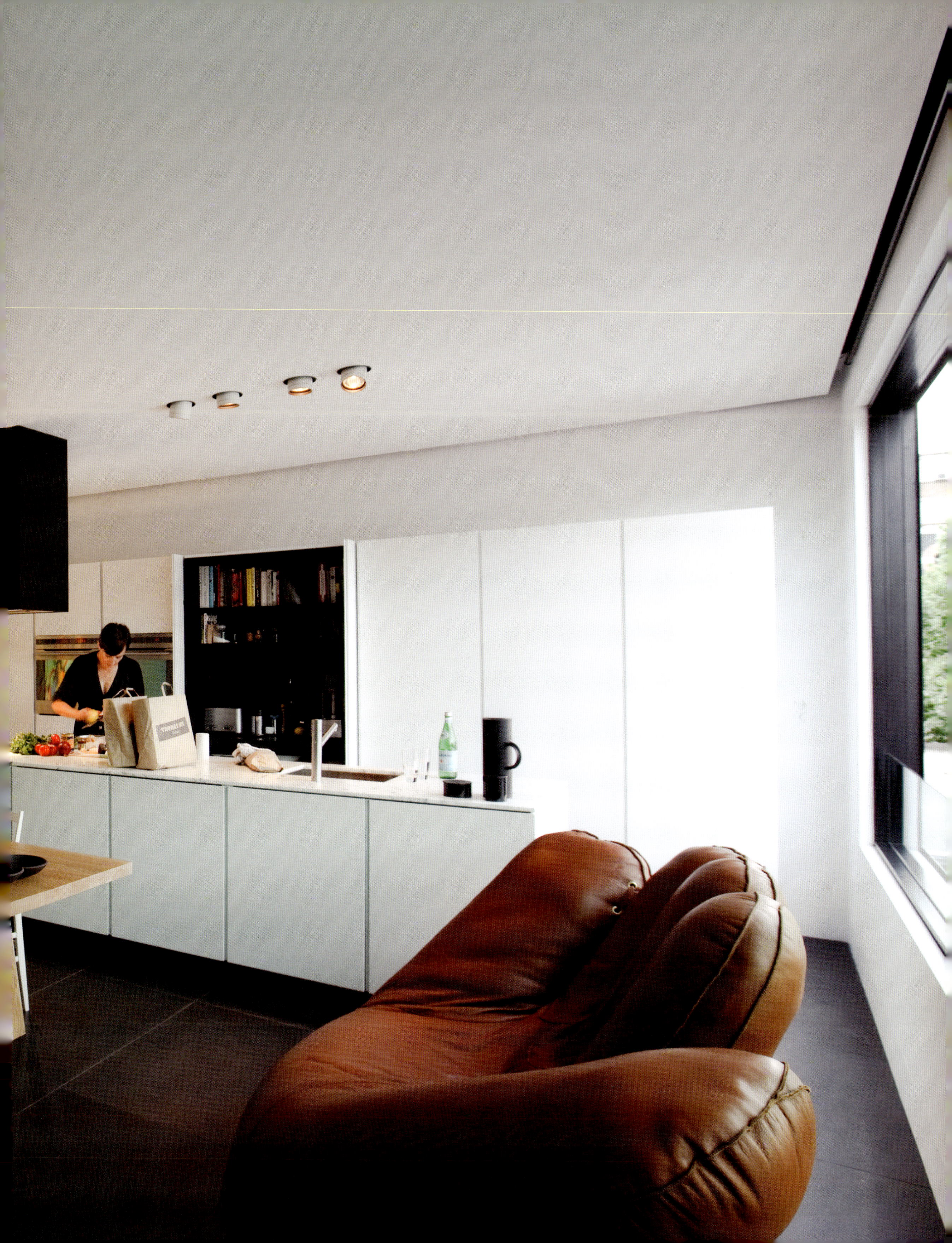

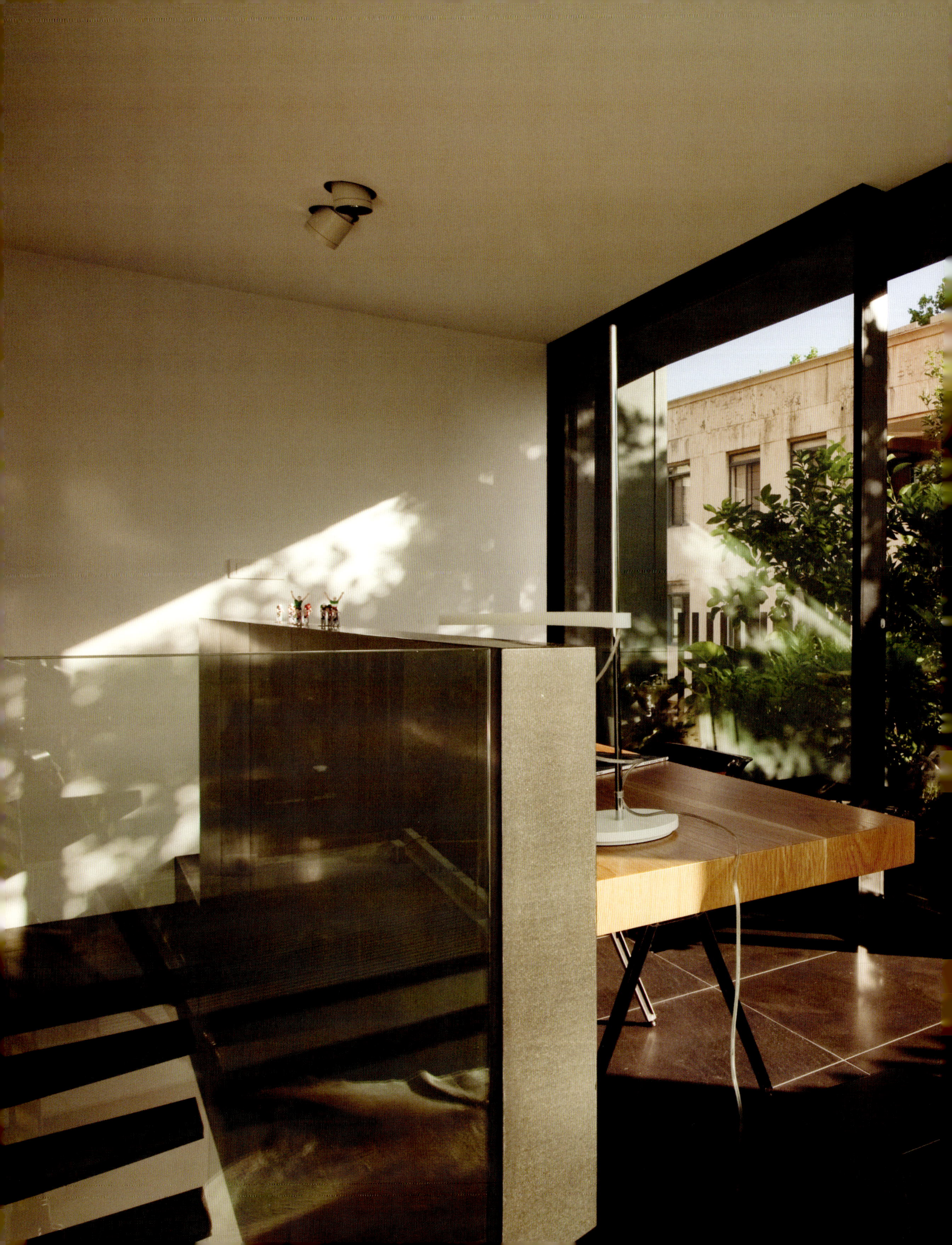

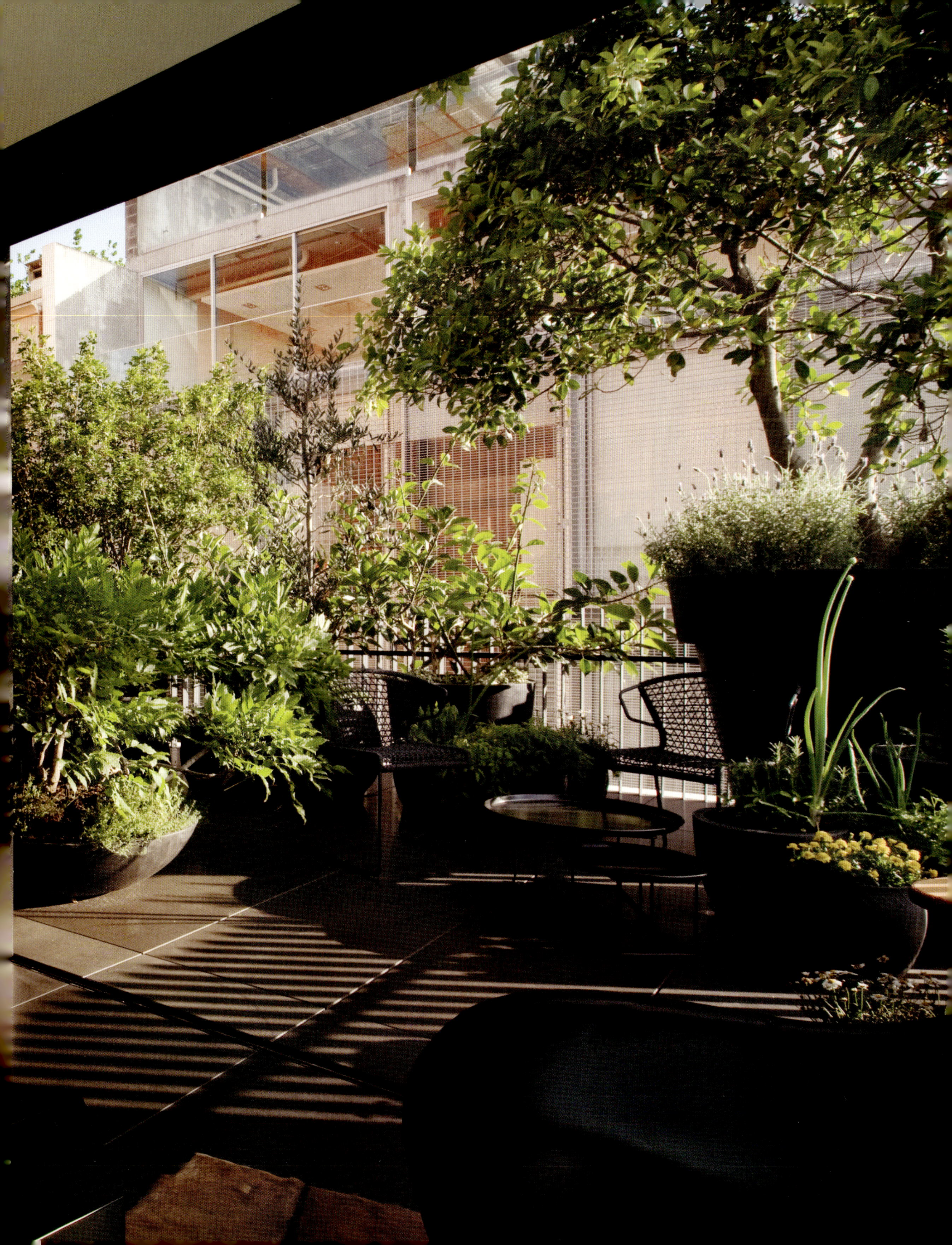

Photographs: Brett Boardman

CASTLECRAG HOUSE

CASTLECRAG HOUSE
SYDNEY, AUSTRALIA, 2011
NEESON MURCUTT ARCHITECTS

The premature passing of Nicholas Murcutt in 2011 robbed Australian architecture of one of its brightest and most prodigious talents. In a career that spanned relatively few years, first solo and then from 2004 with wife and partner Rachel Neeson, the practice built an enviable reputation for designing highly resolved, finely tuned houses. Their Five Dock House and a house at Whale Beach, of 2007 and 2009 respectively, won the Australian Institute of Architects (New South Wales) Wilkinson Award, that state's highest prize for residential architecture.

This house, perched at the edge of an escarpment overlooking Sugarloaf Bay at Middle Harbour, on Sydney's lower north shore, is arguably one of their finest. It is the last house that Murcutt saw completed before his death. Its location is impressive, on the side of a ridge on the beautiful Castlecrag Peninsula, master planned by Walter Burley Griffin and Marion Mahony Griffin in 1921. It is within easy reach, too, of some of the 15 houses built to the Griffins' designs on the peninsula. Hugh Buhrich's own house from 1972, a masterpiece of rough-cast concrete, now regarded as one of the finest houses of 20th-century modern Australian architecture, stands just along the road; while up the hill, separated by a bush reserve, is an earlier house by the German architect.

This house is essentially an addition and alteration to the client's grandfather's original house, built in the late 1940s. But as only one wall and fireplace of the original were retained, the house is a new construction in every respect, its form and plan responding almost entirely to the steep and difficult terrain. Designed as a family home, the house is arranged over four levels stepping down the long and narrow site: a shared family space at the entry level, a parents' retreat above, a children's space one level down and a flat for guests on the lowest level, spilling out to a swimming pool. But it's the planning that is impressive, responding to the three remarkable qualities of the site: a large sandstone rock shelf that partially shields the house from the street, a bushland reserve studded with pink angophora trees and the view over Sugarloaf Bay and Castle Cove below. The result is a pinwheel plan, with views arranged to the rock shelf, the bush and the water.

In situ concrete, brick and sandstone are the main materials employed in the making of the house, and it is clear that the architects delighted in experimentation. The two main external walls are of twice-recycled bricks (the first house was built of recycled bricks due to a lack of building materials in the period following World War II, and many of the same bricks have been re-used here). Sandstone, new and recycled, is used in parts both for external paving and internal flooring, as well as cladding for some walls. But it is the fair-faced concrete, employed in exposed floor plates, massive structural beams left revealed, and structural walls, that gives the house much of its power and warmth.

A concrete plate extending out from the house folds down at one end to signal the entrance canopy at the same time enclosing a car parking space, left open to maintain constant views through to the water, as the Griffin master plan always intended. The attraction of the concrete, however, is never more apparent and irresistible than the moment you step inside through a steel pivot door. Here, you enter directly into a kitchen and dining area, remarkable for its concrete ceiling and deep structural beams that imbue the space with a compressive, cave-like quality. A structural wall of concrete supports a white-painted steel stair on one side, and helps enclose a small family area on the other, with the house's original fireplace and simple timber mantle retained and restored. It is from here that the architects play a game of revealing the house gradually. Go up, along the white-painted steel stair, and you reach the parents' retreat which is more of an enclave than a sleeping zone. The plan then takes you on a circuitous path that includes an artist's studio at the top of the stairs, a study further around, and then the bedroom and a bathroom. Nowhere is the pinwheel plan experienced more powerfully than here, with each room placed to capture a different view.

In what seems somewhat of a folly, a steel bridge leads from the top of the stair to the rock ledge outside for clambering on. An open terrace on the main living level, at which you feel as if you are standing at the edge of a precipice, uses concrete beams as a sun-shading device. Steel stairs take the visitor down to what is, in essence, a subterranean world that incorporates a children's level, with cell-like bedrooms behind timber panelling, weighed down by a deep concrete beam stretching the width of the house. You need to go outside and down a set of stone steps to access a small guest flat leading to a swimming pool. An extant sandstone wall from the original house has been restored and retained, along with original kitchen joinery from the house, as part of the client's determination to keep some memories of the former house. The sense of living inside a cave is never more powerful than here. This capacity to remind extends to the north face of the house, where bands of yellow bricks are laid in vertical patterns, as a reminder of shadows cast onto the original wall by tall angophoras long since removed from the site.

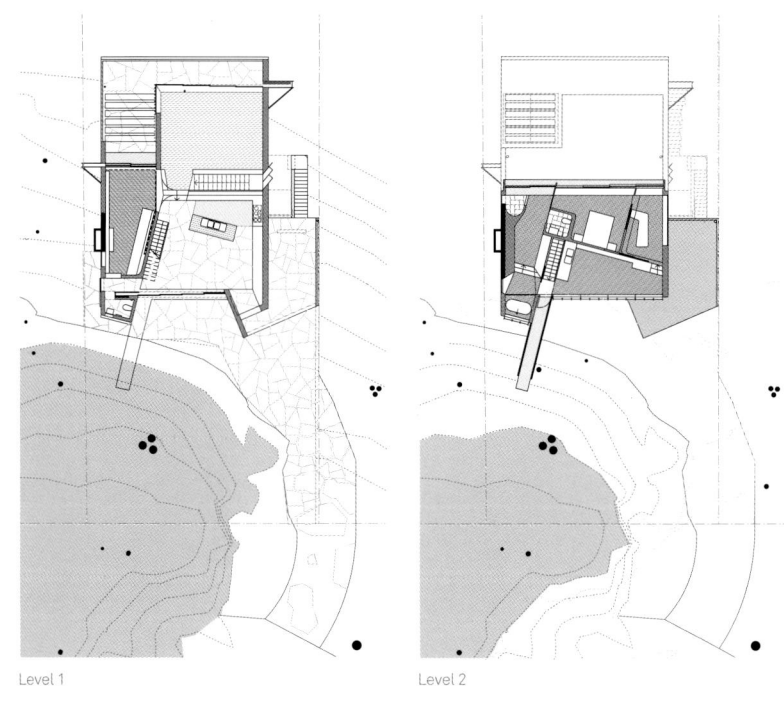

Section elevation

Level 1

Level 2

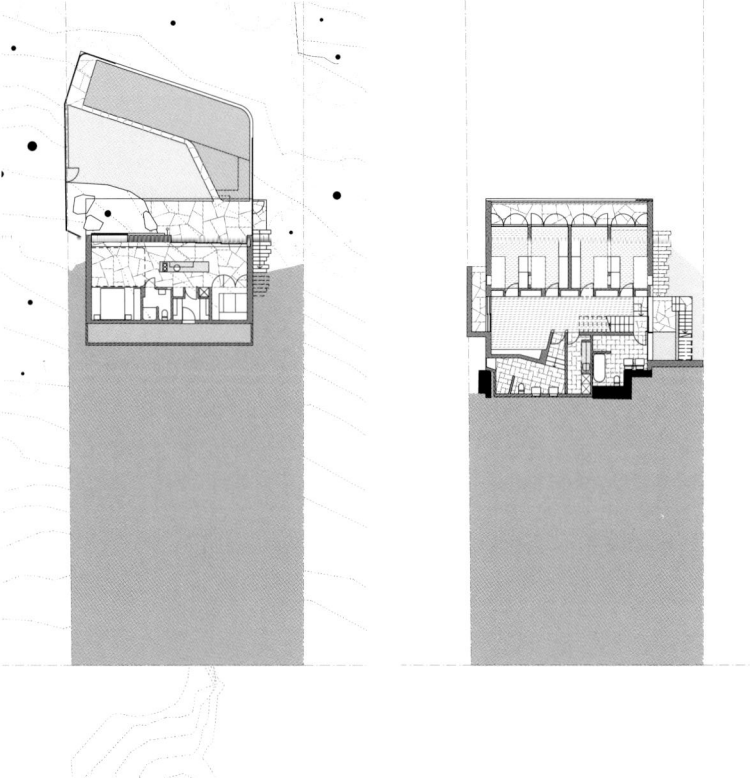

Pool room

Level 0

0   10m

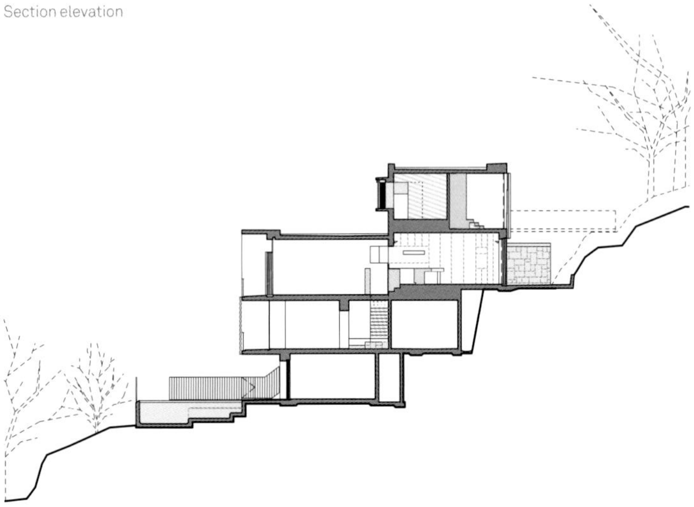

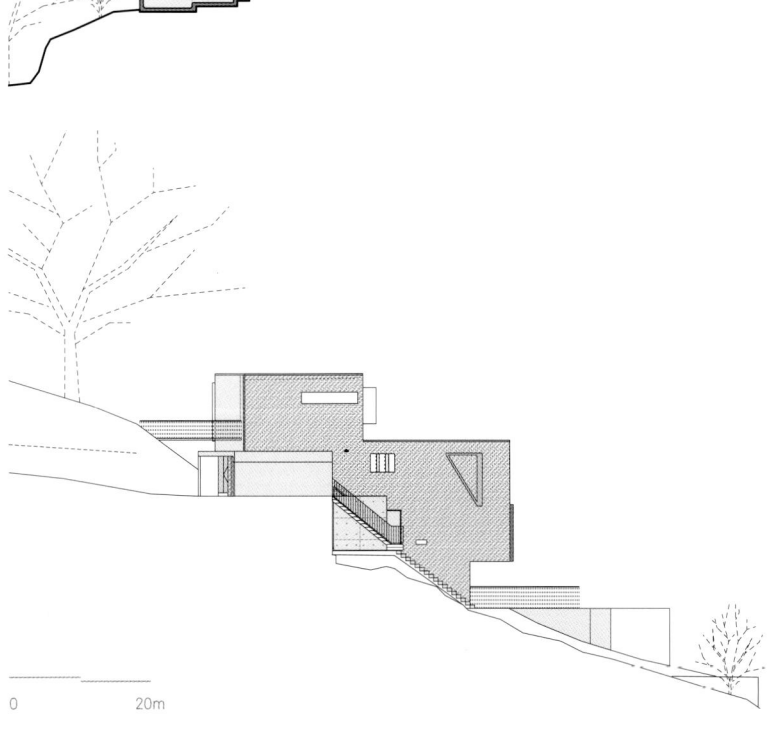

0   20m

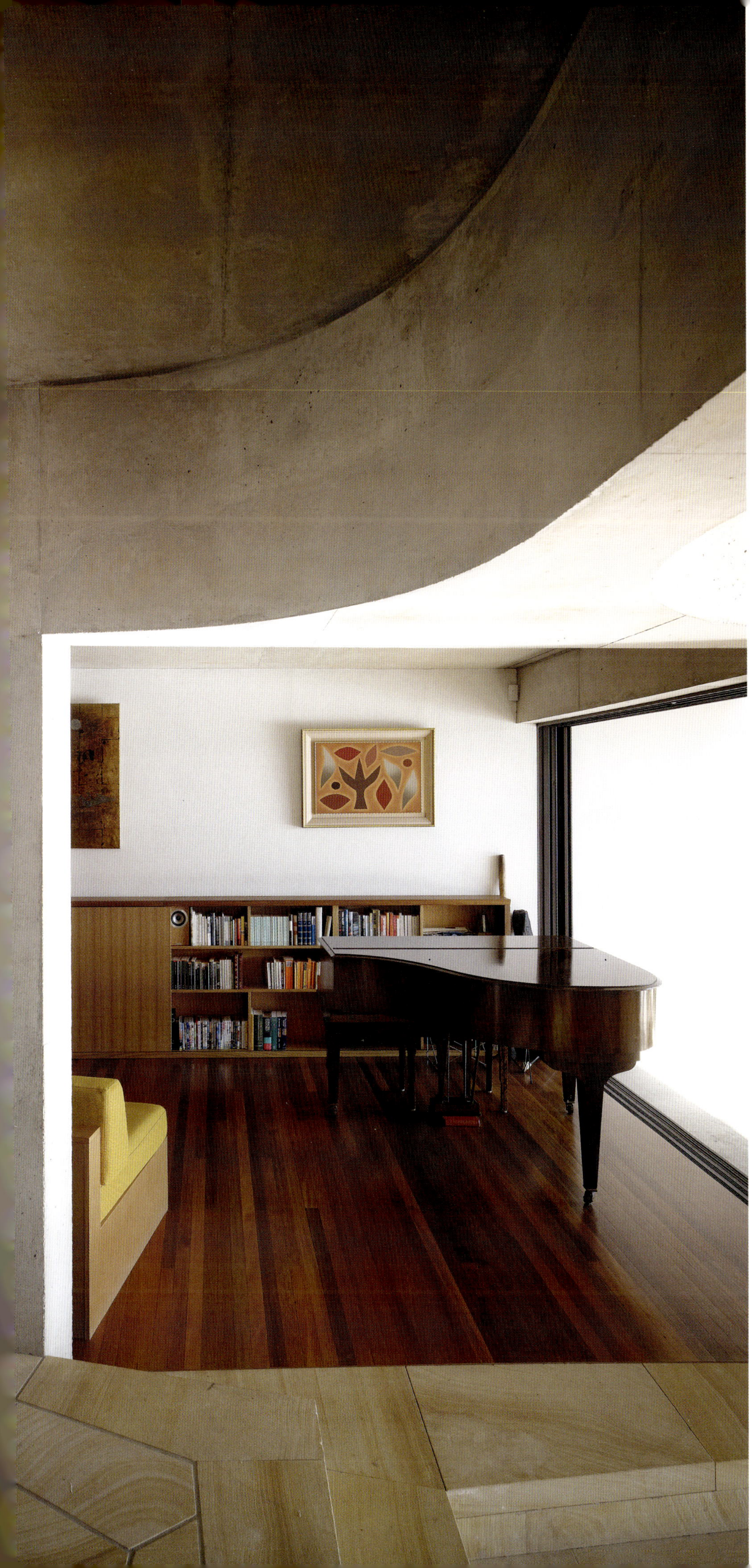
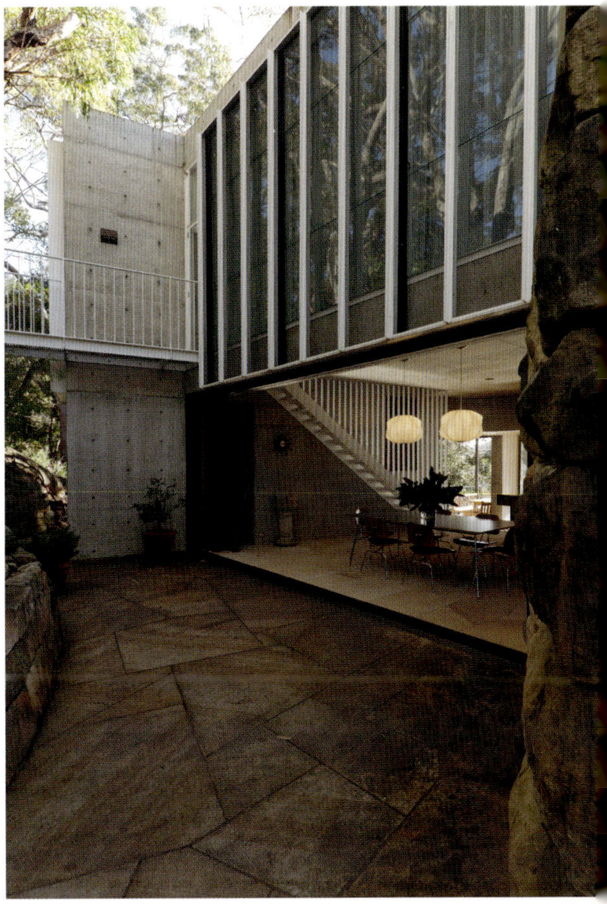
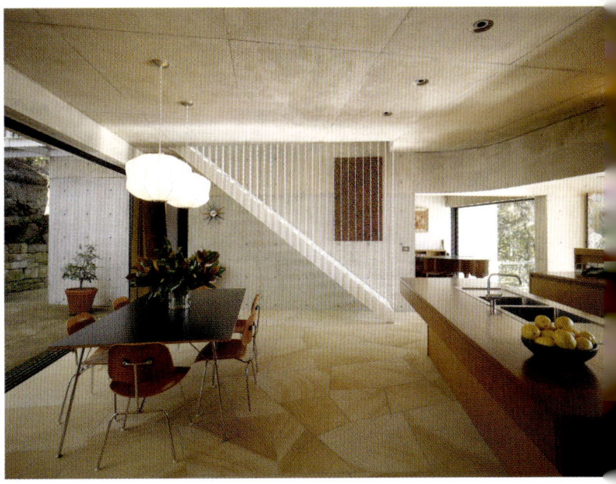
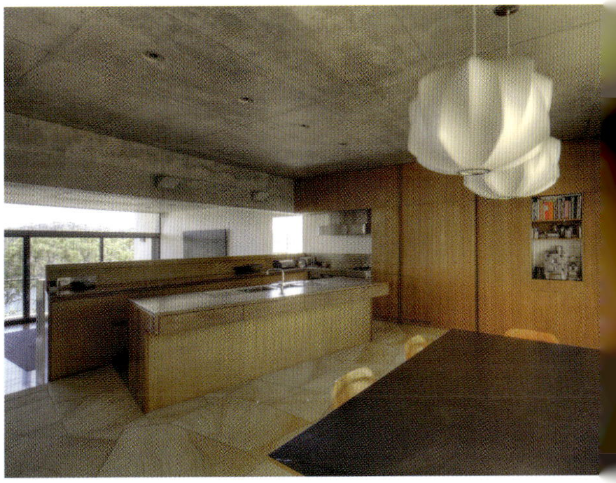

The site has three particularly special qualities: a beautiful sandstone outcrop that largely shields the house from the street, tranquil water views down to Sugarloaf Bay and Castle Cove below, and an adjacent bush reserve studded with pink angophoras. *Rachel Neeson*

    The bespoke quality of the house is best understood in the junctions between new and old, and in material experiments throughout – the preciseness of steelwork, rawness of in situ concrete, texture and colour of sandstone, texture and pattern of recycled bricks. *Rachel Neeson*

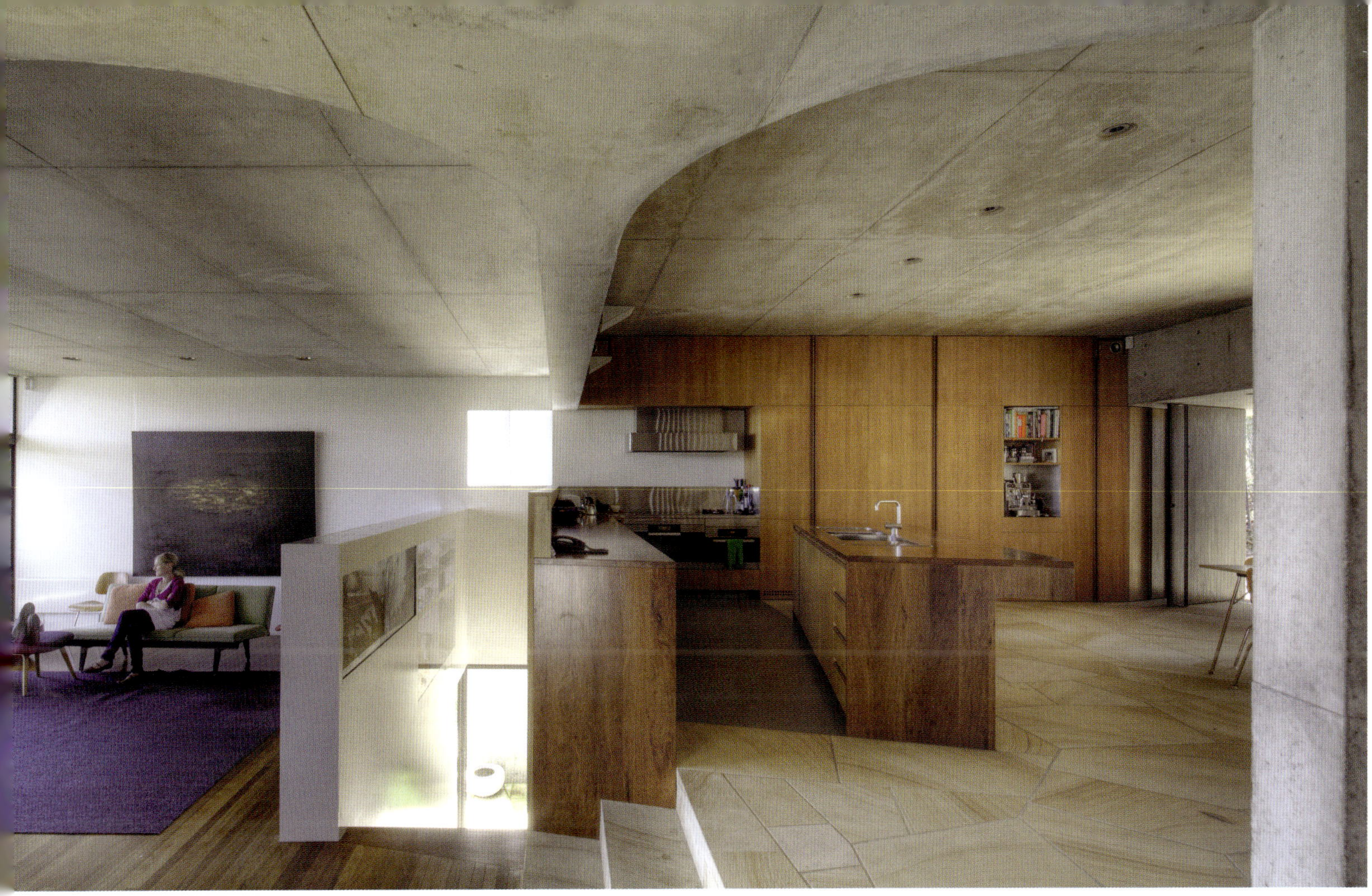

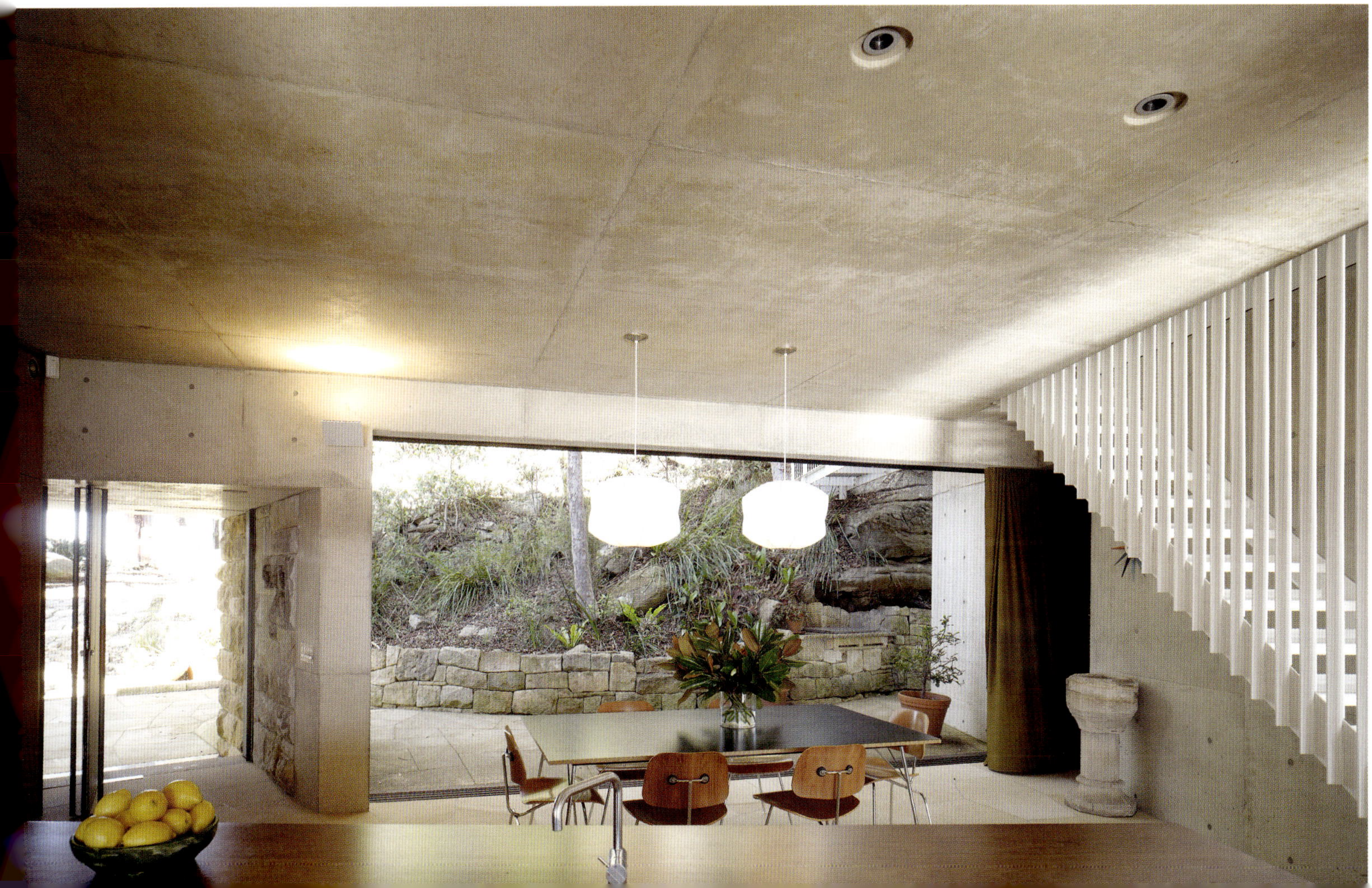

Photographs: Daici Ano

HOUSE O

HOUSE O
TATEYAMA, JAPAN, 2007
SOU FUJIMOTO

There is much to like about the buildings of Tokyo architect Sou Fujimoto. He has carved a big name internationally as a protagonist of what he calls the 'primitive future' – seeking out new geometric orders, composition and spatial relativity through manipulation of basic geometries.

'I'm interested in creating a sort of situation in which human habitation develops around the idea of living inside a nest or cave,' Fujimoto says. He describes a nest as 'a place for people, which is very well prepared, in which everything is assembled and very functional. A cave is just raw space, which people need to explore and find their own comfort within … a situation where people can use space creatively. I prefer cave-like unintentional space, something between nature and artefact.'

One project, House N, comprises three white concrete cubes, one inside the other inside the other, with large openings cut out of the concrete fabric of each to let in light and air. The outermost shell is all-enveloping, creating a covered semi-indoor garden. The second shell encloses a limited indoor space. The third sits deep within the outer two shells, creating a small, secure interior space.

Fujimoto describes life within the house as like 'living among clouds … a distinct boundary is nowhere to be found, except for a gradual change in the domain. You could say that an ideal architecture is an outdoor space that feels like the indoors, and an indoor space that feels like the outdoors. In a nested structure, the inside is invariably the outside and vice versa.'

His most radical project is Final Wooden House, a tiny 4-cubic-metre box set in a copse of trees in Kumamoto, on Kyushu, Japan's third largest island. Resembling an elaborate woodblock puzzle, the house is assembled from massive cedar beams, stacked and piled endlessly to make walls, floors and ceilings, creating, in the process, a series of flexible, interlocking, multi-level spaces. 'I wanted to see if I could make, simultaneously, primitive yet new architecture,' Fujimoto says.

This coastal dwelling in Tateyama, in the Chiba prefecture near Tokyo, is yet another of Fujimoto's plays in the manipulation of composition and space. Set on a rocky outcrop at the edge of the Pacific Ocean, the house is conceived as a continuous single space. Seen in plan it resembles the branch of a tree, leading the visitor on a journey uninterrupted by walls or doors. Separation of functions and privacy are created with each crook and crank and fold in the plan.

Simple and complex at the same time, the house is above all what Fujimoto describes as 'architecture of distance'. Here, in this concrete bunker, his deft manipulation of spaces affords its inhabitants long and near views, and grand panoramic vistas over the Pacific Ocean. 'Creating architecture is nothing more than creating various distances,' he says.

'I thought of creating various oceans: panoramic views of the ocean, the ocean seen from the recesses of a cave, enclosed ocean and a place projected above the ocean. Oriented in different directions, you can find various views of the ocean as you walk through the house. The living area, bedroom and bathroom each have their own unique relationship with the ocean. Comfortable spaces are scattered along this trail. Interminable spaces continuing over and over without any clear borders. I wanted the architecture to be primitive, between natural and man-made.'

Fujimoto's early design strategy, in response to his clients' wishes to make the most of the spectacularly wild coastline, was for a linear form, a simple straight-lined box, stretched across the site, facing the ocean. But views are made from more than single experiences. Fujimoto began manipulating the form, assembling first a series of boxes to control and frame vistas to take in the craggy rocks and irregular water inlet and other key views, finally tying them together in a carefully choreographed sequence that culminated in the tree-branch composition of the final plan.

Fujimoto also wanted the house to appear at one with its rocky terrain on approach from land. So, on arrival, the visitor is confronted by an irregular concrete box, its starkness tempered only by a couple of palm trees and no clue to any obvious point of entry. Once inside, however, the views explode through walls of frameless glass as the visitor moves along the buckled plan. At each fold, the 3-metre-wide section shifts to create greater depth and incident in plan. 'I wanted a feeling of looking out from the recesses of a cave,' Fujimoto says.

With the concrete, too, there are distinct differences between the exterior and interior. The outside is coarsely finished, board-marked with planks of rough timber formwork. The interiors, by contrast, are defined by more precise and pristine surfaces, made by casting the concrete against cedar planks. This subtle shift acknowledges each surface's response to nature and maker, with the heavier texture on the exterior resonating with the jagged rocks outside, compared to the more tactile and human scale inside.

There is rigour and robustness in finishes and detail, too. The roof is of fine steel plate, the windows are walls of 15-millimetre frameless glass, and double-leaf doors are set flush with internal and exterior concrete surfaces to maintain the illusion of mass. Services are reduced and discrete, integrated with walls and floor with finesse. Floors reflect the transition from wild exterior to controlled interior with stone surfaces flowing into white-painted timbers, terminating in a sitting room of tatami mats, as a fitting sign of a truly Japanese interior.

Fujimoto allows himself a solitary moment of expression with the glass front door. As the only frame in the entire house, a consistent section of dark timber wraps around the door head, sill and jambs, responding to human scale without diminishing the architectural strategy of the house.

I thought of creating various oceans: panoramic views of the ocean, the ocean seen from the recesses of a cave, enclosed ocean and a place projected above the ocean. Oriented in different directions, you can find various views of the ocean as you walk through the house. The living area, bedroom and bathroom each have their own unique relationship with the ocean. Comfortable spaces are scattered along this trail. Interminable spaces continuing over and over without any clear borders. I wanted the architecture to be primitive, between natural and man-made. *Sou Fujimoto*

The characteristic of the plan, imagined like the branches of a tree, is a continuous room. All the required spaces – entrance, living area, dining area, kitchen, bedroom, Japanese-style room, study room and bathroom – are arranged in this continuous room. *Sou Fujimoto*

Site plan

01 Parking
02 Closet
03 Tatami room
04 Kitchen
05 Dining room
06 Porch
07 Entrance
08 Living room
09 Study room
10 Closet
11 Bedroom
12 Bedroom

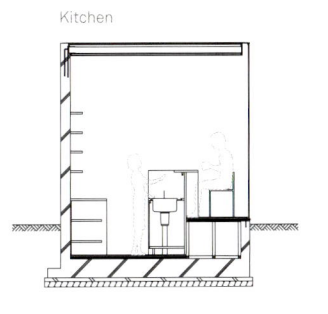

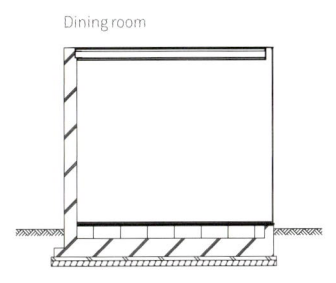

Kitchen

Dining room

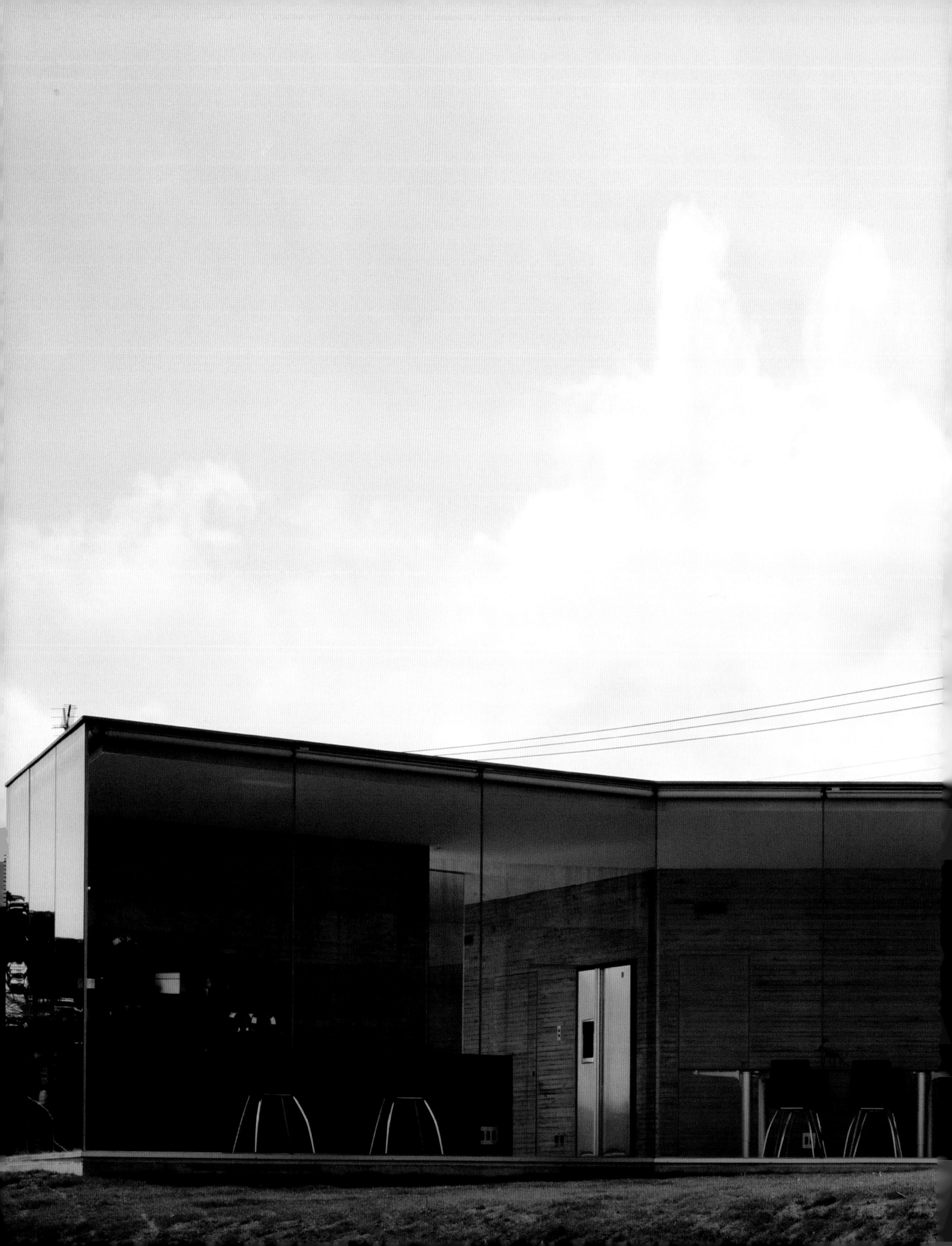

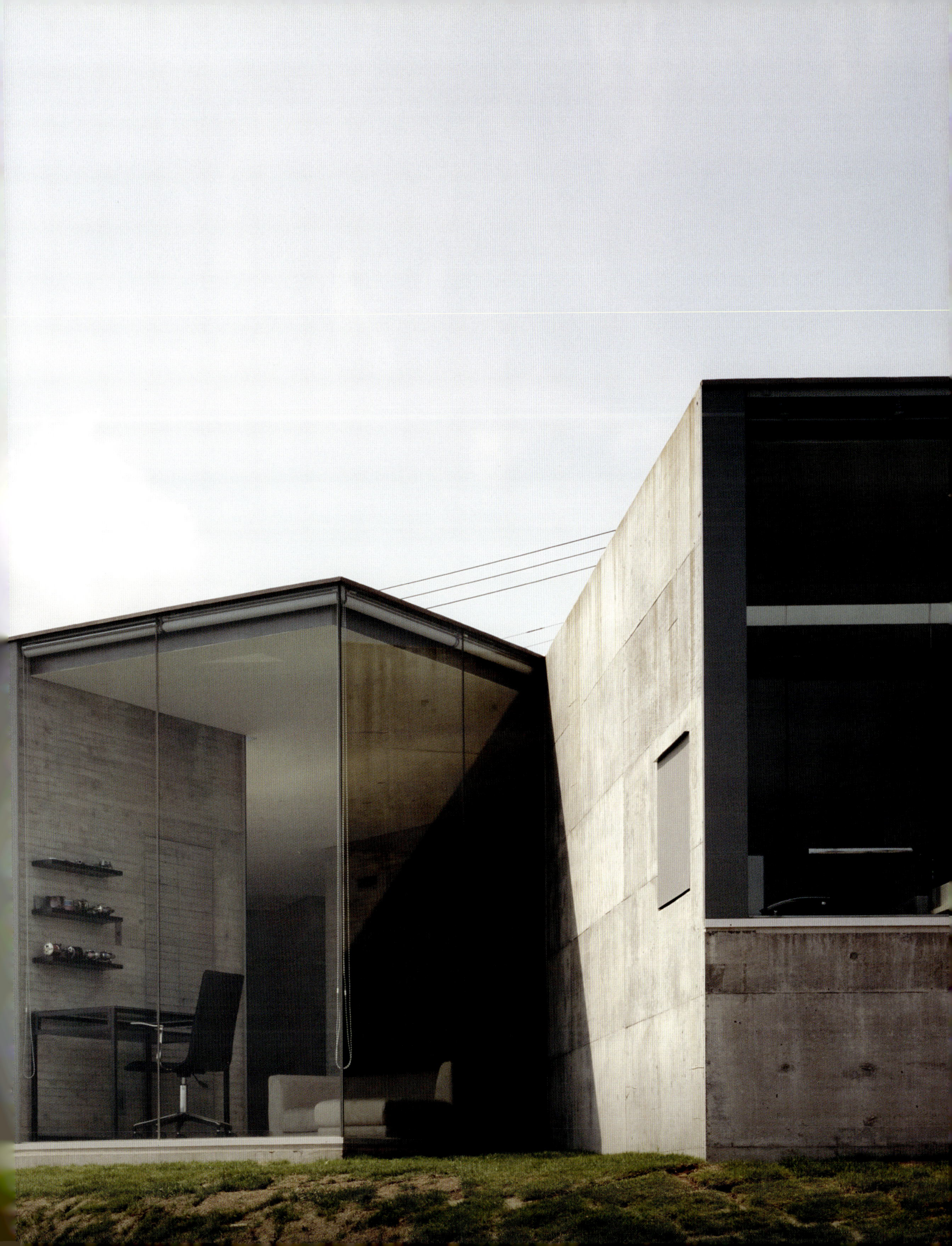

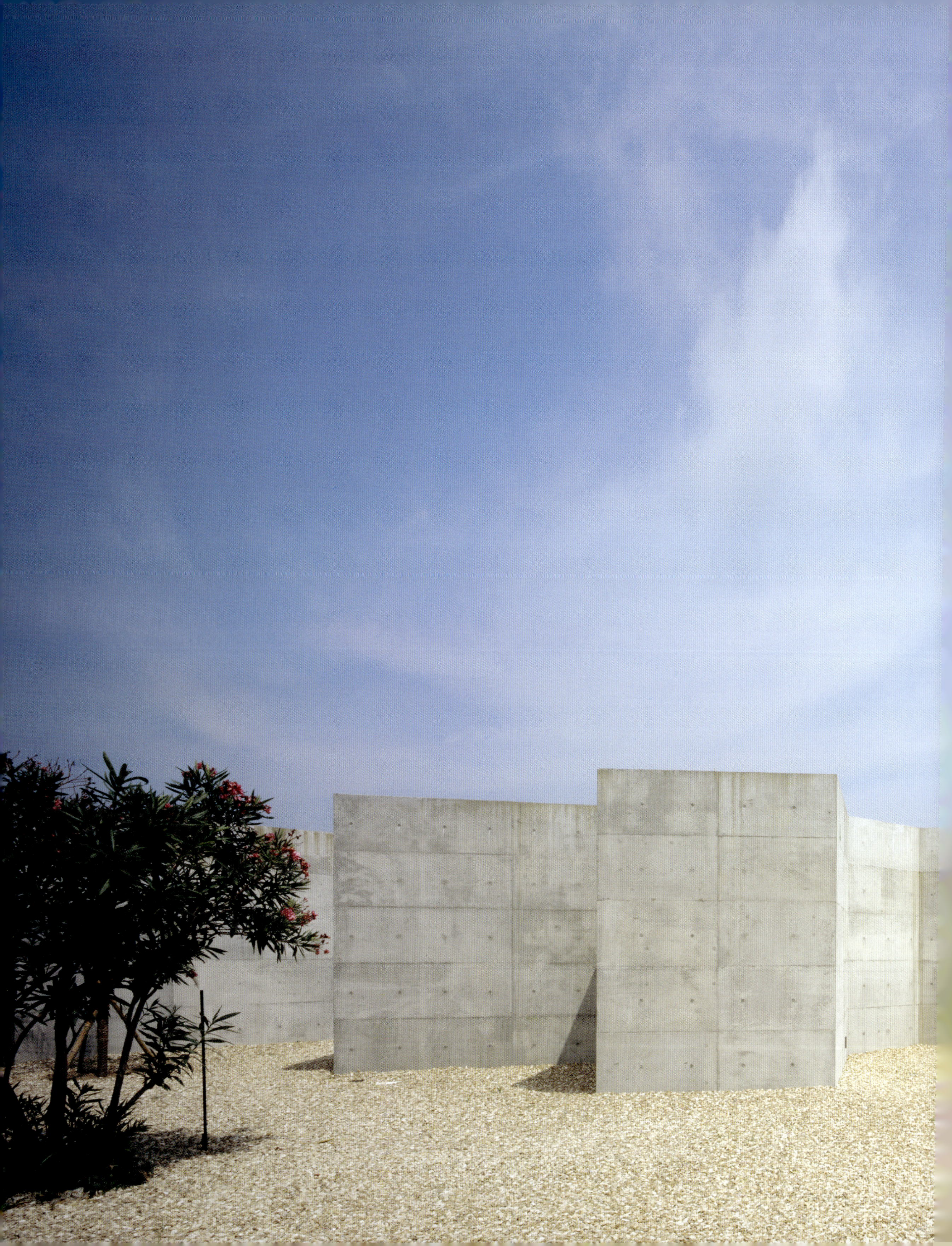

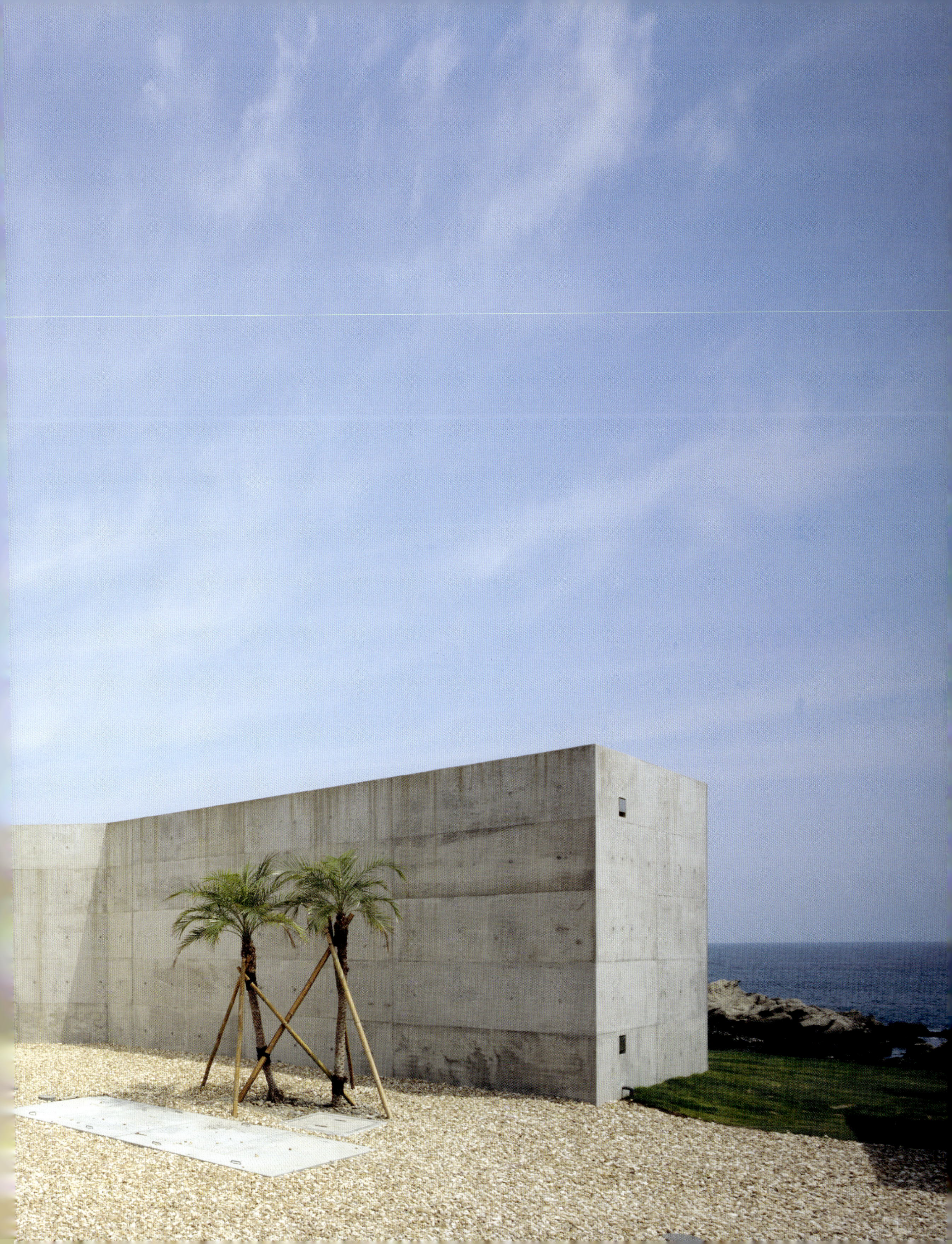

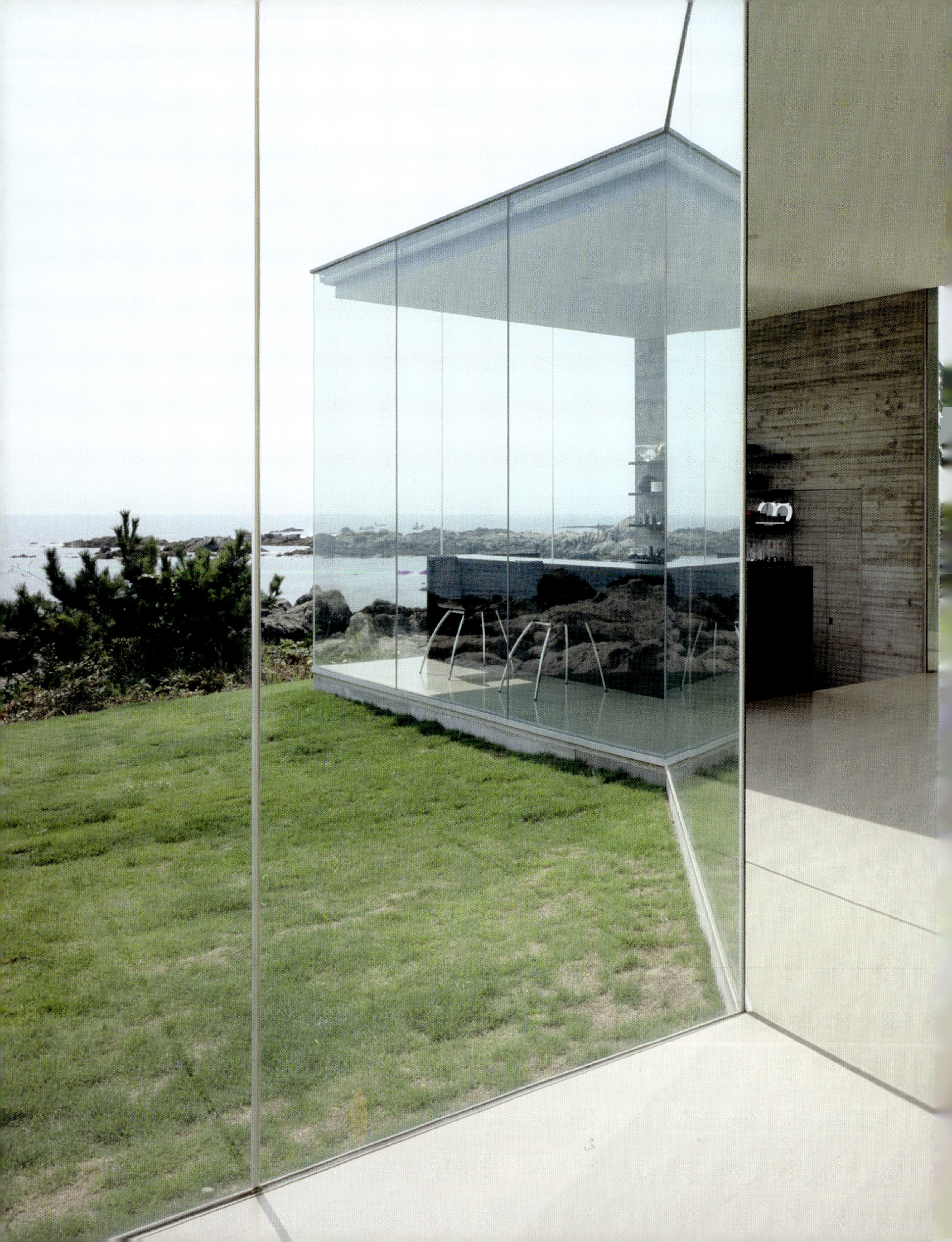

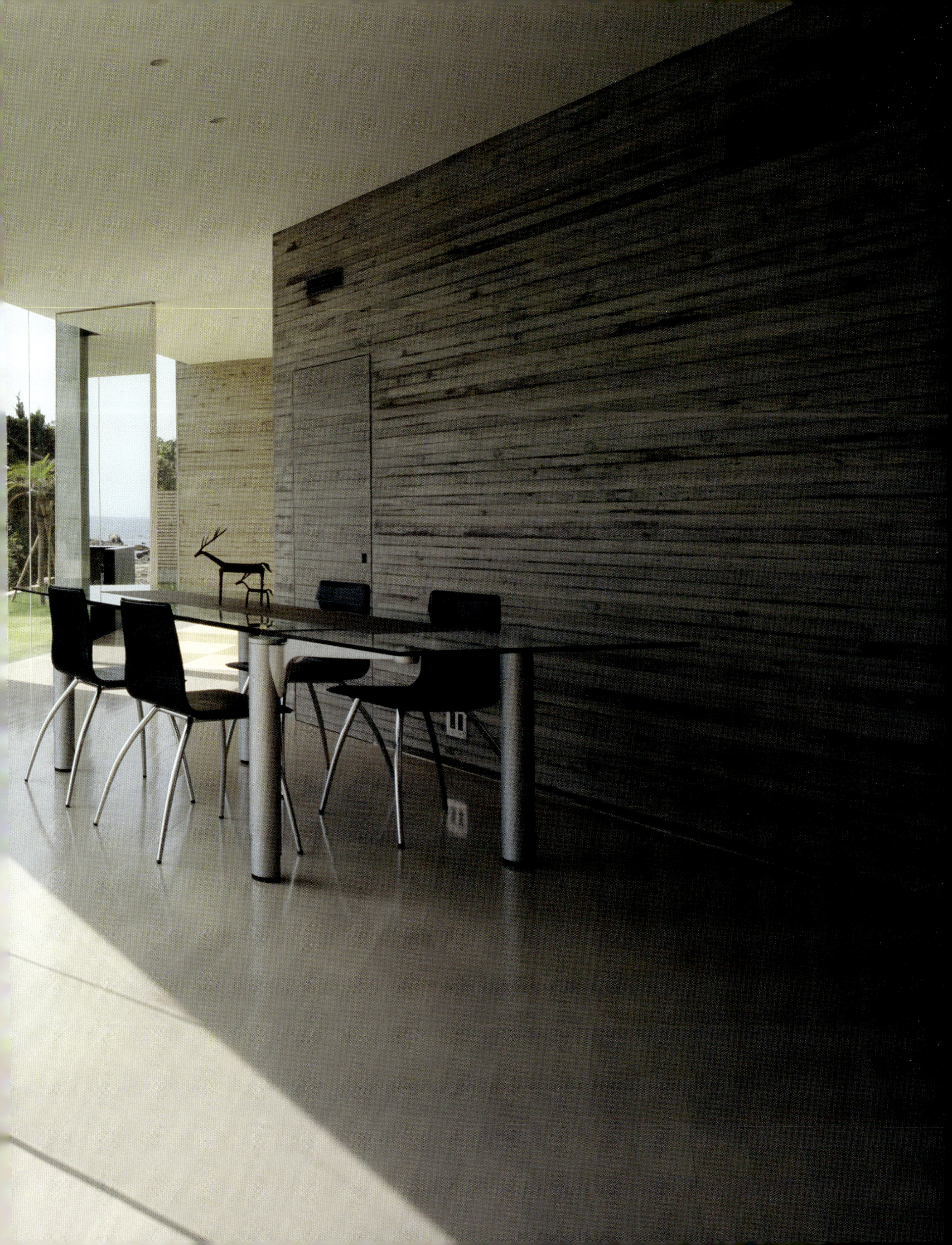

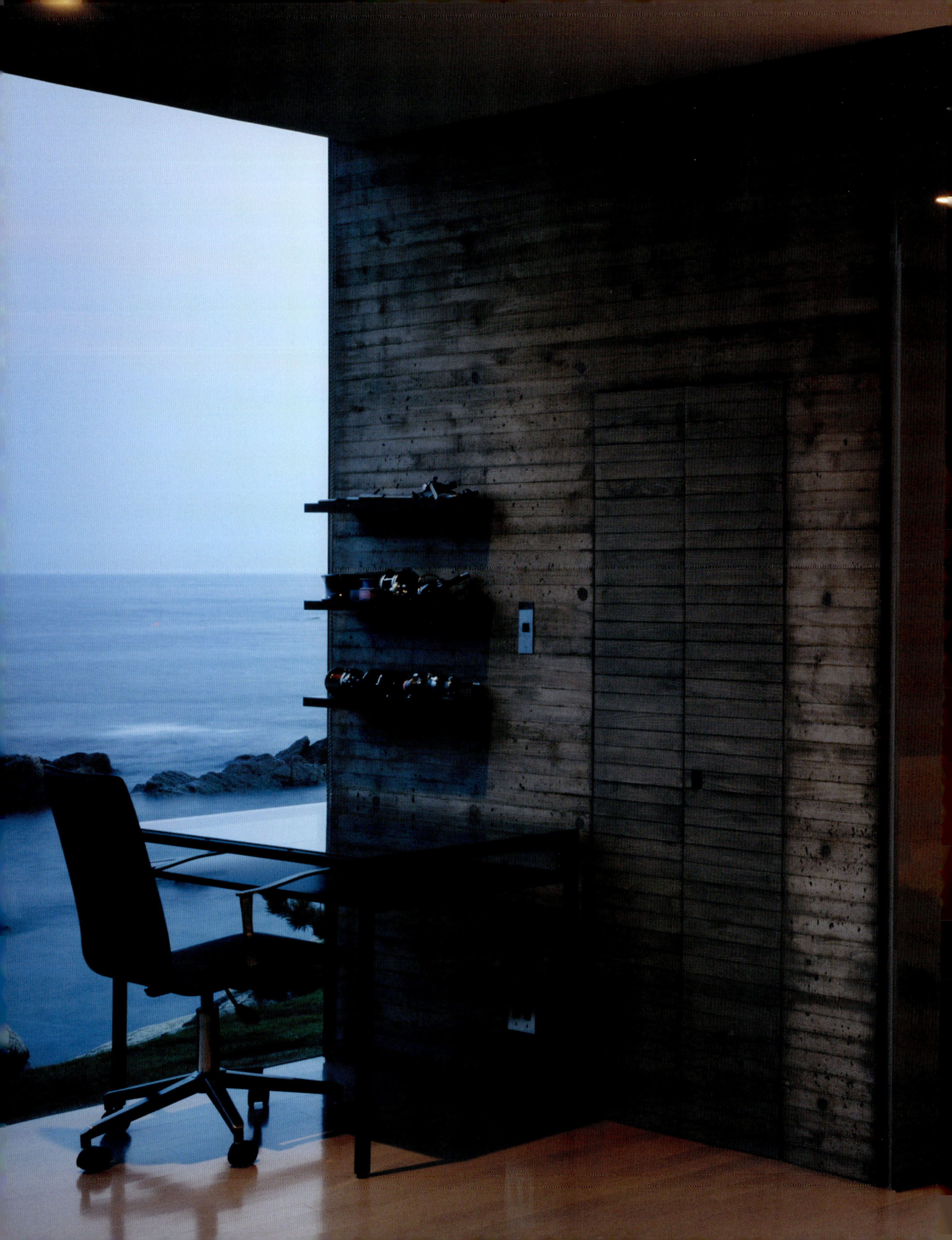

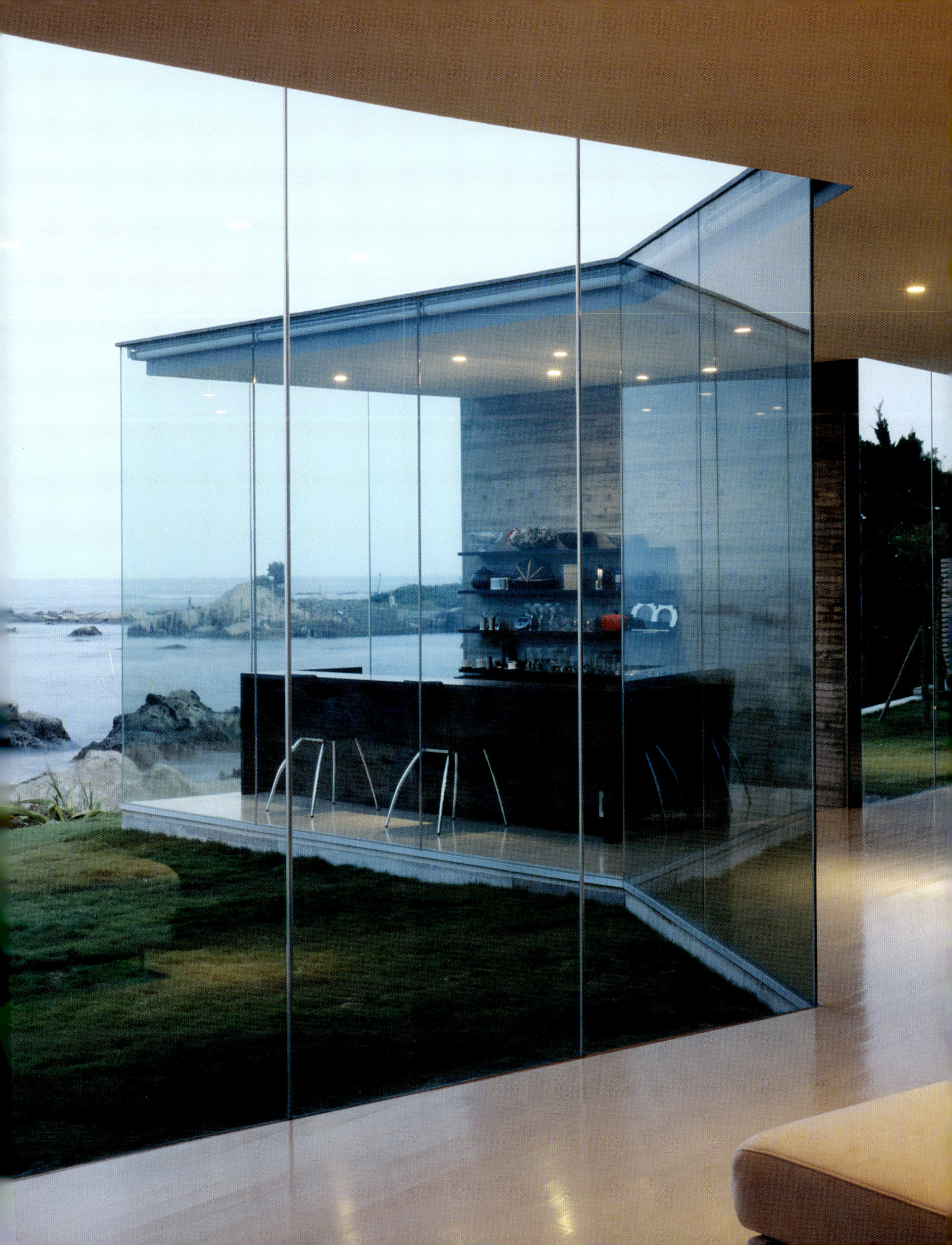

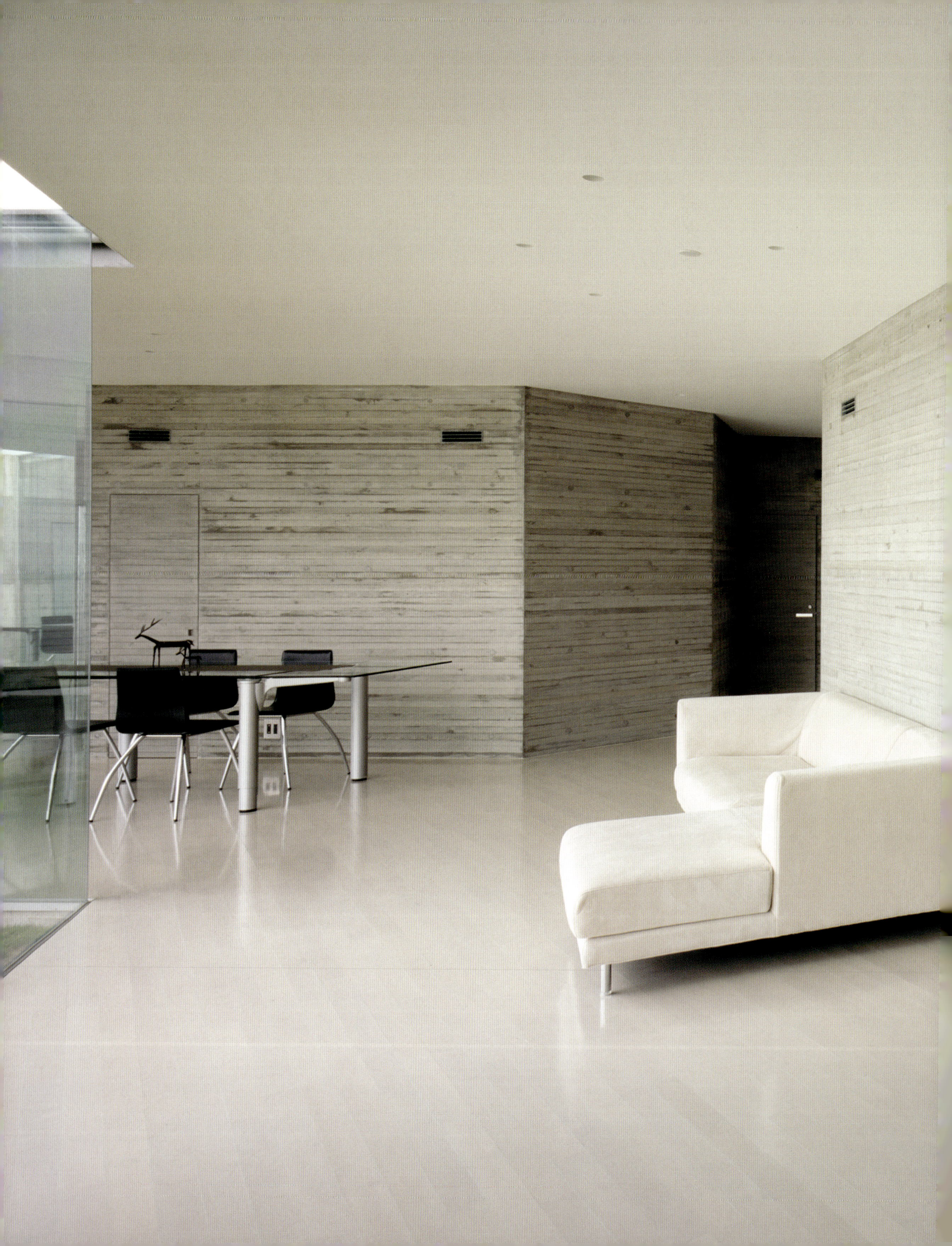

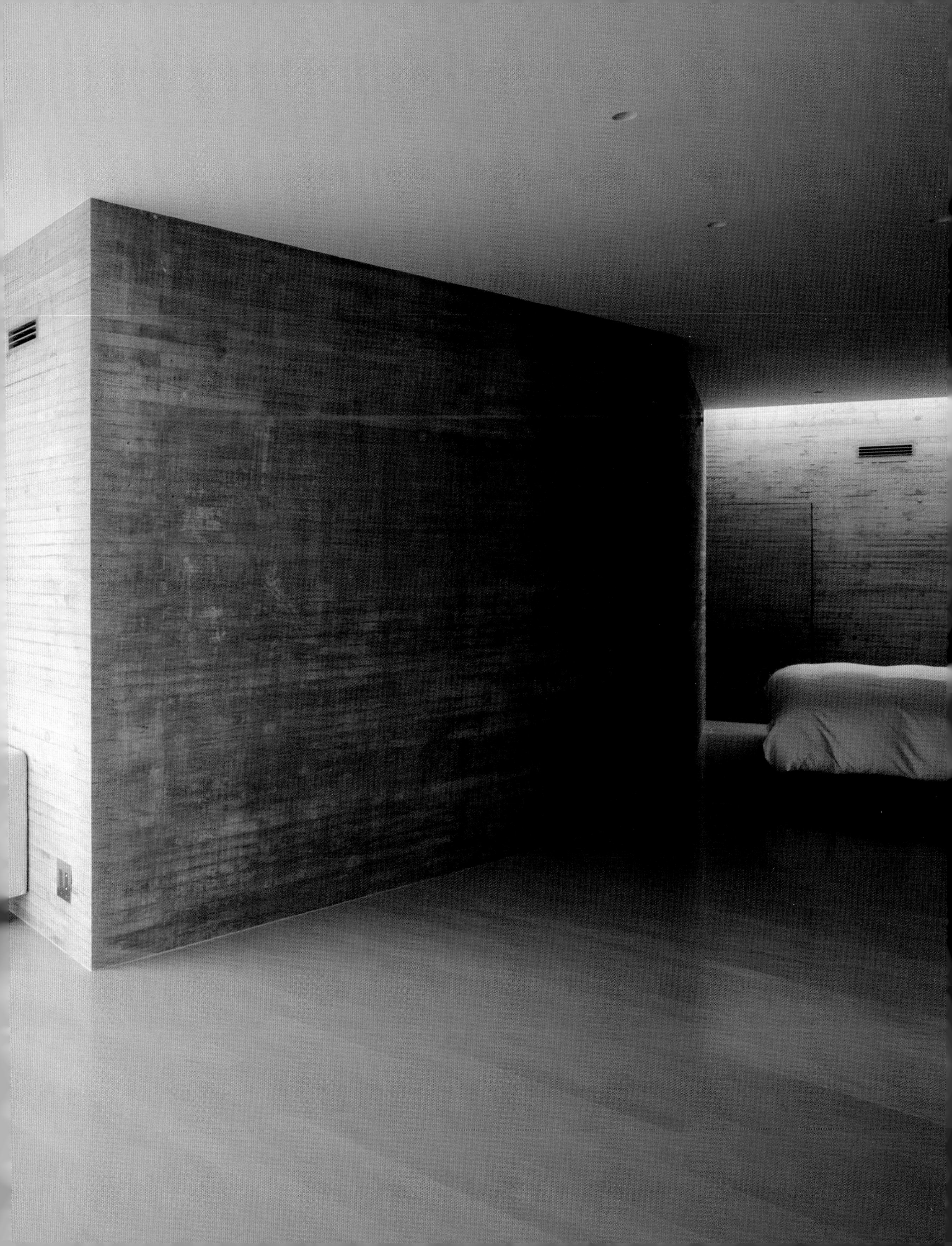

Photographs: Hélène Binet

VILLA WAALRE

VILLA WAALRE
EINDHOVEN, NETHERLANDS, 2015
RUSSELL JONES ARCHITECT

There are echoes of the work of Marcel Breuer and Ludwig Mies van der Rohe in this family house in a forest of conifers at Waalre, near the city of Eindhoven in the southern Netherlands. In particular, it brings to mind Breuer's own house in Massachusetts – his 'volume resting on a landscape' – while a private enclosure on the ground floor evokes the form and scale of Mies's Barcelona Pavilion courtyard.

Designed by Russell Jones, a London-based Australian architect who once worked in the office of Harry Seidler, the house sits on a 7000-square-metre parcel of land among a tranche of house lots formerly owned by Philips, the Dutch electronics giant. In the late 1950s and early 60s, the company sold plots to senior executives to encourage them to build houses close to its facilities, with several of those houses designed by Louis Christiaan Kalff (1897–1976), the company's legendary design director who oversaw the lighting for the Barcelona Pavilion and the Philips Pavilion at Expo '58 in Brussels, among other projects.

The house replaces one designed by Kalff for Frans Otten, son-in-law of Anton Philips, the co-founder, with his older brother Gerard, of Royal Philips Electronics NV in 1912. 'The Kalff house was a pretty good house as it stood,' Jones says. 'In the UK it would have most certainly been heritage listed.' But with several other notable houses designed by Kalff on the estate, the only restriction placed by local planners was that the new house be of greater architectural merit than the one it was replacing.

Early in the design process, it was clear that the position of the Kalff house was the most favourable location for the new villa. A large sand dune along the western boundary, the forest of conifers and the garden planted fifty years ago as part of the Kalff scheme all influenced decisions relating to placement, orientation and form for the new house.

Taking advantage of key natural features, creating a specific and special exterior and interior relationship with the environment, Villa Waalre covers an enclosed area of approximately 1200 square metres over four levels, with only two levels visible on the landscape. Oriented so that the main living, kitchen and bedroom spaces are south-facing and contain large glazed openings, the house is arranged about a ground-floor living space with two wings, and a double-height kitchen, study and enclosed terrace reaching out into the forest. Resting on the two wings is a white box containing the bedrooms, with the master suite placed centrally to look out over the garden. A basement houses a 25-metre swimming pool, gymnasium and photography studio, lit naturally by shafts of light from the roof level. A 'drive-through' tunnel under the western sand dune leads to a large carport and second access from the house to the street beyond.

'There is a gentle, natural richness to the material palette that tempers the rigorous, sculptural form,' Jones says. 'Continuous, textured surfaces that extend from the landscape and run through the interior are bathed in light softened by the forest and the architecture, creating a comfortable, sheltering home that is part of the landscape.'

Fundamental to the project was an early decision to reflect the textural quality of the bark of fir trees in the forest onto the reinforced concrete structure. Formwork of rough-sawn boards was used to imprint the concrete, which was enriched with titanium dioxide, giving it a chalky white hue, while also making it near impervious to water. The textural quality of the sawn timber was extended to all interior joinery, where 150-millimetre fir boards similar to those used in the formwork were used. A special spray-on mix of crushed glass and marble was applied to ceilings, while carefully selected blocks of marble from an Italian quarry were used for every bath, sink, fireplace and kitchen counter.

The thermally separated outer and inner concrete structural walls were articulated to allow for structural and thermal movement, and expressed construction joints were strategically located to further register the planar and volumetric qualities of the building. Concrete cavity walls of 700 millimetres at their deepest and high levels of insulation give the house thermal mass. These passive measures are used in combination with a ground-source heat pump that draws water from sixteen boreholes, and a heat recovery central-heating boiler for the under-floor heating and hot water. Under-floor cooling between the basement swimming pool and the main house above helps minimise heat gain. Air treatment technology and mechanical ventilation facilitate further regulation of the internal environment. Commercially available systems were adapted to enable a fully integrated services design compatible with the architecture and the budget.

First floor

Section AA

Section DD

0   12.5m

Ground floor

Minus 1a

Site plan

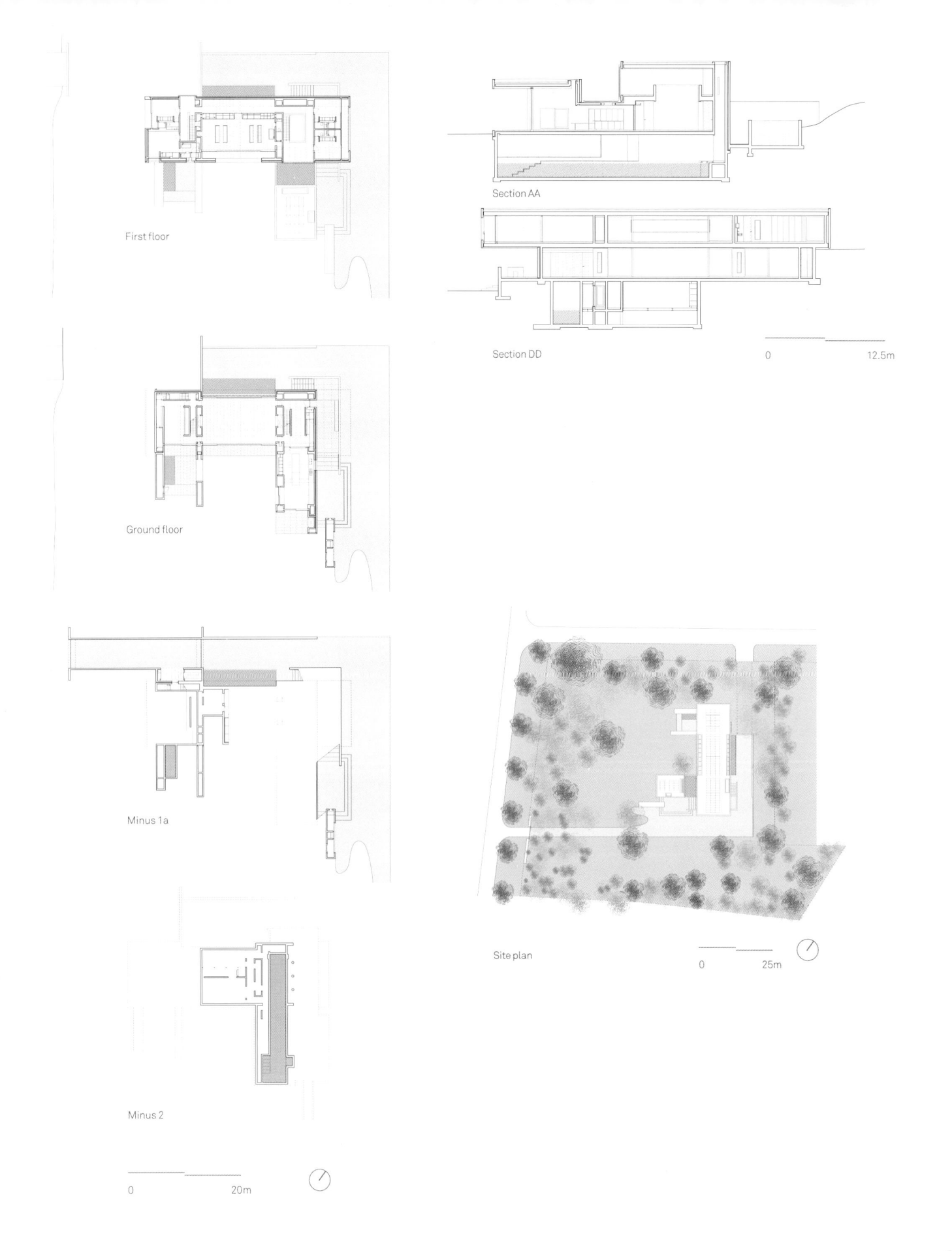

0   25m

Minus 2

0   20m

There is a gentle, natural richness to the material palette that tempers the rigorous, sculptural form. Continuous, textured surfaces that extend from the landscape and run through the interior are bathed in light softened by the forest and the architecture, creating a comfortable, sheltering home that is part of the landscape. *Russell Jones*

The building's environmental performance was an essential part of the design of the project, and balances both active and passive means to create a highly efficient building. Orientation, thermal mass, high levels of insulation, a ground-source heat pump, a heat recovery central-heating boiler and a bank of photovoltaic modules integrate discreetly with the architecture.

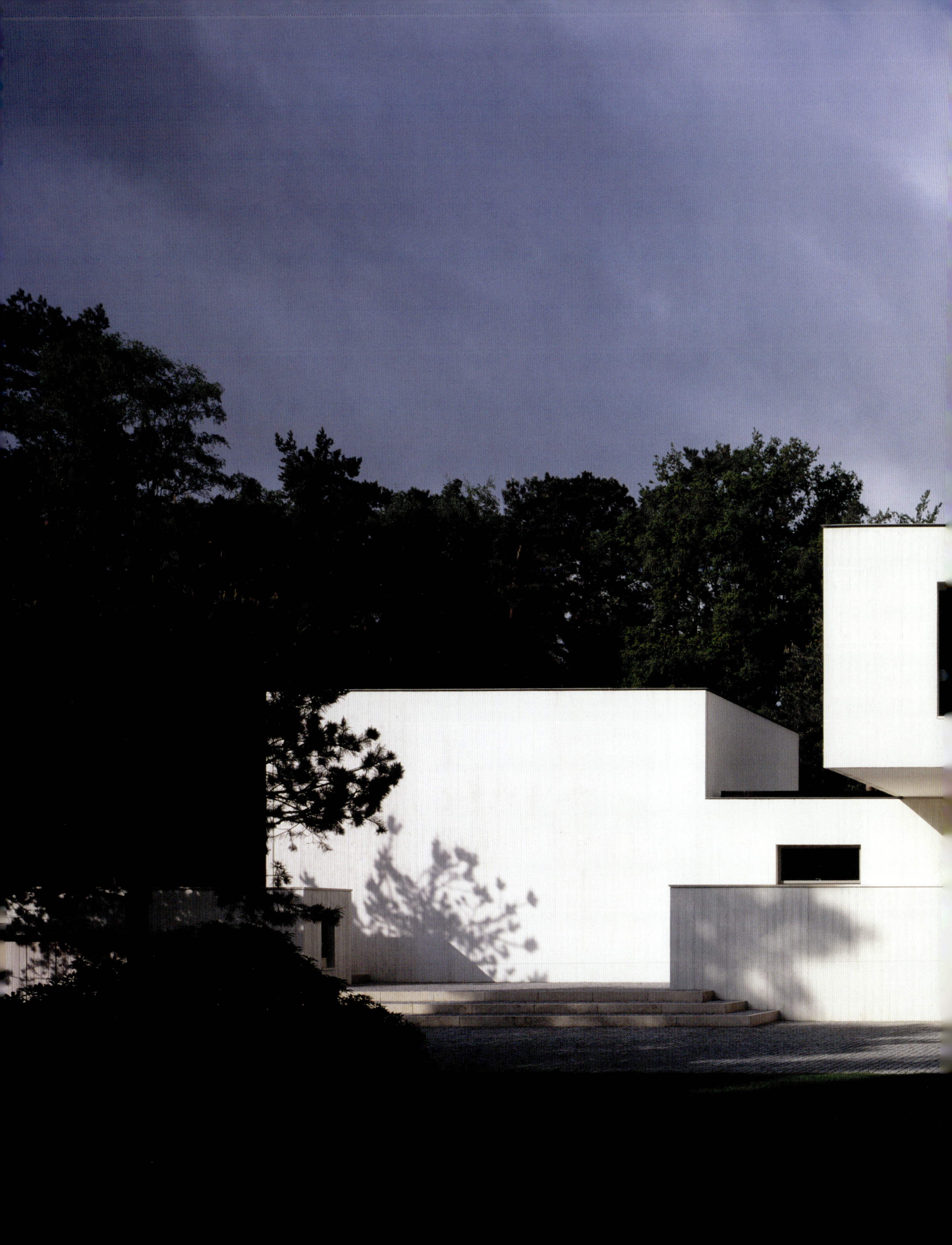

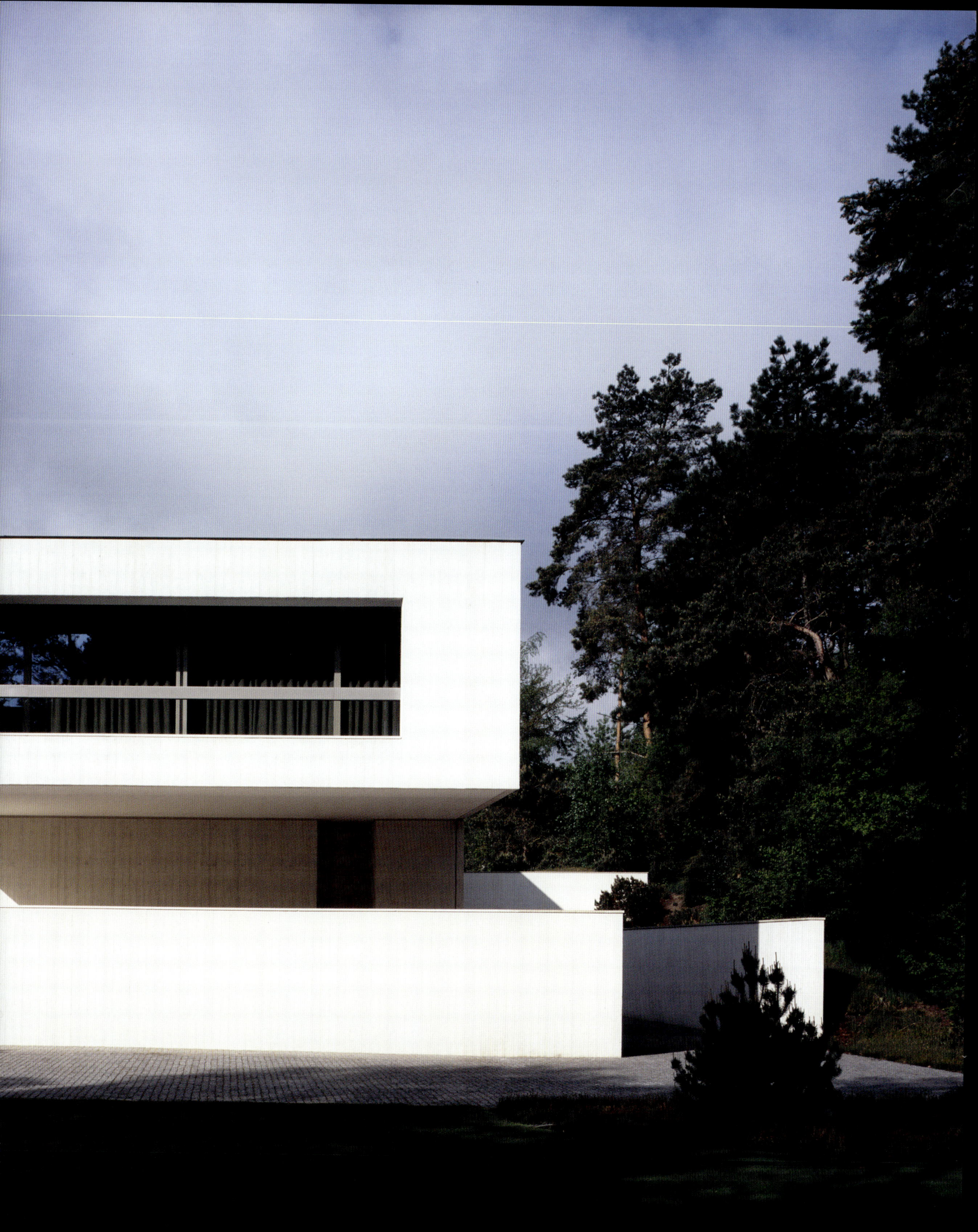

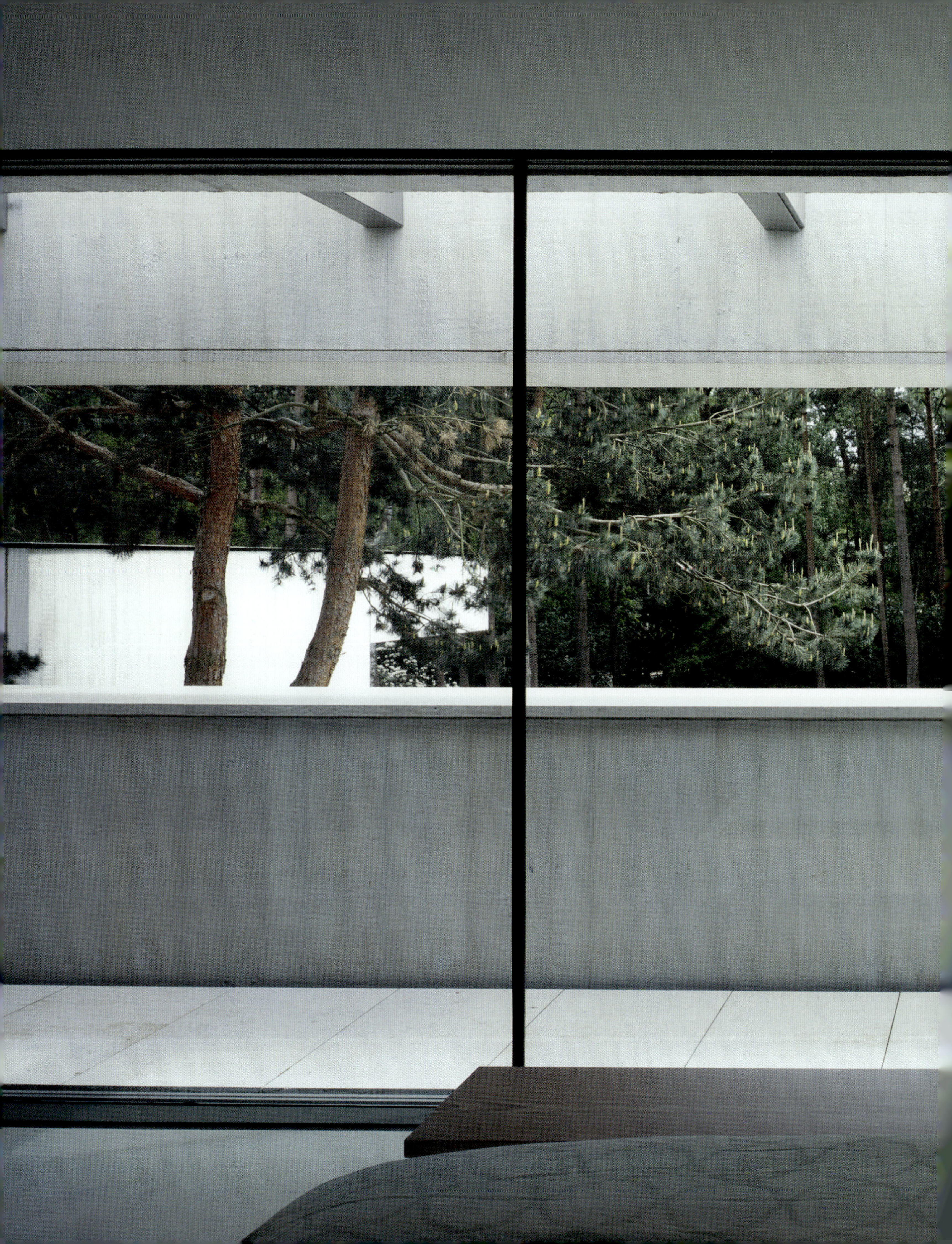

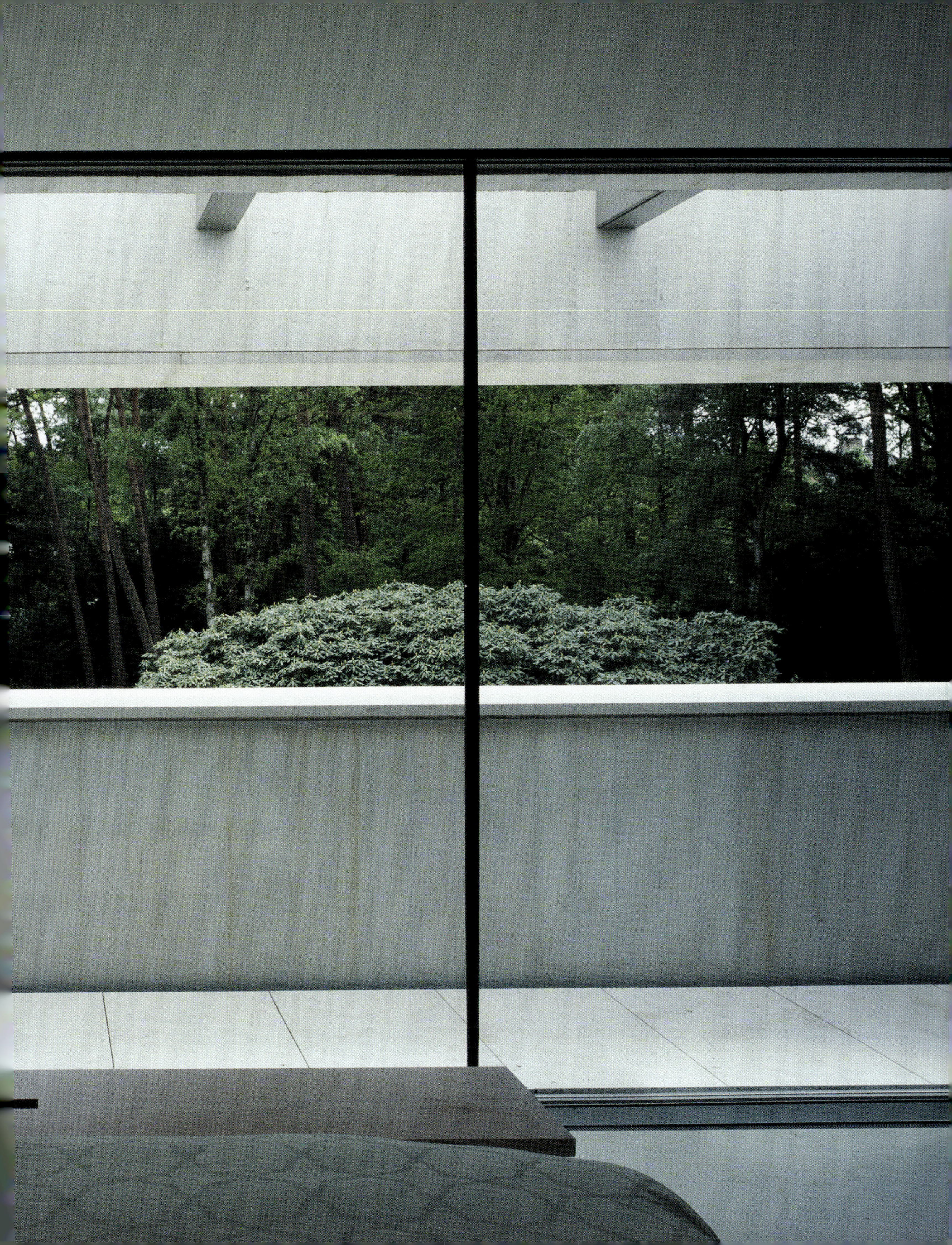

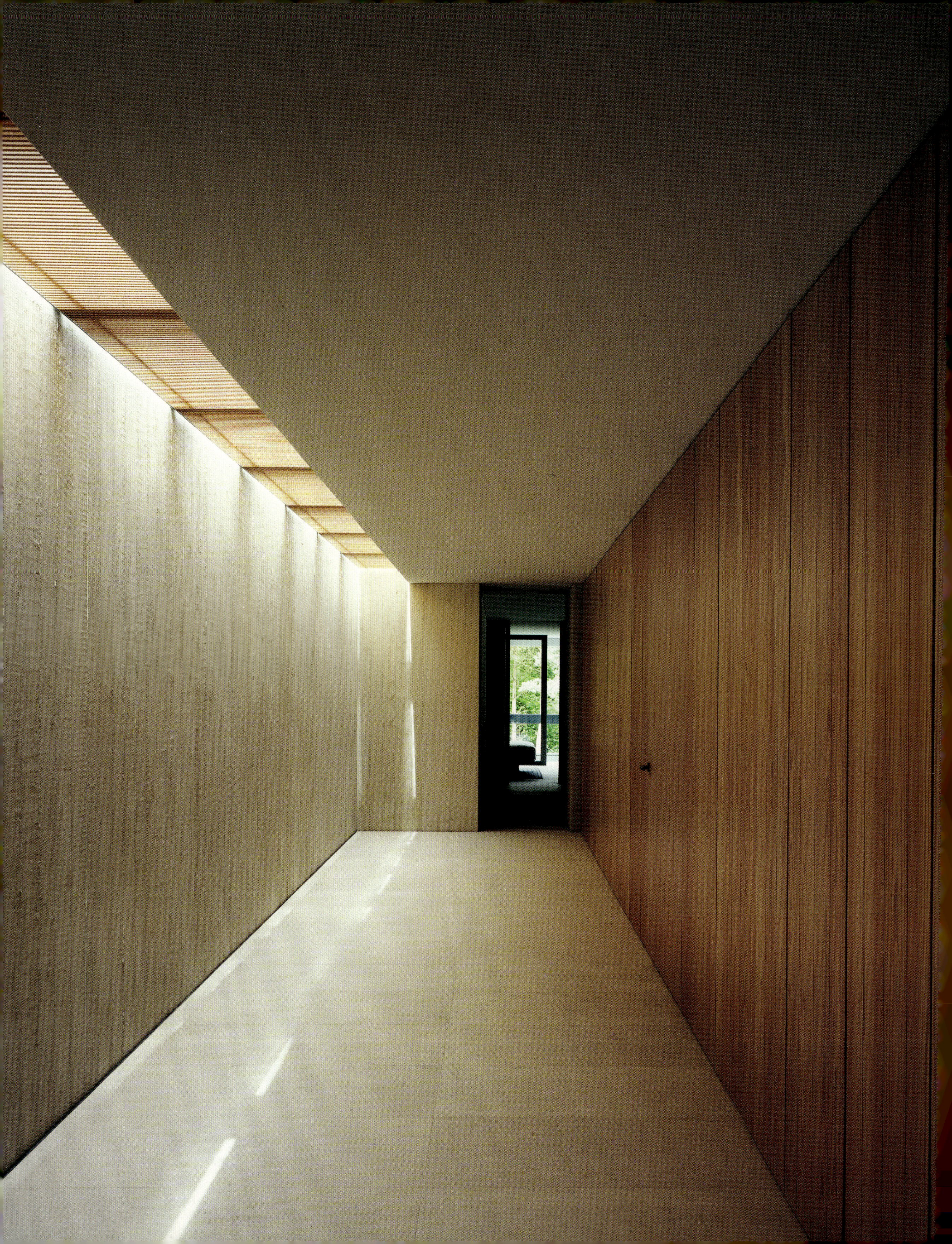

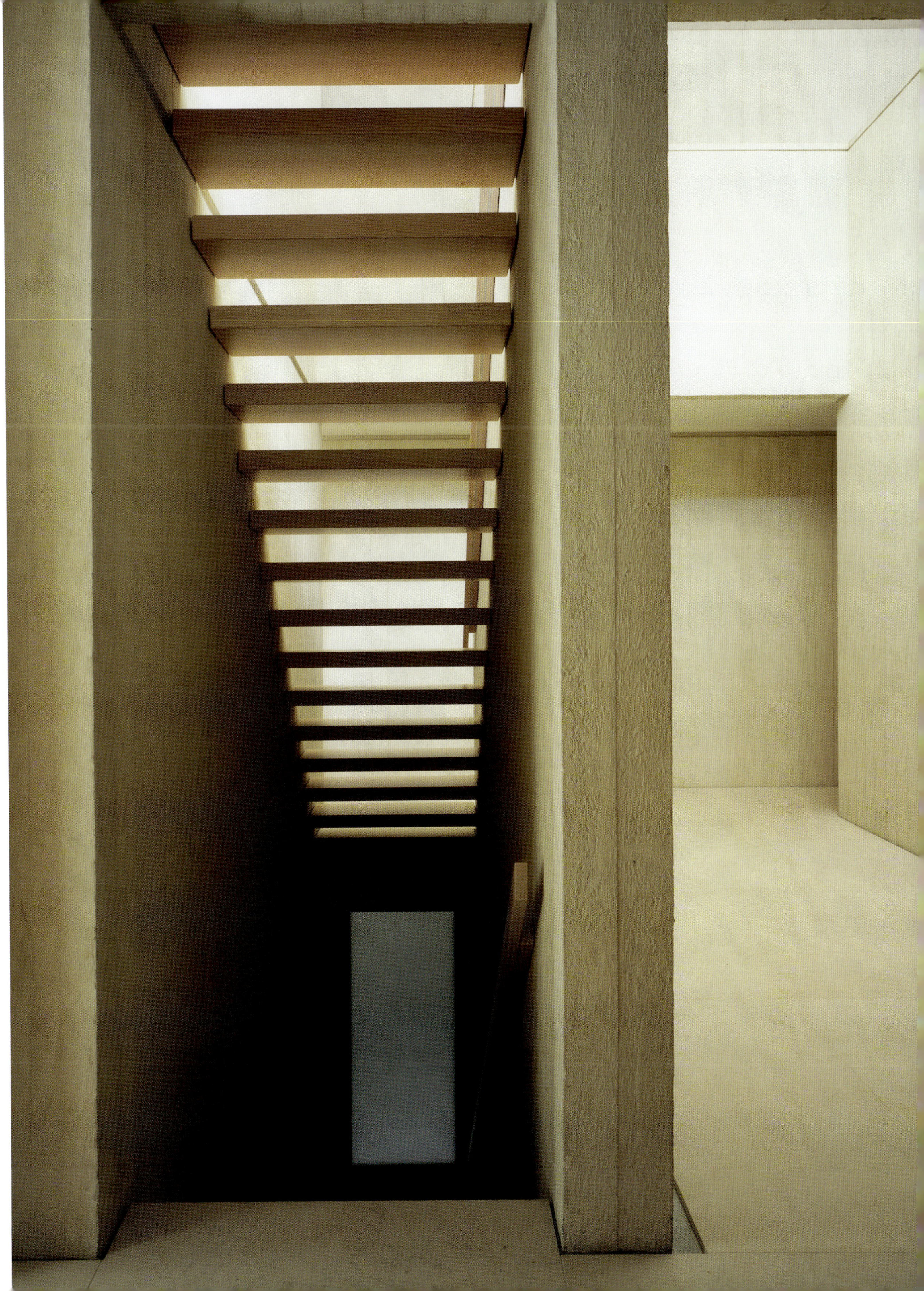

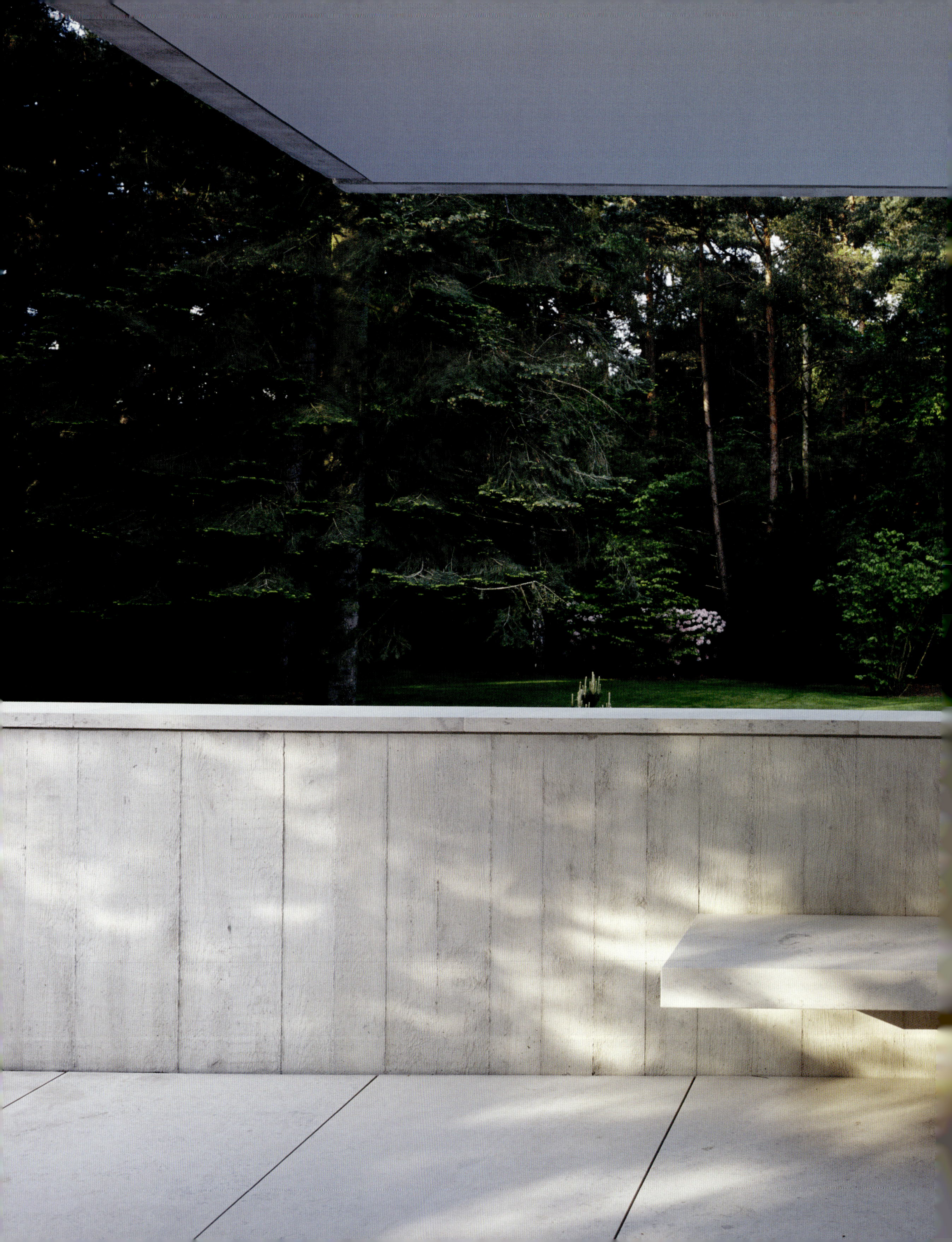

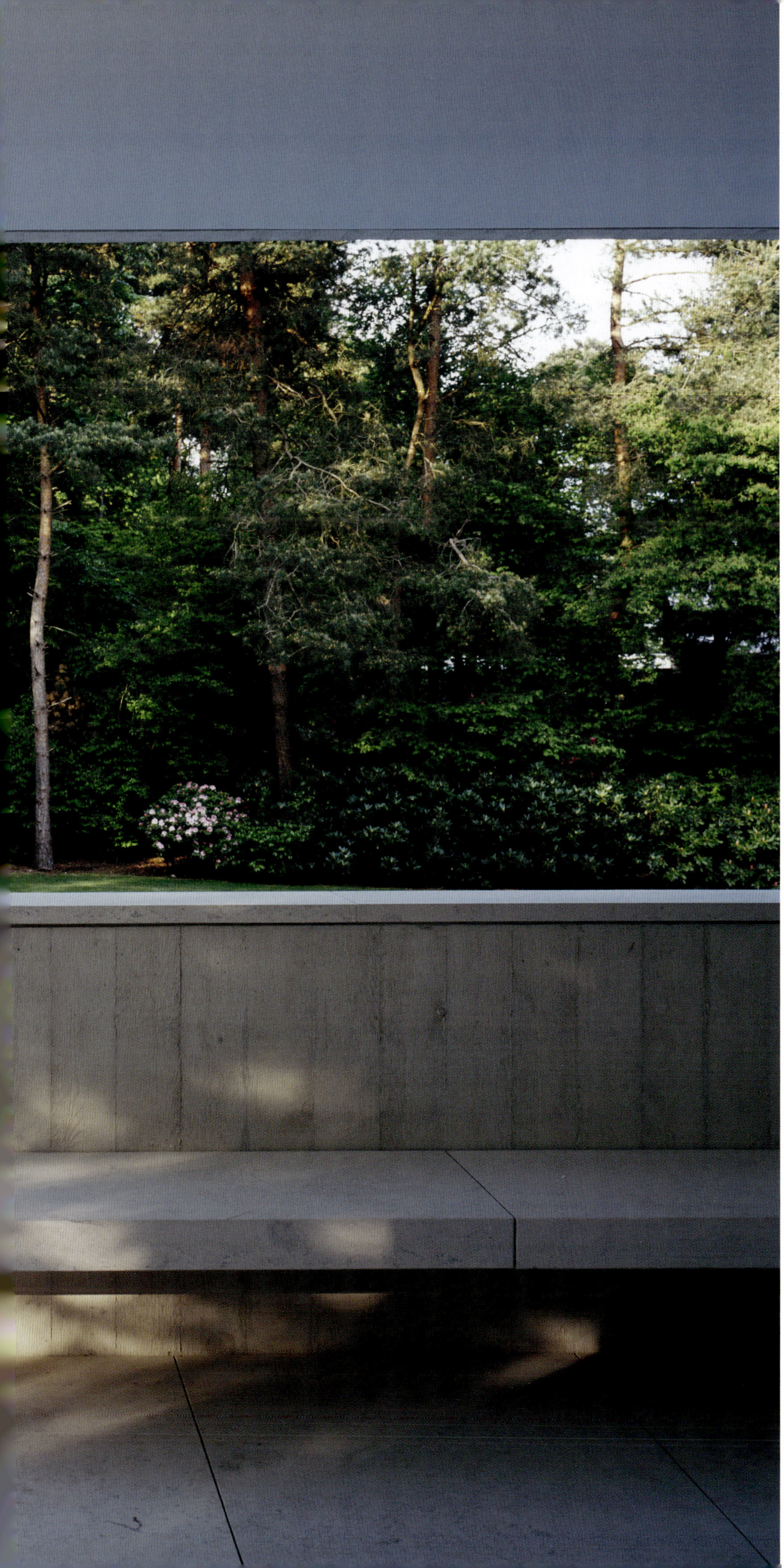

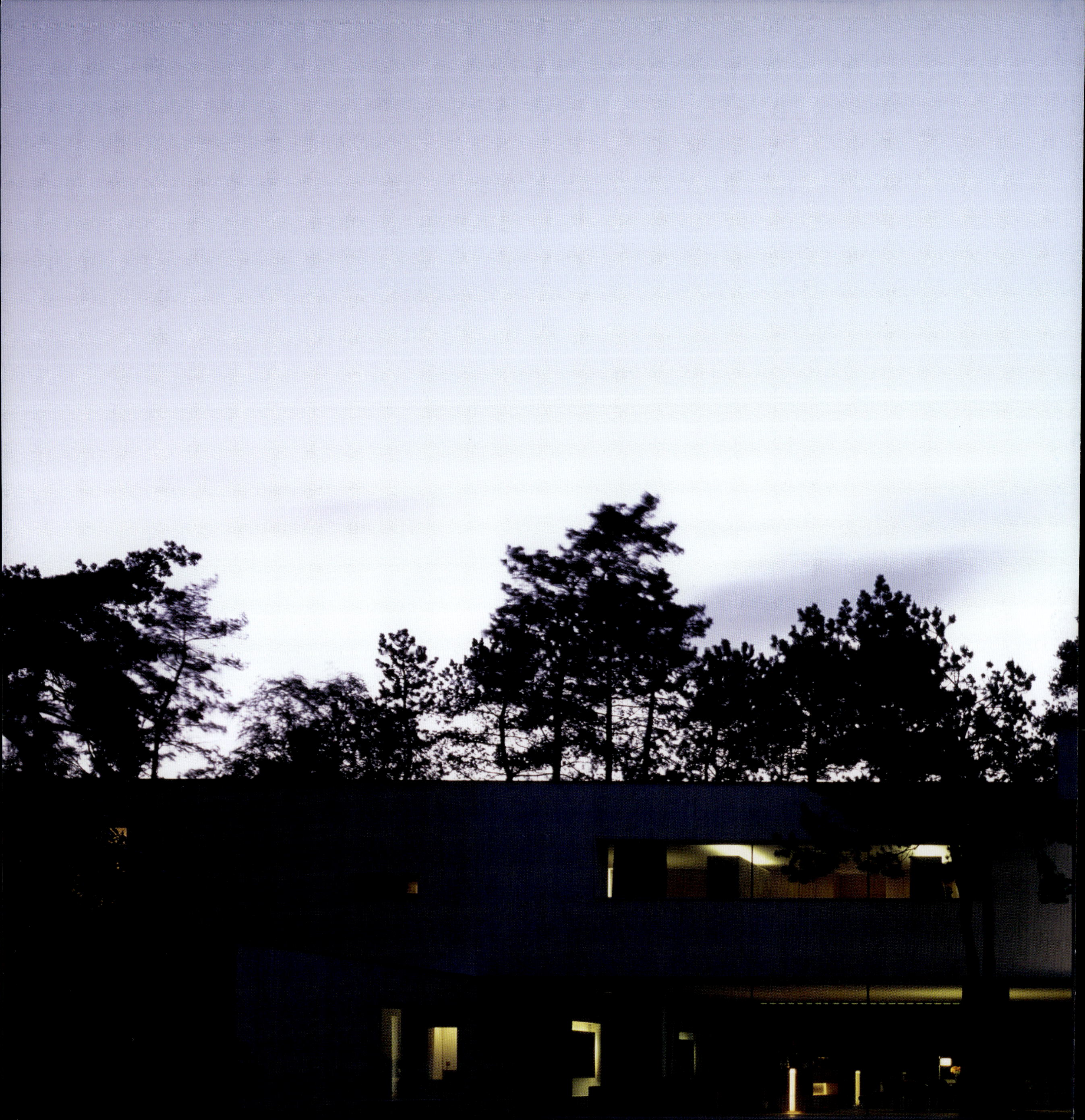

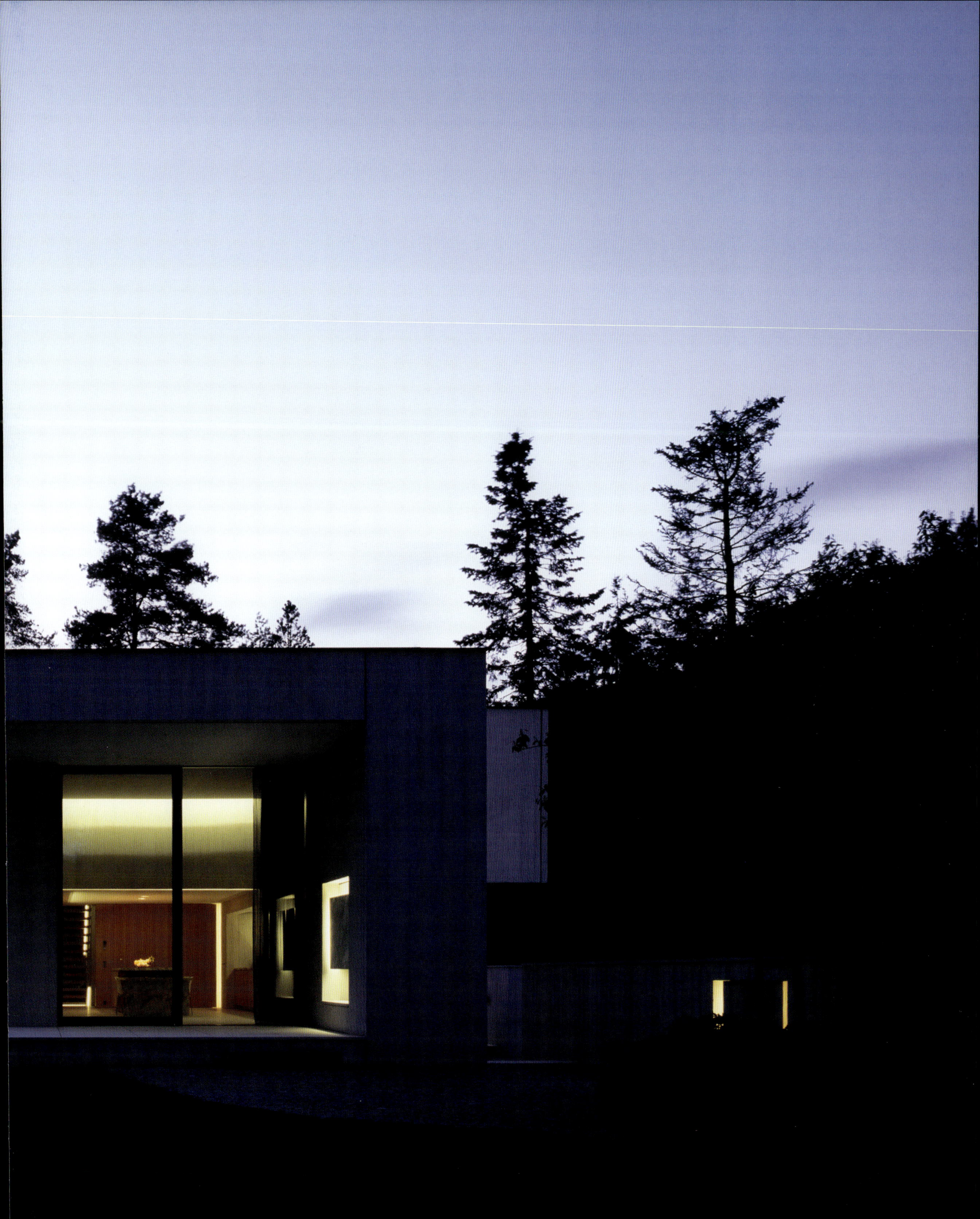

Photographs: Kraig Carlstrom and John Gollings

288

WHALE BEACH HOUSE

WHALE BEACH HOUSE
SYDNEY, AUSTRALIA, 2008
ALEX POPOV & ASSOCIATES

The vaulted form has marked much of architect Alex Popov's work. He used it to great effect in the award-winning Rockpool Apartments (1999) at Mona Vale, Sydney, and expressed it best in the Northbridge House (2003), a beauty set into a cliff face overlooking that city's Middle Harbour. At Northbridge he placed a series of vaults side by side across the block, supported by twenty-two pairs of precast concrete blade piers, to create a number of galleries, flowing into each other, filled with soft, reflected light.

Especially evident in Popov's work are the influences of Jørn Utzon's 'additive systems of assembly' to which he was introduced while working in Utzon's office in Denmark early in his career, and his admiration of Louis Kahn and his ideas of a building as a seamless 'community of rooms'. Kahn's Kimbell Art Museum in Fort Worth, Texas, comes to mind in the Northbridge House.

This new house at Whale Beach, towards the top of the Pittwater Peninsula on Sydney's northern beaches, signals a fundamental shift in Popov's approach: the vault is gone, as is the expressionist steel frame of earlier houses, replaced by a more direct, monumental expression. Sited on a narrow, steep block falling to a surf beach, the house, on first encounter, appears as a black timber box reminiscent of the black-painted timber beach houses of the Pittwater Peninsula in the 1920s. From the street, it sits just below the horizon line, its black form in stark contrast to the deep blue of the Pacific Ocean at its back and more conventional houses at its flanks. It is only remarkable at first glance for a 'spoiler' fin over a simple copper skillion roof, and a black timber 'corral' at the bottom of the steep drive, concealing a turntable for cars. The fin lifts the roof somehow, gives air to it, and works to take the eye past its top edge and define the horizon beyond.

Closer inspection reveals that the house is defined by a massive wall of in situ concrete to one side and a timber wall on the other, and 450-millimetre-deep concrete floor plates to help support its rectangular form. The black timber box has been inserted between, but slightly detached, from the parallel walls. To the south, a glass-louvred breezeway is used to allow easterly breezes in off the ocean and to flow up and through the house. On the north, there's the great concrete wall. It is the determining generator for the architecture. It extends for nearly the entire length of the house, adapting to the fall of the site, starting out at single-storey height and rising to nearly the full three storeys of the house. The wall acts as both a powerful sculptural element and a device to introduce light, air circulation, ventilation and a view corridor to the beach. Connected to the house ever so slightly, it helps to enclose a modest entry hall, where a narrow, angled slot cut into the wall offers a carefully framed view of the ocean.

Washed with soda water to draw out natural salts in the concrete, and hand-buffed to a waxy lustre, the wall gathers light and reflects it softly into the house through large sheets of glass. Jørn Utzon used this method of washing concrete at the Sydney Opera House. More recently, soda-washing was used to return to life the badly stained folded concrete beams and exposed walls of the restored Reception Hall (now known as the Utzon Room) at the Opera House. Exposed concrete ceilings throughout the house are also soda-washed and hand-rubbed in this manner.

The deep concrete floor plates cantilever past the end of the house, facing the ocean, working as abstracted verandahs, blinkered by the extended black-painted timber walls for privacy from neighbours, at the same time giving the building the appearance of floating lightly over the slope of the land. A square cut out of the top floor plate casts light into the terrace below; reflections from a swimming pool dance on its underside.

You enter the house at mid-level, into a flowing living, dining and kitchen zone; then it is either upstairs to the main bedroom suite or down to more bedrooms and another living room, leading directly to a garden and the swimming pool. Typical of all Popov's work, the interior planning is a highly resolved assembly of parts: direct, legible, simply ordered; the palette of materials, as always, restrained. Floors are of light-stained American oak, and the black-painted timber walls outside are repeated inside.

This is one of Popov's most assured houses. His European training, his early work in the office of Jørn Utzon and his admiration of Louis Kahn endow this work with a sensibility far removed from the light steel and glass structures that mark much of Australia's coastal architecture.

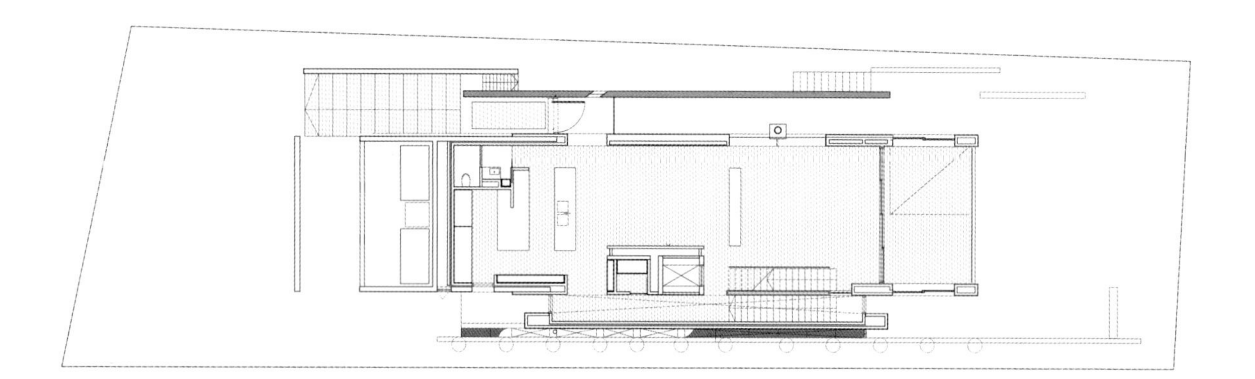

House plan

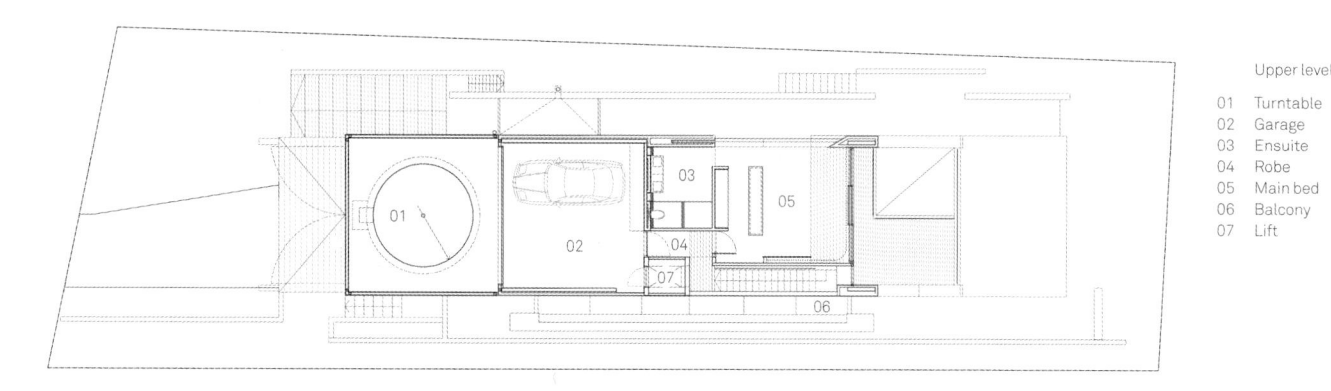

Upper level

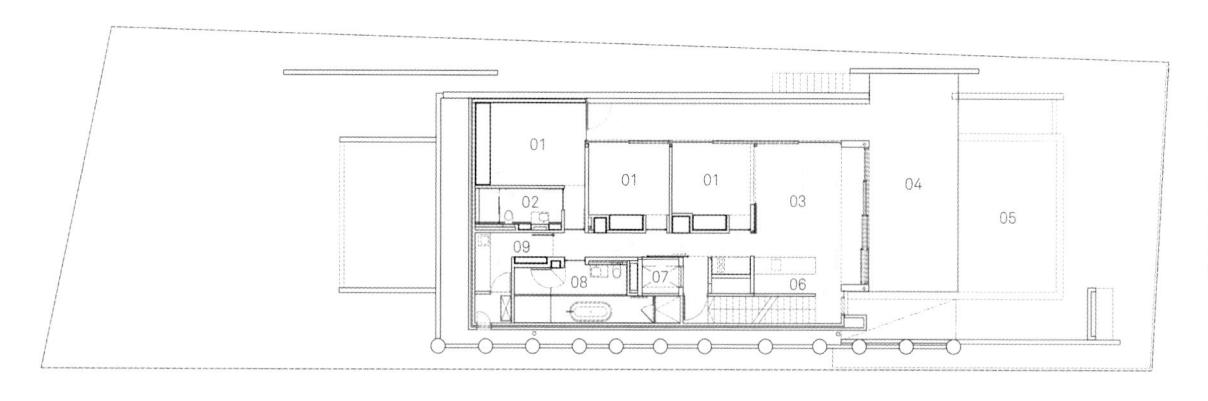

01 Turntable
02 Garage
03 Ensuite
04 Robe
05 Main bed
06 Balcony
07 Lift

Lower level

01 Bedroom
02 Ensuite
03 Living
04 Deck
05 Pool
06 Kitchenette
07 Lift
08 Bathroom
09 Laundry

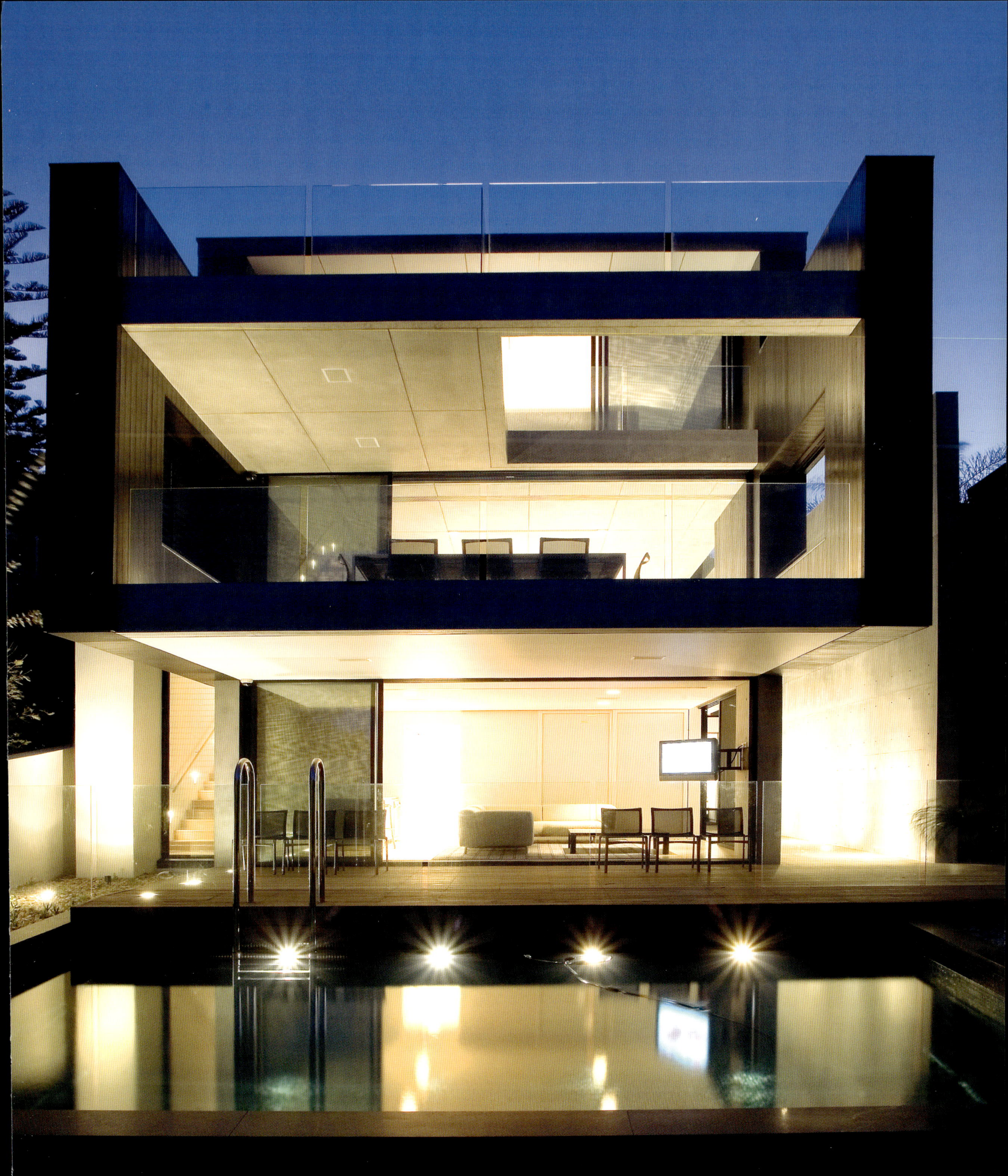

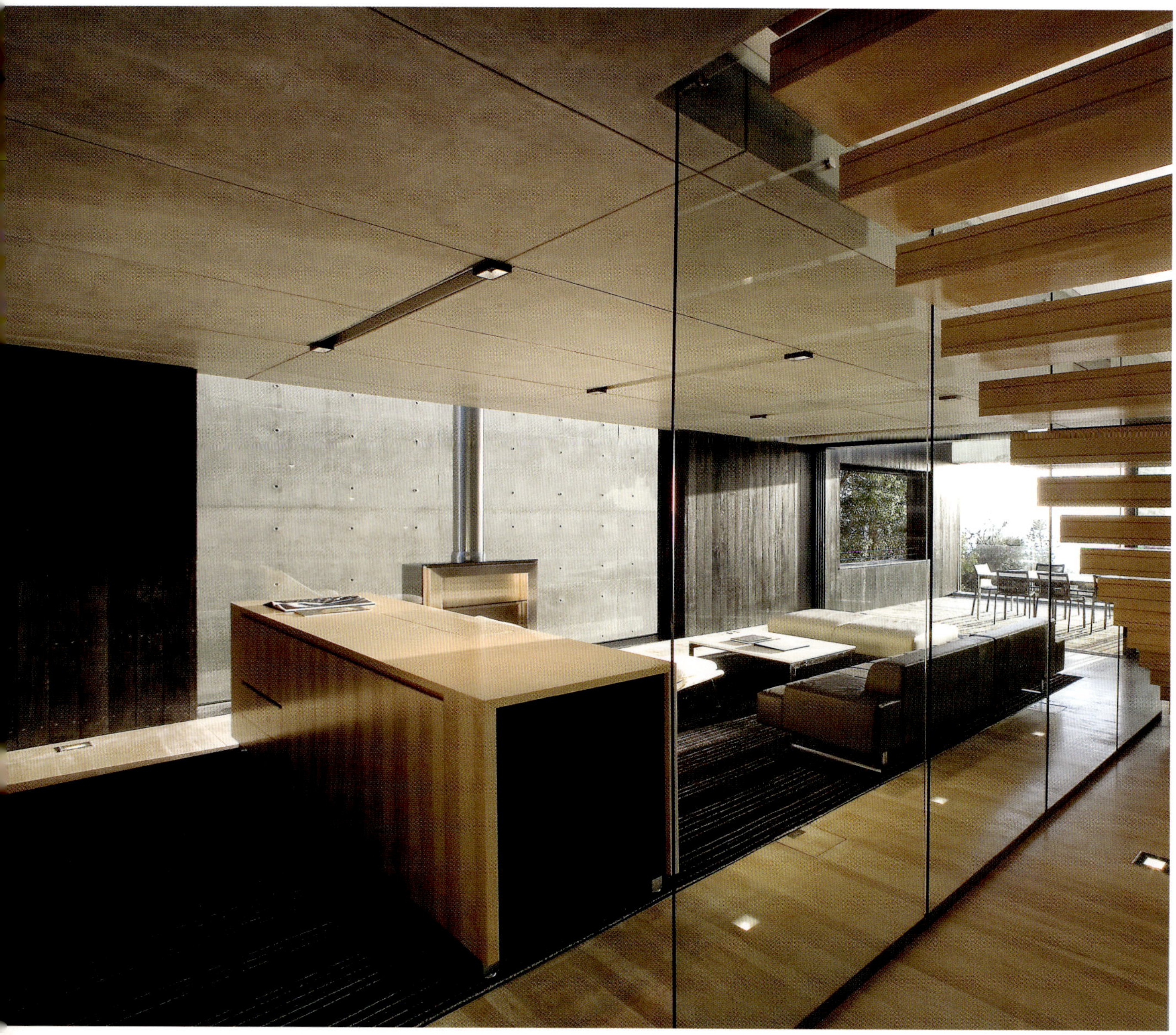

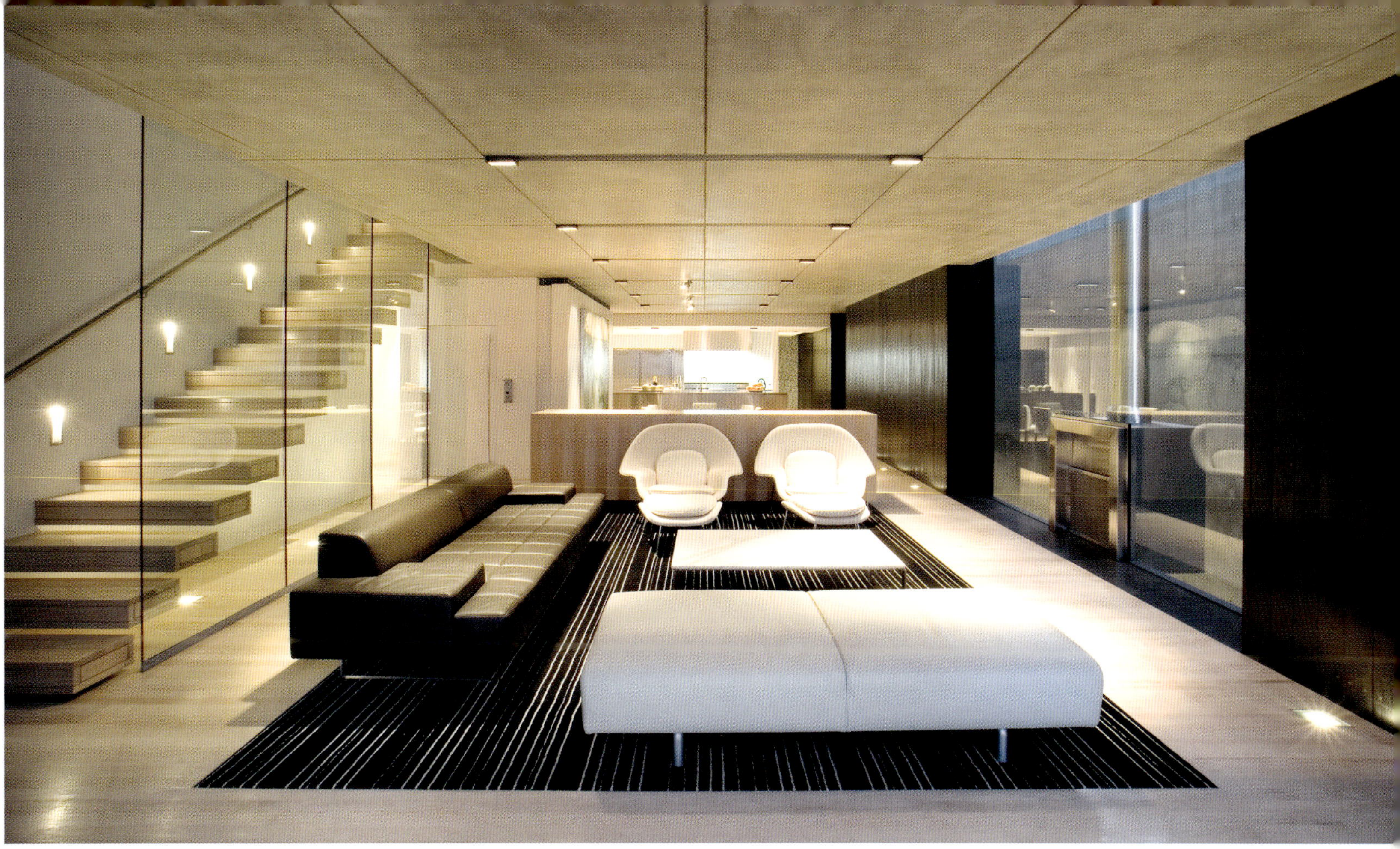

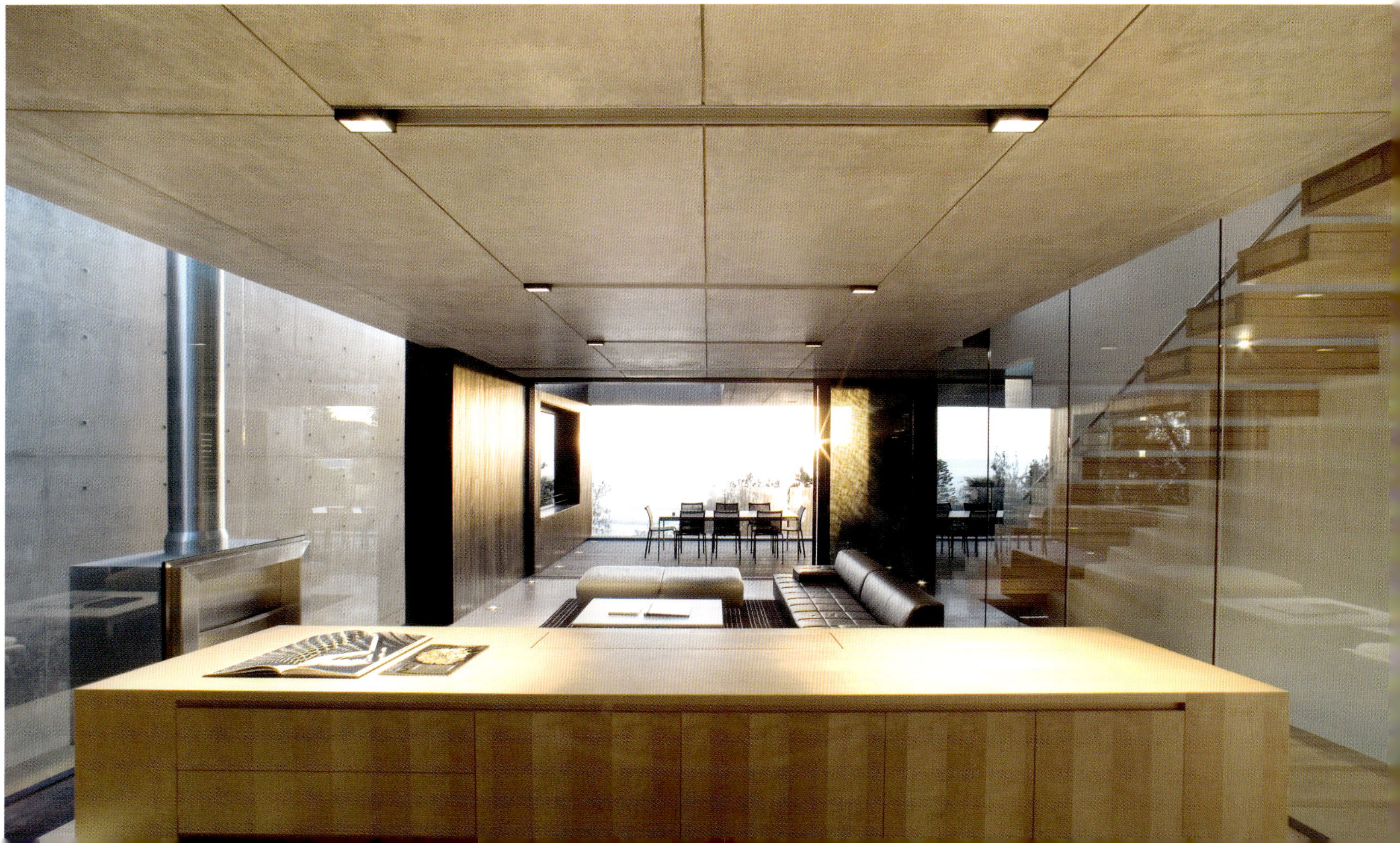

Architecture and physical location have always been inseparable from one another. The location, its characteristics and history are part of the emotive connections that form a sense of place and context. This project articulates the idea of a modernist approach to the Pittwater Peninsula's traditional concept of beachside dwellings. An early idea was of a timber packing case fallen from a ship and washed to shore. Further images of a wooden crate lying in the sand kept the idea principle in place. *Alex Popov*

    The concrete blade wall determines the path of circulation, acting as a device to direct views towards the beach and sea, gathering light and reflecting it into the interior. The reflections from the hand-polished walls and ceilings provide ever-changing plays of light, drawing the sea and clouds into the house. *Alex Popov*

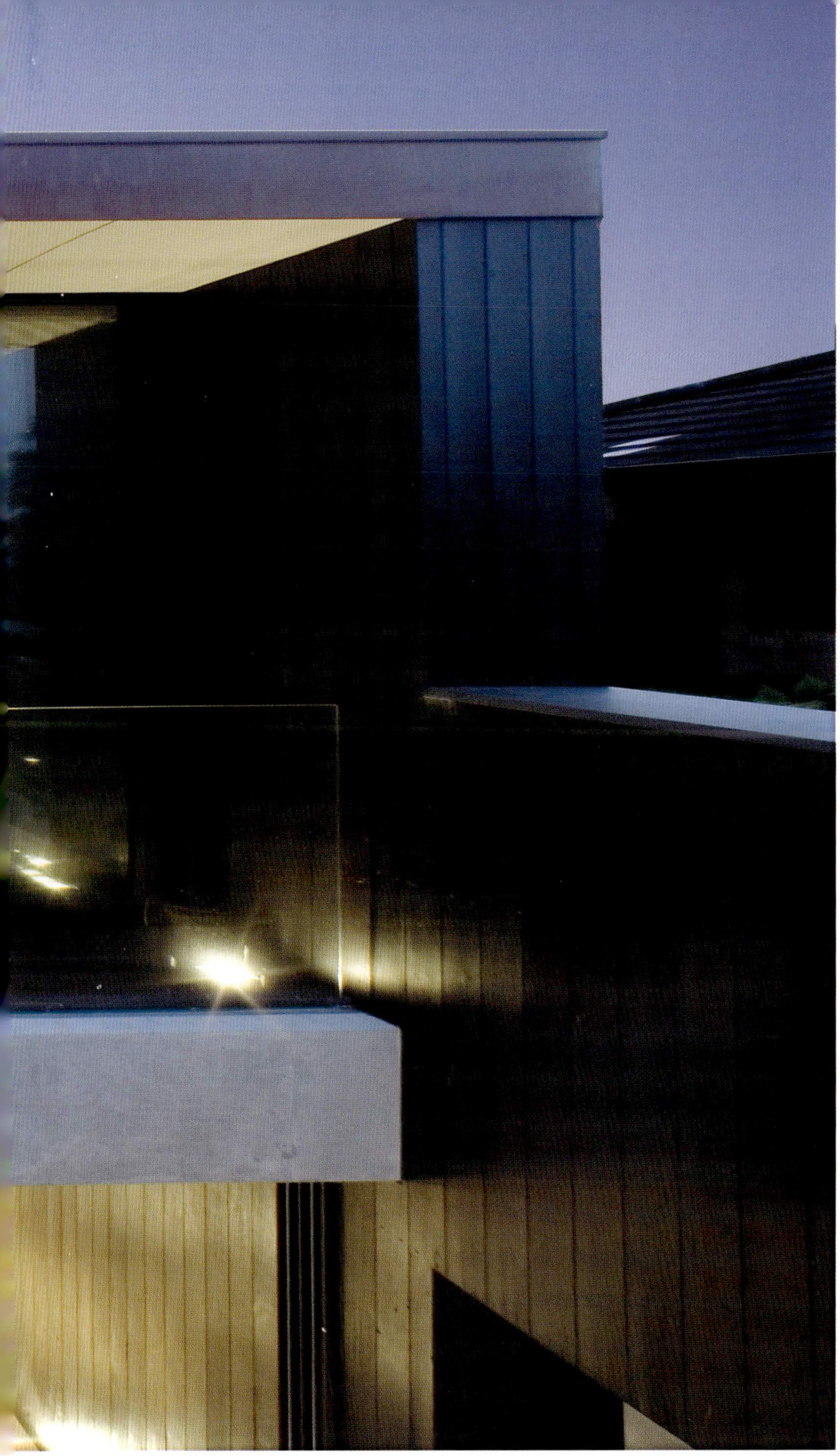

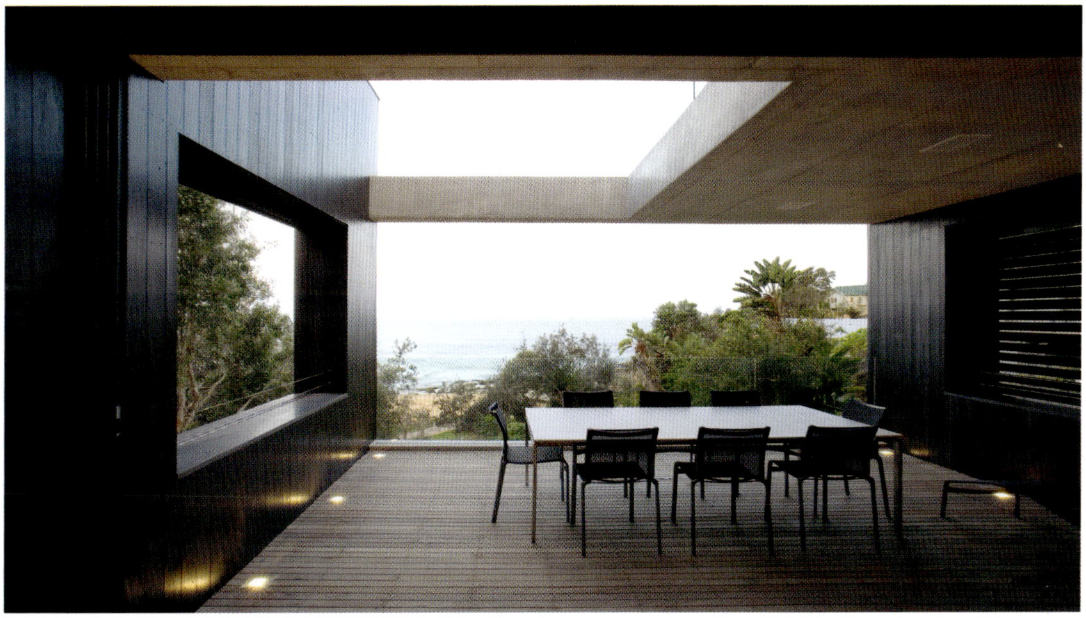

Photographs: John Gollings and Katherine Lu

SKYLIGHT HOUSE

SKYLIGHT HOUSE
SYDNEY, AUSTRALIA, 2011
CHENCHOW LITTLE ARCHITECTS

The facade of this house in Balmain, Sydney, overlooking the Parramatta River across to Cockatoo Island, is just a foil for the architectural drama going on inside. Behind its frilly Victorian facade stands a finely considered and refined modern house, stepping across three-and-a-half levels, remarkable for a deeply folded ceiling and skylights and an in situ concrete shelf – a concrete tray, really – with floating steps, incorporating the house's living, dining and outdoor spaces.

Designed by architects Tony Chenchow and Stephanie Little, this home is an exercise in producing highly resolved architecture within the constraints of a tight, steep site on a heritage-listed street with strict planning controls. The strategy from the outset was to retain the historic facade and construct an entirely new building behind it between rendered concrete-block walls. The requirement was for three bedrooms, two bathrooms, and living and dining zones. Problems arose when the facade itself, supported on bluestone foundations, threatened to collapse and had to be demolished and rebuilt faithfully under the strict supervision of heritage architects.

The plan of the house is inverted, with bedrooms downstairs, living and dining zones on the middle levels and a master bedroom suite on a third level. But it is the middle level that is truly dramatic. Constructed as a suspended slab of reinforced concrete, it serves to create split-level living and dining zones that blur indoor and outdoor spaces with an elegance seldom seen under such restricted conditions. The kitchen and dining area spills out to a tiny enclosed court at one end, while a small central court at the top of the stairs in the middle zone, literally cut out of the concrete slab and open to the sky, is planted with a mature *Banksia integrifolia* tree. From here, a series of floating concrete steps carry you to the living zone with double doors out to a balcony and views over the river across the road. A 'slice' in the stairs allows for sliding glass doors to open or fully enclose the small courtyard. The floor folds and steps and tilts along the ground plane, defining each space. The edges of the concrete tray turn up as an organising datum line flowing throughout the house. On one side it serves as a balustrade over the stairwell, on the other it supports a floating concrete shelf for the display of objects. Here, sliding glass walls are used to enclose or open the spaces this way and that, to enclose the tiny court with the tree, open the kitchen out to the rear court, or separate the living zone up the stairs entirely from the rest of the house. The idea, says Chenchow, 'was to create a fluid sense of continuous space dragging you along from the moment you step inside all the way through to the master bedroom suite at the very top at the rear of the house'.

Diffused light flows into the house through two immense glass skylights inserted into the south-east section of the roof, with the strong northern light tempered by a series of deep plaster folds in the ceiling over the living zone – not unlike internal brise-soleils – that bounce soft light into the house. The deepest of these plaster folds cuts sharply into this space to serve as a delineator between living and dining zones. Seen in section, from outside, the deep V-cut into the side wall gives the roof line the appearance of large, tilted exhaust chimneys. The kitchen and dining area is dominated by a sculptural ceiling that curves and flows, reminiscent of the ceilings of Alvar Aalto, which aids the flow of soft, continuous light into the house. On the third, uppermost level the floor plane tilts out at the edges to form a tray housing the master bedroom, high among the canopy of the tree. The angled edges of the tray aid light penetration into the dining room and kitchen below. The palette of the house is restricted to raw concrete, spotted gum joinery and white paint. This is wonderful, finely resolved architecture, with subtle but critical use of concrete.

Two fluid horizontal planes have been inserted within the party wall: one, a concrete tray forming a ground-floor plane mediating the natural ground levels along the site; and a second, a ceiling plane, which is fragmented to permit sunlight into the length of the building. *Tony Chenchow*

The concrete floor plane has been cut out around a central courtyard containing an endemic *Banksia integrifolia*. The floor steps and tilts along the ground plane, defining each space. On a third, upper level the floor plane tilts on each edge to form a tray housing the master bedroom amongst the branches and canopy of the tree. *Tony Chenchow*

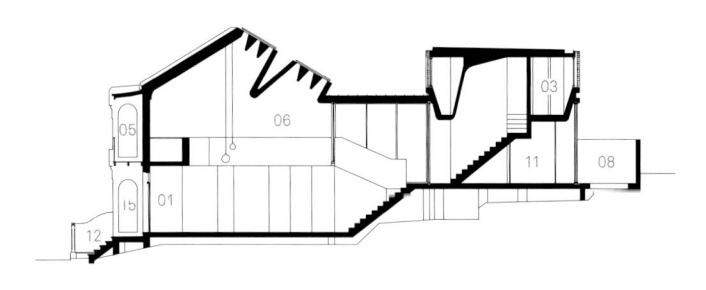

01 Entry
02 Bedroom/study
03 Bathroom
04 Storage
05 Balcony
06 Void
07 Living
08 Courtyard
09 Dining
10 Kitchen
11 Laundry
12 Garden
13 Skylight
14 Roof
15 Porch

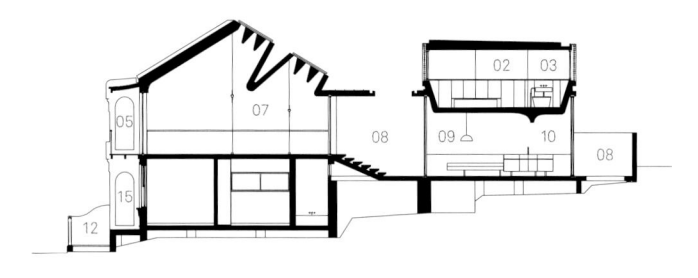

Section AA

Section BB

Ground floor plan

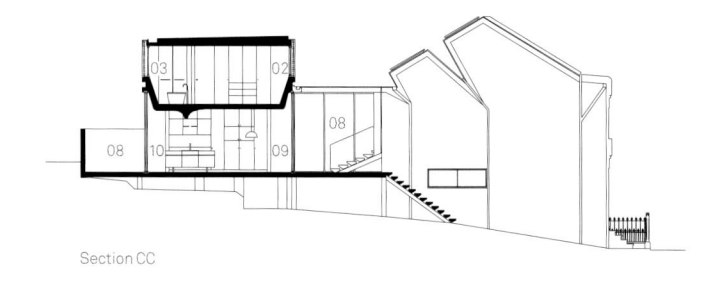

Section CC

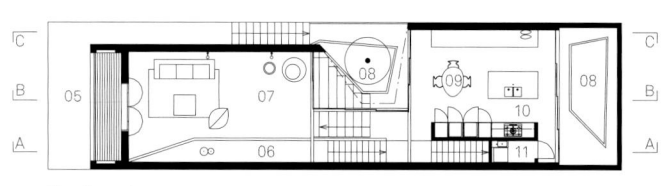

First floor plan

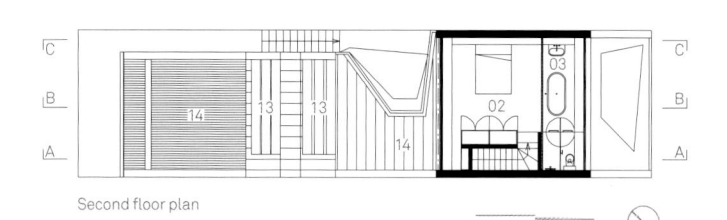

Second floor plan

0   5m

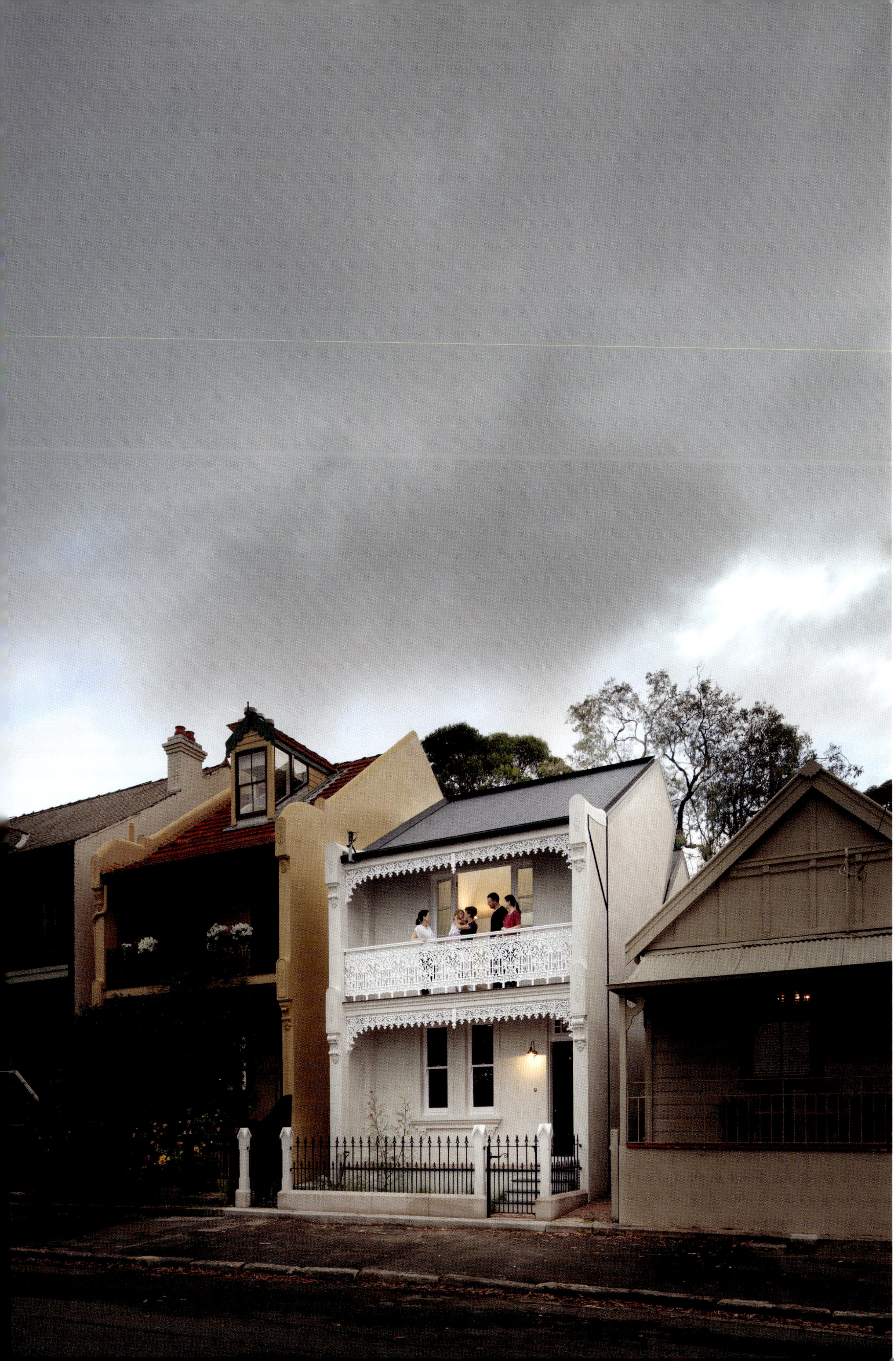

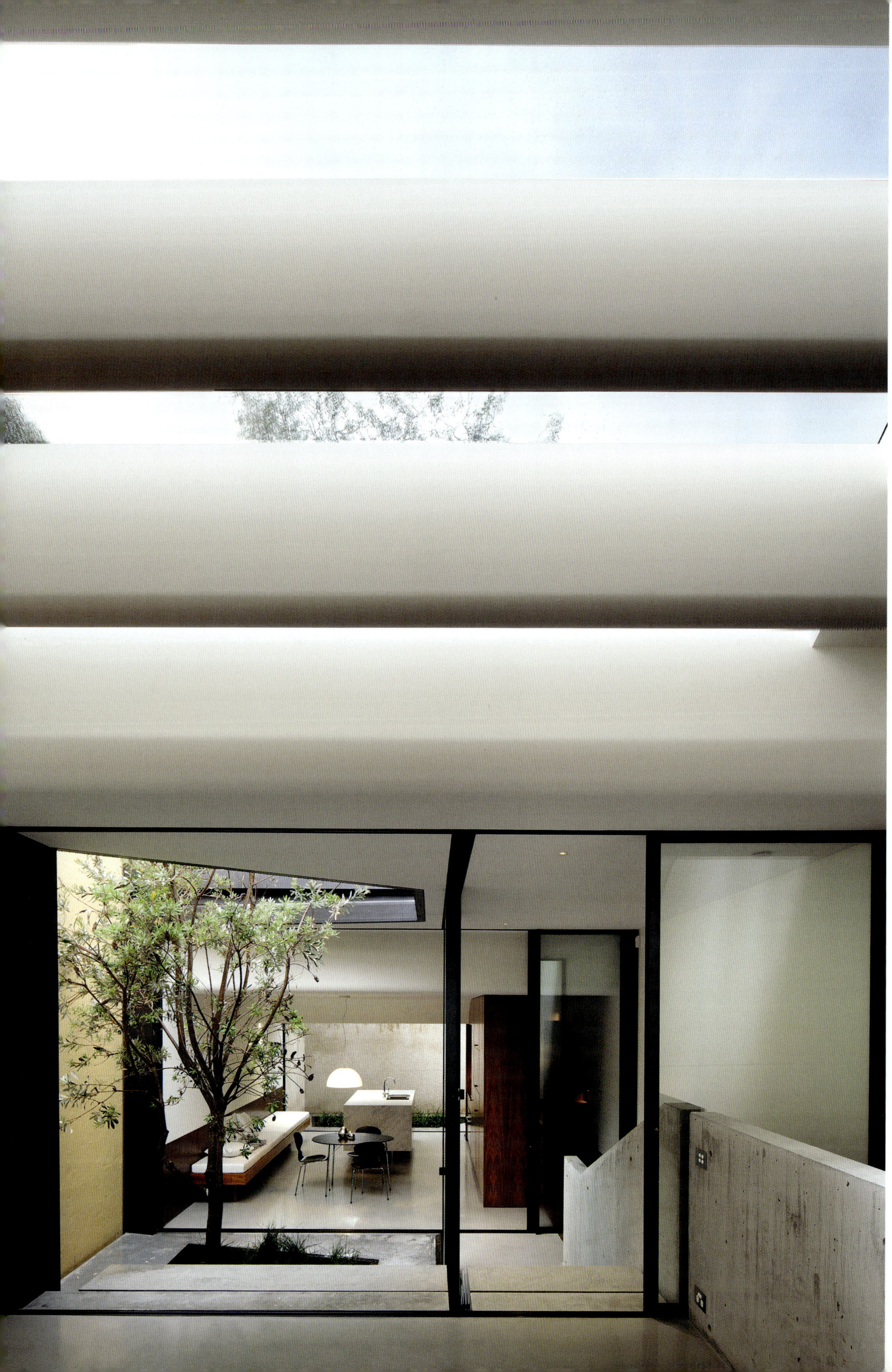

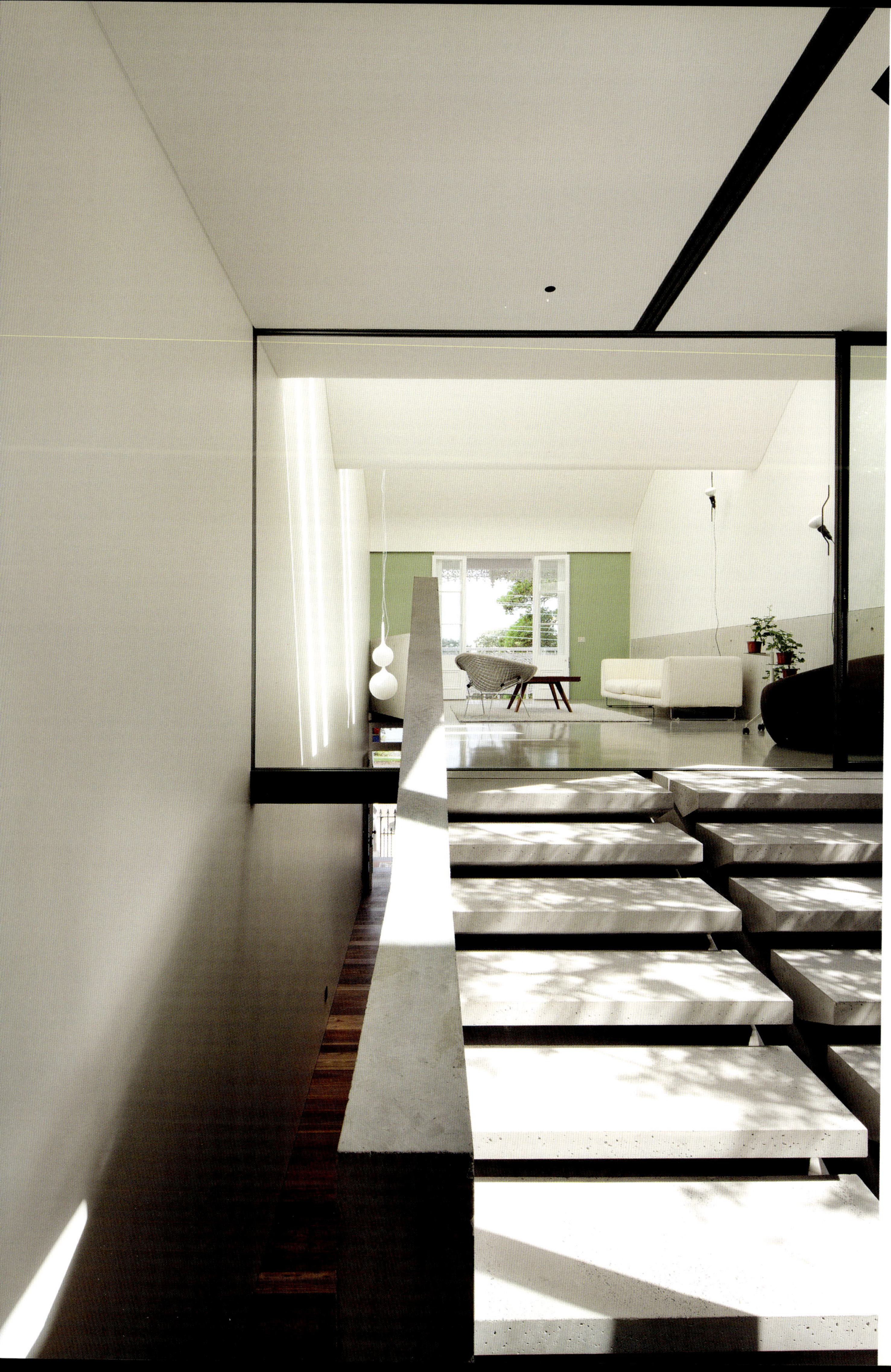

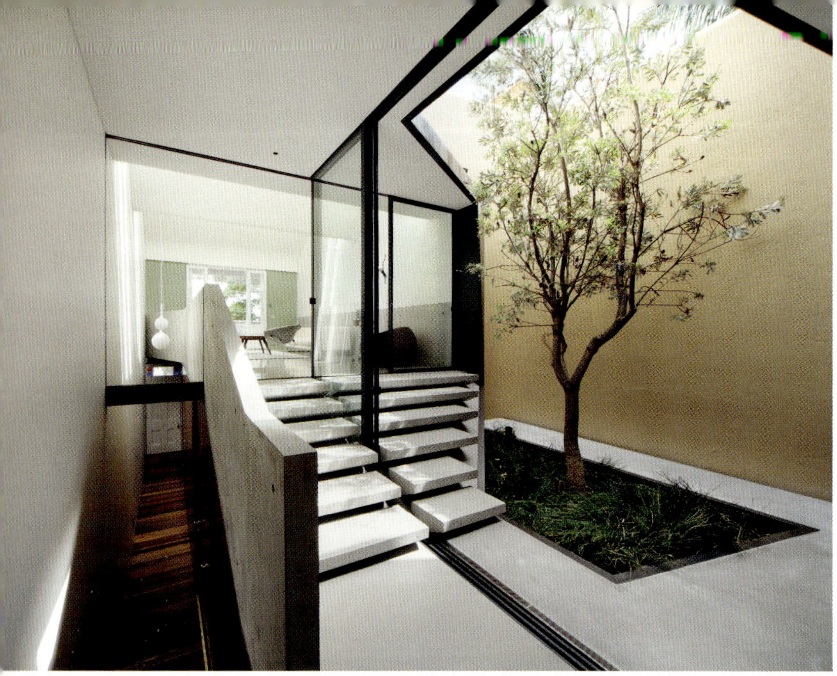

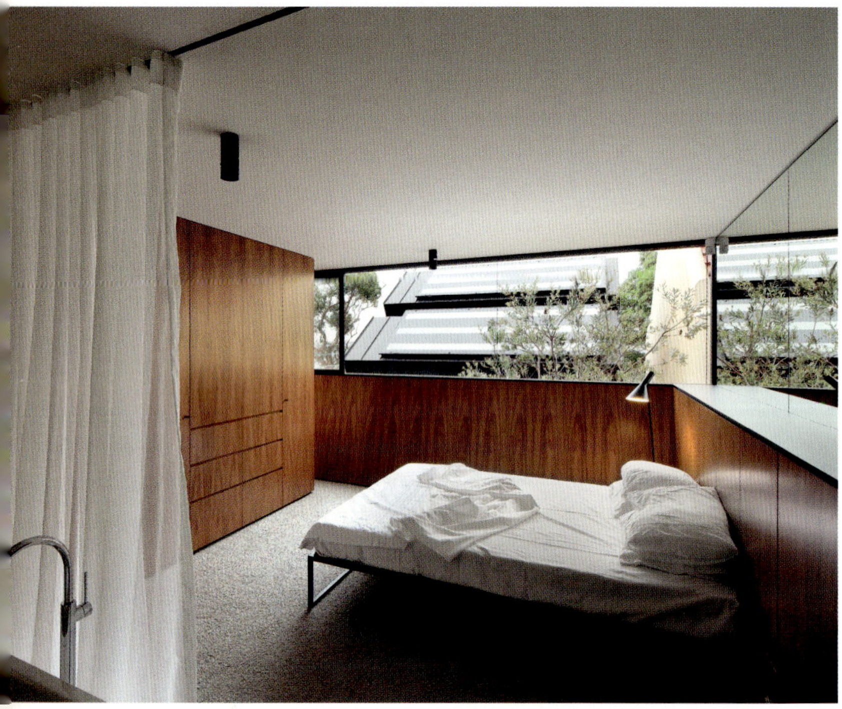

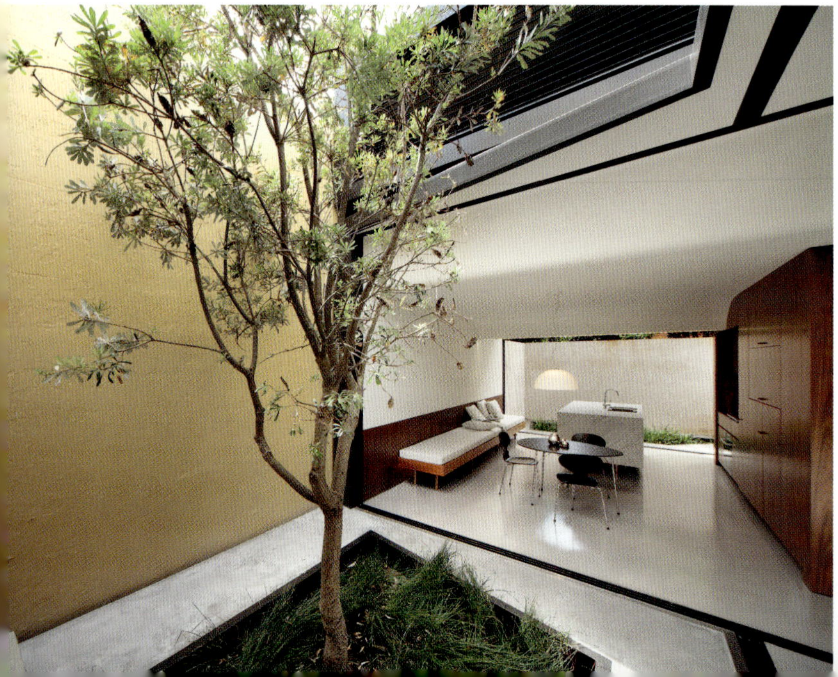

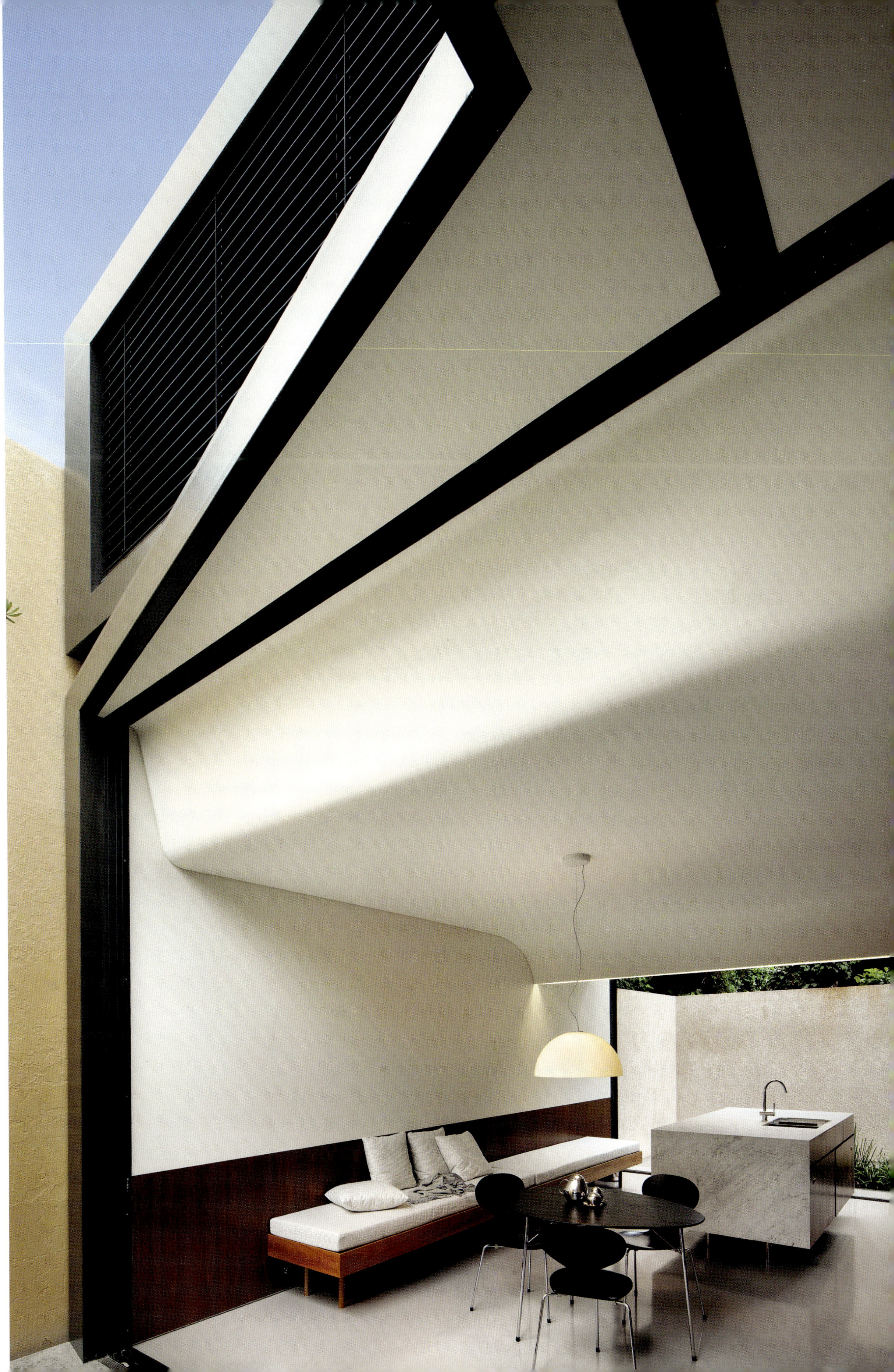

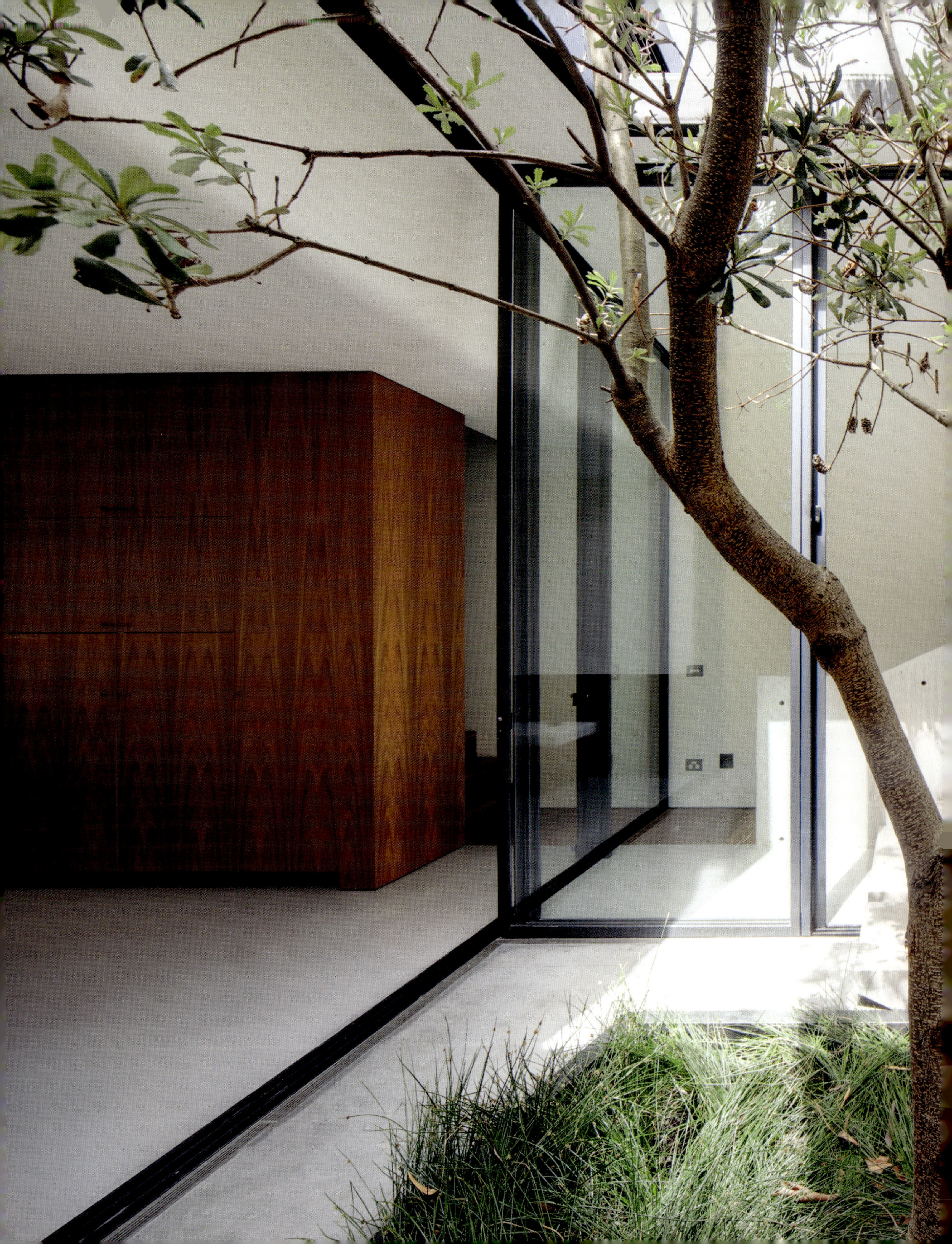

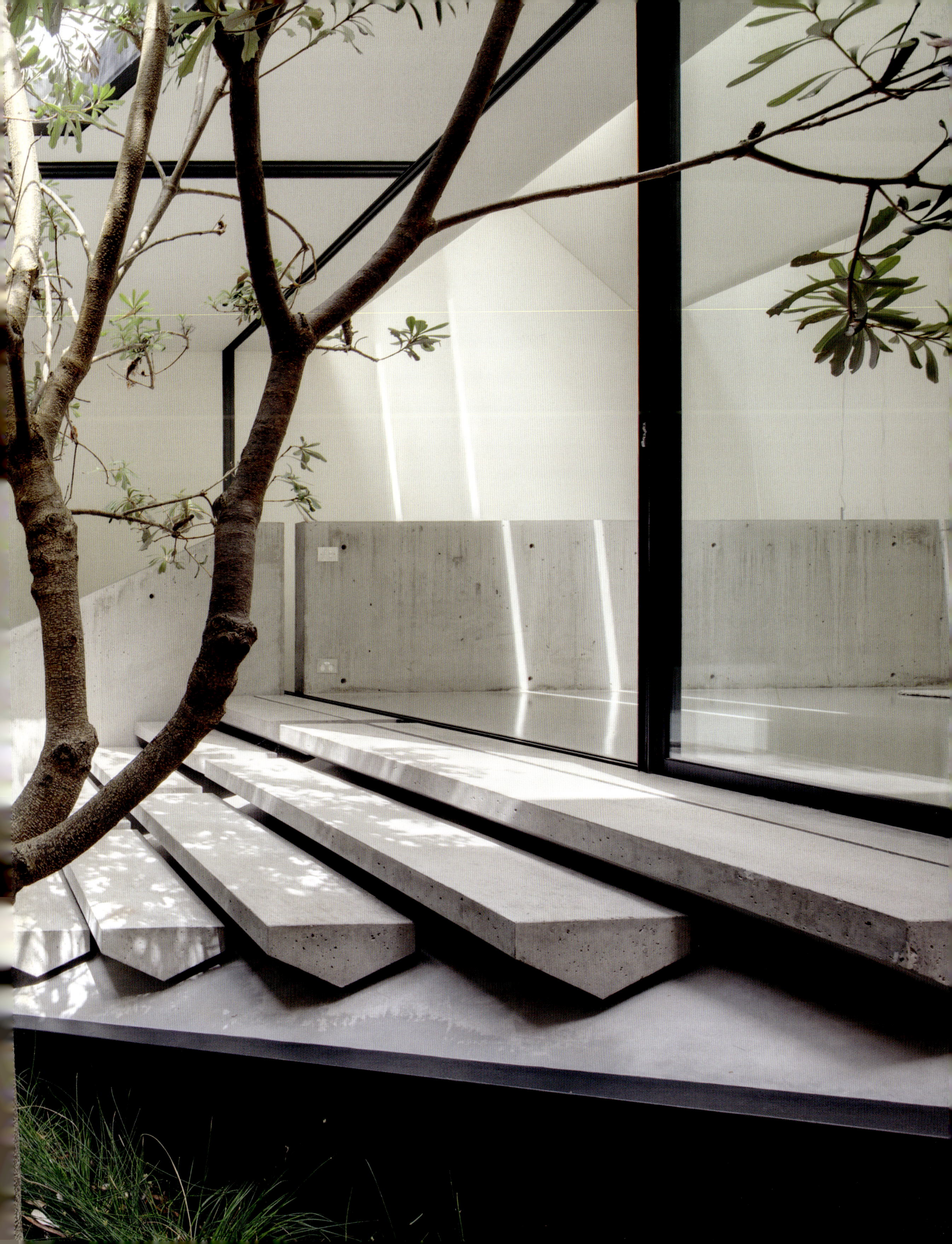

ABOUT THE AUTHOR AND ACKNOWLEDGEMENTS

Joe Rollo is an architecture writer and editor. He reviewed architecture for *The Age* newspaper, Melbourne, from 1994 to 2015. He has written extensively for newspapers and magazines, including *The Australian*, *The Weekend Australian Magazine*, *The Spectator Australia*, *The Australian Financial Review Magazine*, *The Bulletin* and *Wallpaper** magazine. He is the founding editor of *C+A*, an international magazine of concrete architecture, and the author of four books: *Contemporary Melbourne Architecture*, a collection of reviews from *The Age* (1999); *Concrete Poetry: Concrete Architecture in Australia* (2004); *Beautiful Ugly: The Architectural Photography of John Gollings* (2011); and *Harry Seidler's Umbrella: Selected Writings on Australian Architecture and Design* (2019). He holds a Master of Architecture degree (Honoris Causa) from RMIT University. He was born in Sicily and lives and works in Melbourne.

Acknowledgements: This book would not have been possible were it not for a little big magazine that I conceived back in 2004 and continue to edit. The magazine is *C+A*, an international magazine of concrete architecture published by Cement Concrete and Aggregates Australia (CCAA), the peak body representing the heavy construction materials industry in this country. *C+A* is little because it is not a mainstream publication; it is big because of its large format, A3, which makes it almost impossible to ignore. It is big, too, because it showcases some of the best examples of concrete architecture in Australia and internationally, including the houses in this book, which were published in *C+A* over a period of fourteen years. My thanks to Ken Slattery, CEO of CCAA, who has shown unwavering faith and trust in my judgement to decide on what to publish and what to ignore. I am forever indebted to those photographers who provided permission for their images to be published here: Michael Nicholson, Trevor Mein, Kraig Carlstrom, John Gollings, Jeremy Weihrauch, Daici Ano, Brett Boardman, Dwight Eschliman, Benjamin Benschneider, Katherine Lu, Åke E:son Lindman, Archive Olgiati, Nelson Garrido, David Roche, Hélène Binet, Tom Ferguson and Fernando Guerra. Without their memorable images there would have been no book. Their generosity is not forgotten. My thanks to Garry Emery, who has designed the book with the assistance of Alexander Hevey. Garry has designed *C+A* from its inception. The large format was his idea, so, if you have to, blame him. Thank you, also, to my publishing team at Thames & Hudson Australia: Kirsten Abbott, Caitlin O'Reardon and Elise Hassett.

First published in Australia in 2019
by Thames & Hudson Australia Pty Ltd
11 Central Boulevard, Portside Business Park
Port Melbourne, Victoria 3207
ABN: 72 004 751 964

www.thamesandhudson.com.au

Text © Joe Rollo 2019

Images © copyright remains
with the individual copyright holders

All articles reproduced with permission from
Cement Concrete & Aggregates Australia.

22 21 20 19   5 4 3 2 1

The moral right of the author has been
asserted.

All rights reserved. No part of this publication
may be reproduced or transmitted in any form
or by any means, electronic or mechanical,
including photocopy, recording or any
other information storage or retrieval system,
without prior permission in writing from
the publisher.

Any copy of this book issued by the publisher
is sold subject to the condition that it shall
not by way of trade or otherwise be lent, resold,
hired out or otherwise circulated without
the publisher's prior consent in any form or
binding or cover other than that in which it
is published and without a similar condition
including these words being imposed on
a subsequent purchaser.

Thames & Hudson Australia wishes to
acknowledge that Aboriginal and Torres Strait
Islander people are the first storytellers
of this nation and the traditional custodians
of the land on which we live and work. We
acknowledge their continuing culture and pay
respect to Elders past, present and future.

978 1 760760 4 1 0

A catalogue record for this
book is available from the
National Library of Australia

Every effort has been made to trace accurate
ownership of copyrighted text and visual
materials used in this book. Errors or
omissions will be corrected in subsequent
editions, provided notification is sent to
the publisher.

Front cover:
Dovecote. Photograph by Nelson Garrido

Design: Garry Emery and Alexander Hevey
Editing: Lauren McGregor
Printed and bound in China by RR Donnelley